Elementary
Social Studies

Elementary Social Studies

Knowing, Doing, Caring

George M. Schuncke

Western Carolina University

WITH A CONTRIBUTION BY
Jean Benedict Raffa

Macmillan Publishing Company
NEW YORK

Collier Macmillan Publishers
LONDON

Photos: Valerie Balogh

Printed in the United States of America

Macmillan Publishing Company
866 Third Avenue, New York, New York 10022

Collier Macmillan Canada, Inc.

Library of Congress Cataloging-in-Publication Data

Schuncke, George M.
    Elementary social studies.

    Includes index.
    1. Social sciences—Study and teaching (Elementary)
I. Raffa, Jean Benedict.   II. Title.
LB1584.S39 1988   372.8'3044   87-12215

Printing: 2 3 4 5 6 7   Year: 9 0 1 2 3 4

ISBN   0-02-408211-2

To Mark

Preface

Whenever I work with teachers or parents I make it a point to ask them, "When children are done with school, what should we expect of them?" Although I have asked this question throughout the United States, Central America, and the Caribbean, the answers I have gotten are surprisingly similar. Our goals, say teachers and parents, should be to teach children three things:

1. To know about the world.
2. To be able to do something about present and future problems.
3. To care about one's fellow humans.

These goals represent what is expected to result from the *total* school experience. They also represent what I, and other educators, believe to be the primary goals of social studies education.

Attainment of these goals is something that doesn't just happen of its own accord; people don't wake up on their twenty-first birthday and suddenly have the ability to solve world problems. A wide number of different types of experiences are needed to develop the knowledge, skills, and capabilities implied by the goals. To insure that the expectations are met, these experiences should begin early and continue throughout the individual's school life. The purpose of this book is to show elementary teachers how they can accomplish this task in the teaching of the social studies.

To achieve this purpose we focus on the three most important elements of the social studies curriculum: *what* you teach; *how* you teach it; and *who* is taught.

What you teach directly parallels the three global goals. In Section I, which deals with helping children know about the world, the knowledge base of the social studies and the content used to develop this knowledge are considered. Section II examines how we can help students function in the world. Emphasis is placed on those processes and skills that we can help develop in our students so that they can become effective problem solvers and decision makers. Finally, Section III explores the caring, feeling aspect of being human. We elaborate on ways in which these responses can be nurtured in children.

How you teach is examined from several vantage points. How to plan for helping children attain the goals of schooling is considered in some detail, as are ways of effectively carrying out these plans. With the latter we examine the variety of learning experiences and resources that can be used to make learning a vibrant and meaningful pursuit for the children.

Who you teach will not only affect *what* you teach but *how* you do it. Thus, the children are considered throughout the book. We examine those characteristics, both cognitive and affective, that our students will have at a given stage of development, characteristics that must be considered with respect to our teaching approach if our goals are to be met.

This book represents the combined experiences of many teachers and their students. Some of these teachers were brand new; others had mastered their art. All, however, saw social studies as a vital part of the curriculum and worked to make them interesting and meaningful to their students. Hopefully, their insights, examples, and experiences will encourage you to do so, too.

Although I cannot acknowledge all of the teachers or students who did many of the activities in this book, I would like to thank several people who were extremely helpful in its production. Suzanne Krogh and Dorene Ross, at the University of Florida, and Judith Clauss, Richard Craddock, and Lester Laminack of Western Carolina University were generous with their time in critiquing various sections. So, too, were the individuals who thoroughly reviewed the completed manuscript, Professor George Gates of Idaho State University and Dr. William Joyce of Michigan State University. Janice Holt, Peter Freer, and Joanne Sutton were very gracious in allowing photos to be taken of their classes at Fairview Elementary School in Sylva, North Carolina; Valerie Balogh took the photos. At Macmillan, thanks go to Lynne Greenberg and Aliza Greenblatt who saw to everything that goes into publishing a book and especially to Julianne Barbato who not only edited it but also read it critically. Finally, I'd like to thank Scott Huler, the production editor, and Gary Ingle, who not only helped proof the book but assiduously indexed it.

G. M. S.

Contents

SECTION VI Evaluating

1

Elementary Social Studies: What, Why, and How?

After reading this chapter you should be able to:

1. Identify the major goals for social studies in the United States.

2. Provide a rationale for the teaching of social studies in the elementary school.

3. Indicate how this book will help the elementary teacher foster children's attainment of the goals for social studies education.

What do you think of when you hear the term *social studies?* History? Geography? Countries and cultures? Round-robin reading of boring textbooks? Each of you has probably had a different experience with this area and probably has a different definition of what it is. Since the aim of this book is to help you become a good social studies teacher, let's see if we can begin to develop a shared understanding of what social studies are. We can do this by examining and analyzing some activities, observed by this author, in elementary classrooms:

    1 Mr. Wesley's third graders lived in a city that had two sister cities, one in Peru and the other in the U.S.S.R. Prior to the beginning of school he had arranged for his class to correspond with third grade classes in these cities. Although the children were free to write anything they wished to their pen pals, Mr. Wesley gave them a list of questions they were to ask about the home cities of the other eight and nine year olds. These questions concerned topics with which he knew his students would be dealing in their study of communities. As these topics arose, the children used the answers to their questions, as well as other information and materials they had been sent by their pen pals, to supplement the learning activities in which they were engaging. This information helped them build understandings about communities in general.

    2 Groups of Mrs. Clark's fourth graders were acting out aspects of life in the New England colonies. The group playing colonial children couldn't find out what these children studied in school. Mrs. Clark had anticipated their problem and, sitting with the group, she showed them a hornbook and helped them read a handout about hornbooks she had prepared. The children were very interested in the handout and offered

many suggestions when Mrs. Clark asked, "Why do you suppose things like the alphabet and the Lord's Prayer were put on the hornbook?" At the end of this short group discussion Mrs. Clark suggested that the children might want to get art supplies and make their own replicas of hornbooks. The students decided that these would be good props for their play.

3. The building center that had been set up in a corner of Mr. Wellborn's kindergarten classroom was so popular that many of the children were not getting the opportunity to use it during their independent work time. These children were frustrated because they too wanted to help build the model city that had been started with the scrap materials that had been provided. In fact, several arguments had occurred over tools in the past few days.

   During group sharing time, Mr. Wellborn asked the children what the problem in the construction center was. They quickly agreed, "There aren't enough tools, so people can't work in the center when they want to."

   He then asked them to think of what they could do about the problem. They suggested three solutions:

   1. Get more tools.
   2. Only some people can use the tools.
   3. You can only use the tools for ten minutes.

   The children were especially attracted to the first idea, so Mr. Wellborn asked them how they would accomplish it. They were disappointed when, in response to their suggestion that he buy them, he stated that he had no supply money left. They decided to make a list of the tools they needed and ask their parents if they had any extras at home. Mr. Wellborn told them that he would write the notes; then he helped them to consider the next two solutions. As a result of being asked to think of all the "good things" and "bad things" about each suggestion, the children decided that there were reasons why neither of the two would work as far as they were concerned. Mr. Wellborn then asked them to think of some other ideas when they went home.

   The next day several children reported that their parents were willing to lend tools to the class. Some new ideas were suggested and evaluated. Ultimately, the children decided that the best solution would be for Mr. Wellborn to form rotating groups so that, during the week, everyone would have a chance to work in the construction center. They realized that, although not ideal, these two solutions were the best, and so the children were willing to go along with them.

4. Ms. Smith's fifth graders were concerned with the way the deaf children who attended special classes in their school were treated. These children were housed in a separate portable classroom unit, and, as Ms. Smith's children said, were "made fun of" by the other children.

   The fifth graders decided to do something about the situation by inviting the deaf children to join them in their classroom activities. In preparation they learned the manual alphabet so that they could finger spell words to the deaf students. As they got to know the other class better, visits were exchanged between classrooms and many of Ms. Smith's students began to learn American Sign Language from their deaf peers. Gradually, other children in the school began to become interested in what was happening and began to interact with the deaf children. Although some of the other children occasionally teased the handicapped children, the climate in the school became much more accepting.

5. Mr. Wright's sixth graders were angry about not being able to go to the creek that ran behind their school. It was polluted and large signs warned them to stay away. The pollution wasn't difficult to see; people threw junk into the creek and its banks were littered with cans. They felt especially cheated when they learned that in the old days people caught fish and ate watercress that grew in the creek. They decided they wanted to do something about the situation.

As a result of questions asked by Mr. Wright, they realized that they didn't know enough about water pollution to say anything of substance about the pollution in their creek and would need to find out about specific causes of this problem. Using books, pamphlets, and information from the Environmental Protection Agency they gathered specific ideas about potential pollution causes (including some, such as pesticide poisoning, that weren't readily visible). Following this, they decided (again with Mr. Wright's assistance) that they should pinpoint the exact causes of pollution in their creek. This called for a fieldtrip. During this walk Mr. Wright took pictures of the pollution sources pointed out by his students.

Now that they had their evidence they decided that they were ready to show it to people and demand (later tempered to request) that something be done. But to whom should they show the evidence? After some exploration, and several lessons about their county commission given by Mr. Wright, they decided to write letters to the editor of the local newspaper and make a presentation at the county commission meeting.

These activities resulted in a great deal of publicity about the polluted creek and some public action. Although the creek is still not in its once-pristine condition, its pollution is now beginning to be controlled. Interestingly enough, many of Mr. Wright's sixth graders, who are now in high school, work with the local environmental groups that have adopted the creek as one of their causes.

Although these examples don't capture everything that occurs in a good social studies class, an analysis of them will allow us to determine some basic characteristics of social studies. Let's look at the first two examples. What are Mr. Wesley and Mrs. Clark's students learning as they study different communities and colonial America? Is there something that both of these examples have in common? In both cases the students are learning important things about the world in which they live and the people who are inhabiting that world. Even though the fourth graders are studying a group from the past, their study and discussion of what was included in the hornbook will tell them something about people of the present and, probably, the future. They are learning that groups of people teach their young those things that the group believes to be important. In colonial America it was the Lord's Prayer, the alphabet, and numbers. This will help them understand other aspects of the world: why they go to school, why they learn what they learn, and, for example, why Moslem children go to Islamic school. Similarly, the third graders, while studying communities in three different parts of the world, may learn some specific things about those communities. However, the major things they will learn are those things that tend to explain communities regardless of locale: why people live in communities, what characteristics communities have, how communities interact with one another, and so on.

But what about the second two examples? We really can't say that they help the students to learn about the world, and to a great extent—with the exception of Ms. Smith's students learning that people can sometimes be cruel—they aren't learning very much about the people of the world. So, what are they learning? If you think about it you'll notice that in both cases the teachers were helping the students deal with problems they were encountering. In the kindergartners' case, their teacher was helping them make decisions for themselves, a process utilized by rational people throughout the world. Ms. Smith's children, similarly, were working with several very human processes: the development of empathy as they began to put themselves in the place of the deaf children; valuing as they decided what was important to them in this situation; and problem solving as they did something about it. In these examples, then, the children were learning those processes that individuals utilize for living effectively in the world.

At this point it is probably unnecessary to analyze the fifth example to any great extent. You probably realize that it incorporates elements of the four previous examples. The students were determining what was important to them in relation to the creek. They were learning about their world: among other things, how people affect its environment and how people govern themselves. They were also engaging in the basic human processes of problem solving and decision making.

Based on our analyses of these examples can you make a statement about what social studies is? Mine is quite simple: *Social studies are concerned with the study of humans as they relate to each other and the world, and with the processes they use to facilitate this relationship.*

Why Social Studies? _____

The question of why we should include any particular academic area in the curriculum asks that we provide a rationale for it. We must articulate the fundamental purposes served by the area; that is, what individuals might be expected to know and be able to do as a result of their experiences with the subject matter in question. Basically, there are two very broad purposes for social studies education:

1. To help the individual know about the world in which he or she lives, and will live in the future.
2. To help the individual become an active citizen of that world.

In the past other, more specific, purposes have been stated for the social studies. These purposes have included citizenship education, teaching about the cultural heritage, and the development of thinking skills. Unfortunately, although they were stated broadly they tended to be interpreted narrowly. Citizenship education focused solely on the child's state and nation; the cultural heritage tended to be an Anglo-Saxon one; and thinking skills tended to be rigidly defined in terms of what rational citizens did.

Such narrow definitions are not completely appropriate today. More and more it is becoming apparent that we are citizens of a world community and have responsibilities in that community. We also know that, even in the United States, what we are is a result of the interaction of diverse world cultures. In addition, we are becoming more aware of the fact that there may be more to thinking skills than we previously realized. For example, ongoing research on the right, nonrational, hemisphere of the brain (which controls the left side of the body) is helping us to become aware of capabilities that can be developed in individuals to add a whole new dimension to intellectual functioning.

By defining our goals in terms of world knowledge and citizenship we do not discard the goals of the past. We still work toward them in our social studies programs, but go beyond their narrow interpretation. We broaden them to include present *and* future realities. Citizenship education, as it was previously defined, is still a major goal of the social studies and children still learn the rights and responsibilities of American citizens. They also learn of their rights and responsibilities as global citizens.

Certainly, few people would disagree that our goals, as stated, are commendable and do provide a rationale for the inclusion of social studies in the curriculum. Many people, however, tend to remember social studies as part of the secondary school curriculum. They might ask, "Why should it be taught in the elementary school?"

This question can be answered from two perspectives. First, there is the perspective of the child. We cannot deny that children do live in the world. They are interested in it and do want to know about it. In addition, as we saw in several of the examples earlier, they often encounter problems in their own lives. Thus, they have a need to know and do that cannot wait until secondary school to be satisfied.

Second, adults continue to have a need to know about the world and solve problems in it. They might need to know, for example, about the pros and cons of nuclear disarmament, or the positive and negative aspects of living in a bilingual city because they might be asked to make personal decisions about these issue (as voters in several states were in 1982 with the former, and voters in Miami were in 1981 with the latter). They also need to know about the world in order to satisfy their curiousity about it.

Knowledge and the ability to use basic human processes come about as the result of a variety of learning experiences, each of which build on those preceding it. With each, our knowledge and abilities become more sophisticated. There is no reason why they should not start in the elementary school. In this way the experiences children have in the elementary school provide a basis for more sophisticated adult activity. They lay the foundation of knowledge, skills and experience which can be built upon to permit adults to function effectively in the world.

How?

How do we help children attain the goals that have been established for the teaching of social studies? Perhaps the most appropriate way of answering this question is to attempt to isolate the relevant characteristics that are possessed by an individual who has attained them, and then discuss how these can be developed. We would suggest that this individual would have three sets of qualities.

First, this individual would be knowledgeable, having a basic understanding of the world and how it functions. This does not mean that this person would know everything that there is to know about the world or would be an encyclopedia of specific facts. Instead it implies that she would have an awareness of the general patterns of behavior that occur among people and between people and their environments. This knowledge would be used in all aspects of her life.

Second, this person would be a "doer," an active individual who is able to

Doing can take many forms. These students act on their decision to clean up their nature trail.

rely on her own resources to manage her life and deal with the world. This quality would be manifested in many ways. One of these ways would relate to the quality of being a knower. This individual would not only be capable of increasing her present knowledge of the world but also would utilize this capability. Thus, her knowledge of the world would be constantly growing. Another manifestation would be this individual's ability and willingness to deal with problematic situations. Again, she would not only be capable of solving problems and making decisions but also would exercise this capability in directing her own life, as well as in the resolution of those problems and decisions she shares with her fellow citizens. Because she employed these processes on a more or less continual basis, her skill with them would be constantly increasing.

This quality of being a doer should not be construed to imply that this person is a rugged individualist who does everything for herself. Instead, it should be interpreted to mean that this person has a grasp of those processes employed by humans for effective functioning in the world and can determine those situations in which individual employment of these processes is required as opposed to those in which collective action is needed.

Third, this individual would be a caring, feeling person. This quality embodies several related dimensions. One of these dimensions is the possession of a set of values. This person would be aware of those things that she believes to be important. She would know what she believes to be good and right and would attempt to live according to these beliefs. She would also be capable of resolving conflicts that occur within this value system. When two or more beliefs that she holds appear to be in opposition to each other she would be able to deal with the situation and resolve the conflict.

In addition to possessing her own value system and being able to resolve the value conflicts that occur in her own life, this individual would be capable of examining the values held by others. She would be able to analyze the behavior of others to determine what it is they believe to be important. She would use this analytical data as a source for guiding her own behavior, both in relation to the others and in different situations in her own life.

The final dimension of a caring person is that this individual would be capable of perspective taking. She would be able to put herself into another person's shoes and view situations from that person's vantage point. She could employ this ability as she interacted with others. She would also be able to use it in looking at the total world; attempting to interpret situations by examining how people in those situations are actually thinking and feeling.

Although we have discussed these three groups of characteristics separately, it should be obvious that the capabilities implied by knowing, doing, and caring are not used discretely in actuality. Rather, the capabilities are used in conjunction with one another. Our hypothetical person would use her knowledge to solve problems, make decisions, and work with values. She would use problem solving as a way of gaining knowledge, and decision making as a way of resolving value conflicts. The reverse would also be true; the values she has would affect the decisions she makes. The list of relationships could go on and on.

In order to attain the purposes established for social studies education it is necessary to help children develop the qualities of the knowledgeable world citizen. Thus, we will work toward three types of goals that parallel the three qualities of knowing, doing, and caring. These are:

1. *Knowledge,* or *conceptual, goals* include those things that we want children to know as a result of their experiences with us. In the social studies our knowledge base consists of concepts and generalizations drawn primarily from the social sciences and humanities. The concepts and generalizations that we will expect children to learn are those that best explain the world and its people.

2. *Process goals* include those things which we would like our students to be able to do. These goals encompass the capabilities and skills necessary to generate knowledge. They also include processes that allow individuals to solve problems and make decisions.

3. *Affective goals* deal with the caring and feeling aspects of being human. These goals are often interpreted as being specific things that we want children to care about and feel. Although, of course, there are some attitudes, values, and beliefs that we can validly teach as content, these represent only a small portion of affective goals. The major activities encompassed by these goals are ones that provide children with the processes and skills that can be utilized for understanding values, for dealing with values conflicts, for analyzing the feelings of others, and for developing perspective-taking abilities.

About This Book

One assumption that we are making in this book is that by helping students attain these knowledge, process, and affective goals we help them attain our ultimate goal of world knowledge and citizenship. Therefore, the book is structured around considering how you can help children meet these goals. In order to do this we'll consider what you'll be teaching as an elementary social studies teacher, how you'll be doing this, and how you'll know that you've done it.

For simplicity's sake, we've broken the book into sections, each of which considers a specific topic such as the knowledge goals of the social studies. All of these topics address things that you'll need to consider in your work as a teacher. Be aware that you don't need to, and won't necessarily, consider these things in the order we have presented them. For example, although evaluation is the last topic we discuss, it probably won't be the last thing you'll consider in your planning. You'll be thinking of it almost simultaneously as you think of what you'll teach and how you'll teach it. The topics do not represent a sequence to be followed; they are integral parts of the whole of teaching social studies.

The first three sections of this book are respectively entitled "Knowing," "Doing," and "Caring." These sections are devoted to helping you understand exactly what is included in each of the types of goals and how you would help children work toward them. In these sections each goal is examined separately. The "Knowing" section introduces concepts and generalizations, helping you to understand what these things you're supposed to be teaching are and how they fit into the curriculum. Following this, we examine six academic areas, or disciplines, which contribute the majority of knowledge to the social studies. We'll speak of a variety of different topics you might use in your teaching of concepts and generalizations.

We'll end each chapter of this book with a synthesis, wherein we'll consider how you can use the ideas discussed in the chapter as you plan learning experiences for children. This particular portion of our Section I chapters focuses on planning to include conceptual goals in your curriculum.

Section II, "Doing," begins by introducing the different problem-solving processes you'll be helping your students develop. It then moves on to a consideration of different approaches to working with problem solving in the classroom. We'll examine strategies for helping children generate knowledge, as well as work through their own problems. We'll also delineate the specific types of skills you'll need to teach your students. Our synthesis here will be devoted to considering how we incorporate process goals with conceptual goals in our planning.

The range of concerns that comprise the affective goals are introduced in Section III, "Caring." We'll also examine and evaluate different types of strategies that have been developed for dealing with affective concerns. Then we'll move on to discuss specific strategies and materials that can be used with elementary children to deal with affective concerns. Synthesis, for this section, is concerned with ways to insure that affective elements are included in your curriculum.

The fourth section of the book is titled "Planning." Here we tie together what we've considered separately in relation to the three sets of goals by examining the processes that are used by teachers to plan units of study. A step-by-step planning format is introduced, and we consider how you can plan on a daily basis.

Planning is followed logically by a section concerned with carrying out plans. This section, called "Implementing," details the wide range of activities you can employ to promote learning—from student-centered activities, to language-oriented ones, to those that are teacher facilitated. In this section we'll also consider the materials and resources you might use and how you might organize your students for these activities.

The last section of the book, Section VI, is devoted to evaluating learning, and is, naturally, titled "Evaluating." Evaluation will be considered generally, and we'll look at different types of evaluation and the situations in which they are appropriately employed. We'll also examine and critique very specific types of evaluation techniques.

As you read this book you'll probably discover some of my biases very quickly. I'd like to point out three of them and share the reasons for them so that the book might make more sense to you. First, there is a great deal of research data to show that social studies is one of children's least favorite subjects. I believe that one reason for this is that much of what children are expected to do may be beyond their capabilities. I believe that children respond to teaching that is appropriate to their level of development, be it cognitive, affective, or psychomotor. Therefore, in various places throughout the book I'll note what might and might not be appropriate to elementary children in this respect. Second, I believe that we do things best when we know why we're doing them. Because of this, I have attempted to provide rationales for why we include what we do in the curriculum and why we do what we do with children. Finally, I believe that learning is interactive. You learn through interaction with people, in this case primarily the professors and teachers with whom you work and your fellow students. To facilitate this interaction, each chapter ends with a series of activities I've labeled "Springboards to Discussion." You can choose one or more of these to do and, when they're completed, use the information you found in the activities as a basis for discussion with your fellow students.

Springboards to Discussion _____

1. Make a list of what you consider to have been "good" social studies experiences in elementary school. Then, list your "not-so-good" experience. In a group, compare all of the "good" experiences to determine what commonalities they have. Do the same for the "not so goods." Then compare the "goods" with the "not so goods." What differences do you notice? Try to make a general statement about the characteristics that differentiate the two.

2. At the conclusion of this chapter I hypothesized that one reason children don't like social studies is that they may be expected to do things that are beyond their capabilities.

   Interview three children who are in three different grades. Ask them what they like and dislike about social studies. Based on what they tell you, see if you can come up with a different hypothesis as to *why* social studies is their least favorite subject. Then hypothesize how you might help children enjoy social studies.

3. Evaluate yourself in terms of the three qualities the social studies can help develop: knowing, doing, and caring. To what extent do you possess them? Do you think you need to develop them further? How might you do this?

Knowing

2

Concepts and Generalizations: Means to World Knowledge

After reading this chapter you should be able to:

1. Identify the major characteristics of concepts and generalizations, the sources of social studies knowledge.

2. Demonstrate the relationship of factual knowledge to the development of concepts and generalizations.

3. Indicate factors that are pertinent to the learning of specific concepts.

4. Illustrate various approaches to the structuring of concept learning in the schools.

The conceptual goals of the social studies are concerned with the development of a basic understanding of the world and how it functions: how people interact with people socially, economically, and politically and how they interact with their physical surroundings. A wide range of academic areas—including the behavioral sciences and the humanities—are drawn upon for the knowledge they can provide to promote this understanding. It is generally the case, however, that the social studies curriculum relies most upon history and the social sciences for its knowledge base. These six disciplines—history, anthropology, sociology, political science, economics, and geography—will provide most of the ideas and information with which our students will deal.

At some point in your academic career you've probably taken a course in one of these six disciplines. Even if it was an introductory course you probably considered a large amount of substantive information. If you look at a college catalog you'll notice that there are a number of other courses in the same discipline, courses that are concerned with a great deal more knowledge. These might be taken by individuals who wished to broaden their knowledge. They would most certainly be taken by individuals who wished to become social scientists or historians. Fortunately, as elementary teachers our responsibility is not the formation of social scientists, and so we need not worry about teaching *every* idea that the disciplines offer. Our goal is to help children develop a fundamental awareness of the world in which they live, and will live. (We might, of course, help them act as social scientists as they develop this awareness.) Therefore, what we'll want to teach are those ideas that will best develop this awareness. Those ideas are referred to as the major concepts and generalizations of the disciplines.

In this chapter and the next we'll focus on concepts and generalizations. We'll begin with some general background information about them. In the next chapter we'll become more definite, examining specific concepts and generalizations that you'll potentially be working with in your social studies curriculum.

We'll consider three topics in this chapter's general discussion of concepts and generalizations. Since many people either don't understand what concepts and generalizations are, or define them in widely divergent ways, we'll initially attempt to build a common understanding of them. To do this, we'll examine what they are and why they are important. We'll also consider their relationship to factual knowledge, the content you'll actually be dealing with in your curriculum. Following this, we'll look at how people develop concepts, focusing on the mental operations employed in this process. Finally we'll discuss how concept learning can be facilitated in the elementary school.

As you read this chapter you'll be struck by the close relationship of concepts and generalizations. Because of this relationship, and to make your reading easier, we'll often use the term *idea* to refer to both concepts and generalizations.

Concepts, Generalizations, and Facts _____

The development of concepts and generalizations will be one of the goals of your social studies program. It will not be the ultimate goal, though; you won't expect children to learn these simply for the sake of learning them. Instead, you'll use them as a means of helping children attain the broader, more global, goals of world knowledge and citizenship.

As you read about concepts and generalizations you will see that they are eminently suited for this purpose. Both have the power to help us understand particular things or events that we encounter in the world. You will see, however, that their usefulness goes well beyond explaining only single instances. They can help us to comprehend a large number of apparently discrete situations. Concepts and generalizations do this by giving us a framework for understanding, a set of general categories into which our specific experiences can be fit. Thus, they provide us with an orderly way to interpret what is happening in our world.

Concepts

Concepts have been defined in many different ways, primarily because educators haven't really been able to agree among themselves as to exactly what they are. Most definitions, however, do tend to repeatedly note certain common characteristics. These can provide us with a basis for understanding what these things are that we're supposed to be helping children learn.

First, concepts are *abstractions*. They are general ideas or mental pictures we develop about things, events, or activities. When people speak of a "group," which is a sociological concept, most of us have some idea of what it is they're talking about. In most cases, we probably don't need them to elaborate on the characteristics of "group," per se, or to specifically define the group they're discussing. We have a "picture" of what's being talked about, a general understanding of what a group is.

Second, concepts represent *classes* or collections of things that have certain characteristics, or qualities, in common. We develop these classes by comparing specific things with each other to see how they are alike and different. The common characteristics that result from this comparison, sometimes referred to as attributes, allow us to differentiate between that which is the concept and that which is not. In thinking about a "group" we think about an entity that has certain qualities. My group is (1) an aggregation of individuals who (2) are together because of some thing or purpose that they have in common. My group and your group may not be exactly alike, but when you speak of a group I'll have a good idea of what you're talking about because both of our concepts will share many attributes in common.

Third, concepts are *personal*. Although we can understand each other when we speak of groups, because we both share what Martorella (1971) has referred to as the critical attributes of this concept, your concept of group will probably be somewhat different than mine. If you were a sociologist it would probably have many more attributes. If you were a third grader, whose only experience with groups has been with reading groups, it will probably have less. In any case, because of the personal background and experiences we bring to our understanding of the concept it is unique and our ideas of what a group is will probably differ, at least slightly.

Fourth, concepts are *learned through experience*. We develop our mental picture of classes of things (or activities or events or ideas) that have specific characteristics in common by having two types of experience. First, we actually experience specific examples of those things. This allows us to build our category. Secondly, we experience things that do not belong in the category. This allows us to clearly set up the attributes of the concept and to clarify our understanding of it. Thus, we learn what a dog is not only by coming into contact with a number of dogs, but also by coming into contact with cats, horses, and fish. The latter allow us to clearly set up the attributes for the class we are calling dog. My concept of "group" comes from the experiences I have had being in groups, from using groups in my classroom, from seeing groups, and from reading about groups. Your concept may come from similar, and different, experiences.

Finally, concepts are *not words*. Words are used to give labels to concepts, but just because we don't have a word for a specific concept doesn't mean that we haven't developed that concept. For example, when I first learned to ski I realized that sometimes the snow was different than at other times and that it affected what I had to do to stay up (which was my primary goal at that time). Later I learned that experienced skiers had specific terminology for different types of snow. Regardless of the fact that I didn't know the term *corn,* I knew that I had trouble skiing on crunchy, icy snow (which is corn). Words simply allow us to convey our concepts to others.

Incidentally, just because people "have" words does not mean that they understand concepts. Someone, for example, might be able to give a dictionary definition of a group, but not understand in the slightest what it actually is.

To summarize, then, a concept:

1. Is an abstraction.
2. Represents classes of things (or activities or events or ideas).
3. Is personal.
4. Is learned through experience.
5. Is not just a matter of words.

Generalizations

Generalizations are also abstractions and are closely related to concepts. An easy way to understand what these are, and their relationship to concepts, is to actually go through the process of developing a generalization. To do this we'll need to know two concepts—both drawn from sociology—*groups* and *norms.* Having discussed the first concept earlier, we can move to a consideration of what a norm is. To do this, let's examine some examples of norms:

1. While traveling through Kano, Nigeria, I had the opportunity to visit with a local teacher. As we were walking down the street we were approached by a young boy who made a sort of curtsy to the teacher. The teacher explained that the boy was one of his students. Later, I saw a grown man do the same thing to a man who the teacher told me was a religious leader. When I discussed these incidents with my friend, he indicated that among the Hausa—the tribe living in Kano—it was customary to "give obeisance" by doing this curtsy. This obeisance is a mark of respect toward individuals who are known to be of higher status. "Giving obeisance" is a norm for the Hausa.
2. In 1980 a serious confrontation developed between local fishermen on the Gulf Coast of Texas and Vietnamese refugee fishermen who had been relocated there. A government investigation of this confrontation indicated that one of its major causes lay in the fact that the Vietnamese were unwittingly violating local norms as they went about their work. They fished too close to other boats, thus infringing on the generally accepted territory (unmarked in any way) of the other fishermen. They also ran their boats at high speed in the vicinity of other boats when fishing was occurring. Again, this behavior was unacceptable because local practice was to move quite slowly. In both these cases the Vietnamese refugees were unaware of the local norms, did not heed them and, thus, unknowingly caused friction.
3. The advertisement for a brand of cigarettes, purportedly made for women, often shows two pictures of what happened before women

"came a long way" in relation to cigarette smoking. The first picture shows a woman being caught smoking by her husband. The second picture shows the punishment she received for smoking. Smoking cigarettes in those days wasn't the norm for females.

4. In many alternative schools children call teachers by their first names. This isn't the norm in most nonalternative schools, and teachers are usually referred to as *Mr., Mrs.,* or *Ms.* so-and-so.

5. Speaking of the appellation *Ms.,* in the past, women were either referred to as *Miss* or *Mrs.* Now, in a great many sectors of our society, the norm appears to be moving toward the use of *Ms.*

Based on these statements you probably have a pretty good idea of what a norm is. What is it? Can you describe some other examples? Did you think of a norm as some type of rule, written or unwritten, or a standard that guides an individual's behavior?

Let's look at the examples again. What do they all have in common? Other than dealing with norms, with what else are they concentrated? Think for a moment. What's so similar about the Hausa, the fishermen, women in the early part of this century, and children in nontraditional schools? Right! They all belong to specific groups. Now, based on our discussion of norms can you make a statement about groups and norms? Of course you can, and it would probably sound similar to the following: *Every group has a system of norms to guide the behavior of individuals who belong to that group.*

This statement is a generalization. Let's use it for a reference as we consider what a generalization is. First, a generalization indicates a relationship between or among concepts. Our generalization refers to only two concepts, groups and norms, but others can be concerned with a greater number. All generalizations, however, will show the interconnectedness of the concepts they contain. (Can you think, for example, of a generalization that shows the relationship between the concepts of price, the supply of an item and its demand?) Second, as its name implies, this statement is a general one and does not speak to specific situations. As such, it has the power to describe a large number of situations that have something in common. Our generalization holds for the Hausa, for fishermen in Texas, for women in the early part of the twentieth century, and for children in nontraditional schools. It should hold for any situation in which there is a group. Thus, it has universal applicability. Because of this, generalizations will allow us to understand and explain situations we have already encountered; why, for example, people have acted in certain ways in groups we have been in. They also help us to make predictions; we can make some hypotheses about groups we have not yet encountered. You, for example, will be a first-year teacher very shortly. Do you think that the faculty at your school will have norms? How will you behave until you know what these norms are? How do you think you'll act at your first faculty meeting?

To summarize, generalizations are statements that are made up of concepts and that have more or less universal applicability. As with concepts, they are "big ideas" that can be utilized to explain a variety of specific situations, and thus help us to better and more thoroughly understand the world in which we live.

Facts

One of the key characteristics of concepts and generalizations is that they are abstractions. A dictionary definition of *abstraction* would be similar to the following: "an idea about the qualities or properties of a thing, formulated by mental separation from particular instances or material objects." You probably engaged in the process of abstraction as you worked with the ideas about groups and norms, which were presented above. You may have attempted to first determine the similarities and differences among the examples and then proceeded to ascertain why these occurred. At the onset you were focusing on specific examples of peoples' behavior. By the end, however, you were developing general ideas about the world, ideas that tended to explain more than each specific example. You had abstracted.

Children go through a similar process of abstraction as they begin to develop general understandings about the world. For example, a first grader who sees pictures of her classmates' families will begin to note that some families are like her own, while others aren't. Yet she realizes that all of these are families and may try to figure out why this is the case. As she does this, she is abstracting or redeveloping her concept of family based on the new information she has encountered. A result of her thinking is that she comes up with a new idea of what a family is, one which would potentially help her understand the characteristics that families around the world have.

If you compare your experience developing the generalization with the first grader's experience developing the concept *family,* you will see that both have elements in common in addition to requiring abstraction. Neither you, nor the first grader, could have developed the general ideas you did without first working with some type of specific information. The process of abstraction, if you'll pardon the redundancy, requires something from which to abstract. This something is factual data. Facts are the building blocks from which concepts and generalizations are constructed.

Because one of our goals is to help children develop concepts and generalizations, we will rely quite heavily on facts in our curriculum. They will constitute our content, the information the children will work with in relation to an area being studied. Just as you used content about different groups and the first grader used facts about the families of her peers to refine her concept of family so, too, will your students use facts about whatever topic they are studying to develop their own concepts and generalizations.

The idea of using facts as a means of developing broader understandings about the world is in many respects a relatively recent one as far as social studies instruction is concerned. Until the 1960s, facts were to a great extent used as ends of instruction, ultimate learning goals. Children were expected to learn an assortment of facts related to the topic they were studying. For example, as a fourth grader in Baltimore I was required to know the year that Maryland was founded, the names of the ships that brought the founders, where they landed, the name of the state capital, and so on. My experience was not unique. Others, possibly you yourself, can remember countless experiences in which they were required to memorize the names of capital cities, chief exports of countries, and who discovered what, when. Unfortunately, although we can remember memorizing these facts, we usually cannot remember the facts themselves. (Quick—what is the capital of Montana?)

It is not difficult to see why facts truly cannot be considered to be either a logical or a defensible goal for education. On one hand, we know that facts change. For example, at one time it was a fact that New York was the capital of the United States. So too was it accepted as a fact that the world was broken into "frigid", "temperate," and "torrid" climatic zones. Unfortunately it sometimes gets frigid in the mountains of Ecuador, which lie smack in the middle of the torrid zone. (This fact about climatic zones, which I memorized as a child, had earlier been disproved by geographers.) Then, too, we also know that we have a tendency to forget isolated facts. Apparently, they're just not meaningful enough for us to hold onto; therefore, they have little applicability in the future. You may have spent a great deal of time memorizing capitals of the states and been able to recite, quite readily, that Helena was the capital of Montana when you were in the fifth grade. However, unless you had a great need to use this fact relatively frequently (or unless you lived in Montana) it was probably forgotten quite quickly. Finally, facts have limited utility when considered by themselves. They deal with specific situations and don't explain much beyond those situation. The fact, for example, that most houses in Baltimore are made of brick is interesting, but it tells us very little about houses in general, why people build houses of specific materials, or what relationship exists between the environment and the type of house built.

Knowledge of facts, then, should not be considered to be the ultimate goal of our instruction. (Of course, children can be asked to remember some facts; however, they would use these facts for some purpose, such as developing generalizations.) Neither should concepts and generalizations be considered in this way. All three notions are means to the attainment of the broader goals of social studies education: knowledge about the world in which we live and the ability to participate intelligently and effectively as a citizen of it. All three are necessary to meet these goals.

Building Social Knowledge

It should be apparent to you at this point that there is a close relationship among facts, concepts and generalizations. Figure 2-1 illustrates this relationship as we might want to think of it in reference to the development of social studies knowledge.

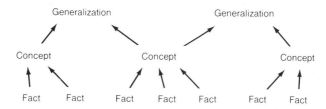

Figure 2-1 The relationship of facts, concepts, and generalizations.

Put quite simply, facts build concepts and concepts build generalizations. In many respects this occurs in a one-two-three sequence. However, the time between learning a concept and the development of a generalization containing that concept can vary. In some cases we could say that both are being developed almost simultaneously. As you may have noted with our discussion of groups and norms, you were basically developing a generalization about the two as you were learning the concept *norms*. On other occasions, some time will elapse between concept development and the formulation of a generalization. That is, you may learn a given concept but never perceive it as being related to the other concepts which constitute the generalization. Thus, if you knew the concept *group*, but were unaware of the idea of norms you could not have begun to develop the generalization until you developed the latter.

Although the diagram and our discussion of it may seem relatively theoretical, all of it does have practical implications as you plan to develop social studies knowledge with your students. These implications include the following.

1. Facts are the base from which your students will work. In your planning you will begin by deciding the "big ideas" your students will learn. Then, you will choose the content, the factual data, most appropriate for developing these ideas. Your students, on the other hand, will begin with content and gradually move to the development of concepts and generalizations.
2. It isn't always necessary for your students to develop generalizations; concepts can be appropriate learning goals. This is especially true with younger children who need to adequately understand a concept before they can begin to work with it. Your goal here will be concept development with the assumption that, at some point later in time, the children will work further with this concept to construct a generalization.
3. It is necessary to know where your children are in relation to the development of a concept. Past experience may or may not have provided them with an understanding of a concept. You would want to work from their present understanding.

All of these ideas will be developed further in later sections of this book as we consider the process of planning for learning in some depth.

Concept Learning

When he was about a year old, my son was given a sun hat to wear on the trips he took around the neighborhood in his stroller. Mark liked that hat, and he liked the idea of having a hat. In fact, for several days just about anything Mark touched was put onto his head accompanied by a big smile and the announcement "Hat!" Many of the things he put on his head slid off, but this didn't seem to bother him too much. Back they went onto his head. Mark apparently had developed a rudimentary concept of hat as "anything I can put on my head." About six months later I jokingly gave him a small book (which he had previously tried to use as a hat) and told him to put the hat on. He told me with a very definite expression that it was not a hat. Mark's concept of hat had changed from anything that went onto his head to something else (possibly, "Anything I put on my head that stays there"). This something else, incidentally, was not the adult concept of hat since he occasionally put baskets on his head and referred to them as hats.

Mark's experience with hats basically illustrates how we all develop concepts. We begin by having an experience, of some sort, with an example of the concept; in Mark's case he had a sun hat put onto his head. From this experience we develop a rudimentary idea of the concept and the characteristics, or attributes, it possesses; "hat" was understood as any head covering. Then, gradually, we have repeated experiences with other examples of the concept, as well as with things that are not the concept, and refine our idea; after six months of repeated experiences, Mark could differentiate some books from hats. Mark's concept of hat certainly wasn't yet the concept possessed by most adults. However, further experiences would allow it to become so.

We can see from this example that one important factor in concept development is experience with the concept. We grow in our understanding of a thing or an idea by repeatedly encountering examples of it. These repeated encounters, however, are not sufficient to guarantee that we will actually form a concept. In order for this to occur we, ourselves, must engage in at least two different types of mental processing: *classification* and *assimilation/accomodation*. Because it is possible to facilitate children's use of these processes, both deserve further scrutiny.

Classification

A concept, as we defined it earlier, represents a group of things that we perceive to belong together because they possess qualities in common. As we initially develop our concept we mentally search for these qualities, attempting to determine not only what is so special about the thing we have encountered but also what differentiates it from other things. The qualities we arrive at are the attributes of our concept. Mark's concept of hat, for example, probably had only one special characteristic, one attribute, in the beginning—anything that could go on his head. This attribute allowed him to differentiate hats from, say, chairs. Later as we encounter other examples of a concept we may isolate more of the qualities that make it special and differentiate it from other concepts. We may also possibly discard characteristics that we initially perceived to belong to the class that was our concept. As we add or subtract attributes from our class, we are refining our concept. Thus, with further experiences Mark was able to add another attribute to his class. Not only was it something that went on his head, it had to stay there. In the process many things that fit his earlier concept now did not.

The ability to classify, to mentally isolate those qualities that allow us to perceive objects or events to be similar, is one that develops over time. In fact, Jean Piaget, the late Swiss psychologist, and his followers indicate that this ability is tied to our total cognitive development. This has implications for work with children, the types of experiences we provide them, and what we can realistically expect of them.

The children we will work with in the kindergarten, first, and second grades (the five to seven year olds) are usually at the upper end of a stage Piaget referred to as *preoperational*. One characteristic of children at this stage is that they learn best by working physically with their environment. They will be able to classify objects and events with which they have had firsthand experience. That is, they can group things that they can relate to by virtue of having personally encountered them in some way. They may, for example, be able to build the economic concepts of needs and wants by cutting pictures out of magazines of things their families must have to live and things they would like to have. When they group these objects they will be remembering experiences from their own lives, things they have encountered with their own families.

A second important characteristic of preoperational children is that they are bound by their perceptions. These children will usually focus on the most dominant quality of an object when thinking about that object. Therefore, they will classify objects based on how the objects appear to them. Although children at the upper end of the preoperational stage may be able to produce subclasses from the classes they have constructed, they will also have a great deal of difficulty in seeing the relationship between the class and its subclasses (such as the class *need* and its subclass *food*.). The preoperational child who has collected ten pictures of food, five pictures of clothing, and two of houses will, when asked if there are more examples of food than there are of basic needs might reply, "More pictures of food." This child is dominated by the most apparent aspect of the situation (in this case the most pictures of a specific need) and cannot perceive that this is part of a larger group. The thing she sees the most of is food, therefore there's more food. She is unable to think simultaneously about the larger concept, needs, and its subclasses of food, clothing, and shelter.

Piaget's *concrete operational* stage, spanning the late second through fifth, and possibly sixth, grades (ages seven through eleven or twelve) is characterized by the children's development of the ability to engage in logical thought. This thought, however, tends to be tied to things the child has concretely experienced and does not occur when problems are abstract or hypothetical. These children, though, can develop hierarchies composed of classes and their subclasses with increasing sophistication. They are able, for example, to break the workers they have seen on their field trip into "people who wear uniforms" and "people who don't" (as one student we observed after a field trip did) or into "producers of goods" and "producers of services," and so on. Children at this stage also gradually lose their perceptual boundedness, the need to base their thinking on the most dominant aspect they have observed in a situation. Because of this, they are increasingly able to deal with these classifications in a logical manner. They are able to understand that a whole class, which contains several subclasses, is larger than any one of these subclasses, even if it is the largest subclass. If asked, for example, if he saw more "people wearing uniforms" (the largest subclass) or "workers" a preoperational child might choose the uniformed group. A concrete operational child, on the other hand, would reply (probably giving you a look that questioned your mental capacity) "workers." This child is able to logically understand that "people wearing uniforms" are workers.

Tied in with this ability to work with classes and subclasses is an increasing ability, on the part of concrete operational children, to engage in multiple classification. They are able to realize that objects have multiple characteristics and can be classified in a variety of ways. These children can take some objects from several groups and place them into a separate group. In examining the goods and services that people use in their community, these children could further break them into "needs" and "wants," or into those provided by "public" and "private" producers.

Concrete operational children are still limited in their classification abilities, however. As with preoperational children they appear to be able to classify, and manipulate these classifications, only with things that are within their lifespaces. They have great difficulty dealing with imaginary or hypothetical classes. It is not until the stage of *formal operations* (which may, but often doesn't, begin at the sixth-grade level) that logical thought can occur without the necessity to focus on the concrete, immediate aspects of a situation.

If we examine these data we can see that they will allow us to make several generalizations about the classification experiences we provide for children. These include the following.

1. Children will work best at classifying those things with which they have had first-hand experiences.
2. As they move to the stage of concrete operations we can expect children to break groups into subclasses; however, children who are still preoperational may have difficulty seeing the relationship between groups and their subclasses.
3. Older children will increasingly be able to deal with multiple classification, and can realize that things can belong to more than one group.

Assimilation and Accommodation

When we encounter something new, be it an object, an idea, or an event, we attempt to see how it fits with what we already know. We search through the concepts we have developed to determine how this experience relates to the classes we have already established. As a result of this search we arrive at one of three conclusions:

1. We recognize that the experience matches others we have had.
2. We can find no relation at all between this experience and the others.
3. The experience has some relation to the other experiences, but it also differs in some way.

Depending upon our conclusion, we will utilize different mental operations to deal with these situations.

In the first case, because the object, idea, or event is so similar to others we have experienced—because it fits an existing class—we already have a concept, or generalization, available that allows us to understand it. The experience matches what we already know so we *assimilate* it. Assimilation is the process of fitting our new experiences to the concepts and generalizations we already possess. As we assimilate new data, we actually aren't learning a new concept or generalization. Instead, we are reinforcing existing ones and becoming more certain of our ideas. Assimilation is, therefore, quite important in helping us make our tenuous ideas more solid. Assimilation also helps us to understand situations relatively quickly. We utilize it to bring existing conceptual knowledge to bear on new situations.

Because of its importance it is necessary that we provide assimilation opportunities for children. When we have helped them to develop a new concept we should provide them with further examples of this concept that have the same characteristics as the original concept. By doing this we reinforce their experience. You can see the usefulness of such experiences by considering what may have occurred as you developed the concept *norms*, earlier in this chapter. You may have developed the concept by the first or second example given to you. If you did, then the subsequent examples helped you ascertain the correctness of your concept; they allowed you to determine whether the characteristics you ascribed to this concept where indeed appropriate.

In the second case, because we have no concept to fall back on, we cannot assimilate. Instead of fitting our experiences to ideas we already possess, we must develop new ideas to fit the experience. In this case we will need to *accommodate*, to develop a new classification. Accommodation, then, is the operation we utilize to begin developing new concepts or generalizations.

We will also accommodate when our existing concepts are not completely sufficient to explain a situation, as happens in the third case. Here, however, we fit our concepts or generalizations to the experience by modifying our existing ideas. We add, or in some cases subtract, characteristics from our existing concepts to allow us to understand. As a result, our concept has changed. The first grader, for example, has an existing concept of family; his own. This concept has the characteristics of including mother, father, and two children. His existing concept will need to change if he encounters classmates' families having, say, one parent or a grandparent in the parenting role. He will need to accommodate these new data. As a result his concept of family will be somewhat broader than it previously was.

Accommodation is important because it not only allows us to develop new concepts but it also permits us to broaden and refine existing ones. A great deal of our teaching in the social studies will be concerned with providing children with experiences that require accommodation. This can be accomplished by having them encounter information that differs from data they have previously encountered. Care must be taken in the selection of these data, however. Learning theory suggests that, if this information is radically different and totally unrelated to the child's past experiences, there is a good probability that the child will not be motivated to attend to it. Without attention, accommodation cannot occur. It also suggests that the more motivating situations will be ones that are just slightly different from what the child expects but still related to the child's experiences in some way. Presenting the first grade child, in our example above, with the families of his peers—families whose makeup differs slightly from his own—would probably cause him to attend to the data.

Concept learning requires both assimilation and accommodation. Unfortunately, there are no hard-and-fast guidelines that suggest that a specific experience will elicit a specific operation. In fact, a given experience may result in one child assimilating and another child accommodating. (The child who comes from a single-parent family assimilates when she is given this example of family; the boy from the two-parent, two-child family probably accommodates.) Thus, it is necessary for the teacher—if he or she is interested in facilitating the development of specific concepts—to initially determine the children's understanding of the concept, and then provide them with the most appropriate type of experience.

Concept Learning in the School

The key to helping children develop social science concepts and generalizations through assimilation and accommodation lies in providing them with cumulative experiences with these ideas. That is, in order to understand concepts fully, it is necessary for children to encounter them repeatedly over a period of time. This implies that children will work with many of the same concepts year after year. A kindergartner, for example, might begin developing a concept of law by considering rules in the school or classroom. In later grades this child might encounter content concerned with community and state laws, ideas about laws of the nation, and examine laws from a cross-national perspective. With each experience this child's concept assumes greater depth, and the child gradually moves to attaining an adult concept of law.

The idea, or concept if you will, of developing concepts and generalizations in depth by having children encounter and work with them year after year is referred to by the term *spiral*. This term is a very apt one in that it suggests a continual movement toward a relatively complete and full understanding of the concepts and generalizations. In each grade these ideas are approached with different content, chosen to provide examples of the concepts or generalizations that contain qualities or characteristics that the children's existing concepts do not. The third grader, for instance, who has previously learned the concept of law by studying school rules will encounter a more sophisticated example of the concept in studying community laws. Each time the child revisits a given concept or generalization, it is encountered with increasing generality, abstractness, and complexity (Taba et al., 1971).

Our knowledge goals, then, will be met through a relatively in-depth development of concepts and generalizations. In order to do this the elementary curriculum cannot be concerned with an overly large number of these ideas. This implies that the concepts selected for the social studies program should be ones that best facilitate our students' attainment of the goals of social studies education. The National Council for the Social Studies, the professional organization of social studies educators, has suggested that the most appropriate concepts and generalizations will be ones that serve the following three purposes:

1. Providing an historical perspective to the child. A sense of the past serves as a buffer against detachment and presentism—living just for today—and thereby assists an individual in establishing a cultural identity.
2. Helping a person perceive patterns and systems in the environment, including a global perspective. It is this ordering function which makes the social universe, even with its increasing complexity, more understandable.
3. Being a foundation of social participation. Without valid knowledge, participation in the affairs of society could be ineffectual and irresponsible. [National Council for the Social Studies, 1979]

Ideally, you are free to choose for your curriculum any concepts and generalizations, from any discipline, that would fulfill these purposes. In reality this would be a major undertaking, requiring that you, in essence, become a master of the social sciences and history. Fortunately, this isn't necessary. The job has been done for you and you will have a variety of sources at your disposal to provide you with very specific ideas as to the concepts and generalizations that should be included in your curriculum. National organizations, such as the National Council for the Social Studies, state education offices, and usually, local school districts publish curriculum guides containing these. Usually professional social studies methods books devote some attention to outlining specific concepts and generalizations that can be utilized (as we shall do in the next chapter). Children's textbooks are also a source. Most teachers' editions of those books lay out the specific concepts and generalizations upon which they focus.

Regardless of whichever source (or sources) you utilize, you will notice at least two things. First, it will indicate those concepts and generalizations that have been recognized as *major* ones. Not only do they serve the purposes outlined by the National Council for the Social Studies, but they are also the most important ideas that the social sciences and history have to offer. These major concepts and generalizations are the ones that have been recognized to explain most effectively the world in which we live. Second, you will notice that there are usually a relatively limited number of these; thus we can teach all of them to some depth. For example, *The Taba Program in Social Science,* an elementary textbook program published by Addison-Wesley (1972), focused on eleven key concepts throughout the elementary years. In the same manner, The Social Science Framework for the California Public Schools lists eighteen broad interdisciplinary concepts to be developed in grades kindergarten through twelve.

Approaching Concepts and Generalizations

The approach most commonly used for teaching major concepts and generalizations in contemporary elementary schools is an interdisciplinary one. Instead of studying specific disciplines, such as history and geography, children focus upon specific areas of interest, or topics, and utilize the most appropriate concepts and generalizations, regardless of discipline, that will enable them to gain a fuller understanding of this area. In studying about some aspects of families, for example, a first grader might deal with concepts and generalizations from sociology (A family is a group), economics (A family has needs and wants), and anthropology (Families do special things on holidays). Obviously, these first graders won't be studying sociology, geography, economics, and so forth as separate disciplines. Instead they will be using the knowledge from these disciplines that is most appropriate to their situation.

This integrated approach to social studies makes a great deal of sense when we think about our purposes for social studies in the elementary school. As we have noted previously, concepts and generalizations are taught not simply to be known or memorized by the children, but to serve the more global purposes of developing world knowledge and citizenship. Situations that call for social action (which is a very important component of world citizenship) usually don't call for knowledge from only one area. We use whatever knowledge is appropriate to the situation at hand. The ability to engage in social action is not something that comes at a specific point in our lives (we don't wake up on our eighteenth birthday as a social actor, for example). It is something that is developed over time and through experience. Using an integrated approach in the elementary school allows us to provide such experiences.

Structuring Concept Learning

Opportunities for social action, such as the example with the polluted stream we mentioned earlier in this book, offer one source to help children develop social studies knowledge, skills, and abilities. These opportunities will tend to occur spontaneously and will require that you "think on your feet" as you help your children plan and carry out the learning experiences that are appropriate to the situation. These social action experiences will represent one strand in your social studies curriculum. Usually, however, there will be another strand. This strand will be devoted to helping children learn about the world. Usually this strand will be institutionalized as the established social studies curriculum in your school.

It is not uncommon for schools or school districts to adopt a social studies curriculum, and guidelines will be published indicating the specific concepts, generalizations, and skills to be developed within this curriculum. Often these guidelines will indicate, for a given grade, appropriate general content areas to be explored and give some indication of the most appropriate topics to be considered in each grade. Usually these suggested topics have been developed so that there is articulation among the grades, so that content in one grade does not unnecessarily duplicate content used in another grade. Rather, the content builds upon and enriches conceptual learnings from previous grades. Topics chosen for particular grades are often chosen using one, or a combination, of the following approaches.

1. *A text-based approach.* Often a specific textbook series will be adopted by a specific school district or school, and topics chosen for each grade will reflect topics dealt with in the text for that grade. With this approach the text is seen as the major learning resource. Teachers, of course, are free to bring in other resources and activities when dealing with specific topics. However, it is usually expected that the concepts

and topics dealt with in the textbook will be considered by the children. This approach is probably the most common one in use today.

2. *A selected-topics approach.* Curriculum committees in a school or district will generate a list of topics they think is appropriate to a given grade. Usually these topics represent a combination of those currently being studied in a given grade plus additional ones that reflect current social needs and concerns. Teachers are usually free to select from these topics as well as implement topics of their own choice.

3. *The expanding-communities approach.* This approach tends to be a modification of the curriculum pattern developed by Paul Hanna in the 1930s. Working from the idea that we live in a series of communities, each of which is contained in larger communities, the sequence of topics to be considered, beginning in kindergarten, is as follows:

   K. The child.
   1. Family and school communities.
   2. The neighborhood community.
   3. The child's local communities: city, metropolis, county.
   4. The state and region of states.
   5. The nation.
   6. World cultures

This approach to sequencing content is utilized in many texts and is the most popular approach in elementary schools throughout the country (Superka, Hawke, and Morrissett, 1980). Unfortunately, it is sometimes interpreted to mean that, in a given grade, only the child's neighborhood community or state is studied. This is not the case. Content that provides a contrast to the specific community can be utilized in developing understandings. For example, a study of the community can incorporate data from a variety of communities in the world.

4. *A social-roles approach.* This is the newest approach to structuring the social studies curriculum. Its intent is to gear content so that it reflects how people actually participate in society. To this end, it suggests utilizing seven social roles individuals assume throughout their lives. These roles include: (1) citizen; (2) worker; (3) consumer; (4) family member; (5) friend; (6) member of various social groups; and (7) self (Superka and Hawke, 1982). Concepts and generalizations are to be developed as students examine the distinctiveness of each of these roles as well as their interrelatedness. This approach has not enjoyed widespread implementation.

5. *Lifelong roles.* This approach, developed by Joyce and Alleman-Brooks (1979), works from the rationale that one of the major purposes of social studies is to help children "become active, knowledgeable, adaptive human beings, capable of functioning within the range of lifelong roles to which they aspire" (p. 5). They believe that the social studies program should be geared to children's needs, both present and future. Children should begin to explore these roles and gradually become more comfortable and proficient with them. The five roles which are the foci of the program are as follows:

(1) Citizen: a member of society, sharing in its rights, responsibilities, and obligations.
(2) Family member: engaging in the relationships and responsibilities of this primary group.
(3) Occupational role: engaging in the activities that provide one's livelihood.
(4) Avocational role: engaging in leisurely pursuits.
(5) Personal efficacy: understanding and working toward self-fulfillment.

The examination of these roles, in both present and future contexts, is to be approached through the study of what Joyce and Alleman-Brooks refer to as organizing themes. These themes include *consumerism, ecology, energy, government and politics, human equality, human life cycle, intercultural relations, our legal system, media,* and *morality.* For example, the role of family member can be approached through consumerism as students look at decisions made by family members in spending money. Or citizenship becomes the focus as students study how they and others fit into and make an impact on our legal system. Joyce and Alleman-Brooks provide a large number of examples of how lifelong roles can be approached through the organizing theme in their book.

Aware that a large proportion of American schools follow the expanding-horizon approach to sequencing social studies, Joyce and Alleman-Brooks indicate that their approach and the former are compatible. Lifelong roles studied via the different organizing themes can be studied in the first grade in terms of neighborhoods, or in the fourth grade in terms of states.

It should be pointed out here that these five approaches to sequencing content are suggested approaches and should not be perceived as sequences that need to be slavishly and literally followed. The easiest way to turn a child off to social studies (as many of us know) is to base the total program on textbook activities. Yet many teachers believe that if a text-based approach is the one recommended, then that is their only source of activities. Similarly, teachers get turned off to social studies when they feel they must follow someone else's plans (as the second approach could imply) or teach only about the children's school when using the expanding-communities approach.

No, these approaches are frameworks, suggesting ideas for topics that could be considered in a given grade. (Some experienced teachers ignore them completely, preferring to use topics that they, themselves, have developed.) As frameworks they simply provide you with broad ideas of what's appropriate.

Synthesis: Child Development and Concept Learning _____

A story is told about John Dewey visiting an elementary school classroom and being invited to talk with the children about their studies. Having found that they had been studying the earth and its physical properties, Dewey posed a problem for them.

"Suppose," he is purported to have said, "you had a shovel that allowed you to dig all of the way to the center of the earth. When you finally got there, what would you find?"

His question drew blank stares, and no responses, from the students.

"Oh, Mr. Dewey," their obviously flustered teacher injected, "the children can't answer because you've asked the wrong question."

She then proceeded to ask the "right" question.

"Class, what is the state of the core of the planet?"

As they had been taught, the children responded, "Igneous fusion."

There are probably a number of reasons why these children could tell, but in reality didn't actually know, what was at the center of the earth. It may be that they were expected only to memorize facts, or perhaps were being taught the concept *igneous fusion* verbally, without being helped to actually understand what it was. It may also be that they were being taught this concept in a way that was inappropriate to their level of cognitive development. These children had probably not yet reached a stage in their development where (as you are doing right now) they could deal with thoughts and concepts abstractly.

The same can be said of the children whom you will teach. Developmental theory suggests that, until the age of eleven at the earliest, students will have difficulty engaging in thought about things that are in some way not directly related to their own lives and experiences. This has strong implications for the teaching and learning of concepts and generalizations. If, in planning to teach these, we do not consider the developmental characteristics of our students, there is a chance that the learning experiences we provide for the students will be inappropriate to them. In that case, as we saw in the example, little if any real learning (and a great deal of frustration on both the part of the teacher and the student) can be expected to occur.

Let's briefly examine some of the developmental characteristics of our students that should be considered in planning learning experiences. In doing this we'll focus on children at the preoperational and concrete operational stages of development. The former would include students in kindergarten, grade one, and possibly grade two. The latter encompasses students in the second through fifth, and possibly sixth, grades.

Children at both the preoperational and concrete operational stages of development learn best by doing, by actually manipulating their environment. Activities developed to teach concepts and generalizations should physically engage the children as much as possible. For preoperational children there should be little reliance on activities that are solely language oriented. When it is necessary for you to verbally describe something to the children, your descriptions should be as concrete as possible. Concrete operational children can engage in language-oriented activities to an increasingly greater extent; reading and writing are most effective when they are tied to firsthand experiences the children have had. Language experiences are most appropriate when they follow, rather than precede, the concrete experiences. Neither the preoperational nor the concrete operational child should be taught concepts by verbal means alone.

The preoperational child is egocentric, believing that everyone thinks as he or she does. This egocentrism is gradually lost by the concrete operational child. Younger children encountering content about people in situations different from their own cannot be expected to completely understand these situations. They will tend to view these situations as being exactly like their own. This is not to say that content about other peoples and cultures cannot be used to develop concepts and generalizations. However, the content chosen to be developed should deal with situations that the child has had previous experience with in his or her own life. Children at the stage of concrete operations can be expected to increasingly be able to deal with this type of content and to view situations from more than one perspective. They can be helped to look at ideas from points of view other than their own.

The classification abilities of preoperational children are relatively limited. These abilities will gradually be developed as the child moves through the stage of concrete operations. Concepts are mental groups of things, objects, events, and so on that have specific characteristics in common. We develop these groups through a process of classification. With preoperational children this classification tends to be relatively rudimentary, being based on only the more apparent aspects of things they have experienced (with the youngest children this would be its shape, its color, or its function). Therefore, classification activities should be with very specific, and very obvious, examples of the concept being taught. Older preoperational children are capable of breaking larger classes into subclasses; however, they may have difficulty in seeing the relationship between the larger class and each of its subclasses. Concrete operational children, on the other hand, are increasingly able to classify and to see relationships among classes and subclasses. They will be capable of realizing that more global concepts (such as pollution) include subconcepts (such as litter and noise pollution). As a result they can be expected to develop more sophisticated concepts than their younger peers. In addition, they are able to perform multiple classifications, to take elements from several classifications and make them into a new class.

Again, classification activities given to by all of these children should work as much as possible from firsthand experiences. These children should not be taught concepts verbally or by being given the definition of the concept.

The preoperational child has a relatively narrow concept of time and space. This gradually becomes broader as the child moves through concrete operations. For the younger child, the past is basically everything that has happened up to the present point in time. This child cannot comprehend the lapse of time between a past event and the present. It is unwise to introduce content about the past and expect the child to realize how long ago something actually occurred. This does not mean that content dealing with past events cannot be used with these children. More emphasis should be placed on the event rather than on the time it occurred. Similarly, these children have difficulty realizing the distance that separates places. To them, a foreign country and a town five miles away may be thought of as being equally far away. Again, this does not mean that content dealing with other nations, and so on, cannot be used with these children; it can if your expectation is *not* that they will comprehend the distance separating them from that place. In the case of both time and space it is probably wise to use the child's here and now as the basis for moving to consideration of other places and time. As this child moves through the stage of concrete operations, both of these types of concepts will become broader.

Springboards to Discussion _____

1. Assimilation and accommodation are often difficult concepts for teachers to understand. In this chapter we said that, in encountering something new, we do one of three things:
   • We recognize that the experience matches others we have had (assimilation).
   • We recognize that the experience has some relation to other experiences, but also differs (accommodation).
   • We recognize that the experience has no relation to other experiences (accommodation).
   One way to make assimilation and accommodation meaningful is to reflect upon instances in our lives when we engaged in these processes. Using the three examples above, think about situations when each occurred. Then, reflect upon what you did and thought in each situation. Also try to remember how you felt. Share your reflections with a partner or in a group and try to come up with some general statements about these processes.
2. Defend the following statement: Although it is acceptable at times to ask students to provide definitions of concepts, this is not the optimum means of gauging student attainment of the concept. Then tell what you consider to be more optimal means.
3. Obtain a copy of Barry Wadsworth's *Piaget for the Classroom Teacher* (New York: Longman, 1978). Read the short introduction to Chapter 20, "Assessing Cognitive Development Using Piagetian Techniques." Then, try a number of the classification assessments with children in different grades. Note the similarities and differences you find. Relate this to statements made in this chapter about children's classification abilities.

References _____

JOYCE, WILLIAM, AND ALLEMAN-BROOKS, JANET. *Teaching Social Studies in the Elementary and Middle Schools.* New York: Holt, Rinehart and Winston, 1979.

MARTORELLA, PETER H. *Concept Learning in the Social Studies: Models for Structuring Curriculum.* Scranton: Intext Educational Publishers, 1971.

National Council for the Social Studies. "Revision of the NCSS Social Studies Curriculum Guidelines," *Social Education,* Vol. 43 (April 1979), pp. 260–273.

SUPERKA, DOUGLAS P., AND HAWKE, SHARRYL. *Social Roles: A Focus for Social Studies in the 1980s.* (A Project SPAN Report.) Boulder: Social Science Education Consortium, 1982.

SUPERKA, DOUGLAS P., HAWKE, SHARRYL, AND MORRISSETT, IRVING. "The Current and Future State of the Social Studies," *Social Education,* Vol. 44 (May 1980).

TABA, HILDA, DURKIN, MARY, FRAENKEL, JACK, AND McNAUGHTON, ANTHONY. *A Teacher's Handbook to Elementary Social Studies.* Reading, MA: Addison–Wesley, 1971.

WADSWORTH, BARRY. *Piaget for the Classroom Teacher.* New York: Longman, 1978.

3

The Knowledge Base of the Social Studies: The Social Science Disciplines

After reading this chapter you should be able to:

1. Describe the major academic disciplines on which the conceptual goals of the social studies are based.

2. Enumerate the key concepts and generalizations of each discipline.

3. Provide examples of the usage of these concepts and generalizations in the elementary grades.

In this chapter we consider the six disciplines that are the major sources of conceptual goals for the social studies—anthropology, sociology, political science, economics, geography, and history. Although each will be examined separately, the format for all is the same. First, you'll find a brief definition of the discipline that indicates the general types of knowledge that it provides us concerning humans and their world. This definition is broadened as, next, a number of concepts and generalizations from each discipline are examined. These were chosen using the criterion of perceived importance in both the discipline and to elementary school children. In making this choice, a variety of resources were consulted. These included professional literature from each of the disciplines; state curriculum guides; and children's social studies textbooks. Concepts and generalizations that were noted to be important by all of these sources were assumed to be major ones.

To show you how they can be applied to your classroom work, every generalization is accompanied by a number of different examples of the types of content that might be utilized to help children in various grades develop the generalizations. Incidentally, as you examine these content examples you should also be able to get some idea of how a spiral curriculum works—how the same generalizations can be taught at greater levels of complexity and with different content as students move through the grades. Specific grade levels have not been attached to the examples. This has been done intentionally to indicate that specific topics need not be the exclusive property of one grade.

In the synthesis section at the end of this chapter we'll consider how abstract concepts and generalizations can be made concrete and meaningful

to children. This section will introduce some of the basic steps of unit planning; that is, steps that are usually taken both by teachers and the writers of
texts used in classrooms.

Anthropology _____

The subject matter of anthropology is humankind—how people live and
behave. Its purpose is perhaps best summed up as providing answers to the
three questions upon which *Man: A Course of Study* (Curriculum Development Associates, 1968) focused. In this fifth grade social studies program
students were asked to consider the following:

1. What is human about human beings?
2. How did they get that way?
3. How can they be made more so?

In order to answer these questions anthropologists study humans from
two perspectives, the physical and the cultural. The first of these is concerned with humans as physical beings. One of the areas considered in
physical anthropology is the evolution of humans, in which the biological
and behavioral differences between people and other primates are docu-
mented. Physical anthropology also probes the differences among humans,
studying the biological variations among the different people on earth.

The cultural approach to anthropology focuses on what humans have
done, and are doing, to adapt and survive in their environments. One of its
subfields, archaeology, is concerned with cultures of the past, and adapta-
tion is studied from a more or less historical perspective. Linguistics. a
second subfield of cultural anthropology, looks at communication as a survival tool, examining the development of and relationships among human
languages. Finally, the subfield of ethnology has as its subject matter human behavior that occurs within cultural groups. It is concerned with documenting the similarities and differences between human groups and provides knowledge about the characteristic ways in which people behave, their
beliefs and values, and how they utilize their physical surroundings.

In the elementary grades, anthropology tends to be approached most frequently from the perspective of ethnology, with content about the behavior
and beliefs of relatively contemporary cultural groups and subgroups being
used. This multicultural approach is important since it allows children to
learn about their own culture through contrast with other groups. It can
pose potential problems, though. Some aspects of the contrasting culture
may seem strange, funny, or even barbaric to the children. This will occur
primarily because they are evaluating the culture in terms of their own.
Because of this they need to be helped to realize these aspects of culture are
the ways that the specific groups have developed to adapt to and survive in
their respective environment. The children can be made aware of the fact
that elements of their own culture, while important to them, may not be
seen as necessary in other cultures. Success in helping children develop the

awareness that a culture makes eminent sense to its members and should not be evaluated from the perspective of another culture is a positive step to the breakdown of ethnocentrism and the development of world citizens.

Concepts of Anthropology

Culture is the distinctively human invention that sets humans apart from other animals. Basically it may be thought of as the way of life developed by a group to ensure survival in its physical and social environment. This way of life affects how individuals perceive and act upon the world in which they live; how and what they think; how they behave in different situations; and even how they speak. In fact, the culture in which individuals are reared is so pervasive that, unless they have contact with other cultures, it is difficult for them to realize that much, if not all, that they do is affected by it. Culture is the natural social element that has surrounded them from birth to such an extent that they are not conscious of it.

Culture is a very broad concept that encompasses a variety of different components or elements. Each of these elements is, itself, a concept. These include the following.

Institutions, which are longstanding ways of doing things developed to ensure the well-being and continuation of a group. The more important institutions include those for caring for and promoting the well-being of the individual (the family); for transmitting skills, beliefs, and values to group members (education and religion); and for resolving conflict and making decisions within the group (government). Although institutions change, as do cultures themselves, they tend to be relatively stable and permanent.

Knowledge includes the repertoire of skills, understandings, and behaviors utilized by the group. Included in this component are such general elements as language and technology, but knowledge also encompasses such specifics as methods of child rearing, food preparation, and healing. Cultural knowledge is transmitted both formally (usually in the context of the school) and informally through families, peer groups, and the communications media.

Beliefs are those things a culture holds to be true. These may or may not be based on factual evidence. Included in this category would be religious beliefs, such as how the world was created, the existence of a supreme being or beings, and ideas about life after death. Conceptions of one's group as being special, or chosen in some way, would also fit into this category.

Values are the clusters of beliefs concerned with what is good, right, or important. Some cultural values would include perceptions about the place of the young or elderly within the group; attitudes concerned with sexual activity among unmarried individuals; beliefs about ownership and use of property; and ideas about the preservation of life.

Customs and Traditions are behaviors and activities, developed over a long period of time, that are used in specific situations. Ceremonies that mark the adulthood of group members, ways of signifying the marriage of two individuals, and activities that take place during a group's holidays would all be examples of these longstanding behaviors.

Artifacts are the tangible things that the group makes use of to meet both physical and aesthetic needs and wants. The tools utilized by the group, ways in which food is prepared, and the arts and crafts of the group would be included in this cultural category.

The preceding concepts help us understand what culture is. The following two concepts help us to understand how cultures survive, yet remain dynamic.

Enculturation is the process through which an individual becomes a member of a culture. That is, it is the way in which the individual is taught and learns the knowledge, beliefs, skills, and expectations of the group. The purpose of enculturation is to allow the individual to function within the group—to behave in ways that do not disrupt its rhythm and, thus, insure its continuation.

Cultural change. Cultures do not remain static; elements (such as beliefs and values) are introduced, modified, or discarded. This change, which can be rapid or gradual, can be due to a variety of factors. New knowledge or technology may be developed within the culture. Increased mobility and communication may allow contact with other cultures that previously was not possible; thus facilitating elements being brought into the culture. Or, a culture may be intruded upon, in some way, by another culture and adopt elements of that culture.

Generalizations of Anthropology

Generalization 1. People living in groups develop a culture.

Concept: Culture (cultural elements)

Content Examples
- The games and activities (which may be considered to be cultural knowledge and customs) played by children around the world.
- Past and current immigrant groups in the United States, focusing on specific elements such as language, customs, and beliefs that differentiated these groups from others.
- The religious beliefs and practices of the Inca, Aztec, and Maya.

Generalization 2. Acceptable ways of behaving are learned within a culture.

Concepts: Enculturation, cultural group

Content Examples
- Games played by children with emphasis on who teaches children to play. The idea that children learn from other children as well as adults would be highlighted.
- Historical content about immigrant groups, such as the Russian Jews in New York City, or data about contemporary groups [Mexican-American or Inuit (Hudson Bay Eskimo), in Canada, for example] that deals with things learned in the mainstream and minority cultures.
- Folktales from around the world that contain a moral related to individual behavior.

Generalization 3. People everywhere have the same basic needs and wants; their culture, however, affects how these are met.

Concepts: Needs, wants, culture

Content Examples
- Special foods eaten by members of the class who belong to different ethnic or cultural groups. If the class is not multicultural, choose foods eaten by selected cultural groups.
- The music (an aesthetic want) of people around the world.
- The types of shelter built by the New England and Virginia colonists and their Native American counterparts from the same building materials.

Generalization 4. Cultures change; although this change is continuous, the speed with which it occurs varies.

Concept: Cultural change

Content Examples
- Toys (artifacts) of today and yesterday.
- Data on the origin of selected words in American English with emphasis on how contact with other cultures affects language.
- Occupations held by women today and eighty years ago.

Sociology

If any one term could be used to describe sociology it would be the *human group*. This group is not restricted to any size—it can just as easily be three children playing on the schoolyard as it could be a tribe or nation. It is studied because it is the context in which human behavior occurs.

Sociology focuses on the examination and study of two general types of group-related behavior. The first of these encompasses the activities in which humans engage to organize, maintain, and insure that the group survives. In other words, sociology is concerned with how people affect the groups to which they belong. With larger groups, for example, this behavior might be studied by looking at universal activities: how group members make sure that the basic needs of the group are met; how the behavior of group members is regulated; and how the skills and values of the group are passed on to new members. With smaller groups, sociologists might look at the processes by which individuals assume or are given group leadership; or they might attempt to identify the types of behaviors that insure the group's goals are met. In attempting to describe how groups maintain themselves, sociologists also examine how groups relate to and interact with other groups.

The second type of group behavior that is emphasized in sociological study is concerned with how the group affects its members and the types of behavior that result from group membership. Sociologists would be interested, for example, in documenting the effects that life in a crowded urban center might have on people's willingness to help others. Similarly, they might be interested in documenting the effects that a child's race might have on how other children in a classroom interact with that child and how the child responds to their interaction.

Sociology, then, is the study of human behavior in the group context—the relationships between humans and their groups, and groups and their members. Its goal is the development of theories of human behavior, statements that explain this behavior within any group.

Concepts of Sociology

Groups, as we said earlier, can be any sized aggregation of individuals. From a sociological perspective, they can be differentiated by whether or not communication occurs within them. Those groups within which communication and interaction does occur are referred to as integrated groups and would include the family; certain classroom groups (those in which children are working cooperatively on a task as opposed to simply being seated together); peer groups; and societies. Nonintegrated groups, on the other hand, are collections of individuals in specific situations where no interaction in occuring. A group of people waiting for a bus or an audience watching a movie would be examples of this type of group.

Groups can also be characterized by the function that they serve. Those responsible for the socialization of an individual are referred to as *primary groups*. They teach individuals the necessary (or primary) social skills. The family, of course, is a key primary group and the elementary class has the potential for being another such group. Usually individuals belong to primary groups for extended periods of time. *Secondary groups*, on the other hand, tend to be less permanent and personal and do not share in the socialization process to any great extent. Throughout life, individuals belong to a variety of secondary groups—from the scouts to the army to the PTA.

A *society* is an integrated group within which interaction and communication occurs to allow the group to maintain itself and continue through time. A society tends to be territorially organized; it is located in a specific area. The interaction that allows a society to exist can be direct, with group members communicating personally with each other. Thus, a family can rightfully be considered to be a small society. Usually a society is thought of in larger terms, though, and we speak of groups such as American or Soviet society. Here communication among individuals tends not to be direct and personal. As long as interaction and communication, however indirectly, is occurring and allows the groups to maintain themselves and persist, these larger entities can indeed be considered societies.

Norms may be thought of as standards of behavior held by groups. In essence, they are written or unwritten rules that tell individuals how to act in specific situations in specific groups. For example, a group of children may have certain rules, never verbalized, about tattling on each other. In other types of groups, norms have been institutionalized as written laws.

Norms, of course, can change over time. Smoking in large groups was, in the past, a very acceptable behavior. Today it is gradually being perceived as inappropriate behavior and as a violation of norms.

When individuals do not act according to group beliefs, they are not acting normally and are potentially subject to sanctions from the group. They are punished in some way for violating the norms. Tattlers don't get played with and smokers are asked to put out their cigarettes. Sanctions are not always negative, however, and rewards are often given for socially acceptable behavior.

A *role* is a set of behaviors that is expected of an individual. In a given situation there are certain norms to which individuals are expected to adhere. In adhering to these norms the individual is assuming his or her role. During a given day individuals will assume a variety of roles—parent, teacher, friend—each entailing specific ways of acting. Some behaviors will cross roles; we can act in somewhat similar ways as parents and teacher. Others, however, will not. We don't usually caution a friend not to spill his milk, for example. Because roles are intimately tied to norms, they too change over time. That is, the expectations for the behavior of individuals in specific situations may become different. Today we are seeing the role of parent becoming less rigid from a gender standpoint. Fathers can perform activities that were, in the past, considered to be part of the mother's role.

Socialization is the process by which an individual learns the norms (and therefore roles), skills, attitudes, and values of the group. It is a lifelong process that begins in infancy and continues as the individual interacts in his or her environment. The family is the first agent of socialization that the individual encounters. Here a variety of things are learned, such as sex-role expectations, appropriate behaviors, and values. As the individual matures, other forces—the media (especially television), school, peer groups, and church—also act as sources of social learning.

Socialization affects how the individual thinks and behaves. Appropriate ways of thinking and behaving are, to some extent, dependent upon the group doing the socialization. Acceptable behavior in one group, such as the peer group, may not be appropriate in another, such as the family. This can pose problems and conflicts for individuals unless they learn to modify their behavior so that it is appropriate to the group and situation.

Generalizations of Sociology

Generalization 1. People live in groups.

Concept: Groups

Content Examples
- Different types of families; including those of classmates as well as of different cultures.
- Historical data concerning settlement patterns of immigrant groups, in specific neighborhoods of large cities and/or in regions of the United States.
- Interest groups that people voluntarily join to protect the environment.

Generalization 2. A society is composed of many interdependent groups.

Concepts: Society, interdependent groups

Content Examples
- Information about the various groups of workers found in schools (societies in themselves)—what they do, why they are needed, and how they help one another.
- Data about the interrelationships of family, learning and governing groups in different communities.
- The contributions of different ethnic groups in the United States in specific areas such as the arts and sciences, and how these contributions affect other groups.

Generalization 3. Social institutions perform the important function of socialization; through this process individuals learn their role and status, as well as group norms.

Concepts: Socialization, role, norms, status (one's rank in a given group)

Content Examples
- The specific types of things learned from families, friends, and teachers.
- Historical data concerning the apprentice system as a means of learning a craft or trade as well as data about contemporary occupations (such as plumbing and weaving) where this system is used.
- The educational and job opportunities of individuals of different castes in premodern India.

Generalization 4. Individuals can assume different roles in different groups.

Concepts: Roles, groups

Content Examples
- An examination and comparison of who does specific jobs in different families.
- Community groups to which children themselves, as well as children of different eras and cultures, belong. Emphasis, here, would be on what the children do and how they act in these groups.
- The activities engaged in by pioneer women and their counterparts who remained in settled areas.

Political Science

Political science studies decision making as it relates to organized groups of people. This decision making is explored by examining the components that make up a political system. These are:

1. The actual process of decision making; how a decision is made for a given group.
2. Who is responsible for making the decision.
3. How the decision is carried out.

These three areas of study are closely related and information gathered about one of them will often help to broaden understanding of the total political system.

When the process by which decisions are made is studied, several ideas are considered. The first of these is why it is necessary for a decision to be made at all, why a particular problem must be considered as opposed to other problems. In dealing with this concern, political scientists attempt to determine what goals the group has and to understand the conflicts that are occurring within the group that requires the specific problem to be resolved. How a particular problem gets to the attention of the decision makers is also analyzed. Information is gathered in relation to who is bringing the problem to the attention of the decision makers and the strategies that they employ to insure that a decision will be made. Finally, the decision itself is analyzed. The rule or policy developed for the total group is examined in terms of how it relates to the initial need and to the means employed to insure that the decision was made.

The study of who makes the decisions for the group basically focuses on the power structure of a group. It attempts to determine who has and does not have authority. It examines how people get power and the authority to make decisions. Information is also gathered in relation to how much power people actually have, what decisions they can and cannot make, and why these limitations exist.

The final concern of political science is how the decision is carried out. In this area emphasis is placed on examining and analyzing the mechanisms employed to put the outcome of the decision-making process into practice. Attention is given to who is delegated the authority to insure that a decision is implemented. Concern is also directed toward determining the affects of the decision on the individuals and groups toward which it is directed.

Political Science Concepts

The *political system* encompasses all of the organizations and processes that contribute to decision making in organized groups—from the setting of agendas for decision making to the actual making and carrying out of the decision. Because it is so all-encompassing it can be better understood by examining three concepts that, taken together, make up a political system.

Political institutions are the elements of the political system that attempt to influence the decision making. Basically, these elements fall into two categories. The first includes those who want their wishes to be carried out—individual voters, interest groups and political parties. The second is made up of those who actually do the deciding. The latter individuals may be elected or appointed from the group.

Government, although often equated with the political system, is in its strictest sense the part of the system responsible for making and carrying out the decisions. In the United States we have a number of decision-making bodies with varying jurisdictions. We have the federal government, state governments, local governments, school boards, and so on. Attached to each of these are agencies responsible for seeing that their decisions are carried out.

Public policy refers to the actual decisions made within the political system that are binding on individuals and groups. Included as public policy are laws, orders, treaties, court decisions, ordinances, or, in the case of school boards, decisions about what will be studied.

Power is a key concept of political science. In fact, many political scientists see its major focus as the study of power: who has it, how they get it, and what they do with it. This concept refers to the ability to influence the thought or actions of others. Power within organized groups is not distributed equally, and individuals and subgroups will have different amounts of it within the political system. It is not uncommon, therefore, for individual or subgroups to band together and use their collective power to influence legislation.

Authority is the right given to individuals or groups to make and/or carry out decisions related to the welfare of the group. In the United States the Congress has the authority to pass laws; it also delegates the authority to enforce these laws to various agencies. Authority can be obtained in different ways—through legitimate channels, including election or succession, or through forceful means, such as a coup or revolution.

Social control refers to the processes by which the behaviors of members of organized groups are regulated so that the groups can meet their goals. Included in these processes are the laws and rules of a society and the sanction or rewards attached to disobeying or obeying these.

Generalizations of Political Science

Generalization 1. Governments are established by people.

Concept: Government

Content Examples
- Games played by children, including those in which children monitor themselves and those in which referees are used.
- The laws of different communities, with emphasis on how they are made, who makes them, and how these individuals are chosen.
- Government in the New England colonies, with opportunity to compare and contrast the democracy of the Pilgrims, as evidenced by the Mayflower Compact, with the theocracy, or church control, utilized by the Puritans.

Generalization 2. Societies have different types of political systems.

Concepts: Society, political system

Content Examples
- A focus on the decision-making aspect of the political system by contrasting how laws are made in different towns throughout the world, with emphasis on who makes the decisions—individuals, small groups, or the total population.
- The election of heads of state in different countries—for example, Great Britain, France, and the United States—with emphasis on the differences in political institutions.

Generalization 3. Every society creates public policies that reflect the values of that society.

Concepts: Society, public policies, values

Content Examples
- The rules children have in their school and the importance of these rules.
- The Bill of Rights, with analysis directed at determining what the founding fathers believed to be important for our country.

Generalization 4. Societies exert social control on their members.

Concepts: Society, social control (a function of government)

Content Examples
- The rules children have in their school and what occurs when these rules are not followed.
- Agencies used by towns and cities to enforce laws, with emphasis on the police department.
- Other types of agencies that carry out policies of state or local government; for example, policies and regulations that have been developed with respect to pollution, and the consequences attached to violating them.

Economics

Like political science, economics is concerned with the study of decision making. Here, however, the emphasis is not on all of the decisions made by organized groups of people; rather, economics focuses on the decisions groups and individuals make concerning how they will use their resources. This type of decision making is not difficult to understand because, whether we realize it or not, all of us make economic decisions on an almost daily basis. We have a specific amount of money (or time) to spend, yet we usually need and want a variety of things that cost more than we have. Consequently, we must choose what is important to us and what we will sacrifice in order to have those things.

On a societal level, of course, economic decision making is much more complex than deciding whether we should go to a movie or buy a book. In fact, it is made of up of a series of decisions, all of which are studied to provide economic knowledge. The following are some of these series of decisions:

1. Like individuals with a limited amount of money to spend, societies have a limited amount of resources. Therefore, choices need to be made as to what to produce with these resources so that the welfare of the population is maximized.
2. Tied in with the question of what to produce with limited resources is the need for a second decision: how much to produce? Societies must

decide upon the extent to which a given resource should be utilized in order to provide goods and services to people.

3. Societies must also cope with the problem of deciding what the criteria for receiving goods and services are. In other words, who gets what is produced?

As a social science, economics is concerned with the study of this type of decision making and attempts to document how societies cope with the problem of limited resources in attempting to satisfy the wants and needs of their members. One function of economics is descriptive: documenting how decisions are reached and how resources are produced, consumed, and exchanged. Another goal of economics is to probe for regularities that allow predictions to be made concerning what might occur given specific circumstances.

Concepts of Economics

Individuals depend upon both physical and human resources to satisfy their needs and wants. *Scarcity* exists when these needs and wants are greater than the resources available. If every individual or group could have all that they wanted of a given resource—without having to sacrifice anything to get it—scarcity, as far as that specific resource was concerned, would not exist. Unfortunately, this situation rarely occurs. In fact many resources, such as water and different types of energy, that were once believed to be unlimited, and therefore not scarce, have begun to become scarce. When scarcity of a resource does exist, individuals and groups are forced to make choices as to whether or not their desire for the resource can be fulfilled. Satisyfing this desire usually requires that something else be sacrificed.

Although *goods* and *services* are two discrete concepts, they are usually considered together because both represent economic resources. Goods are those material things—such as food, an automobile, clothing, and so on—that consumers buy to satisfy their wants and needs. All goods are scarce to some extent because most consumers must sacrifice the purchase of some other goods or services to acquire them. Services are, in essence, the work-for-hire of human beings. Included as producers of services would be such individuals as teachers, physicians, plumbers, and television repairpersons. *Producers* are individuals who provide goods and services that satisfy human wants and needs. Usually producers sell these goods and services; however, they may also exchange them for other goods and services. *Consumers* are individuals who use goods and services, usually purchasing them from producers. In most economic systems all individuals are consumers because they are unable to fulfill all of their needs or wants without depending upon others.

Supply and *demand* are another pair of concepts usually thought of together because they deal with a relationship between producers and consumers that affects the cost of a resource. Supply refers to the available resources; the amount of goods or services that producers are willing (or able) to provide to consumers. Demand is concerned with the amount of these goods and services that the consumer is willing and able to buy. It should be noted that both supply and demand do not reflect the actual resources available nor do they reflect the actual wants and needs of the consumer. Rather, they deal with a willingness and ability to buy and sell the resource. Even if a producer possessed a large amount of a resource but was not willing to provide that resource to consumers (such as occurred with the oil embargo in the early 1970s), it would be in short supply. In a like manner, if consumers were not willing to purchase something, or if they could not afford it, the demand for it would be low.

Exchange is the process by which goods and services are traded for other goods and services. In some cases this exchange is a direct one and individuals barter goods for goods, goods for services, or services for services. Usually, however, it is an indirect one with money being used as a medium of exchange. An individual, for example, will be paid money for a service and use that money to buy other goods and services.

In most cases within modern economic systems people have become specialized, producing a specific good or service. With this specialization it has become difficult for individuals themselves to supply all of the goods or services they need or want. In fact, few (if any) individuals are capable of this. Therefore it is necessary to rely on others to meet demands. As a result, a web of *interdependence* has developed; individuals with a good service provide this to others and, in turn, are provided with goods or services by others.

Generalizations of Economics

Generalization 1. People have unlimited needs and wants but limited resources; therefore, choices must be made.

Concept: Scarcity

Content Examples
- The needs and wants of families around the world.
- Supplies that colonists brought to the New World. The concepts of scarcity and choice can be introduced with these data through an examination of why certain items were brought while others were left behind.

Generalization 2. A society's economic system reflects decisions that society has made as to what is important.

Concepts: Economic system, values

Content Examples
- The variety of services provided by community or state with emphasis on the types of services provided (such as schools and roads), how these are paid for, and why they are provided while others are not.
- Business ownership in the United States and the Soviet Union can be compared to highlight the different beliefs about the place of government in the economic system.

Generalization 3. Producers exchange their goods and services with other producers to meet their needs and wants.

Concepts: Producers, exchange, goods, services

Content Examples
Money as a medium of exchange can be examined in terms of how families get money through work or other sources and what is done with this money.
- The geographical sources of the various foods that children eat.
- Information concerning the imports and exports of the United States. This need not be restricted to goods alone but can include the export of services, such as technical expertise.

Generalization 4. The price of goods and services reflects the relationship between their scarcity and the need or want for them.

Concepts: Cost, goods, services, scarcity

Content Examples
- Differences in food prices, under different conditions, at different times of the year. This should allow comparisons of costs of produce, when it is in and out of season, as well as its costs when it is scarce for other reasons (such as crops being destroyed).
- The invention of the automobile and its costs prior to and after the development of the assembly line can be used to help children realize that the assembly line allowed workers to make more cars than they did previously, and allowed the cars to be sold more cheaply.

Geography _____

The basic emphasis of geography is the study of places on earth. This study is approached from a variety of perspectives. One of these looks at the earth from a biophysical standpoint and is concerned with locating and describing places according to their physical features. Landforms, climate, soils, and vegetation are focused upon, as is the identification and description of the physical similarities of different areas. Although it does contribute to geographic knowledge, this emphasis on the physical alone is a relatively narrow one, from a social science standpoint. It ignores the relationships that exist between humans and the earth they call their home.

Other approaches to geographic knowledge do take the human factor into account, and places on earth are considered as having both physical and human elements. Some approaches look at the reciprocal relationships that exist between people and their environment; how people adapt to and, more importantly, modify their environment. Geography documents the effect that a group's culture has on the decisions it makes in relation to the environment, how different cultures utilize the resources of similar areas in different ways. Working from this perspective, a geographer might examine how beachfront property is utilized by different people in different parts of the world.

Geographers also attempt to describe how places on earth are similar from both a physical and cultural standpoint. An attempt is made to isolate those characteristics that distinguish an area from surrounding areas but make it similar to areas in other parts of the world. In looking at a tourist region, for example, the geographer attempts to pinpoint the factors that cause it to appeal to tourists. To do this a given tourist region is compared with areas surrounding it and with other tourist regions around the world. An attempt is also made to describe the processes or events that occurred to allow this area to become a tourist region.

Places are not studied in isolation, however, since the character of a place—what it is and the use humans have made of it—is dependent upon interactions with other places. A city, for example, may become an industrial center because of its location in relation to sources of raw materials needed for production and because of its accessibility to other areas to which its products may be shipped. Geographers attempt to identify these relationships among different places and unearth factors that encourage these relationships to develop.

The study of places on earth, then, can be utilized to answer many different questions: What are the physical characteristics of the earth? How have people modified their environments? How are different places on earth similar? and How do different places relate to one another? Geography provides the knowledge to answer all of these.

Concepts of Geography

Place refers, in essence, to a piece or area of the earth. We can think of place in two ways. First, we can conceptualize it generally so that it encompasses a variety of areas having specific characteristics in common. Mountains, plateaus, valleys, and so on, would be examples of these general places. We can also consider places more specifically. Mount Rushmore and Washington, D. C., are unique places that occupy specific areas of the world. These latter places can be described in terms of their characteristics and their location in respect to other places in the world.

People live in both a physical and a cultural setting; it is the combination of these elements that makes up their *environment*. The physical setting may be thought of as everything in the environment that is natural, as opposed to having been made by humans. Elements of the physical setting include: (1) The atmosphere, or "air ocean," which envelopes the earth. This atmosphere contains the gases necessary for life and is a source of specific weather conditions and climate of an area. (2) The land, which contains soils and minerals. (3) Oceans and other bodies of water, which contribute to climatic conditions and are a source of food and minerals. (4) The living things on earth, animals and vegetation, which are sources of food and energy.

The cultural setting reflects the human imprint on the natural setting, how people use their piece of the world. Anything that modifies the physical environment—for example, cities and their attending pollution—is part of the cultural environment.

A *region* is an area that contains a unique group of features. These features differentiate it from areas that surround it but may allow it to be considered similar to other areas of the world that are removed from it in space. We can, for example, speak of coal mining regions in both Pennsylvania and Poland, which, although quite a distance apart, are in many respects more similar to each other than to areas near them.

Regions are human inventions; humans decide on the specific characteristics that make up the region. These commonly include: physical characteristics (exemplified by the Sunbelt states or by a desert); places containing common cultures or cultural artifacts (such as Arabic-speaking nations, industrial cities, or Italian-American neighborhoods); or economic and social characteristics (a blue-collar neighborhood).

A region is not limited by size. In the elementary school we can look not only to the child's neighborhood but also to groups of states as regions. The only criterion for describing a specific area as a region is that it have some type of identity that distinguishes it from other areas.

In the modern world it is almost impossible to find a place that is self-contained or does not depend on other places for goods, services, and ideas. Places are related to one another and their mutual dependence requires that they interact with each other. Thus, places on earth are connected to each other. For example, oranges from South America are shipped to Florida to be processed into juice concentrate, which may be bought in San Francisco as frozen orange juice. Citrus specialists from the United States, in turn, may work with South American grove owners to increase their crop yield. Thus, there is *spatial interaction* between the United States and South America.

The degree of interaction between places on earth will be affected by the ease with which materials, people, and ideas can flow from place to place. The greater the accessibility of an area, the easier it is for this flow to occur, and the more interaction the area will have with other areas.

As with the concept of region, spatial interaction is not restricted to areas of a specific size. It can refer to the movement of workers from one neighborhood to another in a city as well as the exchange of technicians from one country to another.

Generalizations of Geography

Generalization 1. Physical and cultural factors are responsible for differences in places on earth.

Concepts: Physical factors, cultural factors

Content Examples
- The types of houses families live in around the world, with emphasis on their physical differences attributable to building materials and climate.

- Types of houses around the world with emphasis on cultural factors—such as level of technology or interaction with other groups—that act to cause similarities and differences.
- The manmade features of different communities around the world.

Generalization 2. Change occurs constantly on earth.

Concept: Change, both physical and cultural

Content Examples
- A daily log of the weather allows children to see the physical changes that occur in their own lifespaces.
- Specific communities of the present and how they were in the past for the purposes of observing changes brought about through cultural factors.
- The Great Plains of today in contrast to what they were during the westward movement.

Generalization 3. Although environment may affect how people live to some extent, people modify the environment to satisfy their needs and wants.

Concepts: Environment, modification

Content Examples
- The jobs people hold in different communities with emphasis on both those jobs directly related to the communities' environments, such as farming and mining, as well as those that are common to most communities.
- Farming communities in the Imperial Valley of California, in Israel, and in Egypt to provide data for the development of the idea that irrigation has allowed farming to occur in many parts of the world where it wouldn't ordinarily occur.
- Exploration of the causes of water and air pollution and ways in which humans can change damaged environments.

Generalization 4. Every region is an area having characteristics differentiating it from other areas.

Concept: Region

Content Examples
- Specific physical areas in the children's neighborhood, town, or city, with emphasis on the specific characteristics they perceive them to have.
- The living patterns of cultural groups in selected cities for the purpose of identifying ethnic neighborhoods.
- The different regions of the United States as well as commonly agreed upon regions of the world, such as polar regions, can be examined to isolate the characteristics which make the specific areas regions.

Generalization 5. Places on earth are linked to each other through the exchange of goods and services.

Concept: Spatial interaction

Content Examples
- The linkages neighborhoods have with other neighborhoods can be examined in terms of who leaves the neighborhood to go to work, who comes in, and what goods—such as food—are brought into the neighborhood.
- The relationship of one large city to others can be studied to see how this relationship affects the meeting of the basic needs of the population.
- An examination of the languages used in various parts of the world and the sources of these languages.

History _____

History may be thought of in two ways. The first of these is comprehensive and includes everything that has happened in the past. Every event, regardless of its impact or significance, is included in this history. These events need not be ones that have been recorded, they simply have occurred at some point from the beginning of time.

When most people think of history, however, they do not consider it from this all-inclusive point of view. They tend to look it at from a second, more narrow, perspective. Here, history is thought of as a record, a compilation of selected statements about events that have occurred in the past. These statements are about humankind: individuals and groups adjusting to their environments and engaging in social, political, and economic activities. They deal with human conflicts and interdependence, human ideas and inventions. They also tell the story of how humans expressed themselves and their quest for values.

This second type of history, the type we deal with in the elementary social studies, can be characterized as having a human element. Not only is it primarily the story of humankind on the move, it is a story that was recorded by humans. Because of this some care must be taken in attempting to make sense out of this story. It should be remembered that the individuals who did the recording were selective—they selected the specific events that would be included in the story and possibly ignored other events that, had someone else been doing the recording, might have been included. Regardless of how objective they might try to be, their statements were influenced to some extent by their circumstances, the time in which they lived, their country, their culture, and so on. It should also be remembered that we, who examine this record, are being influenced by our own perspective. Whether we realize it or not our circumstances affect how we interpret this story.

History, then, is the human story. We can use this story to know about our world as it is and has been. We can also use this story as a source of data to help us deal with decisions concerning present problems. It provides us with alternatives based on human experiences.

Concepts from History

Continuity and *change* are ideas that need to be considered simultaneously because, combined, they form the basis on which the story that is history can be told. Continuity speaks to the idea that time marches on at a steady pace, and that events can be identified as falling in a chronological sequence. One event follows another. As this occurs, things change. They become different to some extent than they were at a previous point in time. This difference can be seen in both the physical and social environments. We know, for example, that at one time the Islands of Hawaii did not exist but were gradually built through volcanic actions. Similarly, we are seeing changes in societal perceptions toward sex roles. Women are assuming greater, and more equal, responsibilities within the society—engaging, for example, in jobs that had long and traditionally been considered men's jobs. And men are beginning to assume responsibilities previously considered to belong to women.

Multiple causation tends to explain the reason for most changes over time. Although events tend to fall in a sequence, it is rare that any one event is the sole cause of another. It is more likely that a variety of separate events — working with, parallel to, or against each other—are the antecedents of the specific event. In most cases it would be erroneous, and misleading, to attempt to find a one-for-one relationship between a specific historical occurrence and a specific cause. Is there one reason, for example, why sex roles are being modified in the contemporary United States? Or is this due to a variety of factors?

The past, of course, is the meat and potatoes of history and historical inquiry. It includes all time before the present moment. In history as a story, the past can be arbitrarily be broken into periods of time based on such characteristics as social, economic, or political development identified by the historian. This allows us to speak of such eras as the Renaissance, or the American Colonial period.

The past appears to be a relatively simple concept to understand because we all have experienced it. However, younger children are relatively limited in the depth to which they can comprehend this concept. For them, the past may be a very narrow band of time, extending only a relatively short period (such as hours, days, or weeks) before the present moment. This does not mean that it is necessary to restrict historical study to only this band of time. We can help children extend their concept of the past, however, by the beginning our study of it within this band.

Conflict results from disagreement and difference of opinion as to what ought to be in a given situation. It can arise between individuals, groups, within a nation, or between nations themselves. It can be based on disagreements over how power is allocated and used, as was the Civil War, which had the question of states' rights as one of its causes. It can arise from differences of opinion as to how the material resources of a society should be distributed, as was the Russian Revolution of 1917. Or it can come about as a result of difference in values and beliefs; whether, for example, abortion should remain legal or creationism should be taught in the public schools along with the theory of evolution.

Conflict is often thought of solely in terms of war. It can, however, be expressed within generally socially acceptable limits. It can be quite destructive to a society, as the Vietnam War was in many respects to the United States. Or conflict can serve constructive purposes and result in change that is socially positive, as did the Civil Rights movement of the 1960s and 70s.

Historical bias is, as we have noted earlier, the selection and interpretation of historical events from an individual perspective. Commager and Muessig (1980) write ". . . that the historian . . . is completely objective . . . is an illusion. There is bias in the choice of subject, bias in the selection of material, bias in its organization and presentation and, inevitably, bias in its interpretation. Consciously, or unconsciously, all historians are biased; they are creatures of their time, their race, their faith, their class, their century—creatures and even prisoners."* Similar, we might add, are those who attend to the story that is history. They, too, interpret it from their own frame of reference.

Generalizations of History

Generalization 1. Change is gradual, continuous and inevitable; however, things vary in the rate they change.

Concepts: Continuity, change

Content Examples
- Physical changes that the children have gone through since babyhood, through a comparison of pictures of themselves over several years, as well as by talking to their parents, examining their baby toys and clothes.
- Information concerning the jobs that people do today, as compared to jobs that were available in the past, with emphasis on jobs that did not exist in the past.
- An examination of farming in Egypt to demonstrate that although some farmers use modern methods of irrigation, others have not changed from irrigation practices that have existed for thousands of years.

Generalization 2. Events rarely have a single cause; instead causes tend to be complex.

Concept: Multiple causation

Content Examples
- Events that occur in children's lives; for example, an analysis of disagreements that occur in the classroom or on the playground to show that these disturbances, although appearing to have a single cause, are usually the result of several things happening.
- Towns in the western United States that grew into major cities compared with those that did not, to allow for the realization that the differences are due to a variety of factors.

*From Henry Steele Commager and Raymond H. Muessig, *The Study and Teaching of History.* © 1980 by Charles E. Merrill Publishing Co. Reprinted by permission of the publisher.

- Data about such groups as those who emigrated to the United States at the turn of the century, the English who moved to Australia, Jews to Israel, Mormons to Utah, or Haitians and Cubans to the United States in more recent times will suggest that people emigrate for many reasons: to leave overpopulated areas; to take advantage of the opportunities of a new land; to escape oppression; or to freely practice their religion.

Generalization 3. Every civilization has had certain basic beliefs about what is important.

Concepts: Civilizations, values

Content Examples
- An examination of the terms found in the Pledge of Allegiance to become aware, on a very basic level what indivisible, liberty, and justice for all mean. This examination should provide children with the understanding that the Pledge tells what Americans believe.
- The early documents of American government, such as the Declaration of Independence and the Bill of Rights, can be analyzed for the purpose of determining what our forebears believed to be important.
- Life in modern Israel and Israel of two thousands years ago, highlighting the value both groups placed on education.

Generalization 4. Conflicts have occurred wherever humans have lived. Conflict is often the source of social change.

Concepts: Conflict, change

Content Examples
- Conflicts in religious beliefs, such as those of the Pilgrims in England, which led to the settlement of the United States.
- The women's suffrage movement from its inception in 1848 to the winning of the vote in 1920. Children can also be helped to understand that there are still conflicts over this issue today and that people are still working for the rights of women.
- Data about the outcome of both the Revolution and the Civil War in the United States.

Synthesis: The Unit as a Base for Developing Concepts and Generalizations

The traditional vehicle for the development of concepts and generalizations in the social studies is the unit. As its name implies, it is the study of one specific topic. Usually, this one topic fits into a larger theme, which is dealt with for the entire year. In the expanding-communities approach, which we discussed in the last chapter, this yearly theme would be families, neighborhoods, and so on. The unit would deal with one specific aspect of this theme, such as how families meet their needs.

Any number of concepts and generalizations may be developed within a unit. For very young children it may be a single concept, such as the family group; for older students, several generalizations. Because of the interdisciplinary nature of the social studies, and of life itself, ideas to be developed in a unit are usually drawn from more than one discipline. Thus, a unit dealing with the development of cities might work with geographical ideas concerning differences in places due to physical and cultural factors. It would also include economic considerations by highlighting the exchange of goods and services from place to place. Finally, it might emphasize the historical generalizations that change is gradual, continuous, and inevitable.

As we noted in the previous chapter, concepts and generalizations are learned by repeatedly experiencing examples of them. In many respects, the social science and history ideas we have discussed are what might be thought of as long-range goals, ideas that students will completely understand only after they have had sufficient learning experiences with them. From a practical point of view, then, the concepts and generalizations themselves are not the immediate and specific knowledge objectives you'll have for your students in a given unit.

The actual ideas you'll be developing with your students may be referred to as *understandings*, or examples of the generalizations. When stated, they rephrase the generalization in terms of specific topics or content. The following is an example of an understanding, based on a political science generalization, which would be used with an upper grade unit concerned with the city-states of ancient Greece:

"Athens and Sparta had different beliefs about sex roles; this affected who could vote."

The generalization on which this is based is:

"Every society creates public policies that reflect the values of that society."

For a primary grade unit dealing with classroom life, an understanding for the same generalization would be

"There are different reasons for having classroom rules."

If you analyze these two understandings you'll be able to see some of the characteristics that they have in addition to being examples of the generalization. First, the understanding contains an example of each concept in the generalization. For the concept *society,* we see Athens and Sparta and classrooms. For values, there are beliefs about sex roles and the reasons for rules. Secondly, understandings tend to be phrased in simple language that is topic specific. They are actually stated in terms that children might articulate. Thus they give an idea of the specific content with which the children might deal. Finally, although they rephrase the generalization in terms of content, they are not meant to be fact statements. Although children indeed could memorize these without much thought, the understandings imply the use of higher thought processes—including the synthesis of data.

If you were to develop your own unit of study, you would be responsible for generating your own understandings from concepts and generalizations. If you used a text as your base you'd find that the job would have been done for you. In the teacher's manual you'd encounter, at the beginning of each unit or sequence of lessons, these ideas referred to by terms such as *main ideas.* The following are some examples of these:

- Natural resources are important to communities.
- People develop ways of working together to solve community problems.
- Communities may fade away as well as grow.

Because they are relatively content specific, understandings provide you with a good idea of what it is that the children will need to learn. They indicate not only specific examples of concepts that need to be dealt with, but also the way in which these concepts would be brought together. For the first understanding, above, children would need to examine sex roles in Athens and Sparta, the belief systems responsible for these roles, and data about who could and could not vote. (Surprisingly, they'd find that women could vote in Sparta but not in Athens.)

An analysis of an understanding will tell you *what* needs to be taught and learned. It might also suggest an order in which different ideas might need to be learned. Thus, an analysis of the classroom-rules understanding would suggest that the children would need to learn (a) the concept *rule;* (b) different rules established in different classrooms; and (c) why these rules exist. Again, if you were developing your own unit you'd need to do this analysis. If you were using a text it will have been done for you.

As far as knowledge goals are concerned, a unit will be based on social science concepts and generalizations but will work toward understandings. Although our expected outcomes will be general—we'll want the children to begin to develop the big ideas from the social sciences—our teaching will be done with specific information. How we plan to do this teaching will be discussed in detail in Chapter 10.

Springboards to Discussion _____

1. In the next chapter we will examine how current affairs can be included in the social studies curriculum. You can begin to see how studying current events can help develop knowledge goals by examining a newspaper. See if you can find items that illustrate different generalizations. You needn't restrict yourself to news items: advertisements, feature articles, and even the comics often will contain examples of important social science ideas. Choose one of your items and describe a way in which you might use it with a specific group of children.

2. Pick a specific grade level in the elementary school, preferably one with whom you have had some experience. Examine the concepts presented in this chapter. Choose the three that you perceive to be most important to children of this grade. Tell why. Then choose the three least important, again providing a rationale for your choice. Share your choices in a group of peers who have chosen different grade levels. Note similarities and differences.

3. Examine the teachers' manual of an elementary social studies textbook. Note the concepts and generalizations that are emphasized. Then examine the scope and sequence chart (usually found at the beginning of the manual), which outlines how the knowledge objectives are devel-

oped in each grade level of the series. Note how the concept of spiral is evident.

References _____

BROEK, JAN O. M., HUNKER, HENRY L., MUESSIG, RAYMOND H., AND CIRRINCIONE, JOSEPH M. *The Study and Teaching of Geography*. Columbus: Charles E. Merrill, 1980.

COMMAGER, HENRY STEELE, AND MUESSIG, RAYMOND H. *The Study and Teaching of History*. Columbus: Charles E. Merrill, 1980.

Curriculum Development Associates. *Man: A Course of Study*. Washington D.C., 1971.

EMBER, CAROL R., AND EMBER, MELVIN. *Anthropology*. Englewood Cliffs, NJ: Prentice-Hall, 1973.

FLESHER, B. M., KOPECY, K. J., AND PAUL, D. T. *A Primer in Economics*. Beverly Hills: Glencoe Press, 1976.

GWALTNEY, JAMES D. *Economics, Private and Public Choice*. New York: Academic Press, 1985.

HANLAND, WILLIAM A. *Anthropology*. New York: Holt, Rinehart and Winston, 1974.

HANNA, PAUL R. *et al. Geography in the Teaching of Social Studies, Concepts and Skills*. Boston: Houghton Mifflin, 1966.

HENSLIN, JAMES J. *Down to Earth Sociology*. New York: The Free Press, 1985.

HURVITZ, LEON H. *Introduction to Politics*. Chicago: Nelson–Hall, 1979.

JAGUARIBE, HELO. *Political Development*. New York: Harper & Row, 1973.

STRAAYER, JOHN A., AND MUESSIG, RAYMOND H. *The Study and Teaching of Political Science*. Columbus: Charles E. Merrill, 1980.

CHAPTER

4

Social Studies Content: Emphases and Concerns

CHAPTER OBJECTIVES _____

After reading this chapter you should be able to:

1. Describe various emphases that have been designated as appropriate for inclusion in the social studies curriculum:
- Global education.
- Multicultural education.
- Current affairs.
- Economic/consumer education.
- Law-related education.
- Career education.
- Energy education.

2. Provide a rationale for the incorporation of these emphases at the elementary school level.

3. Show how to plan to include these emphases in a given class' curriculum.

In Chapter 2 we considered how content was generally sequenced in the social studies. Then, in the third chapter we suggested different content that might be employed to teach the major concepts and generalizations of the disciplines. These examples were chosen to help you see the wide range of specific topics that could be used to help children function in the world. The fact that there is a wide range of applicable topics should not be misinterpreted to mean that all content will be appropriate for elementary social studies. The content you do use should be factually accurate—we don't want children growing up believing that all Indians live in tepees, or that the Dutch wear wooden shoes as they tiptoe through the tulips. It should also reflect a sensitivity to your students' capabilities and needs, as well as the needs of their community, and society as a whole. You, of course, will be the best judge of the needs of the children and their community, so we won't go into specific detail here about what should or shouldn't be considered in relation to them. (We will in a later chapter, though, discuss how to deal with controversial issues—ones on which there isn't community agreement—in your classroom.) This chapter will focus on identified societal and world needs, suggesting different emphases which should come forth in the content you choose and in the understandings you develop.

The seven emphases to be considered in this chapter basically fall into two categories. The first category deals with the development of ways of seeing, thinking about, and behaving in the world. Within this category we'll consider how we help children to become global citizens as well as active members of a multicultural society. We also discuss how we help them develop a continuing awareness of what is occurring in the world. Because your curriculum will be pervaded with content and activities related to this category, major emphasis will be devoted to it in this chapter.

The second category includes specific areas that have been identified by the public, as well as the profession, as being important for inclusion in the social studies. These include economic/consumer education, law-related education, energy-conservation education, and career education. In considering these we'll briefly discuss what each is about and how it is related to the total social studies curriculum.

A concern voiced by many teachers is that, with the need to emphasize all of these things, there might not be time to deal with content customarily thought to belong to the social studies. In the synthesis section we'll deal with that worry, showing how little or nothing from the regular curriculum needs to be sacrificed to include these seven emphases.

Major Areas of Emphasis

A Global Perspective

A primary function of the social studies has always been that of citizenship education—helping students to become active and productive members of the society to which they belong. Traditionally this citizenship education focused on the child's community, state, and nation. There has been a gradual move, however, to conceptualize citizenship more broadly—in terms of membership in a global community. Thus, citizenship education now implies not only learning how to be a citizen of one's own society but also of the world.

Can the world really be considered to be a community, though? Let's examine some data:

1. People throughout the world share the same problems. The rapid dwindling of nonrenewable resources, human pollution of the atmosphere, the restriction of nuclear armaments, and international terrorism are but a few of the concerns shared by all the nations of the world. These problems are ones that will probably not be resolved by one nation alone but require a mutual cooperation on the part of all nations.

2. The people of the world are economically interdependent. Nations are not self-sufficient and there is a great dependence on other nations to satisfy needs and wants. Americans drive cars made in Europe and Asia, fueled by petroleum from the Middle East, Africa, and South America. The United States exports everything from wheat for Russian bread (and vodka) to technology in the form of students returning home to third world countries with degrees from American universities.

3. There is greater opportunity today for people of the world community to interact with each other. Advances in communication allow us to be in contact with other places in the world almost instantaneously. An individual in San Franciso can see an event occurring in London as it is occurring thanks to communication satellites. It is also possible to pick up the telephone in Boston and call, with little delay, Osaka, Japan. Similarly, advances in transportation allow world travel, once restricted to the very wealthy, to be within the means of a large number of people.

4. There is an emerging world culture. People can travel throughout the world and feel comfortable with their surroundings because these surroundings include elements that are quite familiar to them. The clothing styles (such as blue jeans), available technology, music, films, and the plays that they see are similar to those they left at home. Even certain types of food have become globalized, and individuals can (if they wish) eat very familiar foods regardless of the country they are in.

Although our list is not exhaustive, these data do suggest that there are intimate interconnections between the people of the world and that, indeed the world can be considered to be a community. Thus it is necessary to help children to learn to function effectively within this community. They must became aware of who the people who make up this global community are, and to realize the relationship that they, themselves, have with these people. They must also develop the skills necessary to work cooperatively and harmoniously with those people. In other words, they must develop a global perspective, an ability to perceive the world and act in it from the standpoint of a concerned citizen of it.

Helping Children Develop a Global Perspective. Global education is interdisciplinary in nature. It doesn't belong to any one subject area but is shared by all. By their nature, of course, the social studies can assume a large share of the responsibility for helping children develop a global perspective. This can be done cognitively, through the content being studied. It can also be done through activities that help to develop the children's sensitivities to the world and the people around them. Although these two do overlap—that is, sensitivities can be heightened through the content being studied—we can examine these two approaches separately for the purposes of simplicity.

Choosing Global Content. Various social studies educators have suggested specific concepts children need to learn in order to develop a global perspective. One most frequently cited is that of *interdependence*, and it is not difficult to see why this is such an important concept. It speaks directly to the relationships among humans; between humans and their institutions; and between institutions themselves. If we work from the premise that concepts and generalizations have universal applicability, that they are a means of making sense out of the world, then in actuality there are few if any social science or historical concepts that cannot be used effectively in helping children learn about and become citizens of their world. Our job is to choose the most appropriate global content to develop these understandings. For our purposes, appropriate global content can be defined as intellectually valid data about the world.

When we speak of intellectual validity we basically mean two things. The first of these is that the content we use needs to be realistic and factually accurate. Examples that are used to develop concepts and generalizations should be ones that portray the world as it is, not as we or others believe it to be. Reality should not be distorted to develop an understanding. All data sources (including the children's textbooks) should be scrutinized carefully for accuracy of information, up-to-dateness of that information, and freedom from bias. To do otherwise is to open the way to stereotypical thinking and the perpetuation of ethnocentrism.

The second requirement for intellectual validity is a balance of data. In the past, content used in the social studies has suffered from an imbalance. The bulk of the data dealt with North America and Europe. Little emphasis was placed on people or countries outside of this sphere. The development of a world view requires that the child view the whole world. Thus, content about emerging and third world people and nations needs to be included.

Helping Children to Develop a Global Sensitivity. In addition to knowing about the world, global citizenship implies an ability to see the world from a viewpoint that is not restricted by one's own personal, cultural, or national background. An individual who has a global perspective can examine commonalities and differences among cultures without judging them only from the perspective of his or her own culture. This individual also has the capability to examine world problems from a variety of standpoints, his or her own as well as those of others who may think differently.

Young children do not have this ability. The egocentricity of preoperational children doesn't allow them to perceive situations from any but their own point of view. These children are incapable of realizing that other people may see things or think about them differently than they do. In the process of development, of course, they may gradually move from this egocentric point of view and be able, to varying extents, to perceive things from the perspective of others.

The results of research done by Robert Selman (1980) indicate that the ability to perceive another person's feelings and thinking is one that develops through a sequence of stages. These stages begin at a point where the individual is incapable of seeing another's point of view, move to a level where the person realizes that people think and feel differently, and ultimately reach a point where the person is able to perceive how people think and feel from a variety of different viewpoints, including societal and cultural perspectives. These stages are thoroughly discussed in Chapter 8.

Obviously a requisite for the developmment of a global perspective will be attainment of the higher stages of perspective taking. Unfortunately, movement from one stage to another is not something that occurs automatically; just as individuals may never attain the stage of formal operations in their cognitive development, so they may not reach the higher levels of perspective taking. A crucial factor in whether or not this occurs is whether individuals are provided experiences that facilitate stage movement. They need to be given frequent opportunities to think about how others perceive situations and to actually examine the thinking of these others. Activities such as role play and structured discussion (Chapter 9) annd dramatic play (Chapter 11) provide such opportunities.

A second characteristic of classroom activities that facilitate perspective taking is that they allow children to encounter the thinking of different individuals in specific situations. Both Krogh (1982) and Selman and Lieberman (1975) found that growth in this area was facilitated when children were allowed to interact with others as they discussed social problems—such as whether or not to buy a dog for a boy who had lost his. Selman used filmstrips to present the problems while Krogh employed stories that were told or read to the children. Other opportunities for encountering the thinking of others would occur with the discussion of open-ended stories, classroom problems, and characters the children have read about or studied.

This affective approach to helping children develop global sensitivity works from the assumption that there are personal, feeling skills that are needed by world citizens. These skills, of course, can be taught throughout the curriculum.

A Multicultural Perspective

In order to become a world citizen an individual must first become a citizen of his or her own immediate society. For students in many parts of the world, and especially the United States, this immediate society is composed of a number of diverse cultural and ethnic groups. Thus it is not difficult to realize that a necessary requisite for the development of a global perspective is the development of a multicultural perspective. For the students you will be teaching this means that they must be helped to understand and appreciate the different groups in the United States and be able to function effectively with members of these groups.

The groups that compose our society can be divided into two categories. The first category is based on ethnicity. All of us belong to and can identify with some ethnic group. We may consider ourselves to be Anglo-American, Afro-American, Japanese-American, Mexican-American, or German-American among others. Our membership is based on the fact that we identify with the group (which may not be the cultural group into which we were born) in some way. We utilize elements of these subcultures in our daily lives. We may think in certain ways, eat special foods, speak in distinctive ways, prefer certain types of music, and so on. A second category of groups is made up of those to which individuals belong because of some specific, but nonethnic, characteristic. Included here would be groups based on sex (the culture of women), age (senior citizens), or specific physical characteristics (the handicapped). Multicultural education should focus on both of these categories of groups.

The Goals of Multicultural Education. Basically there are three goals for an education that is multicultural: (1) An understanding and appreciation of the different cultural groups that make up our society; (2) self-understanding; and (3) the development of knowledge, skills, and attitudes necessary to function across cultures. Since the third goal in many respects subsumes the first two (for example, self-understanding comes about as we begin to understand others) let's examine the first two briefly and consider the third to some depth.

Understanding and Appreciation of Other Groups. The United States has been likened to a large salad made up of a variety of ingredients. Each of these ingredients adds a distinctive color and flavor to the total salad. The ingredients in this salad, of course, are the diverse groups that constitute American society. Our goal is to help our students experience these groups and, thus, become aware of what they add to the total society.

In order to do this we need to help children become aware of who these groups are and why they are special. By exposing the children to the groups' past, their music, art, literature, folkways, food, and so on, we help them to perceive the richness of each of the ingredients. This learning, however, is not one sided. In the process children learn of the commonalities among people, the elements and ways of life that the children share with these other people.

The goal of multicultural education is to help children understand all of the other peoples with whom they share their society. This understanding encompasses not only the past experiences of cultural groups, but who they are at the present and what their aspirations for the future are. As we help them move to these goals we would like children to begin to identify with these groups, to understand them in a more affective, feeling sense. The end result of this understanding can be a breakdown of stereotypical thinking, racism, and ethnocentrism. It is the eating of a salad whose diverse ingredients go together to provide a very palatable experience.

Self-Understanding. Being reared in a specific culture is analogous to being a fish. The fish's total environment is water, an element that surrounds it from the day of birth. This element is so all-pervasive that, if a fish could think, it probably wouldn't spend much time doing so about water. In fact, it might not even realize that the water was there. It could be said, therefore, that the only time that this realization might occur would be when the fish was somehow introduced to another element, such as air.

Our culture is the water that surrounds us from birth. In order to realize it, and to understand it, we must be exposed to other elements; that is, other cultures. Thus, the second goal builds on the first—while learning about and trying to understand other cultures, children are being helped to understand their own culture. When they are exposed to other cultures they are being helped to understand why they themselves do things the way they do and believe certain things. A result of this is a rudimentary understanding of the commonalities the children share with other people. It is also the beginning of the realization that they differ in some ways from these other people, that they are unique individuals. These two types of realizations are the bases of self-awareness.

Knowledge, Skills, and Attitudes Necessary to Function Across Cultures. This third goal embodies the first two in that it requires that the individual have self-awareness and knowledge of other cultural groups. It goes beyond these goals, however, in that it speaks to the application of what is learned to real-life situations. It says, in essence, that an education that is multicultural should result in the individual being able to interact productively with members of other cultural groups.

The knowledge aspect of this goal refers to a great extent to the type of knowledge discussed in this and earlier chapters. That is, the major social science concepts and generalizations can be used as a means of intercultural understanding. (Although multicultural education is interdisciplinary in nature, we are speaking of it primarily from a social studies point of view. For this reason we are not considering such curricular areas, as language.) Thus, for example, such concepts as culture, cultural change, group interdependence, conflict, social change, and universal needs and wants, can be utilized. Although the major focus is on cultural and subcultural groups, the choice of concepts for fostering intercultural understanding need not be restricted to anthropology or sociology. Indeed, as our short list suggests, every discipline should be utilized. Other concepts previously not identified in this book, such as ethnocentrism, racism, and inequality, can also be emphasized when appropriate.

There are two types of skills required for intercultural understanding: thinking skills and behavioral skills. The former refer to problem solving and decision making. Individuals will encounter problematic situations directly related to living in a pluralistic society, such as whether to vote to make a city officially bilingual, as occurred in Miami a few years ago, or whether Martin Luther King's birthday should be an official United States holiday, a decision that faced the Congress in 1983. They must be capable of dealing with these situations in a rational manner.

Behavioral skills refer to the capabilities needed to insure positive interactions with individuals of different subcultures and among groups. These skills would include, but not be restricted to, appropriate ways of communicating and behaving within a given subculture.

The attitudes part of this goal also covers a great deal of territory. Its aim is the individual's acceptance of others, a recognition of the validity of their life-styles and experiences. This requires that the multicultural curriculum be concerned with helping children develop and critically examine their own values, especially as they relate to people of other groups. It also requires the ability to determine what values others hold. This will allow the individual to understand the background, as well as some of the reasons, for the behavior of others. Finally, the appreciation of others implies an ability to perceive situations from the standpoints of others, to be able to put oneself in the place of another, a characteristic of a global citizen we discussed earlier.

Multicultural Content and Activities. In 1976 the National Council for the Social Studies published its *Curriculum Guidelines for Multiethnic Education*. The major message contained in this document was that multicultural education should not be considered to be an "add-on" in the curriculum. It is not something that you develop special units for once a year, or something that you have special days for every so often. Instead, multiculturalism should permeate the school, and the curriculum of all grades should incorporate multiethnic content.

The guidelines also addressed questions concerning appropriate content and activities for the multicultural curriculum. The following summary, which does not include all of the guidelines presented in the document, suggest some important considerations.

The NCSS suggested that content should:

1. Reflect cultures and ethnic groups within the schools.
2. Continuously illustrate the wholeness of the experiences of ethnic groups—the problems they encounter; their cultural and social patterns; and the diversity and dynamism of their experiences.
3. Illustrate the conflict between ideals and realities in society.
4. Indicate ethnic alternatives and options.
5. Allow for comparisons among cultural groups.
6. Describe the development of the United States as a multicultural society. (NCSS, 1976)

Because multicultural education can be considered to be an aspect of education for a global perspective, the two criteria enumerated for content selection in that area would hold here. Content must have intellectual validity, accurately representing the world and society in which we live. It must also be understandable to the children.

In order to utilize content appropriately you, as the teacher, need to be aware of, understand, and be sensitive to the cultural groups that will provide content for your curriculum. This may require data gathering and study on your part.

The NCSS guidelines also address general types of activities that lend themselves to a multicultural curriculum. Although we will discuss specific types of activities in later chapters, some general characteristics of multicultural activities are worthy of note here. Appropriate activities will:

1. Allow students to develop values, attitudes, and behaviors which are supportive of ethnic pluralism.
2. Allow students to engage in decision-making and social participation.
3. Allow students to try out and reflect upon cross-cultural experiences.
4. Allow children to participate in the aesthetic experiences of various ethnic groups—including those utilizing literature, art, music, dance and architecture.
5. Make maximum use of community resources—including those which can be brought to the classroom, such as members of different groups, as well as those, such as fieldtrips, which allow students to go into the community. (NCSS, 1976)

Awareness of Current Affairs

An important objective of the social studies is the development of informed adults, individuals who continually expand their understanding of the world and its people. One of the ways that they do this is by staying abreast of what's going on in the world. By helping children study current affairs we can give direct experiences that very closely parallel the actual experiences adults have doing this. In the process we are doing two things. First, we are helping them to generate a base of world knowledge that can be expanded up to and throughout adulthood. Secondly, we are facilitating the

Children can be asked to share various aspects of their cultures, such as traditional dress.

development of some of the basic processing skills they will need for obtaining this knowledge.

Developing the Current Affairs Knowledge Base. Children's knowledge of current affairs is often restricted to the here and now, what's directly related to their own lives. They are very interested in happenings in their own families and neighborhoods, and want to share these. For younger children these events represent some of the content of the current events program, and a starting point to the awareness of what is occuring in the wider world. To say that these are the only events that interest children, and about which they want to know, might be underestimating them, however.

Children spend a great deal of time watching television. They also hear their parents and other adults talk about current events. They often want to know about these things that they see and hear. For example, at the age of four my son became quite interested in the space shuttle from watching its take-off and landing on television. He wanted pictures of it in his room and asked many questions—some simple and some fantasy based—about the whole space program. Events in which children show such interest should also be used in a current affairs program with them. These can be used to help broaden their vistas and become stepping stones to a consideration of more global issues.

Of course, not all events will be appropriate for children to consider. To be appropriate, a current event topic should be interesting and understandable to the children. There are three guidelines that should be considered in selecting current events topics to insure that this occurs.

1. The events should be ones they can easily relate to their own lives or to which it is not difficult to establish such a relationship.
2. Events chosen for consideration should not be abstract in nature. Topics in which conflicting ideologies or beliefs come into play are difficult for children to comprehend fully because of the abstract nature of the ideologies. (The civil war in Lebanon is an example of an event in which conflicting ideologies play an important part.) Similarly, events that require children to understand large numbers, such as the number of missiles being considered in an arms limitation talk, would be difficult for them to comprehend. The more abstract an issue or event is, the less likelihood that the children will understand it.
3. The more appropriate current events topics will be ones that help children to develop conceptual understandings, as opposed to simply reporting isolated facts. Understanding about the world is facilitated by an individual having a conceptual framework from which to draw.

Of course, you won't always supply the topic to be considered during current events. Because they are interested in the world, children, even at the earliest grades, can be asked to bring current event items to school to be shared. Unless they are assigned a specific topic or news source, you will find that the items they bring will cover a variety of areas—from a happening in the neighborhood to satellite launchings. Most of these will reflect interests that the children have.

Because you do not have complete control of the content to be considered when children do bring in current events items, you'll need to insure that this content, although interesting, is also understandable to them. Occasionally, they will present ideas that they've seen on television or heard their parents discuss, ideas which they may or may not completely understand. Knowing that children's verbalizations do not necessarily imply an understanding of an event or concept, you'll need to determine just how aware the children are of the topic. This can be done through discussion of the item and through a few well-chosen questions on your part. These questions should probe their understanding of what occurred and what the event means to them. Their responses should give you some indication of their knowledge and interest. If you have reason to believe that both of these are present, then the event can be considered in more detail.

At times you will find that for some reason there appears to be a great deal of interest in an event but little meaningful understanding of it. Because of the children's interest you may want to pursue consideration of it. This may be possible if you can help them discuss the event in terms of ideas that they can understand. That is, you may teach the concepts implicit in the event by using examples of them that the children can understand. A teacher I observed recently helped her students begin to understand why one of their classmates was so upset over the death of his dog. She used the idea of losing something and not being able to have it again to illustrate the concept of death. Another teacher helped children comprehend the limits of freedom of speech by referring to appropriate classroom rules. In both cases, their instruction enabled the children to begin to understand the event through the process of assimilation, which we noted in an earlier chapter.

Suppose, however, you receive little indication that the children understand or are interested in the event? In this case it may be that the children are simply bringing current events items because it is an assignment, something that they "have to do." This suggests a lack of vitality in the current affairs program and could be due to the fact that current events has become a dull routine to the children. As teacher, you may want to question how this came about. Possibly the children see current affairs as having little value. Or they may be reflecting the attention they see you giving it. In these cases it may be possible to renew interest by making the children aware that sharing current events is everyone's job. You should increase this awareness by being an active participant yourself—reporting events, asking questions, and sharing perceptions. Then, you can rightfully ask the children to do the same. The key to a successful current events program is teacher interest—interest in being up to date about the world and in sharing your understanding.

Necessary Skills. We obtain information about the world from a variety of sources; some of which require us to attend through reading, others through listening, and still others through some form of observations. Much of our knowledge of current affairs is derived from the news media, and full utilization of radio, television, newspapers, or magazines as data sources requires that we employ specific skills. These skills need to be learned and practiced. The current events time is an opportune one for teaching such information-gathering skills as those enumerated below.

Television. Questions such as the following can be asked to analyze news stories on television.*

1. *Selection*
   • Why was the story included in the news?
   • Was it important? Was it interesting?
2. *Structure*
   • Why was this event or these issues covered in this news format?
   • How did the visuals and narration enhance the story?

*From James Dick, "Using Television News, Documentaries and Public Affairs Programs in the Social Studies," *How to Do It Series,* Vol. 2:12, 1981. Reprinted with permission of the National Council for the Social Studies.

3. *Depth and Length*
   • Was the subject treated in sufficient detail?
   • Were you able to understand the report?
   • How long was the report?
4. *Objectivity*
   • Is the treatment of the subject fair?
   • Were all sides of the events or issues fairly represented?
5. *Implications*
   • What are the local, regional, national, and/or international implications of these events or issues?

Using the Newspaper and Related Periodicals

1. Learning the organization of the newspaper, including what is contained in the various sections of the paper. Children can be helped to see that news items of widespread interest will be found in one section of the paper while news of interest to such specific segments of the population as business people will be found in others.
2. Learning how to use an index. Knowing what is contained in the newspaper, they can be shown how to locate a specific section or news of interest to a specific group.
3. Selecting main and supporting ideas in stories. News stories usually begin with the five W's: who, what, when, where, and why. Children can learn to use these as the basis for gathering data from news stories. Similarly, they can be taught to utilize topic sentences to determine the main ideas of paragraphs and to look for data to support this main idea.
4. Using headlines as guides to the content of news stories. Headlines are written to concisely tell as much as possible about the content of news stories.

Radio

1. Listening with a purpose. Compared to the visual stimuli provided by television and newspaper—images that tend to be available to the viewer or reader for some period of time—the audio stimulation provided by radio is relatively short-lived. Unlike visual stimuli, the spoken word disappears after it is uttered. In order to capture the information provided by radio news, children must have some idea of what they are listening for. Thus they can be taught to attend to cue words in the news presentation.
2. Taking notes while listening. Because audio stimuli are so short-lived, and don't remain available to the listener, they tend to be more easily forgotten. One way to insure that they are not forgotten is to record them in some way. Since it is not only impractical, but impossible, for them to transcribe news broadcasts verbatim, older students can be taught to take notes on them, outlining important points and ideas.
3. Differentiating fact from opinion. Although both radio and television programs usually indicate when editorial opinions are being given, they are often presented by individuals who have learned to speak convincingly. It is easy to fall into the trap of accepting what is said

with little thought about it. Children can be taught to ask themselves questions about what they hear: Who is the source of data?; How authoritative are they about it?; and Why are specific data being presented? They can also be taught to ask if statements are factually true or if they represent what the speaker believes to be true.

Although they are somewhat medium specific, these skills can easily be used across media. The note taking discussed with radio usage is just as applicable to newspaper reading and television viewing. In addition, there are a wide range of more or less generic skills—such as comparing information from a variety of resources, selecting the most important ideas presented by a given source, or using maps for different purposes—that you'll also want to include in the current events as well as other areas of the curriculum. We'll go more deeply into these data gathering and analysis skills in subsequent chapters.

Current Affairs Approaches and Activities. There are any number of ways in which current events can be included in the social studies program. They can be included in ongoing units of study. They can actually be the basis for units. Or, they can stand on their own as an integral part of the social studies program without being directly related to the content being studied.

Upon examination you will find that many unit topics—be they ones contained in a school district's course of study, in a textbook, or ones you develop yourself—quite naturally lend themselves to an inclusion of current events. Children can be encouraged to seek out news items related to topics being considered. In the primary grades this might be news about one's own family or neighborhood, news that is not necessarily earth shattering but of a type the children understand and wish to share. During a unit concerned with the interdependence of people in neighborhoods, for example, children can be encouraged to report on workers they have observed in their neighborhood or specific instances of neighbors helping one another. In the upper grades, specific topics dealing with local communities, states, and nations can be supplemented with news items, brought by the teacher or students, obtained from the media. I once observed a fifth grade class, which was studying the Bill of Rights, devote several periods to a discussion of rights either being exercised or violated. Students brought newspaper articles that they shared with the class. Then, the class was invited to tell which right was at issue. It was interesting, and thought provoking, to see children actively debate the question of what freedom of speech actually meant! The inclusion of current affairs in established units brings a "realness" to the content and fosters a better understanding on the part of children by helping to present concepts in a concrete manner. Many adults would assume that the Bill of Rights might be too abstract for children. Yet when provided with examples of these rights, and given the opportunity to seek their own examples, these freedoms became very real to children and they could begin to see that the United States Consitution was a living document.

It is possible that current affairs can actually be the source for content for units. Sometimes events are predictable; presidential elections and the Olympics occur every four years; the dates for various space launchings are known well in advance, and so on. Units can be constructed around these events, and social science concepts and generalizations can be developed by using data concerned with them. Some of these data will be firsthand information gathered by teachers and students, but it need not all be. Presidential elections, for example, can be supplemented by information about the electoral process gathered from texts and trade books. They can also be compared with processes used to elect leaders in other countries. Similarly, a unit on the Olympics might deal with both the original and present-day ones.

Happenings in the world are not always predictable, however, and things do occur unexpectedly. Sometimes these events are of great interest to children and beg to be explored further. These too can be sources of units. Possibly these units will be full blown ones in which social studies instruction over a period of time is devoted to exploring the event and developing social science ideas based on it. Or, it may be a minor unit in which a short period of time is taken on a daily or weekly basis to follow what is occurring. Once, while teaching sixth grade, one of my students generated such a minor unit by jokingly bringing a supermarket ad to class as her "local news" contribution to the current events bulletin board, and then announcing the price of round steak. Egged on by her peers she continued to do this on a weekly basis, posting the prices on a special "round steak" section of the bulletin board. At the end of the year we looked at this data in terms of price changes and were able to come up with some understanding of the law of supply and demand.

There will be times when current affairs will not complement unit content or when you feel that they should be given more emphasis. It is very acceptable to include them as a separate part of your curriculum, and many teachers do. A special part of the day, or the week, may be set aside for consideration and discussion of what's happening in the world.

Current Affairs Activities. Two key things that should occur when current affairs are considered are a presentation of the news item and a discussion in which it is analyzed or evaluated. The presentation can be done by groups or individuals and, it goes without saying, should precede the discussion. It doesn't necessarily have to precede it immediately though. In some of the following activities the current events reports can be presented in such a way that individual children can examine them at different times during the day.

A *class newspaper* is a vehicle in which children report events in their own words. Groups of children are given the responsibility of collecting news items, writing news stories, and then duplicating them. The newspaper is then distributed to the class and the articles discussed.

A *class news show* can be either live, videotaped, or audio taped and may contain stories the children have gathered. The use of audio or video recorders allows the show to be viewed (or heard) at different times during the school day and thus can be fit into the schedule of individual students. The news show may be set up as a learning center. *Round-table reporting* can be utilized by individuals or groups of children in order to present their current events item to the rest of the class.

Children can post either clippings from newspapers and magazines or news stories they have written themselves on *news bulletin boards*. These bulletin boards can be designed to reflect different categories of current events (local, regional, national affairs, and so on) or they can be designed as news maps: maps of specific regions of the world or the world itself. In the latter case, the current affairs items would be posted on the location where the event occured.

Computerized news is an activity in which children, through the use of a word-processing program, type their news item onto the computer and store it on a disc (in a current affairs file). This file could then be put back into the computer by a child and the news items displayed on the monitor screen. The computerized news would be used in the same way as the class news show and could be part of a current affairs learning center.

It is not enough to simply have these current affairs activities without teacher guidance and follow-up. Children not only need help in choosing appropriate current affairs for consideration, they also need help in making sense out of them. Thus, as we noted earlier, your responsibility will be to

Computers can be used to word process "electronic news."

help them examine and evaluate these items. This can be done through class or group discussions.

There are four basic questions that should be considered in a current events discussion:

1. What does the news item say? Here, your job is to determine that the children are aware of the basic message contained in the news item. You'll want to insure that they know the facts surrounding an event: the who, what, when, where, why, and possibly how.
2. What does it mean? Knowing the facts of a story does not necessarily mean that the children understand it. Therefore, you will next need to determine their level of comprehension, how they interpret the item and what inferences they can make about it. You'll want to make certain that they have, at least, a basic understanding of what's going on.
3. Why is it important? The question, or a related one, should be used to help children probe the effect of an event—on the children themselves, on others, and on the world.
4. How does it relate to me? Here children can be assisted in examining their roles as citizens—of a community, state, nation and world—to determine if the importance of an event requires some action on their part. Often, this question can lead to decision making, valuing, and social action in their part.

Other Content Emphases

Global and multicultural education and current events, may be considered to be general themes that should permeate our social studies curriculum. In addition to these, there are other more specific concerns for which the social studies has been given some responsibility. We will briefly examine four of these areas of responsibility—economics/consumer education, energy education, law-related education and career education—in terms of what their goals are and how we deal with them in the elementary social studies.

Economic/Consumer Education

Economic/consumer education is concerned with helping students develop the knowledge and skills necessary for economic decision making. It is unfortunate that, in some cases, this decision making has been defined rather narrowly, being concerned only with personal economic decisions. Emphasis in these cases has been placed only on personal buying, spending, and budgeting. This narrow focus has caused critics of consumer education to voice concerns that it might breed economic illiterates, individuals who may, indeed, be smart buyers and budgeters but know nothing of societal and global economic problems.

This narrow interpretation was never meant to be. The Joint Council on

Economic Education, whose membership includes representatives from education, business, labor, and agriculture, has, since 1949, consistently defined the purposes of this area to be twofold:

1. To help students understand and make reasoned judgments about major economic questions facing society. It is expected that students will understand the impact that their economic decisions have on the total economic system and they will understand their relationship, as consumers, to the economic community.
2. To help students make reasoned personal economic decisions, now and as adults.

Thus, the goal is, indeed, economic and consumer education.

Attaining these two purposes requires that individuals possess specific knowledge and skills. Not surprisingly, the former is embodied in concepts drawn from economics. These include all of the major ideas—including scarcity, production, supply, demand, exchange, and price—that were outlined in the previous chapter. Other ideas that are highlighted in this area of the curriculum include labor organizations, investment, advertising, income, credit, and budgeting.

The specific skills emphasized in economics/consumer education are those concerned with decision making and valuing. Proponents of economic consumer education point out that, in developing these skills, it is not necessary to focus on decisions directly related to economics. The aim is to give children decision making experiences that are relevant to and useful in their everyday lives, experiences with processes that they can potentially use as adults. Thus, any relevant decision making experience we give children—be it in relation to how they spend their time or what classroom pet they will choose—will be useful in helping children meet this second goal.

It is obvious that the goals of economic/consumer education and the social studies closely parallel one another. Both emphasize concepts, processes, and affect. Even though experts in this area see it as best taught throughout the curriculum, it is very apparent that social studies can contribute much to its goals being met.

Energy Education

The world is facing a number of energy problems such as dwindling fossil fuels, increasing energy costs, the nuclear controversy, energy-related environmental problems, and the unequal distribution of energy resources throughout the world. These and other problems require confrontation and resolution. Energy education is seen as the vehicle for helping to do this. It is a means by which we can help students understand what energy is and what the social, economic, and political problems that surround the energy crisis are. It is also the means by which students can be helped to develop the skills and abilities necessary to cope with and resolve the short- and long-term energy problems they will encounter.

According to the National Council for the Social Studies, energy education in the context of the social studies should have two broad goals:

1. *Public/citizen competency:* Helping students acquire the knowledge and skills to deal with energy issues which affect everyone;
2. *Personal life-style competency:* Development of the capabilities necessary to deal with energy issues affecting oneself (National Council for the Social Studies, 1981).

The National Council for the Social Studies indicates that these goals will be most appropriately met as students work toward the established knowledge, process, and affective goals of the social studies within the context of the established curriculum.

Most individuals in the energy education area tend to agree with the idea that energy should not be an added-on unit. The energy curriculum for the elementary grades published by the Indiana Department of Public Instruction, for example, suggests that as younger children study families and family concerns, they examine how families use energy and compare these with activities that occurred in the past (Lane, 1980). Similarly, the National Science Teachers Association suggests that, as middle grade children examine how communities meet their needs and wants, they consider the role of energy in meeting these needs (Fowler and Carey, 1980).

Law-Related Education

Just as economics/consumer education is sometimes misinterpreted as dealing with specific consumer issues, so too is law-related education. It is sometimes perceived as being directed only to helping students learn specific laws, or what an individual's rights are in a given situation. This is not the case; law-related education does not have the training of juvenile lawyers as one of its goals. Rather, it is concerned with helping the student learn the basic principles and processes that underlie the legal system. Law-related education is, in essence, citizenship education.

Charlotte Anderson, in an article in *Social Education* (1980), the journal of the National Council for the Social Studies, outlines what she referred to as eleven critical outcomes of this type education. These goals include the following:*

* Perceiving law as promotive, facilitative, comprehensible, and alterable.
* Perceiving people as having potential to control and contribute to the social order.
* Perceiving right and wrong as issues all citizens can and should address.
* Perceiving the dilemmas inherent in social issues.
* Being reflective decision makers and problem solvers who make grounded commitments.
* Being able to give reasoned explanations about commitments made and positions taken.
* Being socially responsible conflict managers.
* Being critically responsive to legitimate authority.

*From Charlotte C. Anderson, "Promoting Responsible Citizenship Through Elementary Law-Related Education," *Social Education*, Vol. 44:5, May 1980, pp. 383–386. Reprinted from *Social Education* with permission of the National Council for the Social Studies.

- Being knowledgeable about the law, the legal system, and related issues.
- Being empathetic, socially responsible and considerate of others.
- Being able to make mature judgments in dealing with ethical and moral problems.

These goals represent ends of law-related education, points toward which the children will gradually move. In the elementary grades these goals can be approached in two ways: in curricular contexts and through participatory experiences where children actually engage in some type of civic activity.

There tends to be general agreement that law-related education need not be a curriculum unto itself. Its ideas and problem-solving processes should be a part of existing courses of study. They can be included in many of the social studies units you teach. So, for example, ideas concerned with rules and laws can be introduced early on as the children work with units concerned with, say, family and school. They can later be more fully developed in units dealing with larger societal contexts.

Career Education

In 1972, Sidney Marland, then Commissioner of Education, pointed out some interesting statistics. He indicated that twenty percent of all high school students graduated with sufficient vocational background to prepare them for specific jobs. Another thirty percent of the graduates went on to college. This meant, he indicated, that when college dropouts were included, over half of the high school graduates were not well prepared to enter the work force (Marland, 1972).

The response to this deficiency was something called career education or career development education. This curricular area is not vocational education; it is not intended to prepare students for a specific occupation. Rather, its aim is to expose students to the world of work, in terms of both paid and unpaid occupations, and to help them examine their places in that world. It encompasses learning about the world of work—including occupational roles and their attendant expectations, satisfactions, and dissatisfactions— as well as a basic understanding of the American system of free enterprise. It emphasizes the development of interpersonal skills needed in the workplace as well as those skills concerned with effective career decision making. It is very concerned with developing individual self-awareness, values related to work, and an appreciation for the role of worker.

This description of the scope of career education, although certainly not exhaustive, does illustrate why career education should be included in the social studies curriculum. Its purposes clearly parallel our goals of knowing, doing, and feeling.

But why do we have to bother with it in the elementary school? Isn't it something more suited to secondary students? The answer to this is quite simple. All of the expected outcomes of career education are developmental in nature. Knowledge about the world of work is developed gradually over time as a result of a variety of learning experiences about that world. The same can be said of self-awareness, the development of decision-making skills, and the generation of values. Thus, to insure a variety of experiences career education needs to begin early and to be continuous throughout the school years.

Proponents of career education do not see it as a separate subject area. Instead, they indicate that it will have its greatest effect when it is included as part of other subject areas. This means, for example, that necessary communication skills would be taught as part of the language arts, or that ways of predicting future occurrences might be shown to children in something so simple as teaching them to estimate answers in division. Career education is not an add-on to the social studies. Instead, career concerns are brought into the existing topics of study.

In our discussion of career education it may seem that this area is directed toward money-earning occupations only. This is not the case! The knowledge, capabilities, and skills that are focused on in this area are appropriate to all aspects of life—the paid jobs we assume, the roles we assume as members of families and larger societies, and the ways in which we use all of our time—be it for an occupation, voluntary work, or leisure.

Synthesis: Incorporating Social Concerns and Traditional Content

As we noted earlier, many teachers worry about how they will be able to incorporate all of these concerns in their curriculum and still be able to deal with the content that has traditionally been thought to be the social studies. It may well be that, to use an old saw, they're trying to teach what a forest is and are doing it tree by tree. That is, they see each of these concerns as pieces of the curriculum to be dealt with separately without realizing how much they fit together.

If you think back on the seven areas we discussed in this chapter, it shouldn't be too difficult to see that each has quite a bit in common with the others. Although the proponents for each may use different terminology, the basic goals they articulate are roughly the same for all. All indicate that children should develop some conceptual understanding, they should gain facility with basic human processes, and they should develop some affective capacities. Each area requires that the children know, do, and feel—the basic goals of elementary social studies.

Regardless of what area or concern the teacher chooses to emphasize, the children should still be moving in the desired direction of rational, active membership in the world.

This still, however, doesn't really respond to the teachers' worries. Or does it? There is another commonality among the concerns that suggests it might. Although it is permissible, and is occasionally recommended, to develop units around specific emphases—such as an energy conservation unit—proponents of each of the foregoing concerns see them best considered in an integrated fashion. That is, they prefer that we not teach global education, per se. Rather, it is more appropriate to incorporate global concerns with the existing content. This means that we don't deal with each concern as a separate unit—teaching seven additional units per year. We use the emphasis to add depth and flavor to whatever it is we're teaching in the social studies. It means that we can address these concerns within the context of existing content.

In the synthesis section of the preceding chapter we said that what you'll be working with are examples of concepts and generalizations (as opposed to *the* concepts and generalizations, themselves) as a means of helping children develop those big ideas. These examples, which we called understandings, are relatively content specific. If your unit topic deals with the interdependence of family members, then your understanding will be phrased in terms of the family. The sociology generalization, "People in groups have roles," would be restated as "People do jobs in familes."

The key to seeing that the seven concerns are addressed is the selection of the content that will be used to develop understandings. Think for a moment. What data about jobs done in families might you see to develop: (1) a global perspective, (2) a multicultural one, (3) an awareness of current affairs? How can you include: (4) one that deals with laws? (5) an economic/consumer emphasis? And how about (6) career and (7) energy awareness?

Now, after you've thought, compare your list with mine.

Global: content dealing with a family or families in a different part of the world, possibly one in which men's and women's occupations do not fit the children's stereotypes.

Multicultural: a family of a different ethnic group than the children. Or, how about a family where one or both parents are physically handicapped?

Current affairs: the jobs done in the children's own families. Or how about the family of a woman politician, say, Margaret Thatcher?

Economic/consumer and career: the occupations people have in these families, and the choices they must make based on their salaries.

You'll notice that no content ideas are presented for law-related or energy education. The ones I generated for them didn't seem to fit with the overall flow of content ideas (even though an example presented earlier with energy education did deal with it). That's okay; although the first three emphases should heavily permeate the curriculum, it isn't necessary to incorporate all seven in every unit. You will want to be sure, though, that all are adequately considered in your total program. You should make certain that you attempt to help children work toward all of the general goals of each area in your year's curriculum.

The preceding ideas are especially appropriate if you're developing your own units. They hold just as well if you're using a textbook as the basis for your unit. In that case, your major job is a bit different, though; instead of generating content you'll be evaluating existing content. Basically, what you'll be doing is determining the extent to which the textbook places emphasis on the seven areas, and (remembering, among others, the criteria for content selection we discussed in relation to global and multicultural education) whether this emphasis is appropriate. You might ask, for example, whether the material in the text helps develop an understanding of cultural pluralism. Is it free from prejudice and bias in relation to race, sex, age, ethnic group, class, occupation, religion, and so on?

If you find that little emphasis is given to an area, or that the emphasis given is inappropriate, you will then need to decide how to supplement the textbook. This means that you'll need to generate additional activities. One source of these activities could be the teachers' manual of the text. In most, if not all cases, these manuals will have lists of suggested readings accompanying each unit. These bibliographies tend to contain books having more information about the unit topic as well as resources that describe different activities that might be done with the class. In addition, they usually list appropriate books for children.

The teachers' manual will usually also contain suggested activities you might wish to use to supplement the unit. Sometimes these activities will help bring the needed emphasis to the content. If the manual provides little help, then you'll find it necessary to develop your own supplementary activities. I'd encourage you to do so because the activities you develop will be more attuned to your students' capabilities and needs. Often these teacher-constructed supplementary activities are the most memorable for students.

If you find that the content of the textbook is completely inappropriate, then you won't want to use it. This practice is defensible because the content will not facilitate the children's movement toward the goals of the social studies.

Springboards to Discussion _____

1. Obtain a children's social studies textbook for a grade in which you are interested. Evaluate a chapter or unit in terms of the seven emphases discussed in this chapter. Focus your evaluation in terms of two basic questions: First, to what extent is there evidence of these emphases? Second, if there is little or no evidence of a given emphasis, is it possible to incorporate it with the given content? How?

2. At the end of the previous chapter we suggested that you examine a newspaper for its potential to develop social studies concepts and generalizations. If you did that (or would like to do it now), you can expand on that activity by planning to use what you found as the basis of a classroom current events activity. For the purposes of this exercise you'll want to consider and list three things: (a) your objective or objectives, what you want the children to get out of the activity; (b) learning activities, what the children will do; (c) evaluation, how you'll determine if the children have met the objectives. (You may wish to consult the section *"Teaching the Unit on a Daily Basis"* in Chapter 10 to help you with this planning.)

   If you are working with a group of children at present, you may wish to implement your plan. If you do, you'll want to evaluate what occurred, reflecting upon what you would do similarly, and differently, were you to do this activity with children again.

3. Do a multicultural survey of a community in which you would like to teach. As an initial part of this survey you'll want to determine what cultural subgroups are present. After you've done this you'll want to consider how these groups can be represented in the curriculum. For the purpose of this exercise you may want to focus less on what might be taught about the group and more on learning resources is might provide (such as guest speakers, people who can do various types of demonstrations, opportunities for field trips, and so on).

References

ANDERSON, CHARLOTTE, C. "Promoting Responsible Citizenship Through Elementary Law-Related Education," *Social Education,* Vol. 44 (May 1980), pp. 383–386.

BANKS, JAMES. *Multiethnic Education Theory and Practice.* Boston: Allyn and Bacon, 1982.

Consumer Education: A Resource Guide for Georgia Schools. Athens, GA: College of Education, University of Georgia, 1973.

Curriculum Guide for Economics and Consumer Education: Grade 2: Money. Gainesville, FL: Center for Economic Education, University of Florida, 1981.

FOWLER, JOHN M., AND CAREY, HELEN H. "Energy and Social Studies: A Match that Works," *The Social Studies,* Vol. 71 (March/April 1980), pp. 56–60.

HICKMAN, WARREN L., AND PRICE, ROY A. "Global Awareness and Major Concepts," *The Social Studies,* Vol. 71 (September/October 1980), pp. 208–211.

KROGH, SUZANNE, LOWELL. "Encouraging Positive Justice Reasoning and Perspective-Taking Skills," *Journal of Moral Development,* Vol. 14 (May 1985), pp. 102–110.

LANE, KATHLEEN. "Teaching-Learning Activities in Energy Education," *Social Education,* Vol. 44 (April 1980), pp. 266–270.

MARLAND, SIDNEY. "Career Education: Every Student Headed for a Goal," *American Vocational Journal,* Vol. 47 (March 1972), pp. 34–38.

MORRIS, DONALD N. "Global Education in Elementary Schools: Implications for Curriculum and Instruction," *Social Education,* Vol. 41 (January 1977), pp. 38–40, 45.

National Council for the Social Studies. *Curriculum Guidelines for Multiethnic Education: Position Statement.* Washington, D. C., 1976.

National Council for the Social Studies. *Guidelines for Energy Education in the Social Studies.* Washington, D. C., 1981.

SELMAN, ROBERT. *The Growth of Interpersonal Understanding.* New York: Academic Press, 1980.

SELMAN, ROBERT, AND LIEBERMAN MARCUS. "Moral Education in the Primary Grades: An Evaluation of a Developmental Curriculum," *Journal of Educational Psychology,* Vol. 67 (1975), pp. 712–716.

Doing

5

The Process Goals: Facilitating Problem Solving

After reading this chapter you should be able to:

1. Describe the three purposes for which individuals use problem solving:
   (a) Information seeking.
   (b) Generating new knowledge.
   (c) Decision making.
2. Identify specific problem-solving activities that are used for all three purposes.
3. Specify step-by-step strategies for doing these activities.
4. Illustrate the use of these strategies in elementary classrooms.
5. Delineate aspects of child development that need to be considered in facilitating problem solving in elementary classrooms.

The "doing" aspect of social studies education is concerned with helping children develop the basic human processes that will allow them to continue to understand and function effectively in the world. Although there are a variety of different processes necessary for this to occur, for our purposes all of them can be subsumed under a general class of activities that may be called problem solving.

In this chapter we'll develop a general understanding of what problem solving is all about. Initially, we'll examine the functions of problem solving, the purposes for which humans employ it. Then, we'll move on to look at the different activities in which we engage as we use problem solving for these different purposes. Although individuals work with problems in different ways, there do tend to be commonalities in what they do. We'll consider those commonalities in this section, outlining some generally accepted models or strategies for dealing with problems. Finally, since our goal is to help children become aware of the purposes of problem solving and experienced in ways of doing so, the synthesis section is devoted to considering the most appropriate ways of doing it with them. This discussion will lay out some general guidelines you'll want to keep in mind as you read the following two chapters (which deal with specific approaches to teaching problem solving).

The Purposes of Problem Solving —————————————————————

Rather than simply discuss the three purposes for which we employ problem solving, I'd like you to attempt some problem solving and come up with them yourself. The following dilemma actually confronted a first-year teacher, Mr. Ross. As you read what occurred, analyze what he did and try to determine the reasons why he asked himself certain questions. That is, ask yourself "What's the purpose behind these questions?" To facilitate your analysis, the important questions will be numbered and printed in **boldface.**

If any one child among Mr. Ross' fifth graders could be considered a discipline problem, it would be Joe. In addition to rather constant acts of misbehavior—talking out in class, disturbing the other children, borrowing their materials without asking—Joe was not liked by the other children. In October, Mr. Ross had administered a sociometric questionnaire that asked the children to name three people they'd like to work with, play with, and sit with in a group. Joe wasn't chosen once; in fact, several children had specifically written on the test that they definitely didn't want Joe for any of these activities. Even if Mr. Ross hadn't administered the test it wouldn't have been difficult to determine that Joe was unpopular. His behavior would have quickly given it away. He was very aggressive with the other children, often for no apparent reason. It was a rare week that Joe wasn't in at least two fights. Unfortunately for Joe, he wasn't very big and tended to lose.

Mr. Ross realized that something had to be done about the situation. The destructiveness of Joe's behavior to the total class environment was becoming more and more obvious. Mr. Ross realized that the first question he needed to answer was:

1. **What can I do to decrease the incidence of Joe's negative behavior? What are some discipline techniques that I can try?** At the same time Mr. Ross realized that even if he found some strategies that might work, and Joe's negative behavior did decrease, the underlying reasons for the behavior would probably still remain. Perhaps Joe's problem would cause him to act out in other, more serious, antisocial ways. Mr. Ross therefore decided to find out what was causing Joe's behavior. To do this he decided that he would need to know:

2. **Are there identifiable patterns to Joe's misbehavior?** Mr. Ross decided that he could deal with both questions simultaneously. For the first he decided to reread a couple of books that he had in his college methods classes, *Teacher Effectiveness Training* (Gordon, 1974) and *Better Discipline: A Practical Approach* (Johnson, 1980). He'd also talk to some of the more experienced teachers in his school and discuss this problem with one of his undergraduate professors.

    In order to get to the second question, Mr. Ross decided to determine if there were specific times, or specific activities, when Joe especially acted out. He realized that he could get this information by keeping anecdotal records—noting what actually happened, when it happened, where it happened, and what activities were going on at the time.

    Mr. Ross' research into discipline techniques was quite fruitful. He had a wide range of suggestions—including everything from corporal punishment to positive reinforcement to conferring with Joe every day in order to co-operatively work out a plan for Joe's behavior. Realizing that he couldn't (or was unwilling to) use all of them he then had to decide:

3. **Of all of these, which do I want to use?** Considering each, he found that some were unacceptable because they went against personal beliefs, others because they would have some type of negative effect—such as taking too much time from the other children—and still others because research results indicated that they were relatively ineffective. Based on his knowledge of Joe and on what he himself found to be acceptable, he decided to try positive reinforcement and a daily goal-setting conference. He then asked himself:

4. **Will these techniques work with Joe?** He rationalized that if they were effective, then the number of instances of negative behavior should decrease. He could check this out using the anecdotal records.

   Speaking of the anecdotal records, these, too, had been helpful in showing a pattern of misbehavior. It appeared that, although Joe misbehaved all week, most of Joe's fights occurred on Mondays and Tuesdays. Knowing that Joe's parents are in the process of being divorced and that Joe spends every other weekend with his father, he wondered:

5. **Is there a connection between the weekends Joe spends with his father and his behavior?** Having found out the weekends Joe has spent with his father, Mr. Ross again examined his anecdotal data and, sure enough, there was more negative behavior right after these visits. This, then, led to several other dilemmas: how to find out why this was the case and what to do about it. Mr. Ross asked himself:

6. **What's the best way of dealing with this situation?** After running through several alternatives Mr. Ross realized that, in this situation, he was over his head. He has neither the knowledge nor the resources necessary to deal with Joe and his family. He decided that the best thing to do here was to refer the situation to the school counselor.

Now, let's examine the questions Mr. Ross asked to determine the reason why he asked them. I have grouped them according to the function they served.

1. **What can I do to decrease the incidence of Joe's misbehavior? What are some discipline strategies I can try?**
2. **Are there identifiable patterns to Joe's Behavior?**

4. **Will these techniques work with Joe?**
5. **Is there a connection between the weekends Joe spends with his father and his behavior?**

3. **Of all of these [*strategies*] which do I want to try?**
6. **What's the best way of dealing with this situation?**

What do the first two questions have in common? Basically, Mr. Ross wanted to know something—he needed information. In the first case this information dealt with available discipline strategies. This was not new knowledge per se; it was available from a variety of sources. All Mr. Ross needed to do was to tap these data sources to get the information he sought. The information needed to answer the second question was not so readily available; in fact, these data represented new knowledge about Joe. To get these data Mr. Ross needed to find and use an appropriate information-gathering strategy. He then needed to carefully scrutinize and analyze the data he gathered.

These two questions and the activities associated with them, point to the first function of problem solving: *information seeking*.

Now, let's move to the second group of questions, numbers four and five. What was Mr. Ross doing here? With each question, he had an idea—a hunch, if you will—that information he already had was what was needed in the situation. So he used this information to come up with knowledge that was new, at least to him. In one case, he was going to determine if certain strategies would work with Joe. In the second case, his awareness of what was happening in Joe's family life suggested to him that there might be some connection between Joe's visits with his father and his misbehavior. In both situations he needed to find the most appropriate way of getting and analyzing the information he needed to see if he was on the right track with his hunches.

What was occurring with this second category of questions, then, was the application of information to new situations for the purpose of *generating new knowledge*.

How about questions three and six? What do they have in common? They dealt with the problem of choosing among various courses of action. With question three Mr. Ross had to decide which discipline strategies were most appropriate for his particular situation. The final question dealt with determining the course of action Mr. Ross should take in relation to Joe and his family. In both cases, Mr. Ross needed to consider the various alternatives open to him and to examine what the consequences of doing each would be. Most importantly, in deciding upon a given alternative he relied upon his own personal values. Thus, he may have excluded some discipline strategies because he valued, among other things, the child's personal integrity as well as the knowledge provided by systematic research.

From these questions it is not difficult to infer that the third function of problem solving is *decision making*.

To summarize, then, the three functions that problem solving serves are:

1. Information seeking.
2. Generating new knowledge.
3. Decision making.

Approaches to Problem Solving

The three approaches to problem solving we will discuss in this section are ones that are commonly used in social studies instruction and serve the functions noted above. These approaches have been given a variety of names in the literature; we have chosen to give them labels that reflect what occurs as they are utilized. *Exploration* is used to gather information; *inquiry* to generate knowledge that is new to the problem solver; and *decision making* is employed to help the individual choose among alternative courses of action (Schuncke and Hoffman, 1980).

There has been a great deal of research on the problem-solving strategies that humans employ. Theorists have postulated a number of requisite problem-solving abilities and have undertaken investigations to determine which of these abilities actually come into play. Their findings have led to the development of a variety of problem-solving strategies, schemes that can be used by individuals (Feldhusen and Guthrie, 1979). Interestingly, there tends to be some similarity among these problem-solving strategies in that they emphasize many of the same activities and operations. This is true for the three models we will consider; each contains four similar steps. Because it would be redundant to discuss these steps (and the activities they embody) with each model we will consider each one once under the rubric of generic problem-solving activities. After this we will consider the three models separately, placing emphasis in our discussion on the activities that are specific to each model. To help you envision how the generic and specific activities fit together, as we discuss each model we will provide an example of specific problem-solving strategies as they would be used in an elementary classroom.

Generic Problem-Solving Activities

Table 5.1 outlines the three models of problem solving in a stepwise fashion. An examination of this chart will show that there are four steps that are common to all. All require that: (1) the individual recognize that a dilemma situation exists and define what the problem is; (2) the individual be aware of information sources that can be consulted for whatever information is necessary to deal with the problem; (3) these sources be utilized; and (4) that

TABLE 5.1   Three Models of Problem Solving

Exploration	Inquiry	Decision Making
Determining the problem	Determining the problem	Determining the decision to be made
Planning to gather data	Planning to gather data	Planning to generate alternatives and consequences
Gathering data	Gathering data	Generating alternatives and consequences
Examining, analyzing, and evaluating data	Examining, analyzing, and evaluating data	Examining, analyizing and evaluating consequences
Synthesis	Accepting or rejecting hypothesis	Choosing according to a value structure
	Generalizing	Acting

Source: Adapted from George Schuncke and Stevie Hoffman, "Developing Problem-Solving Readiness in Elementary School Children," *The Social Studies* vol. 71 (January/February 1980), pp. 23–27. A publication of the Helen Dwight Reid Educational Foundation.

the problem solver work with the data to come up with meaningful responses to the original dilemma.

Problem Determination. Problem determination is the initial step in all of the problem-solving models. Basically, this step is one of formulating a question, or questions, that we need answered. Before we can do anything about a problemmatic situation we have to be aware of exactly what's bothering us, or what we need to know. Sometimes this is a relatively clear-cut situation; the problem or need for a decision presents itself unambiguously. We realize exactly what we need to know or do and can proceed. At other times, we encounter dilemma situations that lack this clarity to varying degrees.

Probably the most ambiguous dilemmas are ones in which we realize that a problem exists, but really can't pinpoint what it is. Two examples illustrate this type of situation.

1. You need to write a research paper for a class but don't know what in the world to write about.
2. Your students are constantly bickering and fighting, but you don't know why.

Obviously, in these two cases (and in others like them) you don't know enough about the situation to do anything. Therefore, the first thing that is needed is data that can make the problem less abstract. In the first case you might read the course syllabus to get an idea of appropriate areas for study. In the second, you might ask your students to provide you with the facts about what led up to a particular disturbance. Analysis of these facts should point to the underlying problem.

There are times, of course, when we are less foggy about the problem and have a good, but general, idea of what it is. Unfortunately, although not completely ambiguous, it is still not clear-cut enough to handle. In this case we need to make the problem more specific. Usually, this specificity can be obtained through an operational definition of the problem—a specific example or examples of it. A teacher, for example, who must find methods for dealing with a child who is a "behavior problem" really can't do anything until she identifies what she means by the term *behavior problem*. Until she operationally defines it as, say, talking out or not being able to stay seated, she cannot speculate on specific ways of dealing with the particular type of misbehavior.

Not surprisingly, the most crucial part of problem solving is knowing specifically what the problem is. The purpose of this step is to ensure that we have this knowledge.

Planning to Gather Data. The three models we are describing here require that information be gathered for problem resolution. These data provide answers to the questions that are the focus of our *exploration;* they are the basis for accepting or rejecting our hypotheses in *inquiry;* and they supply us with alternative courses of action, and the implications of taking these actions, in *decision making*. Because the data we utilize in problem solving are very important we want to insure that we get the most appropriate information available. This requires careful planning and entails three different activities.

In defining the problem situation we basically indicate what questions we need answered, what information is necessary to resolve our dilemma. The first activity we engage in as we plan to gather data is the determination of what sources are available to provide us with this information. This may actually entail some data gathering about data sources.

Once we are aware of the information sources, we must then decide which source is most appropriate for our purposes. This means finding the best information in the most economical manner. In considering what is best our primary concern is on the validity of resources—which one (or ones) will provide us with the most accurate, up-to-date, and unbiased information. To insure that we get valid data it is often wise to rely on more than one source. If several sources appear to provide valid information we could choose among these for those we might use. A good guideline for this choosing is to single out those that require the least expenditure of our personal resources, be they time, effort, or money.

Having identified appropriate resources, our third job is to be certain that we are able to utilize them to their fullest extent. Different information sources need to be approached in different ways and require that we use data-gathering skills that are source-specific. (For example, use of the library requires one set of skills while interviewing necessitates another.) So, at this stage of the planning process we need to know two things: (1) What skills are necessary to get the information? and (2) How are those skills applied to the specific situation?

Gathering Data. This is basically an extension of the preparation step. The plans that have been made are now carried out. The problem solver collects the information necessary to answer questions that were asked initially. During this stage additional questions, based on information already collected, may be generated and additional data gathered.

Examining, Analyzing, and Evaluating the Data. At the end of the data gathering stage, the information that has been collected is in a relatively raw form, analogous to pieces of a puzzle. They need to be put together to form a total picture. The problem-solver's job now is to understand and make sense out of this information and to determine if it provides the specific answers needed. At least four tasks have to be undertaken to do this and the problem solver will engage in these almost simultaneously.

First, it is necessary to get an overview of the data to determine exactly what information is available and whether the initial questions appear to have been answered. This is accomplished by reviewing all information. During this review the problem solver rechecks the sources that provided the information to insure that they are valid.

The second task (which may occur as the first is being undertaken) is a determination of how, and if, the various pieces of the puzzle fit together. Here, similarities and differences among what was found are sought. This second task is basically one of categorization and conceptualization, and the individual attempts to group data according to the ideas they repre-sent. The outcome of this task is the organization of the data in some meaningful way.

As the problem solver engages in the second task, a third task is simulta-neously being undertaken. The data are examined for discrepancies; the individual looks for differences among pieces of information that appear to belong to the same category. When these differences are found it is neces-sary to recheck the data to be certain that the pieces of information are actually concerned with the same thing.

When a discrepancy does exist it is necessary to attempt to resolve it. (This is not to say that all discrepancies can be resolved. Sometimes its necessary to accept conflicting data.) One way to do this would be by recheck-ing data sources, evaluating them on the basis of how the information was obtained and whether the source can be considered to be a valid one. The individual would determine whether the data were fact (as opposed to being opinion or inference) and whether the source of information was knowledge-able in the area. Another avenue to resolving discrepancies among data is to consult additional sources.

The final data analysis task is one of evaluation, determining the extent to which questions that initiated the problem solving have been answered. If they have not, then it would be necessary to return to the data-gathering stage.

The general activities we have outlined here are, as we noted earlier, ones that tend to be utilized regardless of the problem or the approach we take to solving it; they are steps that are utilized in all problem-solving models. Table 5.2 summarizes what occurs in these steps.

Problem-Solving Strategies _____

As you examine the three problem-solving models described below, there are a number of things that should be kept in mind. The first of these is that, although they are outlined in terms of the steps people go through as they engage in each strategy, individuals don't necessarily follow these steps in sequential order throughout. A person, for example, might be gathering data and realize that he or she isn't aware of sufficient data sources. It would be necessary to return to the planning stage. Considering the models in steps, though, will allow you to get an uncomplicated picture of how the specific problem-solving model works.

Another thing that you should note is that, although we are talking about three discrete strategies, there are connections among them. Many times as we are engaging in one strategy we'll find it necessary to turn to another. We might, for example, be *inquiring* to generate new knowledge and realize that we don't have enough background information necessary to hypothe-size. Therefore, we need to get this information through *exploration*.

The most important thing for you to keep in mind is that these strategies can be used for both academic and social purposes; that is, they are appropri-ate for building a conceptual understanding of the world *and* for functioning

TABLE 5.2 Generic Problem-Solving Activities

Determining the Problem

- Specifically delineating the problem to be studied or decision to be made.
- Generating a question or questions to be answered.
- Gathering information to make the problem less abstract.
- Operationally defining the problem.

Preparing to Gather Data

- Determining sources available for answering specific questions.
- Deciding which sources are most appropriate for ones purposes:
  - considering validity of sources
  - considering most economical source.
- Being aware of skills required to utilize source:
  - developing ability to use source.

Gathering Data

- Applying skills to specific sources.

Examining, Analyzing, and Evaluating Data

- Obtaining overview of available data:
  - determining if intitial questions appear to be answered.
- Examining data for patterns or categories.
- Determining if discrepancies exist:
  - resolving discrepancies by evaluating validity of sources or gathering new data.

---

in that world. We can use problem solving with content to help our students develop important social science and historical ideas. We can also use it to help them deal with the real-life problems they encounter. Doing problem solving in both contexts with our students is very necessary because real life requires both. (Mr. Ross, whose problem we discussed earlier, needed to gather theoretical information before he could actually begin to work with Joe.) The classroom examples provided at the end of our discussion of each model will deal with both content and social concerns.

Seeking Information: The Exploration Model

Exploration is used when we want to know about something which we have little or no background knowledge. As adults, all of us probably use this strategy quite frequently—without ever consciously realizing that we're using it. If you've written a research paper you've engaged in the exploration process. If you've ever wanted to know what all the sides were saying about a controversial issue, you were exploring. And if you've ever wanted to find the cheapest way to take a trip you probably did some exploration before you bought the tickets.

The exploration model which, by the way, is probably the problem-solving model used frequently in elementary classrooms, has five steps:

1. Determining the problem.
2. Preparing to gather data.
3. Gathering data.
4. Examining, analyzing, and evaluating data.
5. Synthesizing.

There is only one step in this approach in addition to the four generic steps discussed earlier. That step is the one in which the individual synthesizes the information which has been collected and analyzed. Let's examine it.

Synthesis. The data analysis culminates when the problem solver has specific answers to the questions that initiated the exploration. In the synthesis step these answers are organized in a meaningful way for the individual; the data are put together so that the person understands them and can do something with them. The outcome of the synthesis step is, in essence, some sort of statement that responds to the original problem.

When we use the term *statement* in reference to synthesizing, we are using it very broadly because it can take any number of forms. It may be something written, something constructed, or a course of action. If you were to use exploration to do a research paper for a class, your synthesizing statement would be the paper, itself. For elementary children it might be a bulletin board, an oral report, a dramatic presentation, or even the articulation of a social science understanding. The form that the synthesis statement takes will be dictated by the needs (and to some extent by the creativity) of the problem solver.

The following example shows how exploration occurred when children were dealing with a social problem. This exploration, which we briefly discussed in the first chapter, was initiated when a group of sixth graders expressed concern about the polluted creek which ran behind their school. They wanted to do something about it, Let's examine what occurred through each step:

Determining the Problem. In this step the students were helped to move from a relatively general concern to the formulation of specific questions to be studied.

The students had been discussing the term *pollution* and their teacher asked if, living in a rural area, pollution affected them.

STUDENT 1: Of course it does! Look at the creek.
STUDENT 2: Yeah. My father used to catch steelheads [*trout*] in it.
STUDENT 3: And kids could go swimming in it before it got all yukky.
STUDENT 1: Now we can't even go near it. Look at all the signs.
STUDENT 4: We ought to do something about it!

There was unanimous agreement to this suggestion.

TEACHER: What pollution are you going to do something about?
STUDENT 4: Everything that's polluting the creek.
TEACHER: Well, let's make a list of everything.

The students named garbage, junk cars, and oil as sources of pollution.

TEACHER: Is there anything we missed?
STUDENT 5:   I don't know.
STUDENT 2:   Maybe.
TEACHER: It is possible we missed something.
STUDENT 6:   What is it?
TEACHER: I don't know, but maybe before we do anything else we should find out more about water pollution. What do you think we need to know?
STUDENT 7:   What are the causes of water pollution?
STUDENT 4:   Yeah! And which ones are in our creek?

The teacher then took a large piece of chart paper and wrote on the top: "What are the causes of water pollution?"
"Which ones are in our creek?"
Beneath this the list, "garbage, junk cars, oil" was written.

In this situation, the problem was generated spontaneously from the children's interests and concerns. These, however, are not the only source of questions that can be explored in the classroom. At other times questions might be generated from the content currently being studied. Or the teacher might generally tell the children about a topic they will be studying and ask for questions they might have about the area.

Preparing to Gather Data. With the teacher's help, the students suggested data sources, decided which ones were the most appropriate, and determined the best way to utilize these sources.

TEACHER: Well, how can we find the answers to these questions?

After some discussion the students decided that they had to answer the first question first. Then they could use the information they obtained to help answer the second question.

TEACHER: How can we find the answer? (*He listed their responses on the blackboard.*)
STUDENT 1:   The encyclopedia.
STUDENT 2:   We can ask our parents.
STUDENT 3:   We can write the EPA.
STUDENT 4:   What's the EPA?
STUDENT 3:   I don't know. But every time you hear about pollution you hear about the EPA.

The teacher then briefly described the function of the Environmental Protection Agency and the students agreed that this might be a good source of information.

TEACHER: Any other ideas?
STUDENT 4:   We can read the newspaper and look in magazines.

At the end of this discussion the students had a list of information sources. They decided that all would talk with their parents and read various periodicals while one group checked the encyclopedia. It was also decided that, as a class, they'd write a letter to the EPA.

TEACHER: What shall we put in the letter?
STUDENT 7:   That we're worried about the pollution in our creek.
STUDENT 8:   And we want to know what causes water pollution.
STUDENT 9:   And we want them to tell us what they think might be polluting our creek.

The planning went on, and with the teacher's help they decided that they'd better describe their area. They then discussed what would go into this, including a physical description of the area as well as the businesses and industries located there. Using the outline made during this discussion, the letter was finally drafted.

As you can see, the teacher has a very definite job in helping elementary children move through this stage. First, students are asked to suggest sources of answers to their questions. The teacher may make additional suggestions. Then they are helped to evaluate which sources they perceive as more valuable. Again, the teacher may help with ideas. Finally, the teacher makes certain that the children know how to use these sources. This may mean reviewing specific data-gathering skills, teaching new skills, and giving the children opportunity to practice these skills.

Gathering Data. The children now apply the skills considered in the previous step.

The encyclopedia group found several sources of water pollution, which they listed on a chart. These sources included industrial wastes, oil spills, and sewage.

Each day the children brought newspaper clippings and magazine articles dealing with water pollution and discussed them during current events. This resulted in their putting checks next to the items they had already noted. They also added chemicals and fluoride to the list. In a few weeks they received an answer from the EPA, which listed many of the items they had already found. It added agricultural chemicals, including pesticides and fertilizer, to the list.

During the data-gathering stage the teacher's job is that of a facilitator and resource person; he or she will make certain that the children are doing their data-gathering tasks but helps them with these tasks only when necessary.

Examining, Analyzing, and Evaluating Data. The students are now ready to get an overview of their data, examine it for patterns, and resolve any discrepancies that might appear.

TEACHER: Let's look at our chart now. What do we have?

The list included garbage, junk cars, industrial wastes, oil spills, sewage, chemicals, fluoride, fertilizer, and pesticides.

TEACHER: Let's examine where we got this information to be sure that it's accurate. You remember when we were talking about the difference between fact and opinion. Do any of these represent opinions?
STUDENT 1:   Yeah, we said that garbage, junk cars, and oil were sources, but we were just guessing.
STUDENT 5:   But oil fits into oil spills, so that's a fact.
STUDENT 4:   And what about garbage? Doesn't that fit under sewage?

The students debated this and decided that, even though they might be stretching it, garbage could fit with sewage. They decided that, on land, garbage is litter and litter is pollution, and so garbage could be considered water litter. They used the same reasoning for junk cars.

STUDENT 6:   What about this fluoride one? That came from a letter to the editor. Let's reread the letter to see if it's fact.

On rereading the letter they discovered that it was the writer's opinion that fluoride shouldn't be put into the water supply of a nearby town. They also found out that this was put into the water at the town's filtration plant. Since their water came directly from wells, they decided to exclude fluoride.

The students also found that the EPA had not listed oil as a potential pollutant for their area. Checking back to the articles they had read, they noted that this problem was primarily one associated with oceans and rivers. Therefore, they decided to also exclude oil. They did the same with industrial wastes. With the teacher's help the students then revised their list. They first combined garbage and junk cars into one category called wastes and decided—based on the fact that fertilizer and pesticides are chemicals—to delete chemicals as a category and use the subcategories. Because aside from agriculture there was no industry in their area, they also deleted industrial wastes.

Movement through this step can be facilitated by the teacher asking such appropriate questions as "What did you find out? (see?) (hear?) (read?)" "Did you check all of your sources?" "Does it look as if you have all the information you need?" This would be followed by, "How does your information fit together?" or "How can you group your information together?" The teacher would help the children look for discrepancies by asking, "Do any of your sources say different things?" "How can you find out what's correct?" Finally, the teacher would ask the children to look at their original questions to tell whether their information was adequate to answer them.

Synthesis. The students are now ready to put their data together.

The synthesis done by the students was very simple; they made a list of the potential pollutants in their creek. It read, "Sources of pollution in our creek may be waste, sewage, fertilizers, and pesticides."

As we said earlier, synthesizing can take many forms, and elementary teachers should not discount those that emphasize written language less than other forms of communication.

The students in our example actually had two questions. They answered the first, dealing with types of pollution, but did not consider the second, "Which ones are in our creek?" To answer that question they would use the answers to their first question as hypotheses from the inquiry model.

Generating Knowledge: Inquiry

Inquiry is the process by which we utilize what we know to formulate new answers to problems we have. In essence we develop new knowledge for ourselves. Thus, the students in the example above would use what they had learned about water pollution to identify the sources of pollution in their creek.

Inquiry is one of the primary methods of problem solving employed by social scientists to develop the ideas of their discipline; concepts and generalizations are the results of the utilization of this scientific method. Of course, inquiry is used by individuals other than scientists. Mr. Ross used it when he asked, "Could there possibly be a connection between Joe's misbehavior and his weekends with his father?" In cases such as Mr. Ross' (and the children with whom we work) the knowledge generated may not be new to the world at large. It will, however, be new to the inquirer.

Inquiry has seven basic steps:

1. Determining the problem.
2. Hypothesizing.
3. Planning to gather data.
4. Gathering data.
5. Examining, Analyzing, and Evaluating Data.
6. Accepting or rejecting hypotheses.
7. Generalizing.

The major differences between inquiry and the other problem-solving models is that it focuses on a hypothesis—a solution that the problem solver suggests. It utilizes three specific activities that are concerned with the hypothesis:

Developing the Hypothesis or Hypotheses. The hypothesis is a suggested specific solution to the problem. Often, an hypothesis has been defined as an educated guess and—although some people have disagreed with this definition—it is appropriate for our purposes. With inquiry, the solution is neither a guess nor a straw that we grasp in desperation. Instead it is a suggestion based on information we have that can in some way be related to the problem. Thus, based on their previous research, the sixth graders in the above example could hypothesize that the causes of pollution in their creek were wastes, sewage, fertilizers, and pesticides.

As individuals hypothesize, they synthesize all of the knowledge they have related to an area. They determine how this information relates to the specific problem and then generate a solution that incorporates the most appropriate information.

Movement to the step where individuals plan to gather data is a gradual one because the hypothesis will, to a great extent, suggest the type of data that is needed. Sometimes individuals find it very helpful to develop "If . . . then" propositions as a means of moving to prepare to gather data. These propositions basically state that "if" an hypothesis is acceptable "then" this is what the inquirer would expect to find in the data.

Accepting or Rejecting the Hypothesis. Accepting or rejecting the hypothesis occurs after the data are collected and analyzed. Based on the analysis, the inquirer can now determine if the hypothesis is supported or not, whether the solution to the problem is an acceptable one. If it is not supported, the inquirer may wish to generate a new hypothesis. If it is accepted the inquirer can do one of three things: terminate the inquiry; generate alternative hypotheses; or move to the next step of inquiry.

Generalizing. When researchers engage in the scientific method they take pains to insure that their findings can be applied to some general population; for example, children in the elementary school, males of a given population, or cultural groups. They do this by making certain that their data sources are as representative as possible of that population. Nonscientists engaging in inquiry usually don't take such measures. Their problems are usually situation specific ("What are the causes of pollution in our creek?") The hypotheses they make usually reflect this specificity.

In the generalizing stage a move is made away from the specific, and the question, "If this hypothesis is accepted in this case, can it be accepted in all cases?" is asked. The accepted hypothesis is then reformulated to include all cases and data is gathered to determine if it is supported. If the new hypothesis is accepted the individual develops a generalization.

When many teachers hear the term *inquiry* they think of a type of teaching where little utilization is made of textbooks. Yet, inquiry can occur even when the only data source is the textbook. In the following example we will show how this might occur. We have chosen two textbooks to do this. They are *The Taba Program in Social Science, People in States* (Addison-Wesley, 1972), a fourth-grade text, and *You and Your Family* (Economy, 1982), a first-grade text. The Taba series, incidentally, though relatively old, was chosen because it is one of the few series to actually provide directions to the teacher for taking the children through each step of inquiry. Even if texts do not explicitly indicate that inquiry might be used, and do not provide directions for the teacher, the strategies suggested here will be appropriate.

Determining the Problem. This step can be used as an opener for a textbook unit. Usually it is initiated by the teacher, who will ask the students a question or questions they need to consider. The *Taba Program* book, *People in States*, presents six questions at the beginning of a unit on "The People of Serbia." All of the questions ask the students to hypothesize who will make decisions for groups of people. The first unit of the text, *You and Your Family*, is concerned with how people are alike and different. This concern could be posed as a question to the children by the teacher.

Inquiry is appropriate only if the problem solver has sufficient knowledge to hypothesize. Therefore, questions posed to the children should be ones about which the teacher is relatively certain the children possess the information necessary to hypothesize. This information can come from previous topics studied or from the children's own life experience.

Hypothesizing. The children's responses to the initial question represent their hypotheses. These are noted in some way, either by the students or by the teacher. The fourth graders using *People in States* are asked to write their ideas and then, for each question, are asked by the teacher to tell why they think their reason is acceptable. With *You and Your Family* the children's hypotheses about similarities and differences among humans could be listed on a chart in either written or pictorial form.

As can be seen from these examples, hypothesizing can be either an individual or group activity.

Preparing to Gather Data. Preparing to gather data is a step that is usually not given much attention because the textbook will be the data source and information will be obtained from it. The texts, however, are usually accompanied by annotations that suggest strategies the teacher can utilize to facilitate the children's reading and observation of illustrations. (We will also suggest some strategies to do this in Chapter 12.) In both books data are supplied by both pictures and texts accompanied by annotations for the teacher's use.

In cases where children will be working with the textbook on their own, it may be wise to teach or review specific skills (for example, outlining) necessary to gathering data.

Gathering Data. Gathering data occurs as the children work with their texts. In *People in States* the children's reading is guided by the teacher. Datum is presented separately for each question that was initially asked by the teacher, and the children are asked to check the hypotheses made in relation to the question. In *You and Your Family* the children are asked to refer to the lists of hypotheses as they read and examine photos and pictures.

Examining, Analyzing, and Evaluating Data. Although much of the data in texts for children are presented in a relatively straightforward manner, they are usually presented in more than one form. Teachers can encourage students to compare information presented in different forms, such as the text and pictures, and to determine what is relevant and irrelevant to their hypotheses. Usually teachers' manuals offer a variety of suggestions for helping children engage in these activities. *People in States* asks children to examine additional data, which have nothing to do with the specific question, and to speculate why they do not fit their hypotheses. *You and Your Family* presents children with opportunities to distinguish between data about humans and animals. Guiding questions are presented in the teacher's manual to help them do this.

Accepting or Rejecting the Hypotheses. Often the function of accepting or rejecting the hypotheses is given little emphasis in teachers' manuals and it is up to the teacher to see that it occurs. Children need to be encouraged to look at their responses to the initial question in light of what they have subsequently learned. The inclusion of this step is very necessary, even if no attention is given to it in the book. Otherwise the reason for the inquiry may be lost to the children and they may perceive the activities engaged in up to this point as wasted effort.

Of the two books, only *People in States* pays direct attention to this step. The teachers' manual for this book indicates that, as soon as the students have read the selection dealing with an hypothesis, and have discussed it, they are to check their hypothesis. At that point the students are encouraged to change their responses if necessary.

Generalize. In order to help children develop general ideas—as opposed to those about a specific topic—it is often necessary to go beyond the text. Sometimes teachers' manuals will suggest additional activities of this nature.

At the end of the Serbian unit in *People in States,* students are given examples of decision making in a fictional country. They are asked who will make the decision and why?

The conclusion of the similarities and differences unit in *You and Your Family* provides generalizing opportunities by asking children two questions:

How are you like other people?
How are you different?

Textbooks are a ready source of data that can be used to help children develop social science and history ideas. If you were to examine a number of them you'd find that some help the teacher take the children through each step of inquiry and some do not. What the latter do, though, is provide hypothesizing opportunities at the beginning of units. These can be used as springboards that will motivate the children to deal with the content.

Making Intelligent Choices: The Decision-Making Model

At times problems we encounter may have more than one possible solution. The decision-making process is concerned with this type of dilemma. It entails the generation of the possible solutions to the problem, the choosing of one (or sometimes more) of these as being appropriate for us, and the acting upon this choice.

The choosing that occurs in decision making is not impulsive or whimsical; individuals don't take the first or most seemingly attractive alternative that comes their way. Instead, this choosing is quite deliberate and is based on careful consideration of three factors:

1. All possible courses of action.
2. The consequences of these actions.
3. The congruence of a given course of action with the individual's beliefs and values.

Thus, decision making is differentiated from simple choice taking in that we must thoughtfully utilize both cognitive and affective capabilities.

The decision-making model has six steps;

1. Determining the decision to be made (determining the problem).
2. Planning to gather data about alternatives and their consequences.
3. Generating alternatives and their consequences (gathering data).
4. Examining alternatives and consequences (examining, analyzing and evaluating data).
5. Choosing in accordance with personal value structure.
6. Acting on the choice.

Decision making can be considered to be a form of inquiry in many respects. The alternative courses of action generated by the problem solver can be considered, for all intents and purposes, to be hypotheses. Their consequences are the data that will allow the hypotheses to be accepted or rejected. Decision making goes beyond inquiry, however, in that the individual needs to choose and act on a course of action from among those hypothe-

Students can make decisions in the classroom about many things that affect their lives.

ses that were accepted. It is this choosing and acting which set decision making apart.

Choosing According to a Personal Value Structure. Here we are required to evaluate the alternatives and consequence according to what we believe to be good, right, or important to ourselves. To do this we will utilize different skills, depending upon the type of decision situations. In some cases the situation may be a relatively clear-cut one where we are well aware of what our values are and can act on them with little serious reflection. At other times we are unclear as to exactly what it is we believe. Here we need to analyze the situation to determine what is important to us. One way of doing this is to examine each alternative and its consequences, attempt to determine which one or ones appear to be more acceptable to us, and then determine why they are acceptable. This "why" would most likely be the value that underlies our choice. We could then determine if we find this value to be acceptable to our life and consonant with other beliefs we have and activities we do. If it is, we are becoming aware of a value we hold.

There are still other times when, although aware of what our values are in relation to a given situation, we find that two or more of these appear to be in conflict. For example, a person may have the opportunity for a career advancement—with a larger salary—but this job may mean that the person will be away from his or her family for extended periods of time. In this case the individual might be experiencing a conflict between a desire for career advancement and perceived responsibilities to one's family. In situations such as this we would initially need to be certain that a value conflict does indeed exist. We would need to recheck data that has been gathered, looking especially at the consequences we have generated. This would be done to determine whether the data are factual (as opposed to inference or opinion) and relevant to the given situation. Do the data indicate for certain that the individual will be away from his or her family or is this an assumption that the individual has made? Rechecking our data may result in different consequences and indicate that the apparent conflict no longer exists.

If, upon rechecking our data we find that the conflict indeed still exists, we will need to determine which value is more important in the given situation. One way of doing this works from two assumptions. The first is that we possess values in addition to those in conflict and that some of these may have an impact on our choice. The second assumption is that the more consonant a choice is with all of the values we hold, the more appropriate it will be. In this strategy we examine the alternatives and consequences in terms of other values we hold. We attempt to see if, when these are used as evaluative criteria, an alternative is more acceptable. If it were we would, by inference, be identifying the conflicting value that is more in accord with our other values in this situation, and more important.

Acting. Acting is the second distinguishing characteristic of decision making. Once we have made a choice, we must carry it out. Otherwise the problem-solving has been an intellectual exercise. This is a very defined activity; we have completely thought it through and are well aware of its implications. Like the synthesis step of exploration, and the generalizing stage of inquiry, acting is a very important step because it brings closure to the process. It is also important because it provides the purpose of decision making.

In discussing the other problem-solving models we have examined how these would be used to build conceptual understandings and to deal with social concerns. To illustrate the decision-making process as it might be done with elementary children, I have, again, chosen a social problem. This problem is somewhat different than the one discussed earlier in that it was of a personal–social nature, one that was affecting the childrens' daily classroom lives.

The problem occurred in my own classroom. At the time I was teaching in an agricultural area of California. Harvesting there began in May, continued through the summer, and ended in November. This harvest required a large number of migrant farm workers, many of whom had families. This meant that we had children transferring into the school in late April. As you may know, by this time of year routines are well established, cohesive classroom groups have formed, and people are beginning to anticipate the end of school.

As a teacher, my job was to make the new children feel that they were part of the school and classroom community. This job was made more difficult due to the fact that most of the migrant students were Mexcian nationals who spoke little or no English! I decided to get my students to help with the job. The following are excerpts of what we did.

Determining the Decision to be Made. In the classroom the need to make a decision can come from the students who realize that a problem exists. It can also be suggested by the teacher, as occurred in this case.

With my class, this first step of decision making occurred in the context of a class discussion. This discussion began with a review of what the children remembered of the migrant students' arrival in previous years. The students spoke of both positive and negative occurrences and of their feelings toward the Mexican children. These, too, were both positive and negative. From what the students said it became obvious to me that the most negative aspects were associated with the migrant children's initial entry into the classroom. As the children got to know one another things became more positive. I pointed this out to my students and they agreed that, for the most part, this was the case. I then summarized the discussion by stating that it appeared to me that the quicker we got to know the Mexican children the quicker we'd have more good feelings and less disruption in our lives. The children agreed, and we decided we'd try to figure out how to do this.

Planning to Gather Data. As noted earlier, data can be obtained inferentially, based on the individual's past experiences, or it can be obtained from other sources. We utilized the former.

The class was broken into groups and the children were told that they were to brainstorm different ideas for making the new children welcome. We then reviewed the rules of brainstorming, and the students were told that, when they felt they had a sufficient number of ideas, they were to choose those that they'd like to try. We would role play these ideas.

I also chose one student from each group to role play the new child for that group. (The students chosen were ones who I believed would frankly state their perceptions of what happened.) As the groups were brainstorming I took the "new" children outside of the classroom and told them the role they would take. The boys would be "Fernando" and the girls were "Rosa"—none of them could speak English. I asked them to think how they might feel and act coming to this new school. They shared their ideas with each other.

Generating Alternatives and Consequences. There are two basic approaches to generating alternatives and consequences doing this in the classroom:

1. All alternatives can be first generated, then the consequences of each are considered.
2. Consequences are considered as each alternative is suggested (Schuncke and Krogh, 1983).

Our role play utilized the former.

I brought the "new" children into the classroom, reminding the students that they had considered ways of making new kids feel comfortable. Then I introduced the Fernandos and Rosas to each group.

After the initial surprise that the Fernandos and Rosas couldn't speak English, the students tried out their ideas. In some cases there was painful silence. In others nervous giggling. One group told their names. In another they started playing a game.

After a few minutes I stopped the role play and asked the Fernandos and

Rosas how they were feeling. Their responses ranged from embarrassed (all of the kids in her group were laughing and she thought they were laughing at her) to foolish ("They treated me like a dope") to somewhat comfortable. I then asked the class members how they felt and they too had various feelings to express. We listed on the board the activity the children did and how it made people feel. I then asked the group to think of other ideas they wanted to try, either from the brainstorming or from any new insights they had.

We repeated the role play three times, evaluating what happened at the end of each enactment. Each time we added to our list on the board.

Choosing According to a Value Structure. Sometimes the teacher may focus the discussion on one value, as we did in this case by choosing according to feelings engendered. At other times the teacher need not provide the focus. However, children should always be given the opportunity to articulate why they believe one option to be better than others.

At the end of the role play we reviewed all of the data on the blackboard. Then we evaluated the consequences in terms of personal feelings. The children discarded those that elicited negative feelings (embarassment, feeling like a dope) almost immediately. They also questioned some that had apparent positive feelings. For example, some felt that pairing a Spanish-speaking child with a new child was okay for the pair but excluded non-Spanish speakers. They also generated new ideas based on ones with positive consequences ("How about trios, and if one person doesn't speak Spanish the other can translate?").

Ultimately, the list was whittled down and modified. The children decided that the ideas that remained would work.

Acting. There is a greater probability that an individual will act on a choice when that individual publicly articulates the choice. In a classroom situation it may be well to have the student state the actions they will take.

Shortly before it was known that the migrant children would arrive, we again reviewed the list and discussed how we would implement the suggestions (for example, non-Spanish and Spanish speakers were paired for trios) upon the arrival of the migrant children, the students, with occasional reminders from me, put their plan into action.

Synthesis: Children and Problem Solving —————————————————————

There is a close relationship between knowledge and problem solving. We use our knowledge to deal with the problems we encounter. Similarly, we use problem solving to generate new knowledge. Each complements and facilitates growth of the other. This relationship holds as far as social studies instruction is concerned. From reading this chapter it should be obvious to you that we can help children develop problem-solving capabilities and skills as we simultaneously help them develop conceptual understandings.

In the following two chapters we will consider two ways of developing problem-solving capabilities in the elementary school: with one approach we help children utilize a given problem-solving model by helping them move through all of its steps; with the other we focus on skills needed by all of the models. As you read about these approaches you should bear in mind that their successful implementation will depend to a great extent on how well we adapt them to where the children are. That is, the developmental considerations we discussed in relation to learning concepts and generalization are just as important in fostering problem-solving capabilities. Therefore, let's briefly review some of the more important developmental considerations and examine their implications for problem solving.

Children's conceptions of time and space point to the need for another type of concreteness in problem-solving activities. As we noted in an earlier chapter, for younger children, the concept of time is focused on "now." Space revolves around "here." Gradually, the understanding of these two concepts broadens. This suggests that the problems we choose to deal with should not be too far removed from the children. The problem situations our students encounter should be ones with which they have some familiarity and can identify.

In reflecting upon the problem-solving steps we have discussed in this chapter, it is interesting to note that one intellectual activity may recur several times in all the models. That activity is classification. Children might classify the questions they ask, the data sources they need, and the information they find. We know, however, that the ability to classify is not completely achieved until the end of the stage of concrete operations— occurring at the earliest at the age of ten or eleven. Initially children will be able to form simple classes of things they have experienced. Next they will be able to generate subclasses from larger classes and see the relationship of the subclasses to the larger ones. Finally, they will move to being able to develop multiple classification; they will understand that it is possible to build new groups with items from other groups.

This progression, from simple to multiple classification, is a gradual one that is facilitated by giving the child classification experiences. We can let them classify in ways that make sense to them. We can also give them experiences classifying in ways that they have not yet mastered. We can, for example, help younger children form subclasses. Although we really can't expect them to understand the relationship between the smaller and larger classes we are providing experiences that will act as bases for this understanding.

Preoperational children are egocentric. One aspect of this egocentrism is their belief that what they are thinking is right. They also believe that the world is as they think it is. The combination of these two elements of egocentrism often results in children's engaging in impulsive behavior. That is, they do not engage in problem solving per se. Instead they will, with little thought, grab on to the first, and usually most attractive, solution to whatever problem confronts them. This implies that they will require help in recognizing what the problem is and, more importantly, they will need assistance in planning how to deal with a problem. Spivak and Shure (1974) have found that when this help is given, children (as young as four) can be taught to thoughtfully engage in problem-solving processes.

Another aspect of egocentrism is concerned with the children's social world and their interactions with other people. You may remember from our discussion of social perspective taking in the previous chapter that preoperational children have difficulty taking the perspective of other people. They also have little awareness that other people may think differently than they do. With appropriate experiences they gradually move to a realization that people do think and feel differently in different situations or when they have different information about the same situation. As they near the end of the stage of concrete operations they can think about their own thoughts and can also predict how other people will think about these thoughts. Gradually they may move to being able to look at situations, not in terms of how they are thinking about it, but in terms of how a given group of people—be it a society or a cultural group—would think about it.

The gradually emergent social-perspective-taking ability needs to be kept in mind as we guide children's problem solving. This is especially true in the case of inquiry and decision making when we ask children to look at implications of given courses of action. It would be difficult for younger children to understand the consequences of alternatives or the implications of a given hypothesis if these were phrased only in terms of their effects on other people. According to Moore (1979), children can consider other people to some extent if the problem situation is meaningful and personal to them. That is, if they have had experiences with similar situations and can see the effects of a course of action on themselves, their experiences may enable them to infer consequences on others. They would have great difficulty, however, doing this in hypothetical situations. Gradually, of course, they will be able to look at situations with an awareness of the thoughts and feelings of others.

The limited perspective-taking abilities of our youngest students do not mean that we should never include the thoughts and feelings of others for their consideration. In order for them to grow in perspective-taking ability it is necessary that they be exposed to levels of perspective taking that are higher than their own. Thus it is perfectly acceptable to do this if it is included in a way that does not exclude the child's own thinking about the situation.

Springboards to Discussion _____

1. One of the major differences between exploration and inquiry is the order in which the question that elicited the problem solving is answered. With *exploration* the question is stated and then data gathering, etc., occurs to seek the answer. The answer is essentially the culmination of the activity. With *inquiry,* the question is stated and, then, a tentative answer (the hypothesis) is suggested. Activities that follow are directed at ascertaining the acceptability of this answer.

   In this chapter we illustrated how a unit in a child's textbook may be adapted to an inquiry approach. It can also be adapted to exploration. Using a textbook with which you are familiar, devise a strategy for doing this. Indicate how you will help children move through each step of the exploration process.

When you have completed your planning, read the section on "A Text-Based Context" in the next chapter. Evaluate what you have done in terms of: (1) what you might do differently, and (2) ideas you had that improve upon the strategy presented in that chapter.

2. The three models of problem solving presented in this chapter certainly don't exhaust all ways of dealing with a problemmatic situation. You, in fact, may have found a way that is very appropriate. The following exercise is appropriate to determine if you have.

   (a) Describe a problem you encountered in the past that has since been resolved.
   (b) Indicate the steps you took in reaching problem resolution.
   (c) Evaluate the effectiveness of what you did. Could it be done better next time? How?

   Finally, consider how you might use *your* problem-solving model in your work with children.

3. Examine a children's textbook for its problem-solving potential. Evaluate how it lends itself to using a specific problem-solving model. Also indicate what you would need to do to insure that the problem-solving potential of the text was exploited.

References

FELDHEUSEN, JOHN F., AND GUTHRIE, VIRGINIA A. "Models of Problem Solving Process and Abilities," *Journal of Research and Development in Education,* Vol. 12, No. 2 (1979), pp. 22–32.

GORDON, THOMAS. *Teacher Effectiveness Training.* New York: Peter H. Wyden, 1975.

JOHNSON, SIMON O. *Better Discipline: A Practical Approach.* Springfield: Charles C. Thomas, 1980.

MOORE, SHIRLEY. "Social Cognition: Knowing about Others," *Young Children,* Vol. 34 (1979), pp. 54–61.

SCHOMBERG, CARL E. *You and Your Family.* Oklahoma City: Economy, 1982.

SCHUNCKE, GEORGE, AND HOFFMAN, STEVIE. "Developing Problem-Solving Readiness in Elementary School Children," *The Social Studies,* Vol. 71, No. 1 (January/February 1980), pp. 23–27.

SCHUNCKE, GEORGE, AND LOWELL KROGH, SUZANNE. *Helping Children Choose.* Glenview, IL: Scott, Foresman, 1983.

SPIVAK G., AND SHURE, M. B. *Social Adjustment of Young Children.* San Francisco: Jossey-Bass, 1974.

TANABE, PATSY, AND DURKIN, MARY. *People in States* (The Taba Program in Social Science). Menlo Park, CA: Addison-Wesley, 1972.

6

Teaching Problem Solving Through a Total-Process Approach

After reading this chapter you should be able to:

1. Based on the *Taxonomy of Objectives: Cognitive Domain,* describe questions that teachers can use to facilitate student problem solving.

2. Identify planning strategies that can be used to structure questions that elicit higher-level thinking skills in the problem-solving context.

3. Describe various types of classroom activities that lend themselves to a total-process problem-solving approach:
- Structured discussion.
- Text based.
- Role play.
- Simulations.
- Dramatic play.

4. Delineate planning strategies that can be used to insure that problem solving is included in the social studies curriculum.

There are two basic approaches to teaching and using problem solving in the elementary school. It can be worked with as a total process, with children moving from the realization of a dilemma or problem completely through to its resolution. With this approach the children engage in each step of a given problem-solving model. The examples of problem solving we saw in the previous chapter, such as the one dealing with making new students feel welcomed, utilized a total-process approach. The second means of dealing with problem solving is through a skills approach. Instead of focusing on movement from step to step of a given model, a skill, or skills, required by one of the steps of problem solving is developed. Using this latter approach, for example, we might teach a specific skill, such as interviewing, which would be associated with data gathering. In this chapter we will look at the first approach, *total-process,* while reserving discussion of the *skills approach* for the following chapter.

In dealing with problem solving from a total-process perspective, our job as teachers will be to facilitate the children's movement from step to step. Because we will want *them* to be the problem solvers, the manner in which we do this facilitation will be indirect. That is, we won't necessarily want to tell them what to do; we'll help them to find their own way. To accomplish this we'll resort to asking rather than telling; by using appropriate questions we'll help them move from one step to another.

There are questions and there are questions, but which ones are appropriate? The major part of this chapter is devoted to helping you answer this. We'll examine different types of questions that might be employed in the classroom and suggest how they might be appropriately used to facilitate problem solving. Following our examination of types of questions we'll look at situations where they might be used. We'll examine how structured discussions and textbooks can be employed with a total-process approach. Then we'll consider some action-based problem-solving contexts, including dramatic play, role play, and simulations. The synthesis section of this chapter will be devoted to a discussion of how we might plan to include a total-process approach to problem solving in our curriculum.

Questions to Facilitate Problem Solving _____

When we engage in problem solving we are essentially finding the answers to a series of questions. We begin the process with a central question such as, "What are the sources of water pollution in the creek?" "How are people similar?" or "How can we make the new students feel welcomed?" In order to answer this initial question we then ask a series of questions designed to lead us through whatever problem-solving strategy we are utilizing: "What do I need to know?" "How can I find this information?" "What do these sources say?" "Are they valid?" "How do these data fit together?" and so on.

As adults we are aware of the steps necessary for working with different types of problems. Using this knowledge we can help our students move from step to step by asking them facilitating questions. In the process we will be accomplishing three things: we will be helping them to solve their own problems (as opposed to solving problems for them); we will be modeling appropriate problem-solving behaviors; and we will be providing them with examples of appropriate types of questions they might ask.

What are appropriate types of questions for problem-solving situations? Because problem solving is an intellectual activity, success with it will require that we employ a variety of different thinking skills. Therefore, the questions we use to guide our students should be ones that serve the purpose of either developing different intellectual capabilities or give the children the opportunity to exercise these capabilities.

Benjamin Bloom and his associates, in *Taxonomy of Educational Objectives: The Classification of Educational Goals: Handbook I: The Cognitive Domain* (Bloom et al., 1956), have identified a list of such intellectual activities. In that book, which has since become a classic in education, six classes of cognition were defined. These include:

1. Knowledge.
2. Comprehension.
3. Application.

4. Analysis.
5. Synthesis.
6. Evaluation. [Bloom et al., 1956 p.18]

This taxonomy has two important characteristics. First, the levels are arranged in a hierarchy; knowledge, or remembering, is the lowest level of cognitive activity while evaluation is the highest. Secondly, because they are in a hierarchy, intellectual activities at the higher levels will require that the individual have engaged in lower level thought about the topic or idea under consideration. To comprehend an idea, for example, an individual must know it; and evaluation requires all levels below it.

The taxonomy is an appropriate one to be considered in developing questions. Research results indicate that the utilization of higher level questions within the taxonomy (e.g., those beyond comprehension) tend to have a positive effect on student achievement (Redfield and Rousseau, 1981). Using higher-level questions does help students develop those thinking skills necessary for effective and sophisticated problem solving.

In the following discussion we'll examine the different levels of the taxonomy at which questions may be phrased. Before we do this, however, two important points should be noted. First, the term *question* is being used very broadly. Sometimes comments used to facilitate problem solving may be interrogatives; at other times they may be statements or suggestions. In helping children determine a problem, for example, a teacher might say, "Let's list the facts." This would fit into the category of questioning as we are discussing it here. For our purposes questions will include any comments that facilitate student thought. Secondly, although we will provide examples of questions at different levels you should be aware that, to a great extent, it is not the wording of the question alone that determines the thinking the questions will engender. The level of thought the children have previously devoted to the topic will be one determinant. Another will be the context in which the questions are asked. The question, "What sources of water pollution can we hypothesize to be in our creek?" would elicit one level of thought if the students have just finished a study of water pollution. A higher level of thought would result from this question if it required the students to choose appropriate ideas from everything they know about water pollution, ideas which they had learned in the past.

Knowledge

The lowest level of the taxonomy, knowledge, is concerned with remembering and nothing more sophisticated. The individual is simply expected to recall what was learned in very much the same form in which it was learned. If I were to say to you, at this point, "Name the six categories of the taxonomy," I would be asking you to engage in a knowledge activity.

Bloom and his colleagues have identified three basic types of knowledge:

1. *Knowledge of specifics* (Bloom et al., 1956, p. 63), which would include specific facts (names, dates, locations of places, events) and specific

terminology (definitions, concept words appropriate to a given field of study).

2. *Knowledge of ways of dealing with specifics* (Bloom et al., 1956, p.68), which would include remembering characteristic ways in which factual data are presented (knowing that the symbol for an airport is an airplane on most maps); remembering classes or groups (the two types of workers studied were producers of services); remembering criteria for judging something without actually doing the judging (knowing, for example, the step to take for resolving discrepancies in data); remembering processes (reciting the steps of decision making, for example); awareness of trends and sequences (how a bill becomes a law, for example, or the step that milk goes through from dairy to supermarket).

3. *Knowledge of universals or abstractions in a field* (Bloom et al., 1956, p. 75) is, basically, an awareness of the major concepts or ideas of an area (*group* is a major concept of sociology).

It is important to reiterate that, although knowledge incorporates three different aspects—specific bits of information, ways of dealing with specifics, and knowledge of universals—it requires nothing more than remembering these. So, for example, although an individual could name the steps of the decision-making process, he or she would not need to understand what is required of each step, nor would that individual need to be able to actually go through decision making. Similarly, although the person might know that group is a major concept of sociology, the knowledge category does not require an understanding of the attributes of a group.

Research data (Goodlad, 1983) indicate that there is a prevailing tendency for teachers to ask lower-level questions. Implied by these findings (and probably reinforced by our own experiences as students) is the thought that many of these questions serve little useful purpose, and are therefore inappropriate. This is not to say that knowledge questions are unimportant and should not be asked. They do have their place in teaching. That place, however, is not as an end of instruction; we don't teach facts or skills simply so that children remember them. Instead, they are taught as means to broader understandings. We ask children to remember facts, for example, so that they can use those facts to build concepts and generalizations. Similarly, we ask them to remember a skill so that the skill can be used for some purpose. Knowledge is used as a foundation for other intellectual activities. Therefore it will be necessary to ask knowledge questions to build the foundation, and the number of these questions you will need to ask will be dependent upon the experiences the children have had with the topic under consideration.

The following examples illustrate different memory questions that might be used at different parts of the problem-solving process:

- **Knowledge of specifics**
  - What are the facts in this situation?
  - From our study, what are some sources of water pollution?
  - What can we find in an atlas?

- What will the card catalog tell us?
- What specific information did you find?
- **Knowledge of ways and means of dealing with specifics**
  - What are the steps of brainstorming?
  - How do we end the interview?
  - How do we find "water pollution" in the encyclopedia?

Comprehension

Like knowledge, comprehension can be broken into three different types of intellectual activity:

1. *Translation,* in which the original communication is put into a different form. Sanders (1966) notes that the most well-known form of translation probably occurs in the classroom when the teacher says, "Put it into your own words." There are, of course, many forms of translation other than from words to words. When children tell what they see in a political cartoon (without doing any analysis of it) they are translating from pictures to words. When they act out something that has been read to them, they are translating from words to action. Or, when they make a histogram (a bar graph), they are translating from numbers to a graphic form.

   Translation occurs frequently as children move from preparing to gather data to the actual data gathering. If we teach them a specific skill, say one dealing with using map scale, and they then use this skill as a means of getting their information, they are translating. We might like to think that they are engaging in application (which is the next higher level of the taxonomy) because they are putting the learned skill to use. If we examine what is happening, however, we see that they are simply remembering what they have been told to do and translating it into action somewhat later. As we shall shortly see, application implies greater thought.

2. *Interpretation* is characterized by the individual's understanding of what a communication means. The individual comprehends the different ideas contained in a message, and is able to combine them into some type of meaningful whole. The understanding is a relatively literal or objective one; that is, we comprehend exactly what a message says. As with translation, the communication that is interpreted need not be a verbal one per se. In the social studies, for example, children will need to understand the message contained in pictures, cartoons, charts, graphs, and maps of different kinds.

3. *Extrapolation* occurs as the individual goes beyond the data contained in the message to draw conclusions based on the data. That is, the individual is able to make logical inferences based on what is contained in a communication. Accurate extrapolation, according to Bloom et al. (1956, p. 95) requires that a person "be able to extend the trends and tendencies beyond the given data and findings . . . to determine implications, consequences, corollaries, effects, etc., which are in accord with the conditions as literally described in the original communication."

The three different types of activities embodied by comprehension all require levels of the taxonomy that are below them. That is, translation requires knowledge or memory; interpretation requires translation; and extrapolation requires interpretation. The following questions are examples of ones that facilitate different comprehension activities, which in turn make the problem-solving process easier:

- **Translation**
  - State the problem in your own words.
  - What did you see in the film?
  - Let's put the numbers into graph form.
- **Interpretation**
  - What did the book say about decision making in groups?
  - How did your first solution make the people involved feel?
  - What is the advertisement's message?
- **Extrapolation**
  - You said that you saw these things happen. What do they suggest the problem to be?
  - If this hypothesis is acceptable, what can you expect?
  - Why does the information suggest that oil spills can't be a source of pollution here?
  - If this continues to happen, what will happen later?

Application

Application follows comprehension in the taxonomy. When application is employed, something learned in the past is brought to bear on a new situation. In the social studies, application can occur in three different ways. Students can apply knowledge, processes or skills. When knowledge is applied, understandings developed in the past (either in a curricular context or through life experiences) are brought to bear on new problems. Hypothesizing in inquiry and the generation of alternatives in decision making often call for the application of knowledge. The application of processes would occur in problem solving when the individual chose and used the appropriate problem-solving model for a given dilemma and worked through that dilemma in an appropriate way. Skills would be applied when a student chose and used an appropriate data source.

It is not difficult to see how knowledge and comprehension are required by application. Before something can be used appropriately it must be remembered and understood. Unfortunately, the activity of application is often difficult to engender in the classroom situation—it takes time, patience, and an awareness of what students are capable of doing. In asking students to engage in application activities we must have some assurance that they possess the understandings appropriate for use in the situation. Having this assurance, we need to be careful that we do not prompt students, or give them hints, as to exactly what knowledge or skills or processes they should be applying. This prompting might result in their coming up with an appropriate response. This, however, will at best be at the level of comprehension. A final requisite for facilitating application activities in the classroom is an appropriate classroom climate, one in which students can feel free to suggest and apply their ideas.

The following are some examples of questions that would facilitate application. (As you read them please be aware that they assume that a period of time has elapsed since the student's initial learning of whatever is asked.)

- What are some ways that you can deal with this problem?
- How can you find the answers to these questions?
- Do you know of some alternative courses of action?
- How can you get this information?
- Now that you have the information, what are you going to do with it?

Analysis

Analysis is a level of thinking that is concerned with the critical examination of data. It goes well beyond the simple understanding associated with comprehension in that it entails the breaking down of information to determine its constituent ideas, the ascertaining of the relationships of these ideas, and the critical examination of how they are presented to convey meaning to the data gatherers. Analysis, then, goes beyond understanding the "what" presented in data in that it requires the individual to understand "how" the information was put together and presented.

Bloom et al. (1956) have identified three types of activities entailed by analysis. These include the following.

1. *Analysis of elements* requires that the data be examined to determine both those ideas that are explicitly shown as well as those that are not. When we engage in outlining as we read we are looking for the explicitly stated parts of a communication. Similarly, we might observe a sociodrama to identify the series of events that led up to a conclusion.

   All of the parts of a communication may not be explicitly stated or demonstrated. However, Bloom et al. indicate that things such as assumptions and values "can only be inferred by an analysis of a series of statements. . ."

2. *Analysis of relationships* occurs when the individual determined how the identified elements in a piece of information fit together. As we isolate the ideas in an outline we are usually simultaneously looking for the relationship among these ideas; how, for example, the main idea is being supported. In listening to a speaker we might attempt to separate relevant from irrelevant ideas. During the observation of a sociodrama we might be attempting to fathom the chain of events that led to a given outcome. As we do all of these things we are engaging in an analysis of relationships.

3. *Analysis of organizing principles* basically refers to a probing for the processes that went into the construction of a piece of information, why an individual presented the information in the way it was presented. Included in such analysis would be the identification of bias and values, as well as techniques of persuasion.

Some examples of analysis questions that might be used in the process of problem solving would include:

- **Analysis of elements**
  - Which data tell us the actual sources of water pollution, and which tell us what people think are sources?
  - From what you read, what do you think is important to the Bedouin family?
  - Let's separate facts from inferences.
- **Analysis of relationships**
  - How are all of the people in the pictures similar? How are they different?
  - How can we group this information together?
  - What data support our hypothesis?
- **Analysis of organizing principles**
  - Why do you think the letter writer called fluoride a pollutant?
  - What message is the cartoonist giving?
  - Why do you think this ad shows dead baby seals?

Synthesis

Synthesis is the process by which ideas or data, obtained by the individual, are put together in new ways that are meaningful to the individual. In essence, it is the application of creative thought to ideas or elements that have been previously analyzed. Its purpose is the development of something new to the individual—be it an understanding or some type of product.

Synthesis can occur quite frequently in the problem-solving situation. The act of hypothesizing is one of synthesis if the individual combines different types of information to develop a new solution to a problem. (Hypothesizing, however, would represent comprehension if the individual immediately utilizes information gathered to deal with a problem. The latter would be the case with the students who, having identified sources of water pollution in their research, now hypothesized that these are polluting their creek. Hypothesizing could also be application if the hypothesis represented a solution found to be workable with a past problem that was very similar to the present problem.) Data analysis could entail synthesis as the individual developed new categories of information from that which had been gathered.

Although synthesis is essentially a creative activity it should not be interpreted as one in which the individual has a completely free run to do whatever he or she chooses to do. For example, it does not give the individual the license to give "off-the-wall" answers—those not based on a new combination of ideas—to questions. The individual should be able to document the appropriateness of a response.

There are three ways in which thought that reflects synthesis can be demonstrated.

First it can be shown by a *unique communication*, which is an illustration of the new combination of ideas. Perhaps the best examples of such communications would be paintings or musical compositions. There are, however, many other ways it can be demonstrated—verbally through oral or written communication, nonverbally, or through the construction of some type of product.

Secondly, it might be shown through the *development of a plan or a proposed set of operations,* which would be a step-by-step laying out of a way of doing something. This plan would be one that could later be put into action.

Finally, it can be demonstrated by the *derivation of a set of abstract relations.* This basically requires that the individual independently engage in inductive or deductive thinking. With inductive thought the emphasis would be upon the combination of discrete pieces of information into new categories. As individuals develop concepts and generalizations from data they have gathered they are engaging in this type of inductive thought. Deductive thought, on the other hand, requires that the individual work from the larger ideas, such as concepts and generalizations, to arrive at new ideas. When individuals utilize different generalizations they possess to develop hypotheses they are acting deductively at a synthesis level.

Because synthesis is essentially a creative endeavor it is necessary to provide an atmosphere in the classroom that encourages creativity. Continuous emphasis on student endeavors being "right" and "wrong" would tend to create a discouraging atmosphere. So too would the standardization of student work, with all students turning out the same product. In cases where the students are asked a synthesis question but where the atmosphere is not conducive to it, their response will probably be at the comprehension or, at best, application level.

The following are examples of synthesis questions that might be used during problem solving.

- **Unique communication**
  - How can we illustrate our findings?
  - Will you demonstrate how you'd do it?
- **A plan or proposed set of operations**
  - How can we carry out this solution?
  - Can you think of a way of dealing with the problem?
- **Abstract relations**
  - What hypotheses can you make?
  - Can you make other groups with your information?
  - Give a different example that would fit your generalization.

Evaluation

Evaluation refers to the process by which individuals make educated judgments about the worth of something—be it an idea, communication, or some type of product. The judgment is an educated one in that it is not without some criterion or criteria that the individual develops. Judgments are made as the individual determines the degree to which the idea, communication, product, or whatever, meets these criteria. Thus evaluation as we are discussing it here, is based on more than unsubstantiated personal opinion.

At the highest level of the taxonomy, evaluation encompasses all of the lower levels of the taxonomy. This can be seen by starting at the analysis level. The individuals needs to analyze whatever is evaluated, breaking it down into its component parts, seeing how these parts are related and how they are presented. Then, synthesis is utilized in the generation of the criteria and plan of action for holding whatever is evaluated up to a critical scrutiny involving these criteria.

Bloom et al. identify two different types of evaluation:

1. *Judgments according to internal evidence* occur when data are examined in terms of how they are presented. In this type of evaluation, such factors as the accuracy and the validity of the data are considered. Also considered is the logical consistency that was used to present it. In essence this type of evaluation is concerned with the effectiveness and accuracy with which evidence is given.
2. *Judgments based on external criteria* occur when, prior to the evaluation, the individual sets up standards for examining the data. Then, the data are scrutinized using these standards to determine the extent to which they meet them. These standards can be ones generated by the individual, or they can be ones that are commonly accepted for a given type of data.

The distinction between these two types of evaluation is a relatively fine one. The major difference between the two is when the criteria are developed and used. With the former this occurs relatively simultaneously with the evaluation—as the individual examines the data, the criteria are generated. With the latter the criteria are postulated before the evaluation occurs.

Evaluation, then, requires two things—criteria to be used for the evaluation and a determination of how well the data meet these standards. (Incidentally, since these standards can come from sources other than the individual, it is perfectly permissible for the teacher to suggest them.) The following illustrate some evaluation questions that might be used.

- **Judgments in terms of internal evidence**
  - Which version is the more accurate version? Why?
  - Your two sources disagree. Which one is presented more logically?
- **Judgments based on external criteria**
  - We said that the decision we make needs to meet certain specifications. Which alternatives meet these best?
  - Are there any other reasons why this alternative, even though it has the most positive outcomes, is not acceptable?

To this point we have discussed the levels of the taxonomy in terms of questions we might ask as we ease the children along in the problem-solving process. Since the goal of these questions is to get children to think in specific ways our discussion can perhaps be best summarized by examining some sample thinking activities in which they might engage during the different steps of problem solving. Table 6.1 does this. The rows represent the different levels of the taxonomy while the columns are the different generic problem-solving steps.

TABLE 6.1 Sample Problem-Solving Activities at Different Levels of Cognition

Levels of Cognition	Steps of Problem Solving			
	Determining the Problem	*Preparing to Gather Data*	*Gathering Data*	*Examining, Analyzing, Evaluating Data*
Knowledge	• Remembering specific facts or events that led to specific situation.	• Remembering specific ways in which ideas are presented in data. • Remembering specific ways to deal with data sources.	• Remembering specific techniques practiced.	• Remembering what data source reported. • Knowledge of criteria that makes a source valid.
Comprehension	• Understanding meaning of facts or events that led to specific situation, what the facts or events suggest.	• Understanding what the problem is. • Understanding how to deal with data sources.	• Using data sources based on preparation in previous step. • Translating information from one form to another; e.g., taking notes from interview.	• Interpreting what is present in data. • Translating data from one form to another.
Application	• Seeing relationship of present problem to one encountered in past when there is a close similarity between the two. • Generating alternatives or hypothesis used in past with similar situations.	• Suggesting sources or data techniques learned in the past.	• Using specific strategies and techniques learned in the past without having to practice them.	• Working with data in ways learned in the past.
Analysis	• Determining the different factors that led to the problem situation. • Identifying how these factors relate to one another.	• Determining information that will be needed to support hypothesis.	• Recognizing point of view of data. • Recognizing such things as facts and opinions, assumptions, hypotheses.	• Differentiating conclusions from supporting statements. • Understanding the relationship of different pieces of evidence presented. • Separating relevant from irrelevant statements. • Understanding how data source is constructed.

continued

TABLE 6.1 *Continued*

Levels of Cognition	Steps of Problem Solving			
	Determining the Problem	*Preparing to Gather Data*	*Gathering Data*	*Examining, Analyzing, Evaluating Data*
Synthesis	• Hypothesizing, combining different ideas learned in past.	• Categorizing questions to be asked. • Suggesting original data sources.		• Categorizing data obtained.
Evaluation	• Evaluating available information for internal consistency.	• Setting criteria for acceptance of hypothesis or alternatives. (These criteria would actually be used later in the problem-solving.)		• Judging of data sources based on internal consistency (logic of presentation, etc.). • Determining if criteria for acceptance of hypotheses or alternatives has been met.

Planning to Use Questions in Problem Solving

There are at least three benefits associated with using higher-level questions in the problem-solving situation. First, of course, they serve as a means for helping students work through the problems themselves without being directly told what to do. The problem resolution is their own. Secondly, as we noted earlier, teachers' use of higher-level questions (usually defined as application and above) tends to have a positive effect on achievement. Finally, employing such questions during problem solving appears to sharpen children's abilities to use higher cognitive processes in situations away from the actual problem-solving activity. Muir (1979) designed a social studies test consisting of items which were at the comprehension, application, analysis, and evaluation levels (the design of the test precluded usage of synthesis items). This test was administered to fourth-, fifth-, and sixth-grade students enrolled in what Muir referred to as inquiry social studies programs (programs which, for our purposes, required students to engage in problem-solving processes to develop conceptual understandings). It was also administered to students in noninquiry programs. Muir found that inquiry students performed significantly better on tasks that required higher levels of thought than did the noninquiry students.

Obviously, then, we will want to use as many higher-level questions as possible. How do we do this? It would make things easier if we could say that a given process is initiated with lower-level questions and naturally carried through with questions at increasingly higher levels. Table 6.1 clearly indicates that this can't be the case because it shows that it is very possible to prepare the way for problem-solving using only lower-level activities.

The solution to this problem of how to include higher-level questions actually lies in the nature of the levels of the taxonomy. You should remember that thinking at higher levels encompasses thought at the lower levels; for example, comprehension requires knowledge, and evaluation requires all levels below it. Thus, if we wish to ask students an analysis question, we must be certain that they remember and understand specific ideas about a situation and are able to apply these ideas to new situations. In using a higher-level question to facilitate problem solving we must be certain that they have mastered the lower-level thinking skills required for it. There are several ways of going about this. First, we might start with a given topic at a lower level and develop a sequence of questions that help students move from this to a higher level of thought (Smith, 1976). The fifth grade that did the exploratory study on pollution was helped by their teacher to define the problem in this manner. After a short initiating discussion he asked:

"What pollution are you going to do something about?"
(Comprehension: he was asking for the students' understanding of the
    discussion to that point.)

Then:

"Let's make a list of everything that's polluting the creek."
(Application: the students apply what they have learned about pollution
    to their own case.)

As a result of this application question the students realized that they didn't know enough about water pollution and needed to find out more about it before they could make any statement or do anything about their creek.

A second approach to moving to higher level questions works from the same basic premise as the first approach but depends upon the teacher's awareness of the background of knowledge and skills the students are bringing to the situation. The teacher can ask a question at any level of the taxonomy if there is some certainty that the students will be able to deal with it cognitively (Sinatra and Annacone, 1984). In this case it would be possible to ask, say, a synthesis question without leading up to it with lower-level questions if the teacher were relatively certain that the students had the knowledge necessary to engage in synthesis. By its nature, this approach is more appropriate when the teacher has evaluated student capabilities in relation to the topic or when the teacher is relatively certain the problem is one with which the students have some familiarity. The use of this approach does not preclude employing subsequent higher-level questions. Like the first approach these can scaffold on the initial question.

In their discussion of questions Taba et al. (1971) suggest a third approach to structuring questions, beginning a discussion with what they refer to as an "opening question." This question has two characteristics: it is open and it sets the focus for discussion. For our purposes the open aspect of this question is the most important. The question is phrased in such a way that it can be answered in a variety of forms and at a variety of cognitive levels. "What happened?" would be an example of another such question because it could be answered at the memory level (strict recall of a series of events); the comprehension level (an interpretation of what was observed); the application level (bring past experiences to bear on what was observed); and so on. The teacher would use the responses to the question as data for structuring subsequent questions. Again, questions could be scaffolded.

It would appear that the key to asking higher-level questions is in planning. A teacher's awareness of these questions is not enough to insure that they will be asked. Lange (1982) summarized suggestions for teaching derived from the research on questioning techniques. He indicated that it is well for teachers to think about the types of questions they will ask, analyzing and sequencing them according to difficulty before using them. (And, with children who don't have an experiential background that lends itself to the topic under consideration it might be well to include a large number of lower-level questions in the sequence.) In my own work as a teacher, and in working with other teachers, I have found it helpful if potential questions are considered beforehand. In this manner it is also useful to generate follow-up questions to be used if original questions do not elicit responses at expected levels of cognition.

Contexts for Questions

There are a variety of different ways in which a total process of problem solving can be approached in elementary classrooms. In the last chapter we saw three of these. The teacher of the children finding out about water pollution utilized *structured discussion* as a means of helping his students work through the exploration process. When we considered inquiry, our example was one where a *text-based* approach was employed. Finally, we saw *role play* being used as a vehicle for decision making. In addition to these, there are two other contexts for problem solving that especially lend themselves to the elementary classroom: *simulations* and *dramatic play*.

In this section we will briefly examine these five different contexts. (All, with the exception of a text-based approach, are discussed in detail in other chapters.) With respect to all of the approaches, two ideas should be kept in mind. One is that successful utilization of any one approach will require the use of appropriate teacher questions, questions that guide movement through the different problem-solving steps. The second idea is that we will be using the same basic teaching process with all of these. Within each context we will have a warm-up, in which children are prepared to work within a given problem-solving context; an action period, during which they actively work with the problem; and a debriefing, in which some understanding about the problem situation is generated and closure is obtained.

A Text-Based Context

The text-based approach to problem solving is so named because of its heavy reliance on students' textbooks as sources of data. In fact, at times the text may be the only source. In the previous chapter we noted that, although some teachers' manuals will offer suggestions for using the text as a base, many do not. Regardless, with some planning most can be adapted for use with one or more of our problem-solving models.

In the warm-up the purpose for the problem solving is established. The teacher may begin with a general discussion of the unit the children will be reading, outlining the general topic that will be considered as well as some specific types of information that the students will encounter. The major activity of the warm-up will be the statement of the problem with which the children will deal. This usually takes the form of the teacher asking the students a question, or questions, which they should consider as they read. The students, too, may be asked to generate questions about the topic. All of these would be listed in some way so that they are readily available for student referral.

When the exploratory model is employed the students may arrange the question in categories to make reading easier; however, nothing more needs to be done with these in the warm-up. The children will, one would hope, find their answers in the textual material. Inquiry, on the other hand, requires that the students suggest answers to their questions. These will be their hypotheses and will be noted in some way—either by being placed with the questions that have been listed or by being individually written by the students.

The warm-up for text usage is very teacher directed. Depending upon the capabilities of the students this high level of instructor involvement may extend into the *action period*. The data gathering occurring at this time will be done through reading and possibly some form of note taking, and the teacher may find it necessary to guide the students as they read silently or orally. The teacher would use the initiating questions and hypotheses to structure the reading. Otherwise, the students might read on their own, noting the information that is pertinent to their problem.

At the conclusion of the action period the students will, ideally, have as much information as the text can supply them in relation to their questions and hypotheses. During the debriefing the teacher helps them make sense out of this data. Through the judicious use of questions the children are helped to determine if the problem has been dealt with adequately; that is, if the data respond to their questions and hypotheses. If the problem hasn't been dealt with, the debriefing may become a new warm-up in which plans are made to collect additional data. Thus, the debriefing may serve as a springboard to problem solving in a different context. If the problem has been dealt with, then the teacher might help the students develop some sort of synthesizing statement or generalization. In the latter case, plans may (or may not) be made to gather additional data in order to test the generalization.

The debriefing, of course, should also be concerned with the problem-solving process the children have used. The teacher will want to help the students review the different steps they have taken, evaluate strategies they used as they read for information, and possibly suggest different strategies they might wish to use in future problem solving.

Structured Discussion

As its name implies, structured discussion as a total-process approach to problem solving relies quite heavily on discussion and, at least with children's early problem-solving experiences, teacher questions are used to lead them through each step of the model. (As children become more experienced they may lead themselves through the steps.) Although this strategy relies on discussion, it should not be interpreted as being one of discussion only. Children may engage in other activities that do not require interaction with the teacher.

The format of structured discussion comes from the steps of problem solving. Through the use of questions and statements the teacher helps the students move from one step to the next until they have worked through a given model.

During the warm-up the stage is set for the problem solving. In a structured discussion the warm-up includes all problem-solving steps up to data gathering. The teacher helps the students become aware of the general problem situation and helps them generate questions, which will make this more specific. Then, the students are helped to plan how they will deal with the situation, considering what data they will need and how they will get this information. In addition, because there are data to indicate that students may follow a given problem-solving model more closely if they are told the steps of that model (Glenn and Ellis, 1982) the teacher may also wish to include these directions in the warm-up.

The *action period* of structured discussion encompasses the steps of data gathering and analysis. During this time the children will be actively involved in seeking out the information necessary to answer their questions. Among other things, they might be reading, seeing a film, observing on a field trip, or interviewing a resource person. As they engage in these tasks the teacher assumes a less directive role. Questions and comments made by the teacher will be for the purpose of easing the children toward completion of the planned task. During this time the teacher will also act as a resource person.

The teacher's role will change somewhat following the data gathering stage. Although the ultimate goal will be for the children to work with information on their own, the teacher will be more involved with the data analysis. Through questions, the children can be helped to formulate the tasks they need to do, and then work through these tasks. The teacher might also find it necessary to teach specific data analysis skills at this point.

The *debriefing* of the structured discussion has two parts, one is concerned with the problem and the other is concerned with the process used to deal with the problem. In debriefing the problem, the teacher helps students make sense of what they've found. With the exploration model this might entail the planning and carrying out of the synthesis activity. In inquiry it is the determination of the acceptability of the hypothesis and, possibly, the development of generalizations. For decision making it is the choosing of an alternative (or alternatives) and the planning of means of acting on this choice.

In debriefing the process, the teacher's job is to help the students become aware of the problem-solving model they utilized in the situation. Teacher questions at this point are directed toward helping students realize the different steps they took, and evaluating the different activities in which they engaged in each step.

Simulations

Simulation activities are ones in which individuals are presented with real-life problem situations and are expected to work through these situations as if they were actually in them. Sometimes called *simulation games,* these activities have three characteristics when used in the classroom:

1. They are abstractions of real life; they bring problems that people or groups actually encounter into the classroom.
2. They require that individuals assume the roles (and all the limitations that these roles imply) of the people or groups in dealing with the problems.
3. They require that the students work with the problem. Usually simulations employ a decision-making format.

An activity in which a mini-economy is set up in the classroom and children buy and sell goods and services would be a simulation. So too would be an activity in which children acted out phone calls they would make if they encountered different emergencies (*Help!* Games Central, Cambridge, MA). Discussing a mini-economy or how to make a telephone call would not fit into the category of simulation because neither requires action in the simulated situation.

Usually simulations occur in rounds in which the students actually make decisions and see these carried out in terms of their consequences. These activities are followed by a discussion in which the decision and its outcomes are analyzed and evaluated.

Role Play

Role play is essentially a form of simulations and utilizes the decision-making model. It is primarily used with problems that the children have encountered or could encounter in their own lives. It can also be used to work through content-based problems (e.g., acting out the process by which a bill becomes a law.) In role play, solutions suggested by the children are spontaneously acted out by the children. They are not told what these solutions should be and are given no prompting by the teacher. With content-based problems, they may know what the solutions are and simply be demonstrating how they are carried out.

In the warm-up of the role play the problem is presented to the students and alternative solutions are elicited. These are then acted out with each enactment being followed by a discussion in which it is evaluated. Finally, all of the enactments are evaluated in a post-role-play discussion and children are asked to choose the most appropriate one or ones.

Dramatic Play

Dramatic play is very similar to simulations in that students act out real-life situations. It differs, however, in that the students develop these situations themselves and there are no preestablished problems for them to encounter. Rather, problems occur spontaneously in the situation and are dealt with as they arise.

Dramatic play is initiated through an arranged environment. The teacher provides a variety of resources and materials dealing with a specific topic. These might include costumes, artifacts, books, pictures, and miscellaneous props. The children are invited to peruse these, handle them, and act with them. With the teacher's assistance, primarily through asking or encouraging the asking of questions, this play, which is initially somewhat random, develops some structure. A second grade teacher, for example, developed an environment that initially contained, among other things, empty food cans and boxes, play money, and a cash register. With his help, a few students began playing grocery store. As the play progressed, other businesses, including service-oriented ones, were added to make a miniature business community in the classroom.

The basic teaching process is repeated more than once in dramatic play, with the first dramatic play session being somewhat different than the others. As it begins, the *warm-up* entails the presentation of the arranged environment. The *action period* involves the children's exploration of this environment. The *debriefing* for the first play is actually a warm-up for extending the initial play.

Subsequent warm-ups entail a planning for the play, usually in a group discussion format. This planning is very brief, and the children move to the actual play as quickly as possible.

During the action period the children act out what they have planned to do, spontaneously adding specifics to their general plans.

The action period can be of any duration but is usually relatively short—most episodes are usually completed in about ten minutes. At the end of the play the children are gathered together for the debriefing. During this discussion, problems that occurred during the play (interpersonal problems or information the children need to make the play more authentic) are uncovered. Plans are then made to deal with these problems prior to the next play.

Synthesis: Planning to Use a Total-Process Approach _____

We include different problem-solving processes in our curriculum for two different purposes. First, we want children to experience and learn these processes so that they can apply them in their own lives, now and in the future. Secondly, through the use of these processes the children can develop understandings of the social studies; they build conceptual knowledge through problem solving.

Teaching the Problem-Solving Models

We can help our students become aware of the fact that there are problem solving processes by modeling problem-solving behavior—asking appropriate questions and acting as problem solvers ourselves. There is nothing wrong with a teacher admitting to students that he or she doesn't know something and needs to seek an answer. In addition, we can teach the steps necessary for problem resolution. One way to do this is to simply tell children these steps prior to their actually going through them. Glenn and Ellis (1982) indicate that elementary students tended to independently solve problems more systematically when classroom problem-solving activities were preceded by the students being told the steps of the given model they would use. Students who were not taught a model at all tended to engage in independent problem solving in a random manner.

Glenn and Ellis's research did not address the questions of whether the problem-solving model might be introduced to students at some point other than prior to the activity itself. We have found it useful to discuss the model after the activity by reviewing the steps the students took. This has the benefit of allowing the children to evaluate the effectiveness of what they did and to suggest alternative ways of acting for future reference. (This discussion, of course, would be referred to prior to subsequent problem-solving activities.)

Using Problem Solving to Develop Conceptual Knowledge

At the conclusion of Chapter 2 we examined ways of planning for the development of conceptual understandings. At this point, we can examine how we can plan to use problem solving with children to help them develop those understandings. Again, we'll consider planning in terms of instruction that will rely primarily on a textbook and on instruction that is based on teacher-developed units.

There are two ways that a text may be used to facilitate problem solving: problem questions may be springboards to text utilization; or the text may be a springboard for subsequent problem-solving activities. In the first case, as seen earlier in the chapter, the teacher and students may generate questions about a unit topic prior to reading about it in the text.

The questions that act as the springboards for text-based problem solving can be generated in any number of ways. They may be elicited by the teacher who asks the children to consider and list what they would like to know about a topic. Or, they may be generated from dramatic play, role play, or simulations.

Of course it may well be that, as a single source, the text will not respond to the children's questions. In this case other sources will need to be consulted. Here, and in situations where textual information generates further questions, the book will act as a springboard to subsequent problem solving, problem solving that might be done within the contexts discussed earlier and which will probably use data sources other than the text.

A different approach to utilizing the text as a springboard for problem solving allows students to apply (in the sense discussed earlier as we considered application questions) understandings developed by the book to new situations. Here, the teacher would plan dramatic play, role play, or simulation situations that paralleled (but did not duplicate) situations found in textual material. The students would then be encouraged to work through these. In the process new problems needing to be considered might well be generated.

The basic question a teacher needs to ask when planning to use a text-based approach is exactly how the text can be employed to facilitate problem solving. As we have seen, it can be the data source to facilitate the answering of questions raised by the students and the teacher. A review of the text during planning will suggest what some of these questions might be. We have also seen that the text might be the starting point for problem solving. Thus, during the planning process the teacher might consider ways in which the children could actively extend and apply understandings developed within the textual material.

Planning to include problem-solving processes when developing one's own unit of study is both similar to and different from planning to use a text. It is similar in that the same basic question, "How can I incorporate problem solving?" needs to be asked. It is different in that more attention needs to be paid to the data sources that the students will utilize as they engage in problem solving.

A very early step of unit planning involves the generation of understandings that the students will be expected to develop. Following this, the teacher needs to determine what the students will need to know to develop the understandings. For example, in planning to develop the understanding, "Athens and Sparta had different beliefs about sex roles; this affected who could vote," we might isolate at least three ideas about both Athens and Sparta that would need to be considered:

1. The roles played by men and women in each city-state.
2. The beliefs responsible for these roles.
3. Who voted in each city-state?

(Incidentally, different teachers might analyze this understanding differently; i.e., they might start with the question of who was allowed to vote in Athens and in Sparta and work from there. That's okay because they will be the ones who will teach the unit and have their own thoughts on how to organize it.)

Realizing what the students need to know, the teacher can then move to considering how problem solving can be used to develop this knowledge. One way to do this is to frame the ideas that need to be taught in terms of questions. Thus, the first idea isolated above could be rephrased as "What roles did men and women play in Athens and Sparta?" Then the teacher would determine which problem-solving process would be most applicable for answering the question.

In the previous chapter three models of problem solving were noted. They and their functions were:

- Exploration: developing new information.
- Inquiry: using knowledge in new situations.
- Decision making: choosing intelligently.

The model to be employed with a given question will depend on the function intended by the question. The function, in turn, depends to an extent on the background knowledge of the problem solver. If the students had little background information about Athens and Sparta they would need to get this information. Therefore the questions of sex roles in these city-states might best be answered through exploration. The question that parallels the third part of the analysis of the understanding, the one dealing with who voted in each city-state, could probably be approached by inquiry because when it was dealt with the students would probably have sufficient background information.

Planning to include total problem-solving processes in our units, then, requires that we determine what ideas need to be developed and determine how they will be developed. Please be aware, however, that it is not necessary to plan to include a total problem-solving process for every idea in an understanding. There are many ways of developing ideas and (as we shall see in the next chapter) it may be impractical to use a total process when an alternative approach may be more appropriate.

Springboards to Discussion _____

1. Research indicates that there is a tendency for teachers to use lower-level questions (e.g., knowledge and comprehension). But what about textbooks? Evaluate the questions used in an elementary social studies textbook. What levels are represented? If you find a preponderance of lower-level questions, suggest strategies you might use to include higher-level questions.

2. Plan a decision-making activity that can be done with a group of children. (This decision should be one that they see as important.) Identify potential questions you might use to help the children move through the process and indicate what levels of the taxonomy they fit. (These questions are potential ones and you shouldn't think of them as a script.)

   Tape yourself as you do this activity with a group of children. Evaluate the tape. What level of questions did you actually ask? Did some of the questions you asked elicit responses different from those you expected? If they did, why do you suppose this happened? How did the children respond? Would you make any changes in the activity?

3. Consider the various contexts for problem solving that we discussed in the latter part of this chapter in light of a specific classroom group with whom you are familiar. Rank order the different contexts in terms of your perceptions of their appropriateness to those children. Provide a rationale for your ranking. If possible, share this with the teacher of the group to determine how similar his or her perceptions are to yours.

References _____

BLOOM, BENJAMIN S., et al. (eds.). *Taxonomy of Educational Objectives: Handbook I: The Cognitive Domain*. New York: David McKay, 1956.

GLENN, ALLEN D., AND ELLIS, ARTHUR K. "Direct and Indirect Methods of Teaching Problem Solving to Elementary School Children," *Social Education,* Vol. 46 (February 1982), pp. 134–136.

GOODLAD, JOHN. "What Some Schools and Classrooms Teach," *Educational Leadership,* Vol. 40 (April 1983), pp. 8–19.

HANNA, LAVONE; POTTER, GLADYS; AND REYNOLDS, ROBERT. *Dynamic Elementary Social Studies,* 3rd ed. New York: Holt, Rinehart and Winston, 1973.

LANGE, BOB. "Questioning Techniques," *Language Arts,* Vol. 59 (February 1982), pp. 180–185.

MUIR, SHARON PRAY. "Testing a Case for Inquiry Social Studies in the Elementary School," *Social Education,* Vol. 43 (May 1979), pp. 386–387.

REDFIELD, DORIS, AND ROUSSEAU, ELAINE. "A Meta-Analysis of Experimental Research on Teacher Questioning Behavior," *Review of Educational Research,* Vol. 51 (Summer 1981), pp. 237–245.

SANDERS, NORRIS. *Classroom Questions: What Kinds?* New York: Harper & Row, 1966.

SINATRA, RICHARD, AND ANNACONE, DOMINIC. "Questioning Strategies to Promote Cognitive Inquiry in Social Studies," *The Social Studies,* Vol. 75 (January/February 1984), pp. 18–23.

SMITH, CHARLOTTE T. "Improving Comprehension? That's a Good Question." Paper presented at the sixth annual meeting of the International Reading Association World Congress in Reading. Singapore, 1976.

TABA, HILDA; DURKIN, MARY; FRANKEL, JACK; AND MCNAUGHTON, ANTHONY. *A Teacher's Handbook to Elementary Social Studies: An Inductive Approach*. Reading, MA: Addison-Wesley, 1971.

7

A Skills Approach to Problem Solving

CHAPTER OBJECTIVES

After reading this chapter you should be able to:

1. Describe the four major skills necessary for reading maps and globes:
   - Direction.
   - Understanding symbols.
   - Location.
   - Scale.
2. Identify the subskills it is necessary to possess in order to use the four major skills.
3. Identify the various types of charts and graphs used in the elementary school.
4. Describe strategies for helping children work with charts and graphs.
5. Delineate a strategy for planning to include skills in the curriculum.

As we engage in the different steps of problem solving we find it necessary to utilize different skills. Which skills we utilize will, to a great extent, depend on the nature of the problem. If, for example, our problem has to do with finding the shortest route from one place to another we'd employ specific map-reading skills. On the other hand, if it had to do with determining how to vote on a given issue we'd use different skills such as those associated with reading or interviewing to get information.

It is impossible to give students experience with every type of problem they will encounter in life. What we can do is teach them the appropriate processes that can be utilized in problemmatic situations and help them learn how to generate questions that will ease movement through the different steps of problem solving. We can also teach them the various skills they will need within a given problem-solving step. A skills approach to problem solving does the latter and can be employed as we take our students through a given process *or* outside of the problem-solving situation. It can be used any time our students are gathering or processing information.

Because we consider different skills in different parts of this book (for example, the skills associated with understanding current affairs, which we discussed in Chapter 4, and reading/language skills, which we will examine in Chapter 12), we will focus in this chapter on the two groups of skills that have traditionally been dealt with in the social studies: maps and globe skills and skills associated with working with charts and graphs. We will examine what is entailed by these skills and consider how they might be taught.

As you read this chapter there are three things that should be remembered. First, skills are means, not ends. We do not teach skills for the purpose of teaching skills. We teach them so that they can serve some other purpose, such as helping us analyze information. This means that skills should be taught within some context where pupils can perceive the need for the skill. Second, as we shall see in the following discussion, skills are usually made up of subskills and there is often an order in which these subskills need to be learned to insure skill mastery. Finally, skill acquisition requires practice. Children need a variety of experiences working with different skills.

As usual, we will synthesize our discussion by considering how we can plan to include skills in the curriculum.

Using Maps and Globes

Direction

Being aware of the directions of objects or places as they relate to oneself or to other objects or places is a skill that is used not only with maps but also in our daily lives. We use these to direct other people and to find places ourselves. Most commonly, we use such directional terms as *left, right,* or *straight ahead.* At other times it is necessary to use such compass terms as *south* or *southeast.* It has been my experience that many adults feel uncomfortable with the latter type of directions; they can identify these on maps but become confused when they need to use them in real life.

We can help eliminate this confusion (perhaps even in ourselves) by providing children with experiences that enable them to work with directions in real life as well as on maps. These experiences would include both giving and receiving directions. As with other skills the sequence for teaching directions moves from teaching them within the child's own environment to considering them more abstractly on globes and maps. Even when dealing with directions on maps, however, attention should be given to relating them to the real-life setting; children should be continually reminded that a direction represents something in the physical world.

The teaching of direction begins in the early grades with the use of spatial concepts from the children's own immediate environment. Some of these concepts would include: *left, right, up, down, near, far, over, under, above, below, here,* and *there.* These concepts would be taught in relation to the children, themselves. So, for example, left and right are taught by referring to the child's hands and feet, and then in relation to people or objects that are to the left or right of the child. Similarly, above and below might be considered in relation to the floor and ceiling of the classroom. Because we want the children to learn the directional *concepts* we would not focus solely on the definitions of the concept terms; rather, we would let the children develop their own definitions.

After these concepts have been initially taught, children need practice with and reinforcement of them. This can be done by using them in directions given to the students for classroom activities ("Please put the paints *under* the sink."), and by asking students to use them. Games such as "Simon Says" can also be used as fun ways of reinforcing the concepts. With frequent use the concept terms will become part of the children's vocabularies and the concepts will become part of their ways of thinking about the world.

When there is assurance that the children grasp these spatial concepts, the cardinal directions can be introduced. This is done outside of the classroom and can be accomplished in two ways. During the morning or afternoon the children can be asked to note their shadows. Because the sun appears to rise in the east their shadow will be approximately to the west of them in the morning. Similarly, it will be to the east of them in the afternoon. By turning so that their left side is to the west, they will be facing north. A second way to determine directions is at noon. At this time, since they are in the Northern Hemisphere, the children's shadows will be to the north. Facing the direction of their shadows, they can be instructed that their left hands face west and their right hands, east.

The cardinal directions can then be brought into the classroom. Walls can be labeled and these directions can be referred to, by both teacher and students, when discussing the location of objects in the classroom. Games in which the children move in directions can also be used to reinforce the learning of these directions.

The move to using directions on maps should be made only after the children have experienced the use of directions in their own environments. This move should not be to flat maps, however. Instead it should begin with consideration of the globe because it is a more accurate representation of the world than a flat map. (It does not have the distortion of the sizes or areas that occurs when an attempt is made to reproduce a sphere on a flat surface.) In introducing the globe for the purpose of teaching direction, attention should be given to the North and South Poles. The children should be helped to see that, wherever one is in the world, north will be toward the North Pole and south will be toward the South Pole. This understanding can be facilitated by indicating northerly and southerly directions from various places in both the Eastern and Western Hemispheres. It is reinforced by referring to objects that have been labeled in the classroom. This reference to things in the children's own environment will also help them develop the idea that north is not "up" nor south "down," an idea that poses difficulty to many adults.

While discussing northerly and southerly directions on the globe, parallels and meridians can be introduced as *imaginary* lines that circle the globe and serve as aids for locating places. Parallels can be shown beginning with the equator and it can be emphasized that, as their name suggests, these lines never meet. Meridians can be taught as running north and south and meeting at the poles. The prime meridian, found running near Greenwich, England, may be pointed out. Systematic teaching of the purpose and use of parallels and meridians would be inappropriate at this point, however. This is best done in the upper elementary and middle school grades.

Once they have been discussed with respect to the globe, directions can be introduced on flat maps. This should be done with maps of areas quite familiar to the children. Maps of the classroom (or of their own rooms at home) would be appropriate for this purpose, and directions on these maps can be correctly oriented and labeled using directions posted on the classroom walls. (This, incidentally, may mean that a direction other than north may appear at the top of the map. Again, this will help to dispel the notion that north is up.) Following this, teacher-made maps of the immediate neighborhood, or areas with which the children have a great deal of familiarity, can be labeled. Again, this labeling would be based on directions the children remember from their initial out-of-door experiences with identifying the cardinal directions.

Only after children have experienced maps of areas with which they are quite familiar should directions on commercially prepared maps be introduced. This might be done in the third grade with maps of the children's own community, if available. At this time attention should be directed to the north arrow, or compass rose, and its purpose should be explained to the children. In working with these maps children should orient their direction in the physical world; that is, north on the map should be facing north.

Because our goal in teaching direction is to develop the ability to work with these on maps and in real-life activities, we will also want to teach children how to use the compass. This can be done in the late primary and early intermediate grades when the children are aware of the location of the cardinal directions in their environment. They can be shown how to align the direction marker for north with the needle of the compass in order to determine north. Then, they can be shown how to determine the other directions. (An interesting problem-solving activity for them, using either the exploration or inquiry model, would be to determine why the needle always points north on the compass.)

Compass learning activities can be reinforced in physical education classes with orienteering activities that require a child to follow a course, either walking or running, while using a compass. Directions for this course are given at checkpoints where the children might also be required to do different physical activities.

Although it need not be taught as a follow-up to compass instruction, this would be an appropriate time to introduce the intermediate directions to students. Concepts such as northeast and southwest can be illustrated by pointing out objects located in those directions in relation to the students, and asking the student the direction of the objects. Unless they have had previous experience with intermediate directions the children will tend to answer with one, or the other, cardinal direction. The teacher can indicate that both answers are approximately correct, but really aren't specific enough. Then, either using a problem-solving mode ("What are some ways that we can be more exact?"), or through explanation, the teacher can help students see the appropriateness of combining directions. At this point it can be explained that, for conventional purposes, north- or south- is always used as the first part of the intermediate direction.

The teaching of intermediate directions follows a similar sequence as that of teaching the other types of directions. If begun out-of-doors, the movement is then to the classroom and other familiar areas in the children's environment; then to globes and various types of commercially prepared maps.

In its 1984 consideration of scope and sequence in the social studies, the

National Council for the Social Studies suggested that minimum attention be given to the teaching of directions in the primary grades, but that the instructional effort be intense in grades four, five, and six (National Council for the Social Studies, 1984, p. 269). This parallels rather detailed suggestions made by the NCSS in its *Thirty-Third Yearbook* (1966). The progression we have suggested here complements those suggestions. To summarize, the following outlines the suggested sequence, along with the grade level suggested by the earlier yearbook:

1. Children are taught spatial concepts from their own environment (early primary grades).
2. Children are taught cardinal directions outside, inside the classroom, and in familiar environments (late primary).
3. Cardinal directions are introduced on globes and on commercially prepared flat maps. Attention is given to orienting maps to "real" directions (intermediate grades).
4. Compass usage is introduced (intermediate grades).
5. Intermediate directions are introduced in familiar environments (intermediate grades).
6. Intermediate directions are used by students on globes and flat maps (late intermediate grades).

As we noted earlier, in teaching children the various skills attached to determining directions, attention should be given not only to finding these directions but also to being able to give them. Children should be given ample practice with both skills.

Interpreting and Using Symbols

A map is essentially a representation of the earth or an area of the earth. In order to represent a large area in a manageable way, mapmakers need to select the specific features of the area that will be included on a map. To a great extent this will be determined by the purpose the map is to serve. A map whose function it is to illustrate the populations of different parts of an area may not illustrate the crops grown in this area. Mapmakers also need to choose the specific means by which the features will be represented. In most cases this is not a difficult decision because there tends to be some standardization of symbols used on maps; for example, there are a limited number of ways that a capital of a state will be symbolized (a star within a circle, boldface print).

The symbols we read on adult maps are abstract. They tend *not* to look like the actual things they represent—a dot certainly looks nothing like a city! Because of their abstraction we cannot begin to teach children the adult symbols; instead instruction should be structured so that children initially learn symbols from their own immediate environment.

The most appropriate map-learning experiences begin manipulatively with the children making rudimentary three-dimensional models (say, using blocks of different sizes) of such familiar environments as their classrooms or rooms at home. First experiences with symbols can utilize these models, which won't necessarily be drawn to scale. By placing the models on butcher paper and tracing around the various pieces of furniture, or whatever, the children convert a three-dimensional model into a more conventional flat map. From this they can be helped to see that their tracings are pictures, or symbols, of real things. Thus we introduce a very important map idea—symbols represent real things, located in specific places, on maps.

Another important understanding about maps—concerning map legends—can be introduced in conjunction with these early mapmaking experiences. The children can be helped to see that, if individuals didn't know what the various tracings meant, they wouldn't be able to understand the map. The teacher can help the children realize that they might place the different tracings at the bottom of the map next to pictures or words indicating what the symbols represent. Thus, they naturally develop a legend.

Gradually, the repertoire of symbols that the children learn can be expanded. The new symbols, however, should still represent things with which the children have had some experience, either first hand or vicariously. Chapin and Gross (1973) suggest that the vicarious learning of symbols is probably best accomplished when the students can see the place or things to which the symbols refer in real-life settings. They indicate that films, filmstrips, and slides are appropriate means of bringing relatively inaccessible places (such as, say, mountains to city children) into the classroom.

The expanded repertoire of symbols is not learned in isolation from maps, however. As children develop awareness of different symbols, these should be used in a map context. Early experiences after the construction/mapping of three-dimensional models should be with teacher-made outline maps and, then, with simple maps constructed by the students. In both cases children should be encouraged to act as mapmakers do—choosing specific aspects of an area they wish to include on their maps and, then, developing appropriate symbols for them.

Once children have had experiences symbolizing familiar environments and are aware of the concept *symbol*, they can be introduced to symbols on commercially prepared maps. This is best accomplished with maps that utilize pictorial, as opposed to more abstract, symbols because they can relate these to the work that they have already done with symbols. It is probably wise, even in the intermediate grades, to have pictures available of the places and things being symbolized so that the children can refer to them. Care should also be taken to insure that the maps being used do not have an overly large number of symbols on them. Anderson (1977) indicates that the complexity of a given map increases with each symbol added.

The progression in learning map symbols moves from the simple to the complex, from the concrete to the more abstract. This means that we move from pure pictorial symbols that are readily recognized by the children (for example, the shape of a given object to represent that object), to a related pictorial symbol that represents a place (such as an airplane to represent an airport), to the nonrelated, or not easily related, and more abstract symbols (such as dots used to represent cities).

The more abstract and complex symbols that are frequently found on adult maps should not be taught until children have had a variety of experiences recognizing both pictorial and semipictorial symbols. When these prerequisite skills have been mastered, abstract symbols—such as colors being used to designate political boundaries, or dots to indicate cultural features— can be introduced. Again, because of their inherent complexity, maps used to introduce these symbols should not be overly detailed.

Regardless of the phase the children are in with respect to their understanding of symbols, reference should be made to the legend of the map. Initially, the children will construct their own. When they start using printed maps their attention should be directed to the legend and to finding symbols identified in the legend. Then, as they become more sophisticated in their understanding of symbols they can be helped to infer relationships among them (e.g., the relation of population and industrial centers).

The following summarizes the sequence in which symbols are taught.

1. Children build models of their own environment, using different three-dimensional objects to represent things (primary grades).
2. Model environments are mapped by the children and symbols are drawn in a legend (primary grades).
3. Children are helped to identify symbols they encounter in everyday life. These symbols should be used on maps constructed by teachers or students (late primary, intermediate grades).
4. Pictorial symbols are introduced on commercially prepared maps. Children are taught to consult the legend (intermediate grades).
5. Semipictorial symbols are introduced (intermediate grades).
6. Gradually, adult symbols are introduced (late intermediate grades).

Locating Places on Maps and Globes

There are two types of skills associated with locating places on maps: those dealing with identifying general areas and those concerned with determining specifically where a place is. We engage in the former when we find the United States, Africa, or Italy on maps by identifying them by their shapes. We locate oceans, rivers, and lakes in the same manner. We have some idea of their shape or size and where they are in relation to other places. We find specific places somewhat differently, relying on some sort of grid that breaks the map or globe into manageable parts. Often we use the key located on the map to tell us which part or parts of the grid to consult. Thus, when we're in a strange city we'll consult the key to determine where a specific street is located—this will give us a number and a letter. We'll then look for the block on the grid system corresponding to the number and letter. Our street should be somewhere within that block.

We will teach both general and specific locational skills. As we indicated earlier, the National Council for the Social Studies (1984) has suggested that minimal teaching effort be expended in teaching location in grades Kindergarten through three. In those grades, therefore, we should simply be introducing the two types of locational skills. Starting in the fourth grade, we'd want to place more emphasis on refining the general skills, and systematically teach the process of locating specific places.

Surprisingly, although the skills associated with locating specific places are ultimately more difficult to master, we can begin our consideration of location with them. We'd start with the children's own environments as they learn the spatial concepts considered in our discussion of direction. Terms such as *over, under, near, left, right*, and so on, not only indicate direction but also tell where one object is in relation to other objects. These spatial terms tell the direction we must travel to locate something.

The understanding of specific locations moves from the children's immediate environments to broader ones they have experienced. Children can be helped to conceptualize the relationships of their homes and schools to other places in the neighborhood and community. As a child, for example, I lived "a block away" from school, "up the hill." Landmarks in the community, either commonly established ones, like parks or ones established by the children (movie theatres, etcetera) can also be used to help children begin developing the idea of specific locations.

By the time they get to Kindergarten we would hope that children have memorized and can recite their address. There are any number of reasons why this is one of the first things they should be taught. Often, they can recite their address but really don't know what it means; they've learned it by rote. We can help them to understand that their address represents a very specific location in their neighborhood and community.

The initial exposure children have to identifying general areas—such as oceans, continents, rivers and islands—should occur as they work with globes. After some explanation they can then be helped to identify the same areas on flat maps, noting the similarities in shape as well as the relative location of different areas. Following this, instruction can move to the identification of specific places by shape and/or location. For example, they can be helped to identify the United States by its shape and then the Atlantic and Pacific Oceans by their location relative to the United States.

This identification of places by configuration and relative location can be further expanded by helping children to learn to identify their own state on a flat map by its shape and where it is located in relation to other states. This can then be followed by locating their home community in relation to other communities or physical features of the state. Children can also be encouraged to locate places they have visited.

The process of identifying places in terms of relative location and shape is a continuous one. As content about various places is utilized in the curriculum, these places should be identified on maps and globes and their specific characteristics should be noted. Some teachers require that students memorize the specific relative location of places. (Yugoslavia is on the Mediterranean Sea, bordered by Greece, Albania, Bulgaria, Romania, Hungary, Austria, and Italy.) Others simply stress relative location (a Mediterranean country or a southeastern European country). The latter is probably preferable because it requires less factual information to be memorized (and subsequently forgotten).

Systematic teaching of children to locate specific places in the intermediate grades is initially done by working as close to the students' own environment as possible. We can begin this instruction with a map containing the number-and-letter grid system. As usual, this map should be of the children's own community or of an area with which they have some familiarity. It should have the grid lines printed on it, with one axis being labeled

This ceramic map of North Carolina was made by fourth graders who were studying their state.

numerically and the other alphabetically. The children can be helped to see that the grid lines allow the map to be broken into any number of small, square maps. This idea can be reinforced by having the children pick a specific location on the map and then identify the "mini-map" on which it is found.

Once the students have grasped the idea that the grid system makes large maps more manageable and are able to use the grid terminology, they can be taught to use the map key or index. This will provide them with a list of locations accompanied by a letter and number. The latter will indicate the portion of the map on which the location will be found. Practice can then be given in finding specific places while using the index.

Following this, the students can be introduced to this system with locations that are farther removed from them in space. Highway maps of the students' own state or region are especially appropriate for use at this point, as are road atlases. (With the latter they can be given practice using the atlas index to determine on what page, or map, a given place will be found.) The major problem encountered in using these maps is that, quite frequently, the grid lines are not printed on the map. Initially, it may be well to have the children actually draw number and letter lines on the map and work with these maps until the idea of an imaginary line can be developed. After practice, they can be taught to do this visually. At each step, practice at locating specific places should be given.

A natural next step in locating specific places is the introduction of parallels and meridians. Parallels, as their name implies, are imaginary lines that run parallel to one another and encircle the globe. These can be intro-

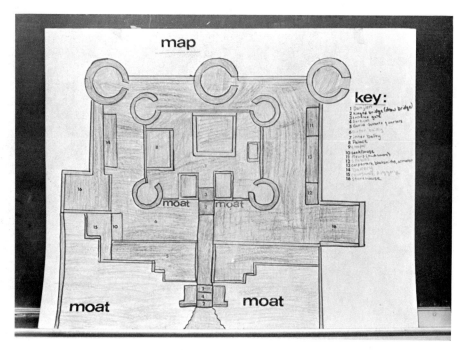

Maps become relevant when they are used for a purpose. In this case a map of a castle was constructed by students during a unit on the Middle Ages.

duced using the equator, the parallel that divides the earth into the Northern and Southern Hemispheres. Meridians also encircle the globe, but are not parallel, and meet at the poles. Parallels and meridians form a grid on the globe but—unlike most flat maps—this grid does not consist of equally sized sections.

In order to use the grid formed by parallels and meridians to locate specific places on earth it is necessary to use the concepts of *latitude* and *longitude*. Starting with the equator, each parallel on the globe is given a number and a letter to correspond to its distance and direction from the equator. Thus, the equator is 0° latitude. The parallel 15° south of the equator is latitude 15°S, while its counterpart 15 degrees north of the equator would be designated latitude 15°N. Children can be helped to identify parallels of different latitude and can be helped to discover the idea that parallels of lower latitude (regardless of whether they are north or south) will be closer to the equator than those of higher latitude. Longitude is based on the prime meridian (or Longitude 0°) which is found near Greenwich, England. Each meridian up to 180° East of the prime meridian would be designated as having longitude *n*°E, while those to the west would be designated as longitude *n*°W. Thus, longitudes 15°E and 15°W would be at an equal distance from the prime meridian. Locating specific places on the globe or on maps requires that we know the latitude and longitude of the place. Initially, we will help children begin the process of location by helping them identify the point where the equator and prime meridian cross. Next, we have them locate the parallel indicated by the latitude. (A north latitude would be away from the equator in the direction of the North Pole; south latitudes would be toward the South Pole.) Once they have located the specific latitude they would move away from the prime meridian in an easterly or westerly direction until they located the meridian indicated by the longitude.

Initial learning experiences in locating with latitude and longitude should be with places the children can locate without moving away from the lines of latitude and longitude to any great extent. Unfortunately, there are few specific places located at the intersections of parallels and meridians, and too few maps give other than standard lines of latitude and longitude. Therefore, it's necessary to use locations as near as possible to these intersections.

Once children have had experiences locating places using latitude and longitude they can be encouraged to use these in the independent identification of specific places. Instruction should be given in the standard terminology to be used for this purpose; the term *latitude*, accompanied by a degree and a direction, followed by the term *longitude* followed by a degree and direction. Thus, Philadelphia is located at Latitude 40°N and Longitude 75°W. Again, it is sufficient for elementary students to locate approximately, using the nearest parallel and meridian.

The teaching of the two types of locational skills can be summarized as follows: Finding places by their shape or location in relation to other places begins with the identification of such things as oceans and continents, progresses to the children's own country and state, and culminates with other places in the world. Similarly, in finding specific places we start with locations familiar to the child—neighborhood and community. As they learn to use grid systems with these areas we gradually move to larger areas, such as their state and, possibly, nation. It is not until the late upper grades of the elementary school that we introduce the concepts of latitude and longitude and the locational skills associated with them.

Scale

Of the skills attached to working with globes and maps, those dealing with scale can be the most complex, and we really shouldn't expect our students to use them with any degree of sophistication until the later years of elementary and middle school. As with other map skills, however, we can begin teaching ideas and concepts related to the use of scale in the earlier grades. The ideas will be developed initially using things and places in the children's own environments.

There are two groups of ideas that need to be taught in relation to scale. The first is the concept of *scale*, or the idea that things can be reduced in size to make them easier to visualize or understand. The second idea deals with working with scale—either systematically reducing things in size or comprehending the actual size or distance of that which has been reduced. We will teach both of these types of ideas in the elementary classroom.

We can begin teaching scale by developing the fundamental idea that large objects can be represented by smaller ones. Photographs are useful for this purpose because they are, indeed, scale representations. The size of the figures in the photos can be compared to the actual size of the object or person photographed. Other items that may be considered in developing this idea of scale are the pictures children draw and many of the toys that they play with (including models that are actually built to scale). It is not necessary at this stage to consider the ratio of a scale (that is, one to ten, or whatever), or the degree to which it is scaled down.

Following the development of a rudimentary concept of scale, the children can be introduced to the globe as a scale model of the world. This introduction may be accompanied by photographs of the earth taken from space. The model aspect can be made more clear by indicating locations on the globe with which the children have some familiarity—the United States, the oceans, a region of states, and, possibly, their own state. Discussion should focus on the fact that it is necessary that all of these things be made small so that they can fit on a globe that is of a manageable size. Therefore, things they know as being quite large, say their city, will be small on the globe.

As we noted earlier in our discussion of the teaching of map symbols, early mapmaking experiences will begin with the construction of three-dimensional models of such familiar environments as the classroom or the child's room at home. These models are then translated into two-dimensional maps by having the children trace around the objects in their models. At this point we won't want to complicate the project by insisting that these models and maps be done to scale. However, after these initial experiences the children can be encouraged to construct maps that are drawn to scale.

There are several things that should be kept in mind as we facilitate this mapping to scale. First, the scale should be one that is manageable, preferably having a ratio of one smaller unit to one larger unit (one inch to one foot, or one block of chart paper to one foot). This will result in a map that is relatively large. Secondly, the map should not be overly complex. This might mean that every object in the environment (especially those whose shape makes measuring difficult) will not be included. Finally, complete accuracy is not necessary if it entails frustration on the children's part. Many objects do not have measurements that lend themselves to initial scaling attempts. It's better to consider a desk top as being a "little more than," or approximately, two feet long than to have children attempt to exactly scale two feet three and three-eights inches.

After children have had experiences making their own maps to scale they can begin to learn to read scale. The scale on the maps used, like the scale on their own maps, should be simple (one inch equaling one block, for example). At this point they can be introduced to the scale notation in the map's legend. This should be in statement form and in graph form as follows:

ONE INCH = ONE BLOCK
_____

They can then be shown how to use a ruler or the edge of a piece of paper to measure scale distances from one place to another, and then convert these to real distances. A variety of measurement experiences should be given to them.

The move to working with scale on commercially prepared maps can be facilitated by using relatively large-scale maps, such as those of the children's local area if available. (If you use maps with a scale of, say one inch–one mile or one inch–five miles you won't unnecessarily bog them down with mathematical computations.) Again, the position of the scale in the legend should be noted, and instructions given on measuring scale distances. First experiences should focus on finding "as the crow flies" distances between two places. Once success has been achieved in finding a variety of distances in this manner, the children can be instructed in determining actual distances that must be traveled between two points. Here, the edge of a sheet of paper should be utilized. The children can be instructed to break routes on the map into straight line segments. That is, in going from *A* to *C* one would not travel in a straight line. Therefore they would need to break the initial two points whose distance needs to be measured (*A* and *C*) into straight-line segments, say, *A* to *B* and *B* to *C*. Then, using the paper they place its corner at *A* and mark the edge where it meets *B*. Keeping the new mark at B they then turn the paper so that its edge parallels the route from *B* to *C*. The paper is then marked at *C*. The distance from the corner to *C* is the scale distance from *A* to *C* which they can then be helped to convert to actual distance.

It should be noted that scale can be indicated in a variety of ways on a map: as a ratio, 1 in./100 miles or 1:100; as a statement, 1 in.–100 miles; or graphically, as we saw previously, with one inch equalling one block. Although all of these can be introduced to children, the latter two—statements and graphs—are the most appropriate for use in the elementary school.

Toward the upper grades of the elementary school, students can be introduced to maps using smaller scales, assuming they have had sufficient experiences with maps employing larger scales. From the maps of their immediate area they would move to estimating distances using road maps of their state and region. Once they were familiar with what actual distances represented (it takes almost two hours to drive one hundred miles) they could use the scale on maps dealing with whatever content they were considering.

Although they might examine a globe as a model of the earth in learning the concept *scale,* teaching the estimation of distances on the globe should only occur after the children have had some experience with relatively smaller-scale maps. This is done because classroom globes as a rule tend to have the smallest scale the children will encounter. One inch on a globe will often represent a distance of five hundred miles or more and the estimation of distance may require sophisticated computation.

The simplest way of measuring the distance between places on the globe is by stretching a string from one point to another, measuring the string according to scale units, and then multiplying these units by the number of miles in one unit. There are, of course, other more sophisticated ways of estimating distance (e.g., the length of one minute of latitude equals one nautical mile; thus 15 degrees of latitude equals 60 minutes per degree times 15 degrees or 900 nautical miles. A nautical mile, however, is longer than the statute mile to which most people are accustomed.) These are more appropriately learned in grades beyond the elementary.

As we work with increasingly smaller-scale maps we can begin to combine the concept *scale* with skills attached to working with scale. That is, we can show our students that scale is a relative idea, and things or distances can be reduced by varying degrees. We do this by providing our students with maps of the same area that are drawn in different scales; for example, their city on its own map and on a state map. Then we can ask them to compare and contrast these maps and come up with different generalizations including:

1. The smaller the scale, the more area can be shown.
2. The larger the scale, the more detail available.

As with the other map skills we have considered so far, there are two related guidelines that can be used in planning to teach scale. First, work from the more to less concrete, from the near to the far. The idea that something can be represented in a reduced size, for example, is more easily grasped by the children when we use photographs of the children themselves for illustration. The second guideline is that we work from the large to the small. Earliest attempts at producing things to scale might start with 1 in.– 1 ft.; later we'll move to 1 in.–1 block or 1 mile. Only after repeated experiences do we introduce the children to smaller scale maps.

Using Charts and Graphs

Charts and graphs are devices which are used to organize and summarize a large amount of data into a manageable form, thus making this data more easily accessible. One of the major differences between the two is that graphs give a picture of some type of relationship, usually a numerical one. A graph, for example, might show the number of students who prefer the different entrees offered for school lunches, and would allow students to make inferences about quantitative differences in taste.

The National Council for the Social Studies' Task Force on Scope and Sequence (1984) indicated that, like map and globe instruction, instructional efforts in relation to charts and graphs should be touched upon minimally in the primary grades and be given greater (but not what they refer to as major or intense) attention in the intermediate grades. Again this does not mean that we cannot give Kindergarten and primary grade children experiences with charts and graphs. We can, and should, as long as these experiences are appropriate.

We will want our students to have two different types of experiences with charts and graphs: making their own and working with those developed by others. Again, there will be a similarity to map and globe instruction in that initial experiences with these devices will be with ones that the children construct themselves.

Charts

Charts may be used for many different purposes: tabulation of items; the recording of experiences; the summarization of data, and so on. They can provide information in many different forms—through symbols, pictorially, or in writing. Sometimes the data presented in chart form can be translated into graph form. In elementary school there is a tendency to use the five different kinds of charts that we will discuss presently.

Experience Charts. Experience charts are usually the first type of chart that children encounter in the elementary school. Their purpose is to illustrate and summarize something the child has learned or experienced. Initially these charts may be simply composed of a picture the child has drawn accompanied by a sentence or two, which is dictated by the child and written beneath the picture by an adult. Later this may be expanded to several sentences or paragraphs dictated by the students, which may or may not be accompanied by pictures. As children become proficient at writing, the experience charts need not be dictated; they may be done entirely by the students.

There seems to be a misconception that experience charts are appropriate only for younger children and are not used in the upper grades. This is not the case. They can and should be used whenever it is appropriate to summarize learning in a verbal form.

Tabular Charts. Tabular charts present information in a columnar form, with each column listing a different type of information. We often see tabular charts used in the sports section of a newspaper to indicate an individual or team's win–loss record. We might see them being used to indicate how legislators voted on different issues. Or, if we read *Consumer Reports*, we'll see such a chart used to indicate the degree to which a given product meets various criteria.

Figure 7-1 illustrates two different purposes tabular charts can serve in elementary classrooms. The first was developed to accompany the discussion of a decision story concerning what a boy should do if he saw another boy break a toy. It illustrates the positive and negative consequence, in terms of feelings, of one student's solution; telling the teacher. The second was made following a field trip. Children listed the workers they saw and indicated whether these were producers of goods or services.

There are no restrictions on the number of columns that can be contained in a tabular chart. However, the more columns it has the more abstract and difficult it becomes to interpret. The data in the tabular chart should be presented as simply and unambiguously as possible.

Retrieval Charts. In many respects retrieval charts are a variation of tabular charts. The retrieval chart differs from some tabular charts in that it will have categories listed on both its horizontal and vertical axes. As a rule, one of the axes will be concerned with specific concepts while the other will be devoted to specific content or data. Figure 7-2 is a sample of a retrieval chart that was made by a fifth-grade class studying community life in different cultures. The row headings, found on the vertical axis, deal with three aspects of a culture while the column headings on the horizontal axis indicate the three different cultures about which data had been obtained. The students in the class filled in each cell of the chart with data they had gathered from various sources.

Retrieval charts are excellent tools for organizing and analyzing data.

Figure 7-1 Tabular charts. (*Source:* From *Helping Children Choose* by George M. Schuncke and Suzanne L. Krogh. Copyright 1983, Scott, Foresman and Company. Reprinted by permission.)

Children can be encouraged to compare and contrast information across categories and come up with similarities and differences among data. Thus, the fifth grades working with the above charts found out that some jobs were similar across cultures. They also learned that basic needs can be met differently in different cultures.

Linear and Flow Charts. These are primarily used to indicate some type of sequence. Linear charts show this progression in a one-two-three form—first this, then that, and so on—and are appropriate for illustrating sequences in which one event or activity follows another. The steps that a letter goes through from being mailed to being delivered could be depicted on a linear chart. So too could the process by which produce gets from farm to market. Flow charts, on the other hand, illustrate a sequence in which it is possible for more than one event to follow a given event. There is no one-two-three sequence; rather, in a flow chart two or three could follow one. You could illustrate the process by which you would teach a given skill to

	Our Community	Amish	Kibbutz
Jobs People Do	1. Houseperson 2. Construction worker 3. Teacher	1. Housewife 2. Farmer 3. Teacher	1. Laborer 2. Metaphlet (nurse) 3. Teacher
Where People Live	1. Children live with families. 2. Single adults may live away from home.	1. Families live together. 2. Children live with families until married. 3. Often families give land to children.	1. Children live together. 2. All married adults stay together. 3. Single people stay with other single people.
What Is Important to Them	1. Nice homes 2. Various things depending on family.	1. Family 2. Religion 3. Land	1. Sharing 2. Land

Figure 7-2   A retrieval chart.

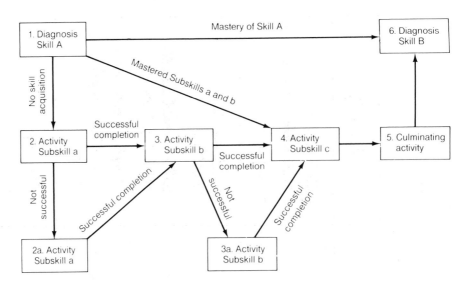

Figure 7-3 A flow chart.

your students through a flow chart. (Figure 7-3 illustrates this.) You would diagnose where the child is in relation to the skill (1). If, after this diagnosis you find that the child has no understanding you would prescribe one series of learning experiences (1 to 2, 3, 4, and 5). If there is some understanding you might use only learning experiences from the series that pick up where the child is (say 1 to 4 and 5.) If the child has attained the skill you would move directly to diagnosis of understanding of the next skill (1 to 6).

Linear and flow charts can be depicted in both pictorial and word form. Because of their relative abstractness it is best not to introduce flow charts in the early grades. Instead, simple linear charts done with pictures, can be employed. These should be thoroughly discussed. When flow charts are introduced in the later grades it is probably best that they illustrate a simple sequence and, if possible, be done in pictorial form.

Time Lines. Time lines are a variation of linear charts designed to show the sequence in which events occur over time. They differ from linear charts in that a specific date is attached to each event. More sophisticated time lines will be drawn according to a scale, with the distance between events on the line corresponding to the specific distance in time.

As we noted in an earlier chapter, children's conceptions of time tend to be very narrow; for younger students the past is "everything before now" while the future is "everything after." Something that happened ten years ago, according to their conception, is probably just as equidistant in time as something occurring a century ago. Children have difficulties understanding such abstract concepts of time as decade and century, difficulties that often don't clear up until college (Chapin and Gross, 1973). Because of these difficulties, care must be exercised in working with time lines. Otherwise, the students will have little or no understanding of the data conveyed in them.

Early attempts at making and working with time lines should focus on events within the children's own experiences, and little concern should be given to the scale of the time line. These attempts may simply be the development of linear charts, showing the order in which events occurred, with no attempt made to attach a time to these events. Gradually, time elements understood by the children may be introduced. For example, the children may make time lines of their own lives illustrating different events that occurred each year with photographs or drawings. Or, they may make a time line of the events occurring during the school day, using different hours as markers. In all cases, these early experiences would work with events roughly equidistant in time.

Gradually the span of the time line can be increased to include events that occurred before the child was born. Still, more emphasis should be placed on the *order* in which the events occurred rather than the temporal distance between the events. As children's concepts of time become more sophisticated, and as they develop a basic concept of scale, this can be introduced—again, with equidistant time elements.

Summary. We can summarize our discussion of charts by indicating a progression in which they might be considered in the elementary school. This would move from the simple to the complex as follows.

1. Experience charts.
2. Simple pictorial linear charts.
3. Simple time lines.
4. Tabular charts.
5. Retrieval charts.
6. Flow charts.

In working through this progression it is best (with the possible exception of flow charts) to have children make their own charts before working with those constructed by others. All experiences with charts should be preceded with other less-abstract activities that deal with the same data.

Graphs

Graphs are utilized to show some sort of relationship, usually numerical, among different pieces of information. Although charts may provide us with numerical data, they do not provide it with the clarity offered by graphs. Graphs provide us with an easily interpreted picture of the data at hand. In the elementary school we will help children construct and develop four different kinds of graphs: pictographs, bar, circle, and line graphs.

Pictographs. As their name implies, pictographs are graphs whose elements consist of pictures. These elements can be presented with varying degrees of complexity. In the early grades there should be a one-to-one correspondence between the picture and the thing it represents. Thus, a first grade class might construct a graph of the pets they have by drawing pictures of each pet, grouping specific animals together, and placing them on chart paper. They would be able then to count the number of dogs, cats, and or other pets owned. Later, this correspondence can be increased from one-to-one to one-to-some-other number, based on the abilities of the children. It should be realized, though, that (as with map scale) the larger the ratio of this correspondence, the more complex graph interpretation becomes. Similarly, pictographs that employ fractional elements—parts of pictures to represent a fraction of a number—will be more difficult for children to comprehend. These should not be used until children have demonstrated an understanding of fractions.

Pictographs can be presented in other than columnar form. One of the most common forms encountered in the social studies class is that of the graphic elements being presented on a map; population clusters, for example, are represented by figures of people located in specific places. In order to analyze and make inferences from data presented in such an integrated manner students will need to utilize both map and graph reading skills, and it will be important to insure that they possess both.

Bar Graphs. Sometimes called histograms, bar graphs present numerical data in the standardized form of a vertical or horizontal bar. In some respect they are more abstract than pictographs; they do not provide an actual picture of the things being graphed. However, for purposes of comparison they can be much easier to read because (with simple bar graphs) it is only the height or length of the bar that will vary throughout a given graph.

Early bar-graphing experiences can work from pictographs with the children counting the number of pictures in a given category and then translating these on a one-to-one basis onto the graph. These initial experiences are facilitated with graph paper containing relatively large blocks. Each block would represent one unit of data. The bars constructed in this way can be labeled with pictures or words.

Various factors can make bar graphs more abstract and affect their understandability to children. One of these will be the number of units of data that are represented by a single unit of the bar. The larger the ratio (i.e., 1 to 1000) the more difficult it will be to comprehend. Thus graphs with a smaller unit to length ratio will be more easily comprehended by younger children. Similarly, bars that have lengths composed of units and parts of units (e.g., a bar representing 1,250,000 people presented in units of a million) will be difficult to understand (and to graph) if emphasis is placed on comprehension of exact numbers. In cases such as this, more emphasis should be placed on comparison of bars and less emphasis on estimating numbers represented by the bars. (If exact numbers are of great importance they will be printed adjoining the bar.) A final factor that will complicate a bar graph and hinder understanding is the inclusion of a variety of variables. Often we see such graphs displaying unemployment figures. One group of three bars might be labeled "males," and be composed of bars representing white, black, and other minority males. A second group of three might be devoted to females of the same categories. Such graphs allow for comparison within groups (white males as compared to black males), between groups (males as compared to females) and between categories in different groups (white males as compared to white females). Although they concisely present a great deal of information and allow for a variety of comparisons, the sheer number of variables sometimes makes them difficult even for adults to understand. Graphs that include such diverse data are more appropriately introduced near the end of the elementary school education and then systematically taught in grades beyond the elementary.

Line Graphs. Line graphs are somewhat more complex than bar graphs. Unlike the latter they do not picture the entire quantity of numerical data. Instead line graphs connect points that would be at the top of the bars in a graph. Line graphs do not offer as clear a picture of quantities as do bar graphs. Because of this, it will be more difficult for students to make comparisons among different pieces of data presented by a line graph. Therefore, children should have a variety of experiences with bar graphs before moving to line graphs. What line graphs, which may be drawn as straight lines or curves, do is offer a picture of patterns or trends.

Circle Graphs. Circle graphs are sometimes called pie charts because of their configuration. They illustrate proportional data—what portion of a given commodity is attributed to a certain factor. For example, circle graphs are often used to show how the national budget is apportioned, with one large slice indicating defense allocations, another much smaller one showing education funds, and so on. Comparisons can be made of the relative sizes of the slices.

An understanding of the data contained in circle graphs requires that an individual understand fractions or percentages. Although younger children do use fractional terms, such as half, and understand some rudimentary concepts of fractions, they do not have the capabilities necessary for dealing with any but the most simple circle graphs (ones with even portions, or possibly ones dealing only with halves and quarters). Thus, although circle graphs may be introduced in the earlier grades, they are best taught in the later grades when the students understand fractions to some extent. As Anderson and Winston (1977) indicate, instruction will be more beneficial at this point because it will reinforce instruction in fractions and percentages.

Summary. If we examine the four different kind of graphs, we can see that there is a logical (and developmentally appropriate) sequence for teaching them. Simple pictographs with elements drawn from the children's own experiences begin this sequence. After children have worked with a variety of different pictographs instruction can be directed to translating the pictures into bar graphs. This would be followed by the development of line graphs. Initially, these would be constructed from bar graphs. Finally, circle graphs would be introduced.

Analyzing Charts and Graphs

There are three basic elements presented in most charts or graphs that help provide a complete picture of the information presented. First, there is the title, which should give a clear descriptive picture of what is being conveyed in the chart or graph. Then there are the vertical and horizontal axes, which are usually labeled to indicate whatever data are being exhibited. Finally, there are the data themselves, the facts and figures contained within the body of the graph or chart. As we help children work with charts and graphs we should systematically teach each of these elements. Children should not only be aware of the purpose of each, but also of its importance to a thorough understanding of what is being communicated.

Once they are aware of the categories of information contained in the graph or chart, they can begin to look for relationships among the data presented. This usually begins with a cursory reading to determine what specific information is contained. Then, they can move to a more in-depth examination of the data. We can help children compare and contrast data to see how the pieces fit together. With charts, this might result in the development of generalizations about the data. With graphs the children might make quantitative comparisons, examining the magnitude of one element on the graphs in relation to others. Such questions as, "What do you notice?" "What differences do you perceive?" and "How does the information fit together?" will help the children in their examination and analysis.

The final step of analysis is concerned with helping the children go beyond the available data. We can encourage students to examine the relationships they uncover and to suggest reasons for these relationships. This may result in extrapolation in which trends in the data are identified and predictions are made. It may also result in the children making inferences from the data.

Synthesis: Planning to Include Skills _____

The skills we have discussed in this chapter are ones we employ as adults. Sometimes we use them in problem-solving situations; for example, we use different map skills as we plan the best route for a trip. At other times, we use them to gather and process information. We read and analyze charts in news articles to keep abreast of what's going on in the world. In all cases, we use a given skill for some *purpose*: it is a means to some end.

This idea of skills being means needs to be kept in mind as we plan to teach. Although our goal will be skill acquisition we'll want children to realize that there is a reason for using the skill. Therefore, we'll want to plan to teach it in some context that will provide the purpose for using the skill. In fact, if we work from the assumption that we are teaching skills now so that children will be able to use them in the future, we'll want to have children work with them in a variety of different contexts. We will want to provide them experiences requiring skill usage that parallel those they will encounter as adults.

Children's textbooks contain many opportunities for skills work. The teacher's manual of any text will usually contain, somewhere near its beginning, charts outlining the skills taught throughout the textbook series as well as the skills taught in the given text. Usually the latter chart gives some indication of the specific skill to be taught as well as the unit within the text in which it is to be taught. The teachers' manual will also contain specific instructions as to how a skill should be taught within the context of a given unit.

At first glance, then, it would seem that planning to teach skills when a text-based approach is used is relatively straightforward—you simply do what the manual suggests. Unfortunately, this isn't always the case. In our discussion of the various skills, we noted the various progressions in which they should be considered (e.g., pictograph, then bar graph, then line graph, and so on). These progressions, in addition to being based on developmental abilities and recommendations of the National Council for the Social Studies, in many cases allow the development of one subskill to be based on the acquisition of other subskills. It may well be that, although the text presents a given skill to be taught, our students will not possess the requisite subskills.

Planning is still needed for teaching skills, then, even when the text is our major learning resource. This planning requires that we consider several different things. First we'll need to determine the knowledge our students will need to have in order to successfully develop a skill. We'll need to consider what requisite understandings and capabilities are necessary. Then, we'll have to determine if our students possess these. If we find that they do possess the requisite capabilities, we can proceed according to the text. If, however, we determine that they are not ready to deal with the skill, we'll have to plan learning activites that will provide the necessary preparation.

We do not need to be restricted to teaching only those skills presented in the text. As we evaluate text content we may see that it lends itself to the development of a specific skill, but does not deal with it. We might choose to introduce that skill to our students. For example, the understanding of a unit concerned with content of an historical nature might well be facilitated by student-constructed time lines. We might also choose to teach specific skills, not presented in the text, because we perceive that our students have, for one reason or another, a specific need for the skill. In both of these cases we would need to go through the same planning steps of determining requisite skills, diagnosis and instruction.

Planning to include skills in units we develop ourselves is very similar to planning to include total problem-solving processes, as discussed in the synthesis section of the previous chapter. We begin with the understanding (which, you will recall, is a generalization that has been rephrased in terms of the specific content we wish our students to develop). Then, we determine what the students will need to know in order to progress in this development. Once we are aware of this we can then determine *how* they will get this knowledge.

As we said in the last chapter, this *how* may be one of the problem-solving processes, but it needn't be. It may well be that this information can be gathered and/or analyzed while using a specific skill. Thus, we might plan for students to develop part of the understanding by using a specific skill.

An example can illustrate this process. In the previous chapter we discussed how we might plan to teach the understanding, "Athens and Sparta had different beliefs about sex roles; these beliefs determined who could or could not vote. We indicated that students would need to know three things: the roles of men and women in each city-state; beliefs responsible for these roles; and who voted. We also indicated processes that might be used to develop this knowledge. However, we could just as easily approach one or more of these with skills. For example, we might decide that information about sex roles and beliefs could be obtained by reading a section of a text with which we were familiar. We might also decide that we can help the children make sense out of what they read through the use of a retrieval chart. Therefore, we plan to introduce our students to the retrieval chart by showing them how it will be constructed, and indicating what types of information they will place on it. In this case we would be using a skill, developing a chart, to organize knowledge necessary for formulating the understanding.

The basic question that we would ask in planning to include skills is, "What skill can be used appropriately here?" Once we have determined the answer to this question we can then proceed in planning to teach the skill in the manner discussed earlier in this section: analyzing the requisite skills, diagnosing, and selecting teaching activities.

Springboards to Discussion

1. In this chapter we have discussed the major skills and subskills necessary for using maps and globes. These subskills will be broken down even further as you teach them; in your planning you'll consider what the children will need to do first, second, and so on. That is, you'll plan for a sequence of activities.

   Choose one of the subskills we have discussed and develop a plan for teaching it. In this plan indicate a sequence of things that the children need to accomplish. Then indicate how you'll know whether or not they have attained the subskill.

2. Examine a children's textbook to determine the skills that it teaches. Note these. Then determine whether they are appropriate for the given grade according to the NCSS guidelines that we have followed in this chapter.

   After you have done this, interview a teacher who teaches the grade of the textbook. In this interview you'll want to ascertain which skills the children have no difficulty learning (you might want to ask the teacher how he or she teaches those skills). Also determine which skills the children have difficulty learning.

   Compare your list of skills learned and the skills with which the children have difficulty, using the sequence suggested by NCSS and reported in this chapter. Indicate similarities and differences.

3. There are any number of different kinds of maps and globes, many of which we haven't discussed in this chapter. Visit the curriculum materials center of your local school district and examine the different types they have available. List these and, later, indicate how you might best utilize these maps and globes. That is, suggest the type of content or learning experience that the map or globe will supplement best.

References

ANDERSON, CHARLOTTE C., AND WINSTON, BARBARA J. "Acquiring Information by Asking Questions, Using Maps and Globes, and Making Direct Observations," in Dana G. Kurfman (ed.), *Developing Decision-Making Skills, 47th Yearbook.* Washington, D.C.: National Council for the Social Studies, 1977.

BACON, PHILLIP. *Focus on Geography: Key Concepts and Teaching Strategies, 40th Yearbook.* Washington, D.C.: National Council for the Social Studies, 1970.

CARPENTER, HELEN MCCRACKEN (ED). *Skill Development in the Social Studies, 33rd Yearbook* Washington, D.C.: National Council for the Social Studies, 1963.

CHAPIN, JUNE R., AND GROSS, RICHARD. *Teaching Social Studies Skills.* Boston: Little, Brown, 1973.

National Council for the Social Studies. "In Search of a Scope and Sequence for Social Studies" (Report of the National Council for the Social Studies Task Force on Scope and Sequence), *Social Education,* vol. 48 (April 1984), pp. 249–273.

SCHUNCKE, GEORGE M., AND KROGH, SUZANNE LOWELL. *Helping Children Choose.* Glenview, IL: Scott, Foresman, 1983.

Caring

8

Affective Goals of the Social Studies

After reading this chapter you should be able to:

1. Identify the components that compose the affective domain as delineated in the *Taxonomy of Educational Objectives.*

2. Describe the various stages individuals go through in the development of:
- Justice reasoning.
- Perspective taking.
- Ethics.

3. Suggest ways in which individuals can be helped to attain higher stages in these areas.

4. Describe the values clarification process.

5. Delineate the conditions for appropriate affective activities for children.

In 1964 a companion volume to Bloom's taxonomy of objectives for the cognitive domain (Bloom, 1956), discussed in Chapter 6, was published. This book, *Taxonomy of Educational Objectives: Handbook II: Affective Domain* by David R. Krathwohl et al. (1964), listed five different types of affective objectives for classroom instruction. These include the following.

1. *Receiving or attending to a phenomena.* Three activities are entailed by this objective: being aware of something that is occurring; being willing to pay attention to it; and, then, actually attending to it. We would be working at this level with our students if we introduced them to the problem of alleviating world hunger and then got them interested enough in the problem so that they generate information to develop understandings about it.

2. *Responding to the phenomena.* Here individuals need to do something about what has caught their attention at the first level. Initially they might respond to the phenomena even if the necessity to do so is not perceived. Then they respond willingly and are satisfied that they have done so. Responding, as defined here, would occur if our students decided to raise funds to help alleviate world hunger and then carried out this fund raising.

3. *Valuing*. At this level the individual believes that what is occurring has worth and therefore becomes committed to it. An example of this valuing level would be seen with our students if, believing that everyone has a right to be free from hunger, they continued working to relieve world hunger even outside of the school setting.

4. *Organization of values*. This occurs as the individual sees how a value relates to other values and incorporates it into a personal value system. Our students would engage in this category of affective behavior if, for instance, they looked at their commitment to working to relieve world hunger (for example, by giving up part of their allowance) in comparison to other commitments they have made (say, commitments to being with friends that might require that they use their allowance) and then decided which was more important.

5. *Characterization by a value or value complex*. At this level the values would become so much a part of the individual that he or she would act on them in a consistent manner. In any situation the student encountered that was concerned with world hunger, he or she would do something to help alleviate it.

As with the cognitive domain, these objectives are in a hierarchical order. Higher levels in the affective taxonomy imply lower levels; to organize our values we must receive, respond, and value.

With the possible exception of the fifth category, which represents a long-range goal of social studies instruction, we will be working rather consistently with all categories of the affective domain in our social studies curriculum. We won't necessarily say we are helping our children *receive* or *respond*. Instead, we'll use such other terms as *developing awareness, appreciations, attitudes,* and so on.

There are many ways in which we will be working toward affective goals. Some we will do consciously; for example, when we help students analyze the behavior exhibited by a group of people to determine what values those people might have. Others won't be so intentional on our part; that is, we will also be unconsciously transmitting the values we have through our actions.

This section of the book will be devoted to a consideration of the former, planned ways in which we can help our children attain affective goals. It will focus primarily on the first four levels of the taxonomy, working from the assumption that these will ultimately lead to the fifth. We won't discuss the levels per se but instead will examine various capabilities that we wish to engender in our students, capabilities that incorporate one or more of the affective objectives.

The bulk of this section is, as is the taxonomy of affective objectives, concerned in one way or another with values. In some segments of society the idea of working with any value at all in the school is a red flag. It is believed that questions of values are best dealt with by the church and home. To a great extent this should be our stance—as teachers we have no right to indoctrinate children with values that might be contradictory to those espoused by the two institutions. A diversity of values is inherent in the nature of our society; many things perceived to be important or right to one group of people will not be seen as right to another group. Values that are not agreed upon by society as a whole should not be taught in the school.

On the other hand, this does not mean that we cannot teach any value in the schools. Our society, as a whole does embrace some core values. These include fair play, justice, free speech, self-respect, decision-making opportunities, the right of privacy, human dignity, and denial of racism (National Council for the Social Studies, 1979). We can teach these values to our students. We can also help our students begin to consider what their own personal values are. We will do this by helping develop those capabilities and processes they need in order to generate their own values. We won't, however, tell them what their personal values should be.

In this chapter we'll examine some of the capabilities and processes that have been identified as contributing to the attainment of the different types of affective objectives. We'll begin by looking at those that are developmental in nature—those that individuals acquire over a period of time if they are given the appropriate stimuli. Included in our examination will be capabilities associated with social reasoning, perspective taking, and moral reasoning. Following this we'll examine a nondevelopmental approach to the teaching of a valuing process, *values clarification*.

The synthesis section will discuss the commonalities among the various ideas presented in the chapter, examing areas of consensus as to what is appropriate in helping individuals attain affective objectives.

The Development of Affective Capabilities _____

Much of the work concerned with the factors that affect our judgment about social and values issues—what is right and wrong, good and bad, important and unimportant—has been done by developmental psychologists. This work has led to the formulation of a number of theories of affective development. These include the stages children go through in thinking about what is just; how individuals develop the ability to see things from the perspective of others; and how individuals mature in their reasoning about what is right and good. Although the knowledge provided by each of these theories actually addresses a different aspect of prosocial reasoning, all complement one another. Taken together they help us understand what is necessary to attain higher-level affective objectives. For example, Damon (1977) indicates that the development of ideas of justice in children is important to the beginning of the development of a sense of morality. Similarily, it appears that an individual's perspective-taking ability will affect the degree of sophistication with which he or she approaches questions of right or wrong (Kohlberg, 1976).

One commonality possessed by all of the theories is that they describe the manner in which individuals think in terms of *stages*. This idea of stages should not be a new one to you; you may remember Piaget's sensorimotor, preoperational, concrete operational, and formal stages of cognitive development. The stages we will discuss will have similar general characteristics to those elaborated by Piaget. Three of these characteristics are important to remember as we consider different types of affective thought.

First, stages are *structured wholes*. If we examine the way that an individual is thinking about, say, how another person is feeling in a given situation, we would be able to pick out specific ideas or characteristics that would identify the individual's thought as belonging to a specific stage. All individuals at that stage would exhibit similar characteristics in their thinking, characteristics that would not radically change until they moved to a higher stage.

An example will help clarify this idea of a structured whole. When my son, Mark, was three years old he hit a little girl in his play group. Although he could see that she was hurt (due to the fact that she was crying) he later related to me that "Laura likes to get hit." His perspective-taking ability was at a very primitive egocentric stage; he could not perceive her feelings since he believed that everyone felt the way he did. In his mind he believed "I like to hit Laura; therefore, Laura likes me to hit her." His level of perspective taking in this, and other situations, could be identified by this egocentric characteristic. Similarly, the thinking of other children sharing his stage would be characterized by this egocentricity.

The second characteristic of developmental stages is that they occur in an *invariant sequence*. An individual will move from one stage of thought to the next higher stage. Although a given individual may spend varying amounts of time at the different stages, that individual will not skip a stage. Thus, after some time Mark moved from the stage of egocentric perspective taking to the next higher stage, where he was capable of realizing that, indeed, Laura could think and feel differently than he did about his hitting her.

The fact that stages happen in an invariant sequence is explained by the third characteristic of developmental stages, their *hierarchical integration*. An individual's thinking at one level encompasses the thinking of stages below it. The manner in which the person thinks at a given level represents a building upon and reformulation of thought that had occurred earlier. Based on the person's previous experiences, and what the person has learned, ideas about a given situation are reconceptualized in new ways.

Having examined the characteristics of stages, we can now consider some of the stages that children and adults go through in their development of different affective capabilities.

Justice Reasoning in Children

Children are concerned with the concept of justice. Their concern, however, is not with the more abstract concept with which adults deal. Instead it is with those problems of fairness that impinge upon their own lives. One of these problems is that of sharing—who should get what, or what is the way of distributing rewards.

William Damon (1977) investigated how children think about this problem of sharing, which he called one of positive justice. He presented children with a hypothetical situation in which a class of students sold the artwork they had made at a school bazaar. Then, in a clinical interview, he queried them on how the proceeds of the sale should be distributed. In this interview he included questions that required the children to consider different circumstances—such as giving money to children who did not do good work or giving more money to a poor child—which might affect their perceptions of how the money should be distributed.

Damon's analysis of children's responses indicated that they did think about sharing in qualitatively different ways and that their thoughts could be categorized as falling in one of six levels. These are shown in Table 8.1.

An examination of the figure shows that children's reasoning about the distribution of goods moves from the egocentric, based on the child's wishes (Levels 0A–0B), to the egalitarian, where everybody gets the same or you get in measure to what you give (1A–1B), to the consideration of needs (2-A) and situational demands (2-B). The child's reasoning gets more complex, and less cut-and-dried, as he or she moves up through the stages.

In addition to investigating justice reasoning with hypothetical dilemmas,

TABLE 8.1 Levels of Justice Reasoning

Level 0-A (Age 4 and under):	Positive-justice choices derive from wish that an act occur. Reasons simply assert the wishes rather than attempting to justify them ("I should get it because I want to have it").
Level 0-B (Ages 4–5):	Choices still reflect desires but are now justified on the basis of external, observable realities such as size, sex, or other physical characteristics of persons (e.g., we should get the most because we are girls). Such justifications, however, are invoked in a fluctuating, after-the-fact manner, and are self-serving in the end.
Level 1-A (Ages 5–7):	Positive-justice choices derive from notions of strict equality in actions (i.e., that everyone should get the same). Equality is seen as preventing complaining, fighting, "fussing," or other types of conflict.
Level 1-B (Ages 6–9):	Positive-justice choices derive from a notion of reciprocity in actions: that persons should be paid back in kind for doing good or bad things. Notions of merit and deserving emerge.
Level 2-A (Ages 8–10):	A moral relativity develops out of the understanding that different persons can have different, yet equally valid, justifications for their claims to justice. The claims of persons with special needs (e.g., the poor) are weighed heavily. Choices attempt quantitative compromises between competing claims.
Level 2-B (Ages 10 and up):	Considerations of equality and reciprocity are coordinated such that choices take into account the claims of various persons and the demands of the specific situation. Choices are firm and clear-cut, yet justifications reflect the recognition that all persons should be given their due (though, in many situations, this does not mean equal treatment).

Source: W. Damon, "Patterns of Change in Children's Social Reasoning: A Two-Year Longitudinal Study," *Child Development,* vol. 51, p. 1011. Copyright 1980 by The Society for Research in Child Development, Inc. Reprinted with permission.

Damon examined children's reasoning in real-life situations where they would need to decide who would get rewards for a job that they had actually done. In this situation the children tended to reason at a somewhat lower level than they did with the hypothetical dilemma. However, the level of reasons were still age related—older children tended to give higher-level responses. They also were somewhat related to the child's level of reasoning in the hypothetical situation; children's actions tended to fall one level below their reasoning.

Damon (1983) indicates that it is important for children to consider questions of justice and fairness in relation to problems in their own world. One reason for this is that sharing is probably the most crucial factor in children's friendships. Another is that the consideration of questions of justice will prepare them "for the later amplification of the justice principles necessary for functioning in the adult social world" (p. 77). Helping children consider what is fair in their lives as children may provide the groundwork for their consideration of what is just and right as adults.

Stages of Social Perspective-Taking

One of the abilities for which the social studies are directly responsible for developing in children is that of perspective taking. Sometimes called role taking, this ability is concerned with being able to understand the point of view and feelings of others. Perspective taking is the basis of empathy, being able to "feel" for another person. It is, as we noted previously in Chapter 4,

This bulletin board helps children see things from their peers' perspectives.

also important to the breakdown of ethnocentrism and to the development of a global perspective.

The development of social perspective-taking abilities in children has been extensively studied by Robert Selman. In his research interviews children were presented with a story in which the puppy of the friend of two boys had run away. The heartbroken boy had told them that another dog would never be able to take the lost one's place. At the conclusion of the story children were asked if the boys should buy a puppy they see in a pet store as a birthday present for their friend. Following this, various questions were asked concerning the feelings of the individuals involved in the situation.

Analysis of their responses to this interview allowed Selman to determine that children do move through developmental stages in their consideration of the thoughts and feelings of others. This movement is one that starts with the individual considering feelings from a very egocentric perspective and can ultimately (but not necessarily) move to the stage where an individual can examine situations from the perspectives of a number of different persons. This movement occurs in the five stages seen in Table 8.2 (adapted from Selman, 1980).

Selman has not only delineated the stages that children move through in the development of perspective-taking abilities, he has also explored ways in which this movement can be facilitated. Like cognitive development—wherein it is very possible for an individual *not* to attain the highest level of cognitive operations—it is also very possible for an individual not to progress beyond the lower stages of perspective taking. Selman and Lieberman (1975) found that this progress could be enhanced if children are given the opportunity to consider and discuss the feelings of others in different situations. Using filmstrips that contained dilemmas to which children could relate (should a girl climb a tree to rescue a cat when her father has clearly forbidden her to climb trees?) as springboards they were able to encourage the children's movement into higher levels of perspective taking through classroom discussion. In a later section of this chapter we will detail some of the characteristics of those classroom discussions.

Moral Development

The study of how individuals develop a sense of morality—how they think about what is good, right, and just—dates back to the ancient philosophers. For our purposes, however, the work of three individuals, Jean Piaget, Lawrence Kohlberg, and Carol Gilligan is most pertinent.

Piaget. Piaget's work with children's moral judgment was essentially a brief excursion away from the work for which he is known best, that of cognitive development. This excursion, however, was not without reason. Piaget found that there was a close relationship between cognitive and moral development, with the former being a necessary prerequisite for the latter. Moral development is intimately linked to cognitive development.

In examining how children respond to such concepts as rules, laws, and justice, Piaget postulated that children moved through two stages of morality separated by a period of transition from one to the other:

TABLE 8.2 Stages of Perspective Taking

Stage 0: Egocentric Perspective Taking (Ages 4 and under)

The child does not differentiate between the perspective of the self and others and perceives no difference between the points of view of both. In addition the child does not reflect on the thoughts of self or others. Essentially, the child believes that, in a given situation, everyone thinks or feels the way he or she does. ("I wanted to hit her, so she wanted to get hit.")

Stage 1: Social Information Perspective Taking (Ages 6–8)

The child realizes that people do think or feel differently because they are in different situations. The child, however, cannot maintain his or her own perspective while simultaneously taking the perspective of the other. This results in the child's focusing on one or the other perspective. ("If I eat the cookie, she won't be happy. I'll be happy. I'll eat it because it will make me happy.")

Stage 2: Self-Reflective Perspective Taking (Ages 8–10)

At this point the individual can understand that people think or feel differently because each has a unique set of values or purposes. The child is able to reflect on his or her own behavior as seen from another's point of view. He or she is also able to take the other person's perspective in order to judge the other person's thoughts or actions. It is not possible at this stage, however, to look at both of these simultaneously from a third-person point of view. In addition, although the child can realize that different, even conflicting, feelings are possible in a social situation, these feelings are seen as occurring sequentially rather than simultaneously. ("If I take the cookie and eat it, then I'll be happy. But then I'll know my sister will be sad, so I'll be sad.") The child does not understand what mixed feelings are.

Stage 3: Mutual Perspective Taking (Ages 10–12)

The individual is able to differentiate his or her own viewpoint from that of others as well as that taken by the average member of the group. It is now possible for the individual to examine interactions from a third person point of view; a point of view that may not be one taken by any specific individual in the interaction. ("People would think that we're both being selfish.")

Stage 4: Societal-Symbolic Perspective Taking (Ages 12 and over)

The third-person point of view is broadened into an ability to perceive how different third persons might view a situation. At this point the individual understands that the group's point of view may be insufficient and realizes the necessity of societal conventions that are understood by all members of the group.

Source: Adapted from Robert Selman, "Social-Cognitive Understanding," in Thomas Lickona (ed.), *Moral Development and Behavior*. New York: Holt, Rinehart and Winston, 1976.

1. *Heteronomy* is the stage in which children believe that goodness is equated with obeying rules, whether or not they are appropriate or relevant. Goodness occurs when rules are obeyed and an individual is bad when rules are disobeyed. Children at this stage believe that it is their duty to obey authority; hence, there is a belief in a strict adherence to what is said by adults. They also believe that rules are immutable—a rule is a rule and it cannot be changed. The determination of the goodness or badness of an act at this stage is done in terms of its consequences, not the intention behind the act. Thus, children at this heteronomous stage would see a child who accidently broke several dishes while helping to set the table as being more wrong than a child who purposefully broke one dish in a fit of anger. *Children at this stage*

do not consider the intentions behind the act. Piaget characterized this stage as being a *morality of constraint.*

Piaget indicated that the heteronomous stage of morality lasts until about the age of six or seven. Thus, it coincides with the preoperational stage of cognitive development.

2. The *autonomous* stage is one in which morality is conceived as stemming from cooperation. The idea of goodness and rightness is based on a social contract among individuals—we do unto others as we would have them do unto us. This stage differs from the heteronomous in that rules are perceived as flexible rather than immutable; thus, they may need to be changed if they treat some individuals more unfairly than others. At this stage authority does not rest with power and might (or with being an adult), but with that which is given for the good of the common order. Finally, at this stage *the goodness or badness of an act is judged by the intentions behind the act, not its consequences.* Thus, the child who broke the one dish in the fit of anger would be perceived as doing a greater wrong than the child who accidentally broke several dishes.

The autonomous stage begins, after a period of transition from heteronomy, around the age of eleven or twelve. Full movement into this stage is contingent upon the development of formal operations.

Kohlberg. Piaget's early work with moral judgment, found in the book, *The Moral Judgment of the Child,* first published in 1932, served as a base for further exploration by other researchers into how individuals reason about what is good and right. The best known of these later researchers is Lawrence Kohlberg, who began his work approximately twenty-five years after the publication of *The Moral Judgment of the Child.* Through analysis of his research interviews Kohlberg delineated three levels of reasoning about what is good and right. These levels were further subdivided into six stages individuals go through in their moral development. The levels and stages are found in Table 8.3.

The three levels of morality delineated by Kohlberg are concerned with how we think about what is good, right, and just. They move from an egocentric orientation to self, to an orientation to the groups to which one belongs, to a realization that there are certain ethical principles that exist regardless of self or society.

As with Piaget, Kohlberg has found that there is an intimate relationship between the stages of moral development and those of cognitive development, with movement through the latter being necessary, but not sufficient, for movement in the former. Thus Stages 5 and 6 require that an individual be in Piaget's stage of formal operations. However, being at the stage of formal operations does not guarantee that an individual will engage in principled moral reasoning.

Kohlberg's research has also addressed the question of how an individual moves from one stage of moral development to another. For this to occur two basic things are necessary: First, an individual needs to be exposed to the next higher stage of reasoning. Individuals can understand all stages below their own and one stage above. This exposure occurs through interaction

TABLE 8.3 Kohlberg's Levels and Stages of Moral Development

Level 1—Preconventional

At this level what is right and just is based primarily on the individual's own egocentric thoughts and feelings. Morality is basically what's good for "me."

Stage 1. *Heteronomous morality.* This has been called the "Punishment and Obedience" orientation. Good is defined in terms of being obedient and avoiding punishment. Good is what is rewarded and bad is what gets an individual punished.

Stage 2. *Instrumental Relativism.* This has been called the "I'll scratch your back, you scratch my back" stage. Right is conceived in terms of serving the needs of the individual and, if appropriate, the needs of others. Fairness occurs when there is an equal exchange—an eye for an eye.

Level II—Conventional

What is good and right moves away from the self-serving needs of the individual and is defined in terms of the standards set by the groups, including societies, to which the individual belongs.

Stage 3. *Interpersonal Concordance.* This is sometimes called the "Good boy/good girl" stage. What is right is conceived in terms of doing what is expected of the individual by the various groups to which he or she belongs—family, friends, and so on. At this stage goodness may be equated with conformity to group norms and rules.

Stage 4. *Social System Orientation.* The term, *law and order,* describes this stage quite aptly because doing what is right is defined in terms of following those rules that have been societally agreed upon, including those laws set by state and church. At this stage it is sometimes possible not to follow laws to the letter, but this would only occur in those extreme cases where the laws of different social systems to which the individual belonged were in conflict. Most Americans, incidentally, are said to be at Stage 4.

Level III—Postconventional

At this level what is good and right may go beyond what is prescribed by society and there is a recognition that there are some principles—such as justice—that can supersede the dictums of a society. (It should be noted that at various times the two stages at this level have been considered as one.)

Stage 5. *Social Contract/Legalistic Orientation.* A consideration of rights, especially "human rights," pervades this stage. The individual still recognizes and respects societal dictums, but this does not occur as automatically as it does in Stage 4. Rather, law as seen as working for the good of all and, when this does not occur, the individual perceives it necessary to change laws so that they do work for the welfare of all. At times an individual at this stage may see working outside of the law as necessary.

Stage 6. *Universal Ethical Orientation.* At this stage the individual's morality is based upon ethical principles that the individual has rationally chosen to guide his or her life. According to Kohlberg (1976a, p. 35), these principles are the universal principles of justice. When there is a conflict between the law and these principles one acts in accordance with the latter.

Source: Adapted from Lawrence Kohlberg, "Moral Stages and Moralization," in Thomas Lickona (ed.), *Moral Development and Behavior.* New York: Holt, Rinehart and Winston, 1976.

with the thoughts of others. Secondly, *dissonance* must occur; that is we must perceive this next higher stage to be more attractive and "better" than our own. Because we see our present stage as less adequate we *accommodate* (in the Piagetian sense) the higher stage. Gradually, further experiences with thinking at the higher stage will permit *assimilation* and allow this level of reasoning to be our own.

These two prerequisites for moral development suggest that it is a cognitive process only. The fact, however, that interaction is required for stage movement to occur indicate that social processes are also necessary. Kohlberg (1976a) has theorized that this is the case and that stage advancement is also tied to growth in role-taking ability of the typed discussed earlier.

Much work has been done with the practical implications of Kohlberg's research, and there have been a number of strategies developed for facilitating stage movement in the classroom. Most of these employ discussion of dilemmas in which such universal moral issues as life and property come into conflict. Students are presented these dilemmas, asked to arrive at a personal resolution and determine reasons for the specific resolution, and to shrae their reasoning. Unfortunately, there has been little work done to determine the effectiveness of these strategies with children below the middle-school years.

Gilligan. In some respects Carol Gilligan's work with moral development may be considered to be a reaction to the work of Kohlberg and other of his associates. Specifically, her concern was fostered by two facts: (1) that the majority of work with stages of moral development had been done with males (for example, Kohlberg's initial work was done with boys aged ten through sixteen); and (2) that when females were included in the research their reasoning tended to be at the stage 3, "Good boy/good girl," level—women appeared to reason below the level attained by most American males.

Gilligan, who was a student of Kohlberg's, theorized that the use of *justice* as the concept upon which morality was constructed may have been the reason for the relatively poor showing among women. Citing a great deal of research on the social development of boys and girls, she indicated that boys are brought up to consider *justice* as a primary factor in resolving disputes. Girls, on the other hand, are socialized to use *caring* as the organizing principle for their interactions. One example Gilligan used to illustrate this was based on what happens when disputes arise in children's games. She indicated that boys resort to citing and arguing rules to determine what is just in the situation. Girls, on the other hand, are less concerned with the rules than with the well-being of the group. To maintain caring in the group they will end the game.

Gilligan argued, in essence, that the moral development of women was being measured by male standards. She indicated that, if this development were gauged using *caring* and *responsibility* (as opposed to *justice*) as a standard, then stages of development of moral reasoning characteristic of females would be identified. This turned out to be the case. Her research was done through interviews with women who were coping with the questions of whether to have an abortion. Its results indicated that there were three levels of development in what Gilligan (1982) referred to as the "ethic of care" (p. 74). The first two of these were followed by a period of transition in which the women reflected on their thoughts in light of the concerns of selfishness and responsibility. These levels were:

1. Caring for the self in order to insure survival. The individual woman is of primary concern at this level and self-interest is the basis of judgment. A woman at this level might have a dilemma about having an abortion because, as Gilligan quotes, "having a baby not only [is] a way of increasing her freedom by providing 'the perfect chance to get married and move away from home' but also as restricting her freedom 'to do a lot of things' " (p. 75).

   This initial perspective is followed by a period of transition in which it is viewed as being selfish. Gilligan indicates that this criticism of self leads to a new understanding of the relationship between self and others (p. 74) articulated at the second level.

2. Concern for caring for the dependent and unequal, with good being equated with caring for others. Gilligan describes a woman working from this perspective who chose to have an abortion, even though she herself did not want to, because of what she saw as responsibility for her lover, his wife, and his children. Having a child could have potential negative effects on these individuals.

   The transitional period following this second perspective is again characterized by questions of the relationship between self and others. At this point the woman asks if it is possible to be "responsible to herself as well as to others" (Gilligan, p. 82). Successful reconciliation of her responsibility to both leads to the third perspective.

3. A realization of the interconnectedness of self and others, with care becoming a self-chosen principle. The woman realizes that there is an interdependence between self and others. At this level there is a con-

Caring takes on added meaning when older students tutor younger ones.

cern for relationships and a condemnation for exploitation and hurt. Gilligan quotes a woman at this stage opting for the abortion because "It will be less of a strain for us individually and for us as a family not to be pregnant at this time" (p. 96).

The three perspectives, then, focus on caring and responsibility. They essentially move from a caring for self, to a more conventional (from the female perspective) caring for others, to a caring that encompasses both the self and others.

Facilitating Affective Development

In addition to the more or less theoretical work done to delineate stages of thinking in relation to distributive justice, perspective taking, and moral development, research has also been conducted to attempt to find ways to encourage student movement through these stages. We can briefly examine some of this research as a means of uncovering some characteristics of learning activities that promote the sociomoral development of our students.

To this writer's knowledge, William Damon has not worked with classroom strategies for facilitating justice reasoning. However, he does indicate, throughout the discussion of his research noted earlier, that any consideration of problems of justice by children must be done with problems from the world of childhood (Damon, 1977). That is, he intentionally had children consider those problems of sharing that children, nor adults, would encounter. His belief was that children have their own social concerns, which differ from those of adults. They reason about these differently than adults reason about their concerns.

Work by other researchers, though, has shown that children's levels of distributive justice can be elevated through classroom intervention. This intervention took the form of having children decide upon the most appropriate endings for open-ended stories that contained a conflict in issues which the children perceived to be important. One story, for example, presented a conflict between sharing and keeping a promise. It required the children to decide whether a girl should give a boy who had no lunch a piece of cake she had previously promised to a friend (Schuncke and Krogh, 1983). The decision making required by this story was aided by having the children role play the various solutions they suggested or by having the children consider alternative solutions in a teacher-directed discussion. Krogh (1985) found that either approach—role playing or structured discussion—was effective in generating stage movement. When compared to control children, who did not work with the problem stories at all, the experimental students achieved significant growth in distributive justice reasoning. Krogh and Lamme (1985) found that this growth could also be facilitated by discussing the issues inherent in children's literature. So, a reading of *The Little Red Hen* was followed by a discussion of the question, "Should the little red hen have shared?"

Robert Selman has used filmstrips containing dilemma stories as a means for generating classroom discussions aimed at helping children develop perspective-taking abilities. These filmstrips present dramatic open-ended stories containing a conflict between two or more values, such as promise keeping and obeying rules. Children were then led in a discussion of alternative resolutions to the dilemmas. In the research using these filmstrips Selman and Lieberman (1975) had several interesting findings. First, the discussions did lead to a growth in perspective-taking ability. Second, and just as important for our purposes, it was found that teachers did not need to be expert at identifying stages of children's perspective-taking development. They found no difference between teachers who had been trained to present the children with a range of levels of reasoning in the discussions and teachers who were untrained. This led them to conclude that the key to effective classroom interventions is not in the knowledge of developmental stages but in the ability to conduct effective classroom discussions (p. 716).

In the results of the same research reported above, Krogh (1985) reported that children who engaged in role playing or discussion of problem stories also grew in their perspective-taking abilities as a result of these experiences. This growth was significant when compared to that of children who had not had the interventions.

As we said earlier, Kohlberg's initial work with stages of moral reasoning was done with boys between the ages of ten and sixteen. This emphasis on children who are at the upper levels of the elementary school is reflected in the research which has been done on classroom interventions to foster the development of moral reasoning. Although guidelines have been given for the application of Kohlberg's theory to elementary classrooms (Galbraith and Jones, 1976), there has been very little research done with students below the sixth grade (Lockwood, 1978). The interventions used with older students employ the moral dilemma—a story containing a conflict in moral issues such as the right to life versus property rights—as their base. In some of the research studies, resolutions to these dilemmas were role played. Other interventions required that these resolutions be discussed in small or large group settings. Both types of intervention appear to facilitate moral development; however, the discussion approached seemed to be somewhat more effective (Lockwood, 1978).

From this brief review of research it is possible to conclude that various types of affective development can be facilitated in the classroom. The interventions used to do this have two characteristics in common, characteristics we might infer to be conducive to effective classroom activities. These included the following:

1. *The presentation of some type of dilemma to the students.* This dilemma will contain a conflict in issues which are seen as important by the students and it will need to be resolved by them. The dilemma will be open-ended.
2. *The working through of this dilemma by the students, either through role play or discussion in a group setting.* We might infer, based on Kohlberg's emphasis on the need for interaction to foster stage movement, that individuals need to be involved in seeing and discussing these resolutions.

A Nondevelopmental Approach: Values Clarification ————————

Any discussion of approaches to the development of affective capabilities would be incomplete without a consideration of *values clarification* because this approach (or at least its name) is probably the one best known to teachers. Unlike the developmental approaches it is not based on stages of thought through which individuals move. Instead it is based on a theoretical consideration of how individuals determine what is important to their lives.

Working from ideas first developed by John Dewey, Louis Raths developed what he called a value theory (Raths, Harmin, and Simon, 1966). This theory is interesting in that it does two things: (1) it delineates the process individuals go through in determining what they value; and (2) it defines what a value is. Interestingly enough, a value is defined as what individuals arrive at as a result of undergoing the process of valuing!

Rath's theory of valuation was described in the book *Values and Teaching* (Raths, Harmin, and Simon, 1966), which introduced the concept of values clarification. The process of developing (or clarifying) a value requires that three different types of actions occur; each of these actions in turn entails different activities. These are as follows.

Choosing: It is necessary for us to thoughtfully select among alternative courses of action. This selection should be made without any external constraints.

Prizing: Once we have chosen we must be satisfied with our choice and be willing to let others know about it.

Acting: It is necessary to follow through on our choice; we have to do something about it. This acting, according to Raths, Harmin, and Simon, should be done consistently (Raths, Harmin, and Simon, 1966, p. 30).

According to this theory, in order for something to be a value it must be chosen, prized, and acted upon. If one of these behaviors is not present, then it is something else. This something else could be an attitude, a predisposition toward some way of thinking or acting. Or, it could be what those associated with values clarification call a value indicator, essentially a potential value.

The values clarification approach uses this valuing process as its base. It entails having an individual work with one or more (possibly all) of the seven activities described above. Thus, one values-clarification activity might focus on having the individual choose, from a list of activities, the five favorite things he or she likes to do. Another activity might ask the individual to publicly affirm some decision he or she has made.

In the past, values clarification has been very popular with teachers. This is probably due to the accessibility of materials and activities. Any number of books, such as *Values Clarification* (Simon, Howe, and Kirschenbaum,

1972) or *Learning to Think and Choose* (Casteel, 1978), contain activities that could be put to immediate use in the classroom. In most cases, the teacher needed only choose the activity and present it to the students.

Values clarification activities basically fall into two categories: oral and written. Oral activities require more knowledge of values clarification on the teacher's part because of the spontaneity of the students' responses; the teacher is responsible for structuring the interaction. Included in this type of activity would be the teacher's use of the clarifying response, the public interview, values voting, and the values whips. The *clarifying response* is one made by the teacher to a statement made by an individual child. Raths, Harmin, and Simon (1966) indicate that such a response, usually very short and directed at one of the seven steps of values clarification, is very appropriate when a student gives some indication of potentially holding a value. Expressions of attitudes, interests, or aspirations would be such indicators. The *public interview* is just what its name indicates. The student is interviewed by the teacher on a topic of the student's choice. In this interview the teacher may attempt to have the student consider one or more of the seven steps of valuing. *Values voting* requires students to vote, by raising their hands, as to how they feel about certain issues ("Raise your hand if you think it's okay to . . ."). *Values whips* work from questions dealing with one of the seven steps raised by the teacher or students ("What are you proud of?"). Students are given a few moments to think of their response, then the teacher "whips" around the room, getting as many responses as possible.

There are many different types of written values-clarification activities. *Rank ordering,* requires students to rank items either presented to them or self-generated, according to their importance. *Forced-choice activities* ask the students to choose between two alternatives, ("Do you prefer to read a book or go out with friends?"). *Continuum activities* require students to indicate where they perceive themselves to fit between two polar opposites (extremely outgoing–very bashful). Finally, there is the *values sheet* in which students are given a description of some type of situation ("Should a mayor invite industry into an impoverished town even though he realizes the industry will pollute?") and asked to give the decision they would make. Values sheets may or may not provide the students with alternative courses of action. Usually, work with a values sheet is followed by a discussion of the students' choices.

Although there has been a great deal of research done with values clarification, the results of this research have been inconclusive. Although it has been found to be effective in certain specific situations (e.g. drug education) Lockwood (1978) indicates that there is little evidence to suggest that values clarification is completely effective in helping individuals develop values. That is, it is probably better used in conjunction with other valuing activities than alone. In addition, for the elementary teacher implementation of values-clarification activities suffers from the same problem that implementation of Kohlberg's approach entails. Few materials have been developed with the younger child in mind. Most are more appropriate for the older student.

Synthesis: Appropriate Affective Activities for Children _____

As we shall see in the next chapter there are a number of different types of affective activities that can be employed in elementary classrooms. Some will require our students to examine and analyze the elements of a situation—to determine how people are feeling or to infer the values that people appear to hold. Others will entail the children, themselves, working through social problems and deciding upon the most appropriate action in light of what they themselves believe to be important. Regardless of the type of activity we use, the research we have discussed in this chapter suggests that activities that will be appropriate for our students will have two characteristics. On one hand, children will deal with content that is relevant to them. Secondly, they will permit the children to work with this content in ways that maximize the possibility of affective growth. We can synthesize this chapter by examining these two characteristics.

Damon (1977) indicates that children are very willing to (and do) consider problems that are taken from the world of childhood. They are very willing to consider feelings, values, and social dilemmas if they understand the situation and can see its importance to their own lives. But what types of situations will children understand? The research reported in this chapter provides several guidelines. First, they will probably be more attracted to situations they can perceive as having the potential to occur in their own lives. This does not mean that they would have had to actually experience these situations. Rather it implies that the children could see that it might happen to them. Thus, they could deal with such situations as the girl climbing the tree to save a cat when her father has forbidden tree climbing (Selman & Lieberman, 1975) or whether to share a piece of cake with someone who has forgotten his lunch when you've promised the cake to someone else (Krogh, 1985). Students could also consider situations found in their textbooks such as how immigrant children might feel when they have to move and leave their friends. On the other hand, they would probably have difficulty with an activity that required them to choose, from a list of ten people, six people who would be allowed into a fallout shelter. This situation would not be very relevant to their lives.

Then, they would be more apt to identify with situations that contain concepts and issues they perceive to be important. These would include such concepts as sharing (Damon), friendship (Selman), keeping promises (Schuncke and Krogh), and caring (Gilligan). More abstract concepts such as liberty and justice (Kohlberg) would be less understandable and thus less attractive to the children.

Finally, in order to be understood, the situations should be presented as simply as possible to the children. Selman and Lieberman (1975) indicate that one of the problems with Kohlberg's moral dilemmas is their complexity. Children tend to get lost in their details and, essentially, are unable to put these together to see the dilemma; they lose sight of the forest for the trees. The children with whom we work are unable to deal simultaneously with a large number of variables. Each concept, or detail, represents a variable and the more details that are presented in a situation the greater the likelihood of decreased understanding of that situation.

The second characteristic of appropriate affective activities for elementary children is concerned with how children actually engage in these activities. Kohlberg's (1976) idea that movement to higher stages of moral thought is facilitated by interaction can, for our purposes, probably be generalized to all types of affective activities. Children need to be exposed to the thoughts of others in order to grow in their understanding of how people think and feel, and what they believe. Thus, to a great extent, the affective activities we present to our students will be social activities; the children will interact with each other *and* with the teacher.

To a great extent the children with whom we work will have neither the attending skills nor the communication and group dynamics skills to deal with discussions of values and feelings on their own (Schuncke, 1981). Until they develop these skills, their interaction needs to be supervised closely by the teacher. This does not mean that the teacher tells them what to think about a situation. It simply means that the teacher, through the judicious use of questions, structures the interaction among the students so that the activity moves forward. Strategies for doing this will be found in the next chapter.

Teachers, of course, can be part of the actual interaction, but care must be taken in how this is done. It is probably not an overgeneralization (at least from my own teaching experience) to say that students often take what the teacher says as dogma. The teacher's sharing in an interaction could potentially forestall any other sharing—the teacher said it, that's it! To ensure that this doesn't occur it is wise to let the students know that all ideas about a situation are worthy of consideration and yours is only one of them. It is also wise to completely share the reasoning behind your idea.

Preoperational and concrete operational children function best in relatively concrete learning situations. In the present context this means that more appropriate activities will be ones that in some way foster active involvement on the part of the students. One type of activity to do this is role playing, with students actually working with different situations. Role play, to be discussed fully in the next chapter, has been used with values clarification, the consideration of moral dilemmas, and situations designed to enhance justice reasoning and perspective-taking abilities (Peterson and McNamee, 1977; Krogh, 1984). A second way to involve students is through the use of visual referents, something the children have seen, or are seeing, to which they can refer during the activity. Examples of such visual referents would be the filmstrips used by Selman and Lieberman (1976) and the graphic illustrations of children's solutions to social problems devised by Schuncke and Krogh (1983). These illustrations are simple line drawings depicting both alternative solutions to the problems and their consequences.

As we have seen in the research discussed in this chapter, many of the activities utilized to develop various affective capabilities work within a decision-making format. Children are presented with a dilemma and are then asked to determine a resolution to it. As we indicated in previous chapters, the children with whom we will be working will not have an understanding of the decision-making process. Without adult assistance they will tend to choose what they perceive to be the most attractive alternative—with little consideration of other alternatives or of the consequences of the alternative they have selected. Therefore, it is important for the teacher to provide that assistance. Through appropriate questions the teacher can help the students move systematically, and thoroughly, through the process.

Springboards to Discussion

1. In this chapter we have indicated that the teaching of values in the schools is a red flag to some people. Suppose you decide to work with your students on the development of a specific affective capability such as justice reasoning or perspective taking. Now you will need to apprise your students' parents of your plans. Write a letter to them explaining what you will be doing. Before you write the letter try to think of any concerns that they might have that you can address in the letter.
2. Read Chapter 8, "Moral Education," in *Caring* (Noddings, 1984), which discusses how the idea and practice of caring can be brought into the school. Then, evaluate a school in terms of the extent to which Noddings's ideas are in evidence. If there is little evidence of the ideas being implemented, suggest how they might be put into practice.
3. Evaluate a textbook for a given grade in terms of affect. Determine the extent to which there are opportunities to develop the capabilities discussed in this chapter. Then, indicate how the text might be supplemented; for example, what activities you might introduce.

References

BLOOM, BENJAMIN S. et al. (eds.). *Taxonomy of Educational Objectives: Handbook I: The Cognitive Domain.* New York: David McKay, 1956.

CASTEEL, J. DOYLE. *Learning to Think and Choose.* Santa Monica: Goodyear, 1978.

DAMON, WILLIAM. *The Social World of the Child.* San Francisco: Jossey Bass, 1977.

DAMON, WILLIAM. "Patterns of Change in Children is Social Reasoning: A Two-Year Longitudinal Study," *Child Development,* vol. 51 (1980), pp. 1010–17.

DAMON, WILLIAM. *Social and Personality Development.* New York: W. W. Norton, 1983.

FRAENKEL, JACK. *How to Teach about Values.* Englewood Cliffs, NJ: Prentice Hall, 1977.

GALBRAITH, RONALD, AND JONES, THOMAS. *Moral Reasoning.* Anoka, WI: Greenhaven Press, 1976.

GILLIGAN, CAROL. *In a Different Voice: Psychological Theory and Women's Development.* Cambridge: Harvard University Press, 1982.

GOW, KATHLEEN M. *Yes, Virginia, There is Right and Wrong!* Toronto: John Wiley and Sons Canada, Limited, 1980.

KOHLBERG, LAWRENCE. "Moral Stages and Moralization," in Thomas Lickona (ed.), *Moral Development and Behavior*. New York: Holt, Rinehart and Winston, 1976.

KOHLBERG, LAWRENCE. "The Cognitive-Developmental Approach to Moral Education," in David Purpel and Kevin Ryan (eds.), *Moral Education . . . It Comes with the Territory*. Berkeley: McCutchan, 1976a.

KRATHWOHL, DAVID R., BLOOM BENJAMIN S., AND MASIA, BERTRAM B. *Taxonomy of Educational Objectives: The Classification of Educational Goals: Handbook II: Affective Domain*. New York: David McKay, 1964.

KROGH, SUZANNE. "Encouraging Positive Justice Reasoning and Perspective-Taking Skills: Two Educational Interventions," *Journal of Moral Education*, Vol. 14 (May 1985), pp. 102–110.

KROGH, SUZANNE, AND LAMME, LINDA. " 'But What about Sharing?' Children's Literature and Moral Development," *Young Children*, 40 (May 1985), pp. 48–51.

LOCKWOOD, ALAN L. "The Effects of Values Clarification and Moral Development Curricula on School-Age Subjects: A Critical Review of the Recent Research." *Review of Educational Research* Vol. 48 (Summer 1978), pp. 325–364.

National Council for the Social Studies. *Revision of the NCSS Social Studies Curriculum Guidelines*. Washington, D.C.: National Council for the Social Studies, 1979.

NODDINGS, NEL. *Caring*. Berkeley: University of California Press, 1984.

PETERSON, JUDITH, AND McNAMEE, SHARIE. "Moral Reasoning and Role-Taking in Young Children Verbally and Behaviorally Assessed," paper presented at the Annual Meeting of the American Psychological Association. San Francisco, 1977.

PIAGET, JEAN. *The Moral Judgment of the Child*. New York: The Free Press, 1965.

RATHS, JAMES, HARMON, MERRILL, AND SIMON, SIDNEY. *Values and Teaching*. Columbus: Charles E. Merrill, 1966.

SCHUNCKE, GEORGE. "Valuing in the Elementary Classroom: Dealing with the Problems," *The Social Studies*, Vol. 72 (May/June, 1981), pp. 137–141.

SCHUNCKE, GEORGE, AND KROGH, SUZANNE. *Helping Children Choose*. Glenview: Scott, Foresman, 1983.

SELMAN, ROBERT L. "Social-Cognitive Understanding," in Thomas Lickona (ed.), *Moral Development and Behavior*. New York: Holt, Rinehart and Winston, 1976.

SELMAN, ROBERT L. *The Growth of Interpersonal Understanding*. New York: Academic Press, 1980.

SELMAN, ROBERT AND LIEBERMAN, MARCUS. "Moral Education in Primary Grades: An Evaluation of a Developmental Curriculum," *Journal of Educational Psychology*, Vol. 67, No. 5 (1975), pp. 712–716.

SIMON, S., HOWE, LELAND, AND KIRSCHENBAUM, HOWARD. *Values Clarification*. New York: Hart, 1972.

9

Affective Activities for the Elementary Classroom

CHAPTER OBJECTIVES

After reading this chapter you should be able to:

1. Describe a strategy for helping children to become aware of people's feelings in a given situation.

2. Describe a strategy for helping children to analyze values that are implicit in given situations.

3. Discuss appropriate values issues to be used with children.

4. Delineate two strategies that can be employed to help children engage in valuing:
- Role play.
- Structured discussion.

5. Describe a strategy for helping children deal with controversial issues.

6. Demonstrate how affective goals can be included in the planning process.

In this chapter we will examine some teaching strategies and resources that can be utilized to help our students attain affective objectives. We won't attempt to match the activities to one or more of the specific objectives described by Krathwohl, Bloom, and Masia (1964) because all of the strategies tend to require that the student meet several of the objectives as they move through the activity. For example, one of the activities we'll consider is designed to help children analyze what people's values are in given situations. In order to complete this activity successfully students need to examine what has occurred in a situation (receiving); make inferences about the values people are demonstrating (responding); and examine how they would feel about a similar situation (valuing). As you read about the activities, however, you may wish to evaluate them in terms of how they relate to the various affective objectives as discussed in the previous chapter.

The activities we will consider in this chapter fall into two categories: those that allow the children to examine and evaluate the affective behavior of others and those in which the children actively engage in social decision making and valuing. One activity we will consider in the former category will help children to determine how people feel in a specific situation. Another activity will help them to analyze the values held by others and reflect on how these values might relate to their own lives. In the second category we will look at two strategies by which we can help children deal with social

dilemmas that occur in their own personal lives while simultaneously determining what is important to them. We will also examine a strategy for
helping them deal with dilemmas that are societal rather than interpersonal in nature. Use of all of these strategies in the classroom will facilitate
the development of the affective capabilities—such as perspective taking,
justice reasoning, moral reasoning, and valuing—discussed in the previous
chapter. We will synthesize this chapter by examining how these, and other,
affective activities might be included in your curriculum.

The activities with which we will be dealing in this chapter are ones we
can plan for in our curriculum. Unfortunately, the scope of this book pre-
cludes a consideration of the many unplanned ways in which affective elements make their way into the school day; how, for example, our behavior
conveys values to students or how textbooks may be tacitly presenting specific values. You, however, can do this to some extent. Although we will
discuss specific strategies and activities in terms of the elementary child,
they are also applicable to adults. You may wish to use them in examining
what is occurring in different situations in your life and in deciding what
you would prefer to have occur.

Examining Feelings and Values _____

One category of affective goals we have for social studies can be best described as concerned with the development of a sensitivity to others. We want
children to realize how others think and feel, and attempt to understand why
they might be thinking and feeling that way. In the last chapter we indicated
that the full attainment of this goal of human sensitivity is something that
will not occur automatically; it is tied to the development of certain capabilities. This development, in turn, requires that students be exposed to different
ideas about how and why people think and feel as they do.

The late Hilda Taba and her associates at San Francisco State College
developed two strategies that can be used in elementary classrooms for
providing this exposure to the thoughts and feelings of others. These
strategies—called *exploring feelings* and *analyzing values*—were developed
as part of the Contra Costa County Curriculum Project, which was later
published as the Taba Social Science Series (Addison-Wesley, 1972). The
format that these strategies take is a series of questions that are asked by
the teacher about some situation with which the students are familiar. (The
questions used in these strategies, incidentally, were derived from observations of teachers working in classrooms.) The strategies can be employed
both with situations that have occurred in the students' own lives as well as
with those presented as part of course content, such as might be found in a
student's text.

In the examination of the strategies that follows we will directly quote
the questions enumerated by Taba and her associates. When you try the
strategies initially with your students you may wish to use the same wording. Our experience has shown, though, that the wording can be revised
somewhat to suit an individual teacher and class style. As long as the

intent of the original question is not lost, it appears that the strategy will be effective.

Exploring Feelings

Consider the following interaction that occurred while I was doing research concerned with organizational structures in classrooms:

> One part of the interview we had with every teacher was concerned with how the teacher organized his or her students for reading instruction. Mrs. X indicated that she used three reading groups composed of high, average, and low readers. We then talked about the names of the groups—the "Airplanes," "Jets," and "Rockets." When I asked her how she decided on the groups' names, she indicated that this was done cooperatively with her students: "I asked them to name something fast," she said, "and they said 'airplanes.' " "Then, I said, 'Okay, name something faster than airplanes,' and they said 'Jets'." "After that I asked them if they could possibly think of something faster than a jet and they said 'rockets . . .' "

Reflect for a moment. How do you think the groups felt about their names? What about the Rockets? And how about the Airplanes? Suppose you were an Airplane, how would you feel? Have you ever been an Airplane, so to speak? If you haven't been, have you ever been in a situation, say a party, where you thought that people didn't think that teaching was a good, or challenging, career? How did you feel? Why did you feel that way?

If you considered all of these questions you've basically gone through the process of exploring feelings. You've done it alone and have your own thoughts. If we had done this in some type of group setting you would have had the opportunity to consider how other people feel about the group names and, possibly, about being thought of as airplanes.

There are several steps involved in exploring feelings. First, of course, students need to be aware of the situation wherein feelings are involved. They might be very conscious of this situation, or it may be necessary for the teacher to bring it to the children's attention, making certain that they are thoroughly aware of what has occurred. Following this there is an exploration of the feelings that might arise as a result of the situation—from the perspective of the most central figure, the individual whose feelings should be most obvious; and from the perspective of others who are involved. Finally, the situation is personalized and individuals are asked to reflect upon whether they have ever been in the type of situation being discussed. They are also asked to consider how they felt and reasons why they felt as they did.

Taba and her associates (1971) have listed the steps necessary for completion of this strategy in terms of the questions asked by the teacher, the types of responses expected from the students, and the follow-through tasks required of the teacher. These are illustrated in Table 9.1.

There are two things that the teacher needs to keep in mind as this strategy is utilized in the classroom. First, an attempt should be made to elicit as many ideas about feelings as possible from the students. This will provide students with a wide range of thoughts and, potentially expose them to perspectives that may be more sophisticated than their own. Second, a

TABLE 9.1 Exploring Feelings

Students are presented with a situation involving emotional reactions on the part of one or more persons. The teaching strategy consists of asking the following questions, usually in this order.*

Teacher	Student	Teacher Follow Through
What happened?	Restates facts.	Sees that all facts are given and agreed upon. If students make inferences, asks that they be set aside temporarily.
How do you think . . . felt?[†]	Makes inference as to feelings.	Accepts inference.
Why do you think he would feel that way?	Explains.	Seeks clarification, if necessary.
Who has a different idea about how he felt?	Makes alternative inferences and explanations.	Seeks variety, if necessary. Asks for reasons, if necessary.
How did . . . (other persons in the situation) feel?	States inference about the feelings of additional persons.	Seeks clarification, if necessary. Encourages students to consider how other people in the situation felt.
Have you ever had something like this happen to you?[‡]	Describes similar event in his own life.	Ensures description of event.
How did you feel?[†]	Describes his feelings, may re-experience emotions.	Seeks clarification, if necessary. Provides support if necessary.
Why do you think you felt that way?	Offers explanation. Attempts to relate his feelings to events he has recalled.	Asks additional questions, if necessary, to get beyond stereotyped or superficial explanation.

* Sometimes only certain of the questions are asked. The teacher should omit questions if students have answered them spontaneously.
[†]These questions are repeated in sequence several times in order to obtain a variety of inferences and fewer personal experiences.
[‡]If students have difficulty responding, you may wish to ask, "If this should happen to you, how do you think you would feel?" or "Has something like this happened to someone you know?" Another useful device is for the teacher to describe such an event in his own life.

Source: Hilda Taba, Mary Durkin, Jack Fraenkel, and Anthony McNaughton. *A Teacher's Handbook to Elementary Social Studies: An Inductive Approach.* © 1971 by Addison-Wesley Publishing Company, Inc. Reprinted with permission of Random House, Inc.

discussion of feelings—especially the children's own—has the potential for overemotional involvement on the part of some students. Taba and her associates indicate that it is important to conduct the discussion in a relaxed atmosphere and be alert to the possibility of overly anxious reactions (Taba et al., 1971, p. 80).

It is not difficult to see how this strategy could be employed in considering the feelings present in situations that crop up in our students' day-to-day lives. Disagreements on the playground, name calling, the loss of a pet, and many other happenings all provide springboards for the discussion of feelings. The discussions, however, should not be restricted to only these types of episodes. As we said earlier, this strategy can also be employed in considering textual content with which the children are dealing.

Because of the nature of the social studies—their emphasis on the human experience—it is not unreasonable to expect that content will suggest situations in which feelings and emotions are involved. Some of this content can be exploited for both its conceptual understanding and its affect. Thus, for example, a topic dealing with neighborhoods might lend itself to the children's considering how it might feel to be new in a neighborhood. In looking at the history of a given community or state the focus might be on the feelings of a member of a group who was displaced in the name of progress; for example, a Cherokee child who followed the Trail of Tears or a child whose family was moved from their neighborhood in the name of urban renewal.

It is not possible to cite examples of all the different topics that would lend themselves to a consideration of feelings. We can, however, provide a guideline for the selection of appropriate content. In the *exploring feelings* strategy emphasis is placed on having the children examine their own feelings in relation to a situation they potentially could experience. This personal experience should parallel the situation discussed initially. Therefore, in evaluating content for its appropriateness to an examination of feelings, we will need to search for parallel instances that might occur in our students' lives. Being new in a neighborhood, for example, is paralleled by being new in a school, a club, and so on. Similarly, being displaced in the name of progress might have its real-life complement in a child's moving from one house to another, an occurrence that many students have experienced.

Values Analysis

In an interesting monograph describing research done with her first grade students, Barbara Porro (1981) indicates some classroom activities and materials that are unwittingly quite value laden. As you examine some of these try to determine the values being conveyed.

1. The career posters in the classroom show these occupations: fireman (male), policeman (male), doctor (male), carpenter (male), nurse (female), and librarian (female).
2. Here are two examples of work problems in the math textbook: (a) Bobby and Allen are building a treehouse. Allen had a board 13 feet long. He sawed off a 6-foot piece. How long was the other piece? (b) Nancy and Mary are making cookies. If they bake 12 cookies on one cookie sheet, how many cookies can they bake on 2 cookie sheets?
3. A parent is going to do a sewing project with the class. She wants to offer the children a choice between making a marble bag or a stuffed doll.
4. The class is going to present a play: Boys are assigned to make scenery while girls are given the job of sewing costumes.

It is obvious that these activities and materials differentiate between roles for females and males. Think for a second. Why do you suppose that they do this? If a teacher saw these as appropriate for his or her classroom, what inferences could you make about what that teacher felt was important?

In her monograph, which is entitled *Non-Sexist Elementary Education,*

Porro indicated that when given the opportunity for free activities, her female students tended to remain in the classroom and engage in quiet activities while males went outside to engage in more physical activities. Suppose this happened with your class? Would you do something about it? If you did, what would it be? Why? Does your response to this situation say anything about what *you* think is important? (Porro, by the way, felt that it was important for students to see that they were capable of all kinds of activities and that they had options.)

The strategy for analyzing values works from the assumption that many of the things that people do and say will convey their values to some extent. This is especially true in decision-making situations where deliberate consideration is given to values as we choose alternatives. It can also be true, however, when we choose how to act in a situation with no conscious reference to what we believe to be important. Take the activities and materials that were presented to give you an experience with values analysis. It would be a rare teacher who would choose to use these specifically stereotypical sex roles; they would be used for other purposes. Yet, they tacitly convey values.

TABLE 9.2 Analyzing Values

Students are asked to recall certain behaviors and to make inferences as to what values are involved, and how they differ from the values of others involved in analogous situations.*

Teacher	Student	Teacher Follow Through
What did they do . . . (e.g., to take care of their tools?)	Describes behavior.	Sees that description is complete and accurate.
What do you think were their reasons for doing/saying what they did?	States inferences.	Accepts. Seeks clarification, if necessary.
What do these reasons tell you about what is important to them?†	States inferences regarding values.	Restates or asks additional questions to ensure focus on values.
If you . . . (teacher specifies similar situation directly related to student, e.g., "If you accidentally tore a page in someone else's book") what would you do? Why?‡	States behavior and gives explanation.	Accepts, may seek clarification.
What does this show about what *you* think is important?	States inferences about his own values.	Accepts. Seeks clarification, if necessary.
What differences do you see in what all these people think is important?	Makes comparisons.	Ensures that all values identified are compared.

* Sometimes all questions are not asked. However, the question exploring the students' own values should *not* be omitted.
† This sequence is repeated for each group or person whose values are to be analyzed. Each group is specified by the teacher and has been previously studied.
‡ This sequence is repeated in order to get reactions from several students.

Source: from Hilda Taba, Mary Durkin, Jack Fraenkel, and Anthony McNaughton , *A Teachers Handbook to Elementary Social Studies: An Inductive Approach.* © 1971 by Addison-Wesley Publishing Company, Inc. Reprinted with permission of Random House, Inc.

Value analysis allows us to make inferences about people's values based on their behavior.

In using this strategy with students we first make them aware of the specific behavior that will be analyzed. Then we ask them to suggest underlying reasons for this behavior, why a person did what he or she did. Based on these reasons we next ask them to make inferences about the person's values, what the behavior suggests in terms of what the person thinks is important. Value analysis does not end with the individual making inferences only about the values of others. An opportunity is given for the student to consider what his or her own values might be in a situation similar to the one analyzed.

As with the *exploring feelings* strategy, Taba and her associates have outlined the *analyzing values* strategy in terms of questions asked by the teacher, student responses, and ways in which the teacher insures that each step has been thoroughly covered. Table 9.2 illustrates this.

The guidelines for choosing situations in which value analysis may be used are the same as those discussed with the exploration of feelings strategy. When appropriate it can be applied to data found in textbooks. It can also be used with other content—the children's own personal experiences as well as other instances of human behavior that they observe. It would also be quite appropriate in helping them understand messages conveyed by the various media such as advertisements found on television and in print, letters to the editor, and so on. The major criterion for deciding whether it would be appropriate to use this strategy would be the relevance of the value being conveyed to the children's own lives. That is, before using this strategy it would be necessary to ask ourselves: (1) would they understand what the value being conveyed is and (2) can we use this situation to help them understand parallel values issues in their own lives?

Summing Up

An examination of these strategies shows that the basic approach taken with both is very similar and requires three things:

1. That the students be aware of behavior that occurred in a specific situation.
2. That the students make inferences about this behavior—either in terms of its effects on people (exploring feelings) or why it occurred (analyzing values).
3. That the students examine the situation in relation to their own lives— how they felt or what they believed to be important in similar situations.

When we introduced these strategies we indicated that the questions developed by Taba and her associates could be modified as long as their intent was kept in mind. In using these strategies with both children and adults we have found it possible to keep this intent in mind by remembering these three stages of the strategies.

Interpersonal Problem Solving and Valuing ──────────────

There is a close relationship between the decisions we make and the values we hold. We cannot thoughtfully choose a course of action without resorting to a consideration of what is important to us. Further, the actual process of decision making often requires us to clarify in our own minds the extent to which we value something; in making a choice we sometimes encounter value conflicts and need to determine what is more (or most) important to us.

The two strategies we will be considering in this section—role play and structured discussion—are based on this relationship between decision making and values. They have been designed to give children opportunities to consider their own values in relation to social problems and to deal with values conflicts when they occur. Their use in the classroom will provide requisite experiences for them to do these things independently, as children and as adults.

One of the criticisms of the two most common strategies to dealing with values in the classroom, *values clarification* and *moral reasoning*, is that the situations they present are often not really relevant to elementary children (Schuncke, 1981). These students can't clearly make the connection between the situation and their own lives. We know, from Damon's (1977) work that they need to make this connection for the valuing acitivity to be successful. The key to having any valuing strategies work is to use it in connection with issues that children, not adults, see as important. Research indicates a number of such issues as being pertinent to children. These include telling the truth, keeping promises, respecting property, sharing, friendship, obeying rules, and obeying authority (Schuncke and Krogh, 1982). In addition, Gilligan's work (1982), although not directed at children, suggests that caring and responsibility are also important issues.

These issues can provide the content for the social problems we present to children. But how do we present these problems? Here, there appears to be consensus. All of the researchers we have identified as working with affective development, plus such educators as the Shaftels (1982) who have dealt with interpersonal problem solving in the elementary school, have found the dilemma to be an appropriate context. Usually, this dilemma is presented as an open-ended story. In this story (which can have more than one or two endings) two or more issues, such as keeping a promise and sharing, come into conflict and must be resolved. The following is an example of such a story.

Who Takes the Cake?

Barbara was singing as she packed her lunch for the bike ride and picnic. She just knew she was going to have a good time with her friends. First she made herself a peanut butter and honey sandwich. That was her favorite kind. Then she washed and dried a very red apple and put it into the bag along with the sandwich. Finally, Barbara cut two big pieces of chocolate cake and packed them in also. She wasn't planning to eat both those pieces of cake. One was for her friend Ginny, who was going on the bike ride, too. Ginny had helped Barbara and her mom bake the cake last night. Barbara had promised Ginny that she'd put an extra piece of cake in for her.

Barbara put her lunch and some orange juice in her backpack, got on her bike, and headed down to Ginny's house. "Have you got the cake?" Ginny asked.

"Of course I do," Barbara answered. "I promised, didn't I?"

Next they went by Jeff's house to pick him up, and finally all three of them stopped by Doug's. There were four of them, Barbara, Ginny, Jeff, and Doug, riding their bikes to the park on the other side of town. When they got there, the kids decided they weren't hungry yet, so they played on the swings and slides for a while. Then they played a couple of games, and by that time they were all hungry and thirsty.

The four kids sat under a big oak tree and opened their packs. For a minute it was very quiet while everyone got out food.

Then Doug said, "Oh, no! I can't believe I did it!"

"Did what?" the others said, all together.

"Forgot my lunch," Doug groaned.

"Hey, that's okay," Jeff said. "I brought an extra half sandwich just in case I was real hungry. You can have that."

"Gee, thanks," Doug said.

Ginny reached in her bag. "I brought a whole bunch of raisins," she said. "I don't need them all."

Barbara looked in her bag. You know what she had, don't you? Just a sandwich and an apple, and, yes, two pieces of cake. She knew she'd promised one piece to Ginny, but here was Doug without any lunch. She figured Ginny wouldn't mind.

"Well, Doug," Barbara said. "I have two pieces of cake. I guess you could have one if Ginny wouldn't mind.

Ginny looked at her. "Hey, you promised!" she said. Barbara could see that she was getting angry. "I helped make that cake, and you promised. You already have enough to eat, don't you, Doug?"

Doug looked kind of embarrassed. "Well, not really," he said.

Barbara didn't know what to do next. Doug was hungry and wanted the cake. But she'd promised Ginny, hadn't she? Can you help her deicde?*

Role Playing

Role playing, also called *sociodrama,* is an activity in which students assume the roles of individuals in dilemma situations and act out proposed solutions to the problem. During the role-playing session those children who have not been given roles act as observers and are given specific things for which they should watch. Role playing is especially appropriate to the elementary school because it allows children to engage in problem solving and learn by actually doing. It allows them to be active participants in the learning situation.

As we will be discussing it here, role playing can be used to help children consider social problems, work them through, and examine their values in relation to a given situation. It is not intended to be a therapeutic instru-

*From *Helping Children Choose* by George M. Schuncke and Suzanne Lowell Krogh. Copyright © 1983 by Scott, Foresman and Company. Reprinted by permission.

ment to help children deal with psychological problems. When used in this manner, role play becomes *psychodrama* and should be used only by well-trained mental health professionals.

Much has been written about the curricular applications of role play. Since space does not allow us as in-depth a discussion of this strategy as some of you might prefer, three resources that do provide a detailed discussion of how role play might be used in the classroom can be suggested. These are Fannie and George Shaftel's *Role Playing in the Curriculum* (1982); Schuncke and Krogh's *Helping Children Choose* (1983); and Chesler and Fox's *Role Playing Methods in the Classroom* (1966). Our discussion attempts to incorporate the cogent points presented in each of these resources.

In discussing the type of open-ended story to be used with role playing we provided "Who Takes the Cake?" as an example. This story deals with the problem of who should get the extra piece of cake that Barbara packed—Ginny, to whom she had promised it, or Doug, who had forgotten his lunch. We can continue to use this story as an example as we discuss the three-step approach to role playing.

The Warm-Up. In their book, *Role Playing in the Curriculum*, the Shaftels (1982) list eight activities that occur during role playing. The first four of these constitute the warm-up as we are discussing it. They are

1. "Warming up" the group (problem confrontation).
2. Selecting the participants (role players).
3. Preparing the audience to participate as observers.
4. Setting the stage.

In helping students confront a social problem it is initially necessary to insure that they are ready to do so. They must be interested in the type of problem situation that will be presented and willing to attend to it. Therefore, before actually presenting the problem it is wise to prepare the children for listening. Schuncke and Krogh (1983) suggest three different ways of doing this, all of which refer to the general topic the open-ended story will be dealing. They suggest: (1) Using a concrete object that will be featured in the story. If the story dealt with, say, a toy or a ball, the teacher might have one of these available and briefly discuss it with the children. (2) Sharing the teacher's experiences dealing with the context of the story. For example, in "Who Takes the Cake?" the teacher might talk about cooking with a friend. (3) Eliciting children's experiences with aspects of the story to which they can identify. With our problem story these experiences might be ones where the children have forgotten their lunches.

In preparing children to listen, the specific problem is not discussed; instead the general situation is considered. This part of the warm-up is very brief and culminates with the teacher inviting the children to listen to the story which is about a similar situation.

Following this the actual problem is presented, either being read or told by the teacher. It ends with an open-ended question in which the children are asked to pose solutions to the problem. In "Who Takes the Cake?" the teacher would ask, "Can you help Barbara decide?"

Usually, there are a number of responses to the culminating question of the story, and the teacher's job is to decide the order in which these solutions will be enacted. It is common practice to initially work with those that the teacher perceives to have socially negative consequences, moving to those that are more socially acceptable. Thus, in a role-play session we observed, the children suggested three solutions to Barbara's problem: (1) Give Ginny's cake to Doug; (2) Give Barbara's own cake to Doug; and (3) Give the cake to Ginny, but tell her how selfish she was being. The teacher in this case decided to work with the third solution first.

Once this decision has been made, the teacher's job is to select the individuals to take the various roles. Usually the student who suggested the solution is asked to take the major role and volunteers are chosen for the other roles. At times, the teacher might ask the students who have not volunteered to take a role. The Shaftels (1982) indicate, however, that the teacher should not allow students to volunteer other children for roles.

There are times when no solutions are suggested by the students. At this point the teacher's approach would be to help the students work to a solution from the perspective of the characters in the dilemma. One way to do this is for the teacher to select students to take the roles of individuals in the story, role play the story, and then at the dilemma point, ask the students what they think will happen next. Or, the teacher might also ask the students to consider what the different characters are like and, based on their judgment, how they would act in the given situation. In "Who Takes the Cake?," for example, a question as to Barbara's character might elicit the response that she's selfish. Based on this response the teacher could then ask "How would a selfish person act here?" to get a solution to the dilemma.

Once a line of action has been chosen and individuals selected to play the roles of the different characters, attention is given to students who will not be actors. They need to be prepared to gather data through observation; being told by the teacher what to look for in the situation. Schuncke and Krogh (1983) suggest that, for younger students, only one type of observation task be given. That is, the observers may be told to look for the feelings of the different individuals involved. For instance, in "Who Takes the Cake?" some children can be asked to observe Ginny, others Barbara, others Doug, and so on. With upper grade students more than one task might be given. Some children might be asked to observe for feelings while others would be instructed to look for consequences.

The last stage of the warm-up is concerned with settling the players into their roles. The teacher's task is to help the students become the character as much as possible. At this point, the players are referred to by the character names and they are given the opportunity to discuss briefly how they are feeling. The teacher might also review with the students the line of action that has been suggested and where the action is occurring. At the conclusion of this stage the students are ready for role play.

The warm-up for role play should proceed at a relatively brisk pace, and there should be little detailed discussion of the problem. The purpose of role play is action problem-solving and the teacher's goal should be to move to this action as quickly as possible. The warm-up will be very teacher-directed in order to insure that this occurs.

The Action Period. The fifth step of the role-playing process, as described by the Shaftels (1982) is *the enactment,* wherein children spontaneously act out the solutions they have suggested. Unlike the warm-up there is little or no teacher involvement; the teacher steps out of the picture and the focus is on the action.

The only major task that the teacher has during the action period is determining when the action should be stopped. Schuncke and Krogh (1983) suggest that there are several indicators that can be employed in making this decision. The most obvious of these is that the action has gone as far as it can go; the children have carried out an alternative to its logical conclusion. If this is not perceived by the teacher it usually becomes obvious as the children either repeat themselves or simply stop what they are doing. Other indicators include the action becoming too physical (or too silly) or the children losing sight of the problem at hand. While both of these require that the action be stopped, the latter may also require that the teacher warm-up the students again, re-eliciting the line of action which was suggested earlier.

The Debriefing. There are actually two types of debriefings that occur in role playing. One is concerned with discussing and evaluating the various enactments that are *part* of the role-play session. The other deals with the *whole* session. Because both of these are important to insuring a productive role-play session, we'll consider them separately.

There are two reasons for the debriefing of each enactment. The first of these is to obtain the students' perception of what occurred, to essentially have the students articulate what they see as the consequences of a given line of action. To do this the teacher, having stopped the action, would first elicit the role-players' impressions. This might be done by first asking each actor to convey his or her feelings about the situation. Then they might be asked to give their thoughts on the effectiveness of the action from their points of view. Following the debriefing of the actors the teacher would turn to the observers and elicit their reactions. They might be reminded of the observation tasks they were given prior to the action period and asked to report on what they saw in relation to these tasks. The teacher should not restrict the discussion to these topics only, however. The children should be encouraged to report on any perceptions that they might have.

The second reason for the debriefing of the single enactment is to decide upon the direction the role-play will take. As the students discuss their perceptions of what they have seen, they may come to one of two conclusions. First, they might feel that all of the consequences of a given alternative have been presented in the enactment and that a logical closure has been attained. In this case, the teacher would move to choosing another solution to be role played and move to a new warm-up. On the other hand, the children might perceive other actions that could result as a consquence of the action they observed. Thus, they would be suggesting a subsequent enactment and the teacher's job would be to warm-up the players again, select new players if necessary, and reprepare the observers. This debriefing corresponds to the Shaftel's sixth and seventh steps of the role playing process: *discussing and evaluating the enactment* and *further enactments.* The *debriefing of the whole* role play occurs when all of the enactments have been completed. It is a period in which evaluation of all of the proposed solutions occurs. It is a time when values conflicts may be considered. It is also a time when the children can be helped to consider what is important to them. This is the Shaftel's eighth step: *sharing and generalizing.*

This debriefing may begin with a brief review of what occurred in the various enactments. The teacher and students quickly enumerate the alternatives and their consequences. Next, the students are asked to examine and compare all of the enactments. Using a question such as, "Which solution do you think worked best?" the teacher helps the students evaluate the appropriateness of the different solutions. As the students do this they can be asked to cite reasons for their preference, why they perceived one line of action to be more appropriate than another. This allows different ideas about what different children perceive to be important to be shared.

Schuncke and Krogh (1983) indicate that this debriefing should be as nonthreatening as possible to the children. They indicate that children should not be required to vote on an appropriate solution because individuals may be tacitly coerced into affirming something to be important that they, in reality, don't believe to be so. They also suggest that children not be required to state what they believe, if they choose not to, or if the teacher feels that such a statement could be detrimental to an individual child's relationship with his or her peers. Instead of requiring that the child make a potentially harmful public affirmation, the teacher can encourage the child to discuss the situation privately with the teacher or with his or her parents.

During both of the types of debriefing (part and whole) the teacher again assumes a directive, facilitative role. The role is directive in that it is the teacher's job to keep the discussion going. This is primarily done through the use of open-ended questions such as, "What will happen next?" or, "Of every idea we've seen, which one do you think worked?" It is facilitative in that, in keeping the discussion going, the teacher attempts to insure that it is the pupil's thoughts that are brought forward for consideration, not his or her own.

Structured Discussion

One of the criticisms directed toward the various approaches to social problem solving and valuing is their reliance on pupil discussion in small groups. Fraenkel (1977) indicates that this does not work well with younger children because they do not possess, to any great extent, the group-process and communication skills necessary for these groups to function effectively and complete the task at hand.

Our experiences indicate that this criticism is valid for the most part when the groups are given dilemmas to work through independently. It is possible, however, to discuss social problems and value dilemmas in the elementary classroom if this discussion is led by the teacher, and is conducted in a manner that is appropriate to the levels of development of the students. *Structured discussion,* described by Schuncke and Krogh (1983) is a strategy that permits this to be done. The term *structure* is used to designate the set pattern of activities in which the students engage as they go through this strategy. This pattern is based on the decision-making process in its simplest form: they first encounter a decision to be made; then suggest alternative solutions and their consequences; and finally choose. The structure of the discussion should not be confused with its content. The students work with their own ideas. The teacher structures *how* the students think, not *what* they think.

The Warm-up. The warm-up for the structured discussion entails two activities on the teacher's part: preparing the students to encounter a social decision situation and sharing that situation with them. With one possible exception, both are done exactly as they are done with role play. In preparing the students to listen the teacher discusses the general context of the problem, or some central element with which the problem story will be concerned. Here a concrete object—such as a ball or a toy—might be employed as a springboard. With some stories the teacher might share a personal experience that is generally related to the experience the characters in the story will have. Or the teacher might wish to elicit the children's own experiences with problems similar to that to be encountered, such as having a toy that someone broke. Although the problem context might be identified in this beginning part of the warm-up, no attempts are made to describe solutions. This will occur with the specific problem, itself, during the action period.

The one difference in procedures employed during the warm-up for structured discussion may occur during the preparation for listening. As a final step before sharing the story, the teacher might wish to introduce the characters, as well as any objects important to the story, in the form of pictures. With the story, "Who Takes the Cake?," for example, the teacher would have pictures of two girls, two boys and a piece of cake. The story would be introduced by the teacher identifying each picture separately, by a character name, indicating that they had a problem concerning a piece of cake (while showing the cake picture), and asking the students to listen to the problem to see if they can come up with a solution.

These pictures need not be elaborate; they might be magazine cut-outs or simple line drawings on the chalkboard. Their use is especially appropriate with younger children, however, because these pictures provide a visual referent, something concrete to which the children can identify. Thus, although the words spoken in the story are heard only for as long as they are uttered (a very short time), the pictures allow the situation to remain concrete.

The warm-up ends with the teacher relating the social decision problem to the student.

The Action Period. The greatest area of differentiation between role play and structured discussion occurs during the action period. Whereas the former requires that the student suggest alternative solutions and then act them out, these solutions are considered only through discussion in the latter.

There are two different orders in which alternatives and consequences may be considered during the discussions, orders that parallel the ways adults actually engage in decision making. The first is one in which the consequences for each alternative are generated as that alternative is suggested. In the structured discussion the children would be asked to supply a solution to the dilemma and, then, to indicate what they perceive the resulting consequences of that solution. Once this has been done, another solution would be elicited. Of course, there is no restriction on the children adding consequences to alternatives they have previously considered. The second order for considering alternatives is a very systematic one. The children are first asked to generate as many alternatives as possible and, then, to supply the consequences for each alternative. When the structured discussion is done in this way it is possible to group alternatives ("Are some of these similar?") to avoid redundancy. It is also possible to arrange them in the sequence with which they will be considered.

Both of these ways of considering alternatives and consequences can be used with children at any grade level. Both provide the children with a model that can be used in decision making. We have found, however, that younger children tend to prefer the first, each alternative and its consequences, order. They appear to want to see their solutions carried through immediately.

As we noted earlier, the spoken word tends to be fleeting and there is a good possibility that much of the discussion may be forgotten if the children are not given some other means to remember it. Thus, the alternatives and consequences need to be listed in some way so that the students can refer to them. One way to do this listing is to construct a three column chart on the chalkboard or chart paper. The first column would be for the alternatives and the remaining two for positive and negative consequences. The latter columns can be headed with labels such as positive and negative signs or smiling and frowning faces.

As the alternatives and consequences are suggested they would be placed in appropriate columns. Schuncke and Krogh (1983) suggest that, for younger children, this is best accomplished through pictures. Using copies of the pictures introduced in the warm-up, facial expressions or symbols can be superimposed to convey the children's ideas. (The pictures used with their stories are expressionless, having no mouths. These are drawn in based on suggestions made by the children.) With children who are able to read, the alternatives and consequences may be listed in printed form.

In an earlier chapter we noted that children who are at Piaget's stage of concrete operations have difficulty dealing with more than one variable at a time. In a decision-making situation such as *structured discussion* a consequence, such as feelings, may be considered to be a variable. If more than one type of consequence—say feelings and the possibility of being caught at something—is considered there is the distinct chance that the younger children's thinking might become confused. In trying to determine the most appropriate course of action, for example, the younger child might focus on one type of consequence for one alternative and a different type for another. They would essentially be ignoring different consequences at different times, making thorough decision making difficult, if not impossible.

In order to prevent this type of mental confusion the teacher might wish to designate one type of consequence that the children will consider. Schuncke and Krogh (1983) suggest that, for younger children, this be the feelings of the individuals involved in the situation. This suggestion is based on the fact that a consideration of feelings allows the children to be exposed to the perspective of others and thus may facilitate the growth of perspective-taking ability, discussed in the previous chapter. Feelings, however, need not be the only type of consequence to be considered. Depending upon the problem situation other types may be more appropriate. In any case, one key to successful structured discussion with concrete operational children is to keep the consideration of alternatives as simple as possible.

Upper-grade students may be able to deal with more than one type of consequence and should be encouraged to do so. They can be encouraged to suggest the types of consequences that would be considered for a given problem. In fact, *structured discussion* can be an activity that allows children to engage in the type of evaluative thinking described by Bloom and his colleagues in their *Taxonomy of Educational Objectives: Handbook I: The Cognitive Domain* (1956). You may remember that at this, the highest level of taxonomy, the individual determines the extent to which an idea, product or whatever meets criteria that he or she has previously established. Types of consequences designated for consideration prior to the discussion may be thought of as these preestablished criteria.

The teacher's responsibility during the action period is to get the children to consider as many alternatives and consequences as they are able. This may mean that he or she will provide the students with items to consider in the consequences; for instance, the teacher might ask the children to consider the feelings of a person they had not mentioned. This, however, would be done in a nondirective manner, and the teacher would give no indication of how he or she thinks that the students should respond. Open-ended questions, earlier discussed in relation to role play, are very appropriate for this purpose.

The Debriefing. In a structured discussion the debriefing is very similar to that of role playing. It begins with a review of what has occurred so far. Using the chart as a guide, the teacher and the students quickly enumerate each of the alternative solutions and its attendant consequences. As this is being done, the students are encouraged to make comparisons among the different solutions, noting the effects of each relative to the others.

Following this review, the students are asked to choose what they perceive to be the most appropriate solution. In articulating their choice the students should be encouraged to indicate why it is better than the others in their mind. It is not necessary at this time to seek a class consensus on a solution, according to Schuncke and Krogh (1983), because this might tacitly encourage some students to adopt a position they do not hold. Nor is it necessary for every child to contribute a thought, because, in cases where an individual's decision may deviate from that of the group, this may set the child up for possible unnecessary peer pressure. Individuals, however, can be encouraged to discuss their ideas with the teacher or with their parents, if they care to do so.

Dealing with Controversy: Using Valuing with Problem Solving

As adults we are frequently faced with the problem of determining where we stand on a particular issue. In a college town, for example, individuals had to decide how they would vote on a referendum that, if passed, would allow no more than three unrelated adults to live in a rented house or apartment. Many college students, who composed the bulk of the renters in the town, saw this not only as an economic threat but also as discriminatory. So too did their landlords. Neighborhood associations and many homeowners, on the other hand, perceived it as a means of protecting their living environments. In the weeks preceding the referendum all presented evidence and made points of view known. The voters had to determine where they stood on this issue.

Of course, there are many ways of determining where we stand on such an issue—from working only from our emotions to thoroughly and critically thinking the issue through before deciding. If we work from the latter perspective we will need to employ a variety of problem-solving processes. Because issues are not value free, we will also need to consider values, determining the values and issues that are implicit in the situation. And, we will ultimately need to decide and act. To deal effectively with controversy, then, we need to combine processes.

As with any type of problem solving, we learn how to deal with controversy through experience. We can provide students with these experiences. Of course, the controversy we will help them consider will be one that will be appropriate to them; issues they perceive as being real and having an effect on their lives. Many environmental issues fit into this category, as do some current events. The question of whether or not American athletes should have been forbidden to attend the 1980 Olympics in Moscow, for example, was one in which upper elementary children were very interested in 1980. So too is the question of protecting various animals, both from what is perceived by some as unnecessary slaughter as well as from being used for research purposes. I observed a group of third graders, for instance, seriously working with the question of whether or not baby seals should be slaughtered for their fur.

The process of dealing with controversy to be discussed here is similar to ones suggested by Banks (1977) and Kaltsounis (1979). It has four basic components that embody both problem-solving and affective processing:

1. Exploration.
2. Value analysis.
3. Personal valuing.
4. Choosing and acting.

An examination of these components suggests that we are essentially engaged in a decision-making activity. In some respects this is true. However, in many decision-making situations we may not be placing as great an emphasis on values, especially in analyzing the values of others, as occurs here.

Exploration

This step is focused on finding out as much as possible about the issue. Although a controversy often appears to be a yes or no question we may find, as we explore this question that there are a wide range of alternatives and consequences, any one of which may have the potential to alter our thinking about the issue. Therefore, we initially want to seek out as many of these as possible.

An example, seen with a fifth-grade class, illustrates what occurs at this point. This class lived in a community that was considering building a coal-burning generator. The children became concerned about this when, during current events, one student shared a news item that indicated a possible relationship existed between coal emissions and acid rain. Although they immediately became anticoal generator, their teacher convinced them that, possibly, they were hearing only one side of the story and that it might be better if they looked at all of the options and the effects they would have. After planning to gather data it was decided that the current events period would be a time for sharing. A bulletin board was constructed so that the information could be posted and analyzed. This bulletin board was initially broken into two columns, headed "Source of Electricity" and "Effects." Later the teacher helped her students make subcategories of the "Effects" column in order to determine whether each was positive or negative.

Value Analysis

Gathering data is an ongoing process as we attempt to make sense out of a controversy, and we will analyze this data as we collect it. We'll need, for example, to look at the validity of sources, resolve discrepancies among pieces of information, differentiate fact from opinion, and so on. At some point, however, we'll need to look at all of the data we've collected in order to make our decision.

In a controversial situation it is probably safe to assume that much of the information we have collected may have been produced for a specific purpose. Unless we are absolutely certain of the objectivity of the data source it is probably wise to consider the motivation behind the presentation of the specific information. We'll need to analyze the information for the values being implicitly espoused by it.

You may remember, from our discussion of questions, in Chapter 6, that thinking at the analysis level requires three things: (1) isolation of the ideas in a piece of data; (2) determining the relationships among these ideas; and (3) explaining the relationships and inferring underlying values. The *value analysis* strategy developed by Taba and her associates (1971) is very appropriate for helping children make inferences about the values messages implicit in the data they collect. It can be applied to news items, printed advertisements, letters to the editor, as well as other types of media information.

The fifth grade teacher whose students were gathering data on different sources of electricity for their community developed a worksheet to help the students do this analysis. On this worksheet the children were asked for four things: (1) an outline of the main points contained in the data; (2) what these points suggested as being important; (3) whether the child perceived these things as important; and (4) why. Using this worksheet, a child was able to summarize a long rambling letter to the editor, as follows:

1. Main points:
   a. Electric bills are high because of oil use.
   b. Foreigners get rich from high oil prices.
   c. Coal is cheap and can be bought in the United States.
   d. Buying coal puts Americans to work.
2. Values:
   a. Saving money.
   b. Not buying from foreigners.
   c. Buying American products.
   d. Putting Americans to work.

In reflecting on her own values the child indicated that saving money was not as important as the writer indicated if it meant that we would lose resources, such as forests, to acid rain. She then reflected in a similar manner on each of the other values she had isolated. Her worksheet, as well as ones done by other students, were placed next to the information items on the bulletin board.

Valuing

Having collected as much data as possible, and analyzed it for the information it contains and as to the values implicit in it, it is now time to begin considering where we stand on an issue. In order to do this, however, we must have a clear idea of what our own values are. One way of accomplishing this is to consider the values uncovered in the value analysis in relation to what we believe to be important. In doing this we need to examine the value positions in two different ways. First, we need to consider whether the values that have been espoused are congruent to values we hold. If the data suggest that something is important in this situation, are we able to agree? Second, if we are able to agree with those values, what is the extent of our agreement? Do we perceive their relative importance in the same way or are there differences in our perceptions?

It is not enough, however, to examine and evaluate only those beliefs that have been presented to us. We need to go further, considering whether other values we hold are pertinent to the situation. If, as a result of this search, we indeed find other values that we think have a bearing on our choice, we need to ascertain how important these are. Here we essentially attempt to determine an order for our priorities, given the present situation.

The valuing step follows the value analysis quite naturally. If Taba's *value analysis* strategy is employed, students are given the opportunity to reflect on the congruence of their beliefs and those suggested in the data with which they have worked. As we saw in the example above, this reflection was part of the value analysis worksheet the students were asked to complete.

The teacher of the class used these worksheets as a springboard for further consideration of what the students perceived to be important in the situation. In a large group discussion the teacher reviewed each of the worksheets, allowing the students to clarify what they had written and encouraging input from other students. This input permitted other ideas about what was important to be considered. The consideration of the worksheets was then followed by the teacher asking if there were other things that were important to the situation that had not yet been suggested. This question allowed the students to articulate other values they felt had a bearing on the question of whether the coal-burning generator should be built.

Choosing and Acting

Having generated alternatives and consequences, examined these in terms of what people perceive to be important, and evaluated them in terms of what we believe to be important, we can now choose what our stand on the issue will be. This will be relatively easy at this point since we have done all of the groundwork necessary for making the decision. What might be difficult, however, is determining how we will implement our choice, how we will act on it. This may require, in essence, that we engage in decision making anew, examining and evaluating alternative courses of action we might take. It is important, however, that we do act, otherwise our decision making has simply been an intellectual exercise.

At times a unanimous decision will be made by a group of children as to how they should deal with an issue. When this occurs it is possible to decide upon actions that the group can cooperatively take. (We observed the class, mentioned earlier in this book, who were concerned about their polluted creek decide on group projects that could be done to publicize the pollution.) At other times there will not be such unanimity; some children may see one alternative as best, others another. In this case, the teacher should not insist upon consensus, since this might have the effect of coercing children to act against their beliefs. Or it may have the effect of indoctrinating children with a belief they do not hold. Instead, it would be more appropriate to allow the children to work individually, or with other individuals who have similar beliefs, in planning a course of action that they should take. The teacher might elicit, or suggest, different types of action that could be taken. This was done by the fifth grade teacher who found that some of her students favored the coal generator and others the existing oil generator. She suggested that each group write a letter to the editor of the local paper.

Synthesis: Planning to Include Affect ————————————————————

Affective goals can be approached in two ways in the social studies curriculum. We may simultaneously work toward them as we work toward conceptual and process goals. Or they can be approached separately. With the former we help children consider feelings, values, and so on as they develop knowledge about the world and its people. Although knowledge and process development may occur with the latter approach, this is not its primary intent. Instead the focus is on having children consider social and values issues per se as a way of developing affective capacities. Because both of these approaches are valid ones for the elementary social studies we can examine how to plan to include each in our curriculum.

Planning to Integrate Knowledge, Process, and Affect

You may remember from previous synthesis sections that the planning process is similar regardless of whether the goal is the writing of a text-book unit or a teacher-made unit for specific given class of students. To review briefly, we said that, once a unit topic has been chosen, we determine the concepts and generalizations that are to be developed within the context of the topic. Next, these are translated into what we referred to as understandings, restatements of the major ideas in terms that are content- or topic-specific. These understandings are then analyzed to determine how problem-solving processes and skills might be utilized by the children in developing them.

Planning to include affect occurs in much the same manner as planning to include problem solving. Basically, it is a process in which the planner attempts to match appropriate affective activities to the content that will be studied. That is, the planner tries to determine which type of affective capability—be it one dealing with feelings, values, and so on—can be appropriately developed with the content under consideration.

This determination begins with an analysis of the understandings developed for the unit. Unlike the analysis done for problem solving—where specific ideas contained in the understanding might be isolated—this most frequently is done with the total understanding, the complete idea to be developed. This idea is probed for its potential to spark affective concerns. Usually this probing takes the form of questions, such as, "Does this understanding lend itself to a consideration of feelings, an analysis of values, and so on? How?," which are asked by the planner. The answers to these questions suggest the specific affective concern or concerns, which can be built into the unit.

An example will clarify this process. For this illustration we can use an understanding we worked with in previous synthesis sections, "Athens and Sparta had different beliefs about sex roles; this affected who was allowed to vote." First we can think about this understanding in terms of the different types of affective strategies we have considered—exploring feelings, analyzing values, social decision-making and valuing, dealing with controversy—and ask whether it appears to lend itself to dealing with any of those areas. It would appear to be especially suited to value analysis because, in developing the understanding, the students will be working with data about beliefs held by different groups of people and the behaviors associated with those beliefs. They will be able to use these data to make inferences about the values of the Athenians and Spartans. The use of the strategy will also help them consider their own values in relation to sex roles.

Before considering how we might deal with affect separate from other goals, two points need to be made about planning to integrate them with other types of goals. The first is that, although we have discussed this integrated planning as being initiated with a consideration of conceptual goals, this need not always be the case. It is perfectly acceptable (and sometimes advisable) to begin with affect or process. You may feel that your students are lacking in affective capabilities and that you need to work with these.

Therefore, you might choose one area of affect to deal with and *then* select the ideas and content that will lend themselves to the development of these capabilities.

Our second point has to do with children's textbooks. Although they do address knowledge and process/skills goals to a great extent, they tend *not* to do so with affect. An examination of teachers' guides to current texts will show that only cursory attention is given to this area, and little help is given to the teacher as far as working with affect is concerned. Therefore, if you wish to include affect in your curriculum the major portion of the planning will need to be done by you.

Affect as a Separate Entity

In some cases it is not possible to develop affective capabilities—especially those concerned with social decision making and valuing—to a desired extent within existing content. Because of this, some teachers choose to develop a separate strand that places emphasis on affective concerns. At given intervals (say, once weekly or biweekly) a period is reserved for working exclusively within this strand.

Even though it might not occur as frequently as "regular social studies," planning is still needed if this affective education is to be effective. It is necessary to have clearly stated goals and ways of helping children meet these goals; haphazard activities usually have haphazard results.

There are two sources for the goals of your affective curriculum. One of these will be your students. You may perceive, from their behavior and activities that they are lacking in certain capabilities. They may, for example, show a lack of concern for other people's feelings. Or, they may engage in antisocial behavior. This would provide diagnostic data for you, suggesting affective areas that need to be considered. The second source will be your knowledge of different affective capabilities, such as those discussed in the previous chapter. You may choose to focus on attainment of a specific capability—such as perspective taking—and use this as a goal for your affective curriculum.

Your next task will be to select an activity or activities that will help develop the capability. This might be role play or structured discussion of an open-ended problem story. Research has shown these to be effective in developing perspective-taking and justice-reasoning abilities in children (Krogh, 1985). Or, you might choose some type of vignette emphasizing feelings or values—such as a story or narrative—to relate to the children for the purpose of exploring feelings or analyzing values.

In planning your affective activities attention should be paid to considering strategies for getting your students to interact with one another and with you. As we said in the previous chapter, it appears that one important factor in facilitating growth in affective capabilities is providing students with the opportunity to encounter the thinking of others. This will occur in a situation where there is an open sharing of ideas. Incidentally, you needn't worry to any extent that children who are thinking at lower levels of, say, perspective taking will influence children at higher levels. There is a great deal of research evidence to indicate that the probability that this will occur is low—individuals tend to be attracted to reasoning at a higher level than their own.

Springboards to Discussion ——————————————————————

1. Choose a story from Schuncke and Krogh's *Helping Children Choose* (1983) that would be appropriate to a given group of children. Using the warm-up, action period, debriefing sequence discussed in this chapter, conduct a role-play or structured-discussion activity with those children. Tape this activity. Then, evaluate the tape in terms of your effectiveness as a leader and their response to the activity.
2. Examine a children's social studies textbook for its potential to act as a springboard for the *exploring feelings* and *analyzing values* strategies discussed in this chapter. Does it present content that lends itself to these affective activities? Then try to find other resources—such as children's literature—that might be available in classrooms and which would lend themselves to using these strategies.
3. In discussing the strategy for dealing with controversy we indicated that it was a way of combining valuing and problem solving. In our chapters dealing with problem solving it was noted that it was very important to consider problems that the children perceived as being real to them. The same can be said of controversial issues. Brainstorm two lists of controversial issues to which children could relate to, one for primary grade students and one for upper graders. Provide a rationale for your choices.

References ——————————————————————————————

BANKS, JAMES A. *Teaching Strategies for the Social Studies.* Reading, MA: Addison-Wesley, 1977.

BLOOM, BENJAMIN S., et al. (eds). *Taxonomy of Educational Objectives: Handbook I: The Cognitive Domain.* New York: David McKay, 1956.

CHESLER, M., AND FOX, ROBERT. *Role Playing Methods in the Classroom.* Chicago: Science Research Associates, 1966.

DAMON, WILLIAM. *The Social World of the Child.* San Francisco: Jossey-Bass, 1977.

FRAENKEL, JACK. *How to Teach about Values.* Englewood Cliffs, NJ: Prentice-Hall, Inc. 1977.

GILLIGAN, CAROL. *In a Different Voice: Psychological Theory and Women's Development.* Cambridge: Harvard University Press, 1982.

KALTSOUNIS, THEODORE. *Teaching Social Studies in the Elementary School.* Englewood Cliffs, NJ: Prentice-Hall, Inc., 1979.

KRATHWOHL, DAVID R., BLOOM, BENJAMIN S., AND MASIA, BERTRAM B. *Taxonomy of Educational Objectives: The Classification of Educational Goals: Handbook II: Affective Domain.* New York: David McKay, 1964.

KROGH, SUZANNE. "Encouraging Positive Justice Reasoning and Perspective-Taking Skills: Two Educational Interventions," *Journal of Moral Education,* Vol. 14 (May 1985), pp. 102–110.

PORRO, BARBARA. *Non-Sexist Elementary Education: A Research Report and Teacher's Guide* (Research Monograph No. 34). Gainesville, FL: P.K. Yonge Laboratory School, College of Education, University of Florida–Gainesville, 1981.

SCHUNCKE, GEORGE, AND KROGH, SUZANNE L. "Value Concepts of Younger Children," *The Social Studies,* Vol. 73 (November/December 1982), pp. 12–15, 110.

SCHUNCKE, GEORGE, AND KROGH, SUZANNE. *Helping Children Choose.* Glenview, IL: Scott, Foresman, 1983.

SHAFTEL, FANNIE R., AND SHAFTEL, GEORGE. *Role Playing in the Curriculum.* Englewood Cliffs, NJ: Prentice-Hall, Inc., 1982.

TABA, HILDA, et al. *A Teacher's Handbook to Elementary Social Studies: An Inductive Approach.* Reading, MA: Addison-Wesley, 1971.

Planning

10

Planning for Learning

After reading this chapter you should be able to:

1. Describe various sources that can be consulted for unit topics.

2. Delineate the various steps to be taken in planning a unit of study.

3. Describe the steps required in planning to teach the unit on a daily basis, the daily lesson plan.

4. Suggest means of working toward a personal planning style.

The customary way of structuring learning experiences in the elementary social studies curriculum is through the unit approach. As its name implies, a unit is the study of a single topic. This topic may or may not be related to the other topics being studied during the year. If we were to use the expanding-communities approach to sequencing learning (see Chapter 2), all of the units we would teach would tend to focus on the community designated for our grade. Most of a first grade teacher's units, for example, would deal with aspects of family and school. On the other hand, if a teacher developed units only from the children's and his or her own interests, there is a good probability that many of them would be topically unrelated.

The time required to teach a unit may vary from one or two days for younger children to several weeks for more mature students, depending upon the topic, the goals we set, and the content to be considered. Regardless of how much time is required and the depth to which the topic is explored, all units will require that we do some planning to insure that we provide our students with the most appropriate, and enriching, learning experiences. This chapter is devoted to considering how we go about this planning.

We'll start by examining the various sources that might be consulted for unit ideas and content. This is followed by a description of a step-by-step process of planning a total unit of study. Finally, we'll detail how you might plan to teach your unit on a daily basis.

The process described in this chapter encompasses all of the steps required to insure successful learning experiences. The sequence with which these steps are approached varies among teachers (Lydecker, 1981). Ultimately, you, too, may wish to vary your approach, so in the synthesis section we provide some ideas that you may wish to consider as you do this.

Unit Planning _____

The planning strategy to be discussed in this section works from the premise that planning starts with the teacher having some general ideas about the content to be taught and the goals the students will attain. These ideas are gradually refined into specific learning activities in which the students will engage.

Beginning to Plan: Selecting a Topic

A very early task facing the teacher is that of choosing the unit topic, the specific theme around which content will be structured and ideas developed. There are any number of sources that can be consulted in our search for unit topics. The following sections briefly describe some of these.

Textbooks. Most classrooms come equipped with a set (or sets) of social studies textbooks, and these are good sources of unit ideas. Usually, in fact, they are divided into units. These units contain the data necessary to develop specific ideas and skills (which are usually thoroughly outlined in the teachers' manual accompanying the text.) The teachers' manual also usually contains additional information to reinforce the textual content—readings to provide a greater depth of content understanding for the teacher; activities which may be used to complement the text; and suggested supplementary materials, such as films, filmstrips, and books, which the students might utilize.

Curriculum Guides. Many school districts provide, in addition to textbooks, curriculum guides for each subject area. These may contain, among other things, general goals and objectives for each grade and suggested unit topics to be considered in each grade. Often they will contain general background information for the teacher as well as suggested activities, resources, and materials that can be employed within the units.

Available Resources. Regardless of where you teach there will be resources other than the textbook available to you to help you plan your unit. Your school library will have books, as well as other materials, available for your use in planning and teaching. In addition, many school districts have an instructional materials center where teacher resource materials, films, filmstrips, trade books, games, simulations, and other printed and nonprinted media can be borrowed. Sometimes these centers will have realia of different types—such as artifacts, models, and reproductions—that can be borrowed for classroom use. In many cases these centers are staffed by media specialists who are willing to help you find information and materials about a topic.

The community in which the school is located may also be a rich source of information and materials that would suggest unit ideas. It may contain, among other things, people who would be willing to do demonstrations or be guest speakers; organizations that can supply data and information about different topics; and places that would be appropriate for field trips.

Interests. The classroom is not a vacuum. Children come to school with many different types of interests. They want to know about a variety of things, many of which at first glance do not appear to fit into the existing social studies curriculum. Yet, if we examine these interests we often see that they can serve as a context within which ideas about the world in which we live can be developed. Take, for example, a child's interest in computers. This interest could serve as a basis for development of ideas about changes in technology (history); cultural changes due to inventions (anthropology); the various types of interdependence attributable to the computer industry (economics, geography). It is possible to adapt our curriculum if we remember that our goal is world knowledge and that a variety of content can be used to develop this knowledge.

Children's interests are not the only ones that need to be considered. You, too, will have interests that can be exploited in your curriculum. In fact you will probably find that your enthusiasm for an area will convey itself to the children and become infectious. Again, the major criterion for using these interests as sources for units would be the extent to which they facilitate the development of world knowledge.

Persisting Social Concerns. The world today faces a number of such long-range problems as environmental pollution, dwindling energy resources, and the proliferation of nuclear arms. Children are aware of these problems and, to varying extents, have an interest in them. Social studies units are an appropriate context for extending this awareness and interest.

Recurring Events. There are a number of events that happen on a regularly recurring basis. Or an international and national scale, for example, there are the Olympics, presidential elections, and various holidays. On a local scale, there might be various festivals, such as days celebrating the cultural heritage of a given area. Often there is a great deal of publicity given to these events and children are very aware of them. Frequently, however, they know little about them; for example, how they originated or why they are occurring. An examination of these in some detail may provide our students with any number of social science and historical learnings.

These sources should give you some idea of different potential unit topics. Your job will be to decide which topics will be appropriate for inclusion in your social studies curriculum. Two guidelines can be suggested to help facilitate your decision making. First, the topic should be one that can be related to your students' lives, now and in the future. The children should be able to see that the topic, and the content used to develop the topic, has some importance to them. As an adult, you should be able to see the potential the content might have for their future lives, how it might help them function in the world as adults. The second guideline relates to the goals of social studies education. The unit topic should be one that lends itself to the development of social science and historical ideas. It should also be one in which cognitive as well as affective processes and skills can be developed.

As a teacher, you should be able to articulate how these guidelines are being met. In fact, many curriculum planners and schools suggest that teachers address these two guidelines in writing. This is called the *rationale* for a unit.

The following example examines how a teacher might go about choosing a unit topic and developing a rationale for it. We will continue to follow this example through all of the steps of unit planning.

> The curriculum for Ms. Lowell's school district indicates that, in the sixth grade, some content emphasis should be given to the countries of the Caribbean basin, with emphasis on, among other things, the various peoples of the Caribbean and the relation of these countries to the United States and the rest of the world. This suits Ms. Lowell perfectly. While serving as a Peace Corps volunteer in Jamaica, she had an opportunity to travel to several different Caribbean countries and has since visited others. The textbook used in her grade devotes several sections to Caribbean lands. In addition, there are several Jamaican exchange students at a nearby university who, Ms. Lowell is certain, would be willing to be resource persons for her students. Based on all of these factors, Ms. Lowell decides to develop an introductory unit devoted to the physical characteristics of the region and the cultural backgrounds of its people. She begins her planning by writing the following:
>
> - *Topic:* Caribbean Lands and Their People
> - *Rationale:* Children come into contact with aspects of the Caribbean on a daily basis—from the food they eat to the music they hear to the people in their neighborhoods. Even though some of the students' families have emigrated from the region, many students have misconceptions about it that result in stereotypical thinking. This unit, while primarily developing geographical and anthropological ideas, will help them realize that the Caribbean countries are a vital part of the American community.

Selecting Goals

The planning process moves from the general to the specific. We start with some general ideas about what we'll teach and gradually refine these ideas until we have specific learning experiences in which the students will engage. Of course, as Taba and her associates (1971) indicate, the teaching process will be just the opposite; the students will start with specific learning experiences and use these as a basis for the development of general ideas. Having started with a general area to be studied, the topic, the next step in planning is to generally determine what the students might learn.

This second step of unit planning is the selection of learning goals, the things that we wish our students to know and be able to do as a result of working within a given topic. In most cases, we will indicate three types of goals that we wish our students to attain: (1) conceptual goals, the ideas and understandings we wish them to generate; (2) process goals, the problem-solving processes and skills we wish to develop; and (3) the affective processes and capabilities we hope to engender. When we plan we usually tend to make decisions about these goals simultaneously. For purposes of clarity, however, we'll consider each type of goal separately.

Conceptual Goals. The selection of conceptual goals is a three step process: (1) choosing the concepts and generalizations to be developed within the context of the unit; (2) translating these into understandings or examples of the concepts and generalizations that are phrased in terms of the unit topic or content; (3) analyzing these understandings to determine more specifically what the students will need to know.

There are two basic questions that you'd ask yourself as you choose the concepts and generalizations to be taught in your unit. First, you would naturally want to know which ideas are most appropriate for inclusion in the unit. If you work closely with a textbook or curriculum guide, this question will usually be answered for you—each will indicate specific ideas to be taught. If you are developing your own unit you should be able to see a clear relationship between the topic and the ideas. One should lend itself to the development of the other, and vice versa. Thus, Ms. Lowell might choose a generalization concerned with culture that affects how people meet their needs because her unit topic encompasses people of different cultures. She can understand how this generalization would fit her topic. On the other hand, she might have difficulty perceiving a match between a political science generalization dealing, say, with social control and her topic. (This is not to say that this latter generalization might not be related; just that the planner cannot see an unambiguous relationship!)

There is a second concern tied to the question of whether there is a fit between the generalizations and content. This concern regards the relationship among generalizations. Once you have selected generalizations, you'll want to ascertain whether they fit together. Here, you'll be looking for a "flow," if you will, a relatively natural progression in which the development of one generalization appears to facilitate or be facilitated by, the development of others. In examining your generalizations you should be able to visualize how the unit will progress.

The interdisciplinary nature of the social studies would suggest that you also evaluate the generalizations chosen to be developed in the unit in terms of whether they come from a variety of disciplines. It isn't necessary to have generalizations from all of the social sciences in all of your units; sometimes an area just isn't appropriate to a unit topic. If possible, however, you should be wary of developing units that rely on only one discipline.

How many generalizations should be chosen for a given topic? This is a difficult question and there aren't any set answers to it other than an offhanded one that says, "As many as are needed to develop the topic." An indirect way of answering, though, is to look at the amount of time that children can realistically be expected to work on a specific unit. Although a unit can last anywhere from one day to six weeks, its length should be dictated by the children's cognitive capabilities. With younger children a unit lasting one or, at most, two weeks and developing one or two generalizations is probably most appropriate. Older students are capable of working for a longer period of time on a single topic and can consider several generalizations.

Having chosen the generalizations for your unit, they can now be stated as specific knowledge goals, referred to as *understandings*. These are restatements of the generalizations phrased in children's language and in terms of the unit content. If you are using a textbook as your resource, you will find that these are usually provided in the teachers' manual. If you are developing your own unit, the process of formulating understandings is a relatively simple one, which becomes less and less difficult with experience. It entails three steps.

In order to see these steps as they would actually occur in the planning process we can use one of the generalizations that Ms. Lowell chose to work with in her unit, "Caribbean Lands and Their People." For this unit she chose to develop generalizations from anthropology (Carribean cultures and how people live), geography (the physical and cultural features of the lands); and economics (how people meet their needs, the interdependence of the Caribbean with the rest of the world). Let's examine how she developed an understanding from her first generalization, "People everywhere have the same basic needs and wants: their culture affects how these are met."

As an example of a generalization, the understanding directly parallels the generalization. It will contain examples of each of the concepts in the generalization. Therefore, the first step in building an understanding entails the identification of the major concepts upon which the generalization is built. For Ms. Lowell's generalization these were *people*, *basic needs and wants*, and *culture*.

Having identified the concepts, you now need to ensure that *you* understand them. This may sound simplistic and unwarranted. The truth of the matter is, though, that we often use concept names as we think and talk but are unable to articulate exactly what we mean by the concept. We cannot state what its characteristics are. (*Culture* is a good example of a frequently used concept word that people have difficulty explaining.) If we are going to teach a concept we need to comprehend it. To insure that we do possess this comprehension, and the second step in developing an understanding requires that we operationally define it. We do this by providing, for each concept in the generalization, an example of the concept that is specific to the unit topic.

You will also need to consider at this point how complex you wish the understanding to be. You may note that the generalization here shows a relationship between people's needs, people's wants, and their culture. It might be, for a given class, that the consideration of the relationships of three concepts would be somewhat confusing. In this and similar areas, the generalizations could be simplified by converting it to *two* related generalizations, each of which shows the relationships of two major concepts.

1. People everywhere have the same basic wants; their culture affects how they are met.
2. People everywhere have the same basic needs; their culture affects how they are met.

With other generalizations, such as, "Social institutions perform the important function of socialization; through this process individuals learn their role and status as well as group norms," the simplification could result in two relatively different generalizations.

1. Social institutions perform the important function of socialization.
2. Through socialization individuals learn their role and status, as well as group norms.

Because the need for simplification depends on your perception of student capabilities, it may not be needed with every generalization. You should be aware, however, that this simplification may allow more than one understanding to be developed from a generalization.

Ms. Lowell decided to simplify her generalization so that it focused only on people's needs. She then defined the concepts in her generalizations as follows: People, in this situation were the inhabitants of Caribbean countries, Caribbean cultural subgroups. For basic needs, she decided to focus on food because she is aware that it is an appropriate means highlighting subcultural differences. Culture, she decided, would be exemplified by how different subcultural groups cook.

In generating examples to act as operational definitions of your concepts you will, in some cases, be faced with the question of how specific they should be. To answer this question you should remember that our ultimate goal is world knowledge and concepts and generalizations are employed as means to meet that goal. Our goal is *not* the memorization of facts. If your examples are so specific that children may have difficulty developing more global ideas from them, then you probably wouldn't want to use them. However, if you could see that the specific examples would help develop the generalization, then they would be appropriate.

The last step of the process is the statement of the understanding. The concept examples are not put into a sentence that could be understood by the children Ms. Lowell's statement was, "People of different Caribbean lands eat the same foods, but they are prepared in different ways."

To reiterate the process briefly we can say that construction of an understanding requires:

1. Identification of the major concepts in a generalization.
2. Operationally defining these concepts through general examples to insure teacher understanding.
3. Development of a topic-specific statement, using the examples.

The final step in the generation of conceptual goals is referred to as the *analysis* of the understanding. During this step the planner identifies what the students will need to learn in order to develop the understanding. It entails two related tasks: identifying content to be dealt with and arranging it in some type of logical sequence.

In the first part of the analysis the general concept examples identified in the development of the understanding are elaborated upon further; specific content that the children will encounter is selected. This selection is done critically to insure that the understanding can be developed relatively unambiguously by the children. It is done while keeping the total understanding in mind. For example, because the intent of her understanding is to high-light cultural differences, Ms. Lowell will want to select Caribbean cultural subgroups whose differences will be quite apparent to the children. She wouldn't focus solely on groups having an Hispanic background. The choice of content is also made selectively; with an eye open for those content examples that can be used most economically. Ms. Lowell won't want to have her students deal with say, ten examples of the same subgroup when two carefully chosen ones will effectively do the job. (This careful selection rather than broad coverage of concept examples is referred to as *postholing.*)

In the second part of the analysis the planner lays out the order in which content will be encountered by the students. This order is one the planner perceives will allow for a logical progression from the specific ideas presented in the content to the general understanding. This logical sequence, among other things, is one that, if possible, allows later content to build upon that which was encountered earlier.

In her analysis, Ms. Lowell realized that her students would need to know three things: (1) what some representative Caribbean subcultures were; (2) the foods they ate with emphasis on culturally based differences among them (she felt that these differences could best be highlighted by foods having similar basic ingredients but different preparation); and (3) the reasons for the similarities and differences among the foods.

With this listing the initial planning for conceptual goals is completed. It has moved from a general identification of ideas to be developed, to the articulation of these ideas in terms of a specific topic to the identification of content appropriate to the development of these specific ideas. The progression is one that moves from a generalization to specific content. Figure 10-1 illustrates this progression.

Process Goals. Process goals, as you may remember, are concerned with those processes and skills that allow us to be effective problem solvers. Although we now discuss them subsequent to a consideration of conceptual goals, you should be aware that, in actual planning, we think about the two

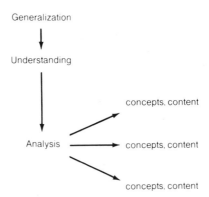

Figure 10-1 Planning for conceptual goals.

functions relatively simultaneously. As you are choosing the concepts and generalizations to be developed you will be thinking of processes that can be used to develop them. In some cases you will use a process or skill as a basis for your choice of concepts and content; you want to emphasize a given process, and so you select ideas you believe can best be learned with this process.

You may remember, from our consideration of problem solving, that there are two ways that it can be taught. The first is by a *total process approach* in which students are helped to work through all of the steps of a given problem-solving model from problem determination to problem resolution. The second is a *skills approach* and is based on the idea that there are certain skills, such as those associated with data gathering, that individuals use regardless of the problem-solving model being employed. These skills can be taught without necessarily having the children engage in a total process.

In choosing conceptual goals we are basically considering the *what* of the unit—what ideas the student will develop and what content will be used to do this. Process goals, on the other hand, are concerned with the *how*; how the ideas will be developed and how the content will be utilized. The two approaches to problem solving provide us with a framework for considering this *how*. In our planning we can examine what we want the students to learn and then determine if it is possible to approach these ideas with a total process, such as exploration, or a given skill, say one associated with analyzing graphs.

Planning to include process goals is relatively simple and begins as we analyze our understanding to determine what we want our students to learn. As we isolate each idea we consider the most appropriate way in which it can be developed. That is, we determine if some aspect of problem solving can be employed by the students so that they can actively develop the idea themselves. Essentially, we pair *what* will be learned with *how* it will be learned and note this in our plans.

Three things should be kept in mind as we plan to include process. First, every idea does not need to be paired with a problem-solving skill or process. In some cases we may use other, more teacher-directed strategies such as exposition to develop it. Secondly, it's necessary to remind ourselves of our students' developmental capabilities. You may remember that some skills are more appropriately taught in the later grades; we do not want to include problem-solving activities for which they are not yet ready. Finally, as you select a process or skill to be developed you'll want to evaluate its appropriateness in terms of economy of learning. You'll need to determine if it helps develop the idea in the least time-consuming and involved manner. Even though an idea lends itself to being developed using the exploratory model of problem solving for example, there may be other just as appropriate ways that are quicker and less painstaking yet still develop process capabilities.

Let's examine how Ms. Lowell would plan to include process in her unit concerned with "Caribbean Lands and Their People." You may remember that she indicated three things the children needed to be aware of to develop the understanding: (1) representative Caribbean subcultures; (2) the foods they eat that have similar ingredients but different preparation; and (3) reasons for similarities and differences among the foods. In considering each of these she decides that for the first idea she will introduce the notion of subcultures by telling the students that, initially, the Caribbean was inhabited by the Arawak and Caribs, groups which no longer exist. These were replaced by groups of people from other lands. She will then present them with the problem of finding the origins of groups who live in the Caribbean today through *exploration*. She will break children into teams, with each team being assigned a different locale. For the second idea she will ask the students to *gather data* from their textbook about foods produced in the Caribbean. She intends, at this point, to present them with a retrieval chart in which the subcultures will be listed at the top and the foods on the vertical axis. Following this the teams will again be asked to *explore* the question of what is made with these foods by the different subgroups. She intends for the data gathering of this exploration to be one in which a variety of sources and skills are used. These will include *interviewing* a resource person, *following directions* in a cookbook and cooking, *observing* demonstrations as well as other data-gathering activities the children might suggest. The result of this exploration will be illustrated on the retrieval chart in any manner that the students choose. The retrieval chart will then be utilized for a total class discussion. The children will be asked *to evaluate all of the data gathered through comparison and contrast.* She intends to use the *developing generalizations* strategy (Taba et al., 1971), which is discussed in the next chapter, as a means for facilitating this discussion. As she thinks of the processes and skills she'll use she notes them next to the concepts and content she has isolated in analyzing the understanding.

Earlier we noted that the process of planning a unit is one in which we gradually move from the general to the specific. An examination of Ms. Lowell's planning up to this point reflects this idea quite well. We can see that she's moved from a general topic to some relatively specific ideas about *what* will be learned and *how* it will be learned. Figure 10-2, which extends Figure 10-1, presented earlier illustrates this movement.

Affective Goals. For the purposes of our discussion the final decision that needs to be made in the process of selecting goals for a unit is concerned with the selection of the affective goals. As we indicated earlier with process

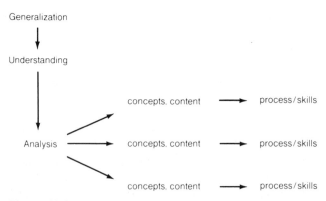

Figure 10-2   Planning for conceptual and process goals.

goals, though, affective goal selection will occur relatively simultaneously with choosing our two other types of goals. Sometimes, in fact, it will precede the selection of the former; we may have affective concerns with which we wish to deal and utilize these concerns as a basis for our choice of content and process.

The activities in which we engage while planning to include affective goals are very similar to those entailed in planning for process. Basically, we evaluate what we want our students to know with an eye for how this will lend itself to a consideration of feelings and values, or to the development of such affective capabilities as those dealing with perspective taking. Like process, of course, there may be situations where the inclusion of specific affective goals will not be appropriate. In this case we need not include them. As we said in our synthesizing discussion of affect, it is perfectly permissible to deal with these concerns as a separate entity in our curriculum.

This type of planning begins with an evaluation of the ideas and content generated in the analysis of the understanding that was done in reference to conceptual goals. Emphasis is placed on content at this stage of planning because it is the content that will embody different types of affect. The planner's job is to probe for the different value and feeling concerns it might convey to the children and then to determine how these different concerns might be used instructionally. One way to do this probing is to look for situations in the content that could parallel, in some way, situations in the children's own lives. (As we said earlier, it is these parallel areas the children will see as most relevant and be most willing to consider.)

One of the content areas that Ms. Lowell's students will consider deals with the origins of the various Caribbean subcultural groups. She is aware that some of these groups, especially the African-based groups, were brought to the Caribbean against their own wills. She thinks that this content will lend itself to helping develop empathy on the part of the children. They can be assisted in examining how the slaves might have felt, being forcibly uprooted from their own homes. She sees that this might somewhat parallel feelings that the children might experience if, as frequently occurs, they moved from one home to another. Therefore, next to the concept, content and processes already noted, she indicates that affect will be dealt with by having the students explore feelings in terms of how it feels to be uprooted.

With the consideration of affect, the goal setting for the unit is complete. Figure 10-3, which extends the earlier charts illustrating the goal-setting steps, summarizes this process.

Once the goals for the unit have been set, consideration of specific ways of implementing them can begin.

Setting Objectives

The analysis of the understanding allows the planner to generally determine the following: (1) what the student will need to know, the concepts and content that need to be considered in developing the understanding; (2) how the concepts will be learned, the processes the student will employ; (3) the affective concerns and capabilities that might be engendered as the students work with the content. Once these have been delineated it is possible to consider the specific ways in which they may be accomplished by the stu-

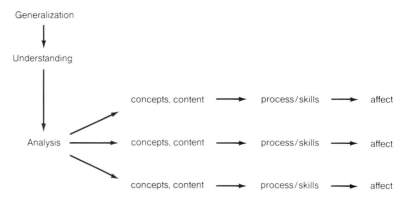

Figure 10-3 Developing unit goals.

dent. This consideration begins with a refinement of these general goals into specific *learning objectives*.

A learning objective is basically a statement made by the teacher indicating the specific ideas, processes, skills, and capabilities to be developed by the student. Let's analyze some examples actually used by teachers to determine the major characteristics of such statements.

From a first grade unit, "Types of Families":

- The student will depict his or her family in picture form.
- The student will describe two other family types.

From a third grade unit, "The Farm Community":

- Given examples of various foods in different stages of production, the student will correctly differentiate between processed and nonprocessed foods.
- Students will develop hypotheses concerning the types of food grown in different climates.

From a sixth grade unit, "Panama":

- The student will describe in writing, the difference between a physical and cultural environment.

All of these examples have two things in common. First, they indicate a *specific learning outcome* (Gronlund, 1978), telling exactly what the student should know or be able to do if the established learning goals have been met. The first graders will know what families consist of, the third graders will know the difference between processed and unprocessed foods, and the sixth graders will know the differences between cultural and physical environments. Secondly, the objective specifically articulates the *student behavior* or *performance* that will indicate that the learning outcome has been achieved, how the teacher can ascertain whether or not the student indeed understands. It does this through the use of nonambiguous terms such as *describe, differentiate* and *hypothesize,* as opposed to the more general and vague terms such as *knows, understands,* and *comprehends.*

Although an objective, of course, will give some indication of the type of learning experience the student should have, it indicates neither teacher performance nor the learning process. An objective indicates an end point of instruction, not the means that will be employed to reach that end. Thus, the objective concerned with the students differentiating between physical and cultural environments does not say how the teacher will teach these concepts or what the students will do to develop them.

You may have noticed that the objectives listed above differed in the degree of specificity employed to describe student behavior. This varies among teachers. In some cases they will describe the specific behavior of the student ("describe," "depict"), tell how the behavior will be demonstrated ("in writing," "in picture form"), and then note some quantitative indicator of when the objective is attained ("with 80 percent accuracy," "two types."). Others will indicate the behavior and how it will be demonstrated ("list in writing"). Still others will simply indicate the behavior—"develop hypotheses," "describe"—without including anything about how it will be demonstrated or giving any numerical indicator of when it will be attained. The form that a teacher's objectives take may reflect policies of the school district in which he or she works; some are very definite in how objectives are to be stated. Or, it may reflect personal preferences. Regardless of how objectives are actually stated, the teacher does need to have some idea, in mind if not in writing, of how the student will demonstrate the learning outcome.

The process of developing objectives for a unit flows quite naturally from the analyses of the understanding. Each of the ideas and processes isolated in the goal-setting stage of planning is now translated into a specific learning outcome. This outcome will need to be accomplished if students are to develop the understanding in the manner initially conceived by the teacher. As a result of this translation the teacher will have a list of objectives paralleling the analyses. These may include concepts to be learned as well as processes, skills, and capabilities to be developed.

This translation from analyses to objectives can perhaps be better understood with an example, so let's return to considering Ms. Lowell's planning for her unit, "Caribbean Lands and Their People." In analyzing her understanding she indicated that she wanted her students to be aware of various Caribbean subcultural groups. She therefore states this as a conceptual objective:

1. The student will identify four different Caribbean cultural groups.

She then indicated that she wanted the students to do this through the process of exploration. Therefore she formulates a process (or skills) objective:

2. The student will employ the exploration process.

She also wanted her students to begin developing perspective-taking abilities by exploring how it might feel to be uprooted from one's homeland and transported to a new land. This becomes an affective objective:

3. The student will state an hypothesis as to how it feels to be uprooted.

For some parts of her analysis Ms. Lowell may have more of one type of objective than another; it isn't necessary to have all three types of objectives all of the time.

As we have indicated, objectives point to learning outcomes that need to be achieved if the earlier established goals are to be met. Some of these objectives may have already been achieved. A child, for example, may already know a concept required for developing the understanding and this concept may not need to be taught. The teacher's job will be to diagnose if, indeed, the child does understand the concept. Thus, objectives do not suggest learning activities per se, and the attainment of every objective need not result from a learning experience engaged in during the unit. The objectives simply point to what needs to be accomplished before or after the unit is completed. They point to what needs to be evaluated to insure that the goals have been met.

The process of moving from the analysis of the understanding to objectives is summarized in Figure 10-4. Although it illustrates a one-to-one correspondence between components of the analysis and objective this, of course, is not always the case. Some components will generate more than one objective.

Considering Diagnosis

As we indicated in the previous section, it is possible that our students may have already achieved some of the objectives that have been set for the unit. It would be unnecessary for the planner to develop learning activities for those objectives. Therefore, at this point in the planning process, rather than move directly to generating learning activities, our task will be to speculate upon how we might determine which of the objectives have been met. This diagnosis entails consulting two different types of sources.

The first of these are sources *external* to the child, sources that could document learnings that the child has supposedly achieved. The chief of these is the teacher, who would consider the learning experiences he or she knows the students have already had. These are evaluated in terms of the present unit objectives to see how they might have contributed to their

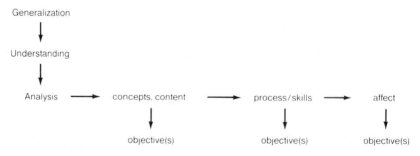

Figure 10-4 Restating unit goals as objectives.

development. Thus, if one of her objectives is concerned with identifying Caribbean countries and Ms. Lowell had taught a previous unit dealing with the Caribbean, she would have some assurance that they had already met the objective.

Another resource to be consulted by the planner would be the textbook series with which the children have worked. The teachers' manual for a given grade will present a scope and sequence chart for the total series. This will indicate the objectives of various types that are developed in each text. An examination of this chart for the previous grades' objectives will give some indication of objectives the students potentially have achieved.

A third source will be the scope and sequence found in the school's curriculum guide, if there is one. Again, this will suggest objectives that potentially have been attained.

A final information source would be the teachers who have previously worked with the students. They may have indicated (in the children's cumulative folders) the objectives the children have achieved. This indication and/or consultation with them should provide the planner with needed data.

The second, and major, source of information about what they have learned is the *children themselves*. Initially, you will need to ascertain for certain that they have indeed attained the objectives external sources suggest they have. Your job is to consider which strategies you might use to get this information. As we shall see in Chapter 14, which discusses evaluation in depth, these strategies might be informal ones, such as a group discussion, or of a more formal nature, such as a written pretest. How formal your evaluation strategy will be will depend to a great extent on how certain you are that they may indeed have attained the objective. A good rule of thumb for diagnosis states that the less certainty you have, the more structured the diagnosis should be.

You would not stop considering your students as sources of diagnostic data only for those objectives identified by other sources as having potentially being met. You would also want to think of the children as primary sources, being able to provide information you had not obtained previously. Therefore, you'll want to consider ways of getting this information, ways of asking them what they know or are able to do. Again, this may be done formally or informally.

Figure 10-5 graphically extends the process of planning to the diagnosis stage.

Selecting Learning Experiences

Diagnosis will help you ascertain those learning objectives the children will have met prior to actually working within the unit. Usually, they will not have met all of the objectives; thus, your next task will be to determine how they might be assisted in achieving the remaining ones. It will be necessary for you to select the learning experiences that will be used to develop specific concepts and processes, as well as the total understanding.

There are any number of specific types of learning experiences that can be used to make social studies exciting and meaningful to children. We have discussed some—such as role play and structured discussion—in previous

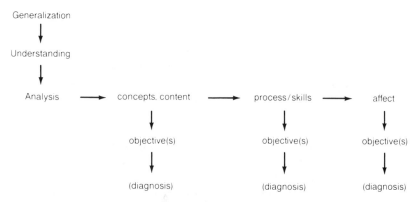

Figure 10-5 Considering diagnosis.

chapters. In chapters subsequent to this we will look at the range of them in some detail. Therefore at this point, rather than delineate specific activities that can be used with units we will focus on some of the general characteristics that all should have if they are to serve their purpose, regardless of the content or the level of the children being taught.

The first quality of an appropriate learning experience is that it directly addresses the objective. Learning activities must be of such a nature that there is no question of the specific performance behaviors they will engender in students. The planner should be able to see an unambiguous connection between what will be occurring as the children engage in the experience and what is needed to be learned. If, for example, Ms. Lowell has developed an objective that requires that students identify four Caribbean countries, then she needs to choose an activity that allows this to be done in a relatively straight-forward manner. Perhaps this activity would require working with maps of the Caribbean basin. Similarly, if she wants her students to hypothesize about how it might feel to be uprooted, she would make sure that they have a learning experience that provides them with sufficient data to make such an hypothesis. What she wouldn't do in either case is to have activities of such a nature that the children would have to quizzically wonder what in the world they're supposed to be getting out of them.

It may seem as if there is a one-to-one correspondence between a unit objective and a learning experience. This is not necessarily the case all of the time; the attainment of some objectives may require that children engage in more than one activity (in this case, each activity would essentially have a subobjective). The hypothesizing objective, stated previously, would require that children obtain data and then work with that data before developing the hypothesis. Although in most situations it is not difficult to determine intuitively how many activities would be required to develop an objective, at times this may not be readily apparent. Jack Fraenkel's (1977) discussion of learning activities suggests a strategy that can be employed when this occurs. He has indicated that activities can be conceived as serving four different functions. One type of activity, such as a listening or observing activity, is directed toward the *intake* of information. A second serves the function of helping students *organize* what they have learned. Included here would be an activity such as categorizing. The third category of activity allows for the *demonstration* of what has been learned; for example by making a mural or through dramatization. The last type is concerned with having the students *create* something new with what they have learned. An inference that can be made from Fraenkel's work is that these four categories tend to fall in a more or less taxonomical order. To organize information we must have taken it in; to demonstrate it we need to have taken in and organized. Thus, we can determine the types of activities required by the objective by examining the objective itself. We must ask ourselves which of the four functions it implies and where this function fits in the taxonomy. Then, we would need to insure that the lower functions have been achieved. If, for example, an objective requires that students organize information we know that our students will need to possess this information. If we know that they don't have the requisite data, then we will need to plan for experience having activities in both the intake and organizing categories.

The experience, then, should be directly related to *what* needs to be learned. It should also directly address *who* is doing the learning. Experiences should be developmentally appropriate. They should also be representative of the different ways in which people learn. As adults some of us learn better visually, say through reading, while others function best in an aural mode, through listening. Some of us prefer to be shown the steps of a process before we engage in it, while others prefer to discover the process for themselves. The same can be said for children. In our classrooms we will have students with a variety of different learning styles. All of the activities in a unit should not have the children doing exactly the same thing; for example, reading. Instead, different activities should allow for learning in different ways. By doing this we increase the probability of all students learning.

The selection of learning experiences in unit planning follows directly from the setting of objectives. Each objective that the children have not already attained will generate one, or more, of these experiences. The planner's job is to select (or create) experiences that help the students meet objectives in the appropriate manner; that is, appropriate to the objective and the child.

Teachers differ in the specificity with which they describe the learning experiences in their unit plans. Some prefer to briefly outline it without going into any great detail. They sketch out what will occur and indicate the materials and resources they will use. Ms. Lowell might do this with the activity concerned with helping children identify different Caribbean countries. Her activity might appear as follows:

- *Objective:* Identify four different Caribbean countries.
- *Experience:* Study of Caribbean basin using political maps.

Teachers who choose to outline their experiences in this skeleton form will later add detail as they do their daily or weekly lesson plans. Other teachers prefer to provide the detail within the unit plans themselves, describing exactly what the students will do as well as the specific materials and

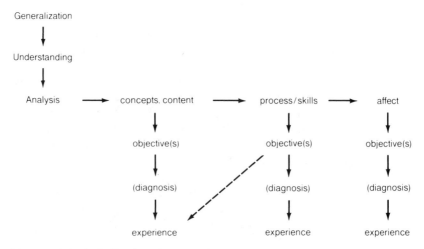

Figure 10-6 Including learning experiences.

resources required by the activity. They then need to do less detailed work as they construct their daily lesson plans.

The step of selecting learning experiences, as it fits into the unit-planning process, is illustrated in Figure 10-6. The dotted line moving from the process objective to the concept/content experience indicates that some experiences, because they may contain more than one activity, may serve more than one type of objective.

Choosing Evaluation Strategies

Evaluation is concerned with the determination of the extent to which a given child has attained a given learning objective. Although it is sometimes mistakenly thought of as occurring only after instruction has been completed, this is not the case at all. Evaluation is an ongoing process that actually begins prior to instruction and continues, within a given unit, until the child provides evidence that he or she has met the goals that have been established.

The initial stages of this continuous process are concerned with diagnosis—it is necessary for us to determine exactly where our students are in relation to the goals that have been established. The next type of evaluation, called *formative evaluation*, occurs as our students engage in different activities. It is concerned with ascertaining progress toward the goals that have been established for the unit. Our unit culminates when the children have developed the understandings, skills, and capabilities we set forth in our initial stages of planning. We determine this with *summative*, or terminal, evaluation procedures.

These three different types of evaluation, to be discussed in greater depth in Chapter 14, need to be considered during the planning process. Thought must be given to the most appropriate evaluation strategy to give us the information we need. Two questions can be used to guide this thinking:

1. For what will I be looking specifically?
2. What is the best way to ascertain this?

The first question, of course, refers to the learning objective, which, if it has been formulated appropriately, should indicate the specific student behavior that the teacher will need to consider. Thus, if one of Ms. Lowell's objectives in her unit is the identification of four Caribbean countries, she knows that they will need to indicate, in some way, four countries.

To answer the second question we choose an evaluation strategy. With the exception of diagnosis, which will occur prior to the generation of experiences and whose results may actually suggest experiences, this choice tends to be a natural outgrowth of the development of experience. In fact, on many occasions the experience will suggest the evaluation strategy. If, for example, it focuses on making a mural, our evaluation strategy may be the examination of the mural for specific elements. If it is one in which the children are learning a specific skill, then we might observe them using the skill.

Figure 10-7 illustrates where evaluation might be considered most appropriately in the planning process. This illustration is somewhat deceptive, however, in that it does not show what occurs in the teaching process if an objective is not met. Here, we might visualize an arrow that goes back to the stage of planning activities, because it would be necessary to develop an additional activity, or activities, to insure attainment of the objective.

Planning to Initiate the Unit

The last step of unit planning is actually concerned with the very first thing you'll do as you teach your unit—insure that your students are inter-

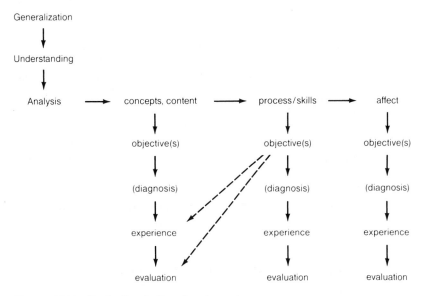

Figure 10-7 Evaluation in the planning scheme.

ested in the topic and are ready to learn about it. You'll do this by helping them generate questions that they'd like answered as they study the topic, or speculate upon areas within the context of the topic that they would like to explore.

There are various ways in which you might initiate a unit. As we indicated earlier in this chapter, one source for unit topics is the children themselves. They have had past experiences that can act as the bases for further learning. They are also interested in any number of things that lend themselves to exploration within the context of a social studies unit. If you decide to use one of these child-generated topics, then your job in initiating the unit will be a relatively simple one. You will only need to have them articulate specifically what they would like to get out of the unit. Later in this section we'll discuss how this might be done.

Of course, there will be other situations where your unit topic may not appear to directly address the interests you know your students to possess. In this case, you will need to create interests. There are any number of ways that a creative teacher might do this. We will discuss some of these ways in the following three sections.

An Arranged Environment. A variety of different materials concerned with the unit topic are brought into the classroom for the children to examine and develop questions about. A fourth grade teacher in California used an arranged environment to kindle interest in a "Gold Rush Days" unit. She included actual mining implements, such as pans, picks, and a very large device called a cradle (which was invented to do panning on a large scale). She displayed pictures and different types of trade and fiction books (including one that contained Mark Twain's stories of gold-rush days, such as "The Celebrated Jumping Frog of Calaveras County"). She also had a box of the type of clothing worn during that era that the children could try on. All of these, plus maps of the gold country, were placed in a corner of the classroom that the children could visit during various parts of the day.

Bulletin Boards. Bulletin boards would deal with various aspects of the topic and might be designed very much like a two-dimensional arranged environment, containing different types of general information—in the form of pictures, pamphlets, maps, and so on. They might also be designed to pose questions that would be dealt with in early unit activities. Ms. Lowell, for example, might construct a simple bulletin board composed of a map of the Caribbean labeled, "Do you know the countries of the Caribbean?" Or, they might be designed as skeleton bulletin boards that are added to as a unit progresses. Ms. Lowell might also construct a large bulletin board labeled, "The Caribbean and Its Peoples," containing only a map. Then as various parts of the unit were studied, other elements would be added (for example, pictures of various Caribbean cultural groups could be connected to countries on the map by strings.)

Simulations and Role Play. Through the use of simulations and role play, children would be given an opportunity to act out a situation, or problem, that is related to the unit topic or deals with concepts they will encounter in the unit. A group of fifth graders, for example, might be asked to put themselves in the roles of early colonists to the United States and decide what they will bring to the new land. The ideas they generate during this simulation could be hypotheses that would be tested as they engage in different unit activities.

Print and Nonprint Media. Print and nonprint media can whet the children's appetite for learning more about the unit topic. Stories, films, filmstrips, and so on can often be used as a basis for generating questions or concerns that bear further exploration. For example, I once used a very short but detailed film to initiate a unit on "Scientific Observation," that examined how social scientists gathered data. The children were given an opportunity to watch the film and then were asked questions about its details. Their inability to answer these led to my introducing the unit topic to them.

Of course, there are many other ways of getting your students interested in a topic, and you can be as creative as you care to be. You should, however, use two guidelines in developing your initiation strategy: First, the initiation is not the unit; its purpose is to get the students ready to work in the unit. It shouldn't attempt to teach concepts or skills. Rather, it should act as an introduction to the context in which these will be learned. In most cases, the initiation activity itself will be rather short. An arranged environment may be in the classroom for a week and the students may examine the materials frequently. However, when it becomes the focus of attention, say in a teacher-led class discussion, that discussion will be relatively brief and will focus on questions and concerns the students have. The second guideline, related to the first, is that the initiation should raise questions, not answer them. It should sufficiently pique the interest of the students so that they will want to consider the unit topic in more depth. In planning an initiation you'll want to speculate upon its interest-raising potential.

You'll also want to consider, as you plan your initiation, how you'll help the children move into the unit from it. One way is to have the children develop questions that they'd like answered. In other situations they can develop hypotheses that they can test. You might also have them generate topics (in this case, subtopics of the unit topic) that they'd like to explore. Or you might provide them with an overview of what they'll be studying. All of these strategies—be they questions, hypothesis, or topics—can be listed, say on a chart, so that the children can refer to them as they move through the unit.

Unit Planning: A Summary

With the selection of your initiation strategy your unit is essentially planned and you're ready to provide your student with meaningful learning experiences. You've moved from some very general thoughts about what you'll teach and how you'll teach it to some very specific ideas about what the children will actually be doing and how you'll know that they've learned what they're supposed to learn. Having discussed the process in great detail in this section we can now summarize it as a nine-step process. These steps are:

1. Choosing a topic.
2. Selecting general goals.
3. Developing understandings.
4. Analyzing the understandings in terms of concepts, processes, and affect.
5. Developing objectives.
6. Considering diagnosis.
7. Developing learning experiences.
8. Choosing evaluation strategies.
9. Creating an initiation strategy.

This list may seem lengthy and, indeed, in the early stages of your teaching you'll find that unit planning is time consuming. You'll find, however, that with experience it becomes less so. Steps are combined and you'll become more fluent in generating experiences. In addition, you'll find that you usually don't teach a unit just once. Many units will be taught over and over again with variations that are added as a result of the previous teaching. (It has been my experience that, even if you don't plan on teaching a given unit again, the children will often request it. They've seen evidence of it or heard about it and want to do it too!)

Teaching the Unit on a Daily Basis

As we've said several times in this chapter, unit planning moves from the very general (topic, goals) to the very specific (planning activities and evaluation strategies). Teaching the unit, on the other hand, moves in the opposite direction. Specific activities are used as a means for the development of general understandings about the world.

Regardless of how thoroughly you've considered the activities in your unit plans you'll need to think about them just before your students actually do them. You'll want to plan in detail how each activity will be carried out. With some slight variation, this daily planning is very similar to unit planning. It entails consideration of four different things:

1. *Objectives.* There should be a purpose for each activity that you have your students do, and you should be aware of what that purpose is. Therefore, an objective is stated for each day's lesson. This objective may be one you stated in your unit plan. Or, it may be one that enables your students to work toward this previously stated objective. For example, if one of your unit objectives was that the students would employ the exploratory process, an objective for a specific activity might deal with one step of this process. For your daily plans you might have the following objective: "The students will choose appropriate data sources to answer their questions."
2. *An activity.* You will next want to indicate how the students will work toward the objective, telling very specifically what they will do. Teachers vary in the amount of detail they actually include in their written plans. Some sketch the steps of the activity in outline form.

For example, with the objective concerned with choosing data sources a teacher might simply note in his or her plan book: (1) review questions; (2) discuss data sources and make student groups; (3) group work; (4) group reports. Other teachers, especially ones who are using a specific type of activity for the first time, will provide themselves with additional directions and information. For instance, with respect to the second notation in the plan book they might list data sources for themselves and note points to be covered about each. They might also list group-work skills and behaviors .they will discuss with the students.

3. *Evaluation procedures.* A lesson plan will also include some indication of the strategy that will be employed to determine if the objective for the activity has been met. In many cases this will have already been decided upon in the unit plans. At times, especially when the students are working with a subobjective, you will need to consider this anew. Regardless, it is during the daily planning that a detailed consideration is given to how the strategy will actually be carried out.

   As we shall see in Chapter 14, evaluation should not be exclusively equated with testing. There are a variety of ways of gauging student progress that don't require tests—for example, through observation, the collection of work samples and discussion. In your plans you'll want to decide which of these strategies is most appropriate to your situation.

   Again, the amount of detail devoted to evaluation in the teacher's written plans will vary from teacher to teacher.

4. *Materials and Resources.* The practical aspects of a given lesson also need to be considered in the daily plans. Here you'll want to indicate what tangible items the children will need to complete the activity. These could include anything from books to maps to paints and glue. You'll indicate these in your plans so that you'll be certain that they are available. There is nothing more frustrating (and disruptive) to a class than to begin a lesson and realize that you haven't, say, gathered the tempera paints that the students need for the mural they're supposed to construct. This step of lesson planning is one most frequently ignored by beginning teachers, incidentally. They quickly learn to include it though.

Having discussed the four elements of a daily plan, let's examine one done by Ms. Lowell for her "Caribbean Lands and Their People" unit. In her unit plans she indicated that her students would explore the origins of the different peoples of the Caribbean. At this point her students have identified different Caribbean countries and have expressed an interest in exploring different ones in depth. She has broken her class into interest groups, based on the country of individual children's choices. She introduced the idea of exploring ethnic origins by asking the students to talk about their own ethnic backgrounds and then telling them that, like the United States, the Caribbean countries are made up of diverse peoples. With her encouragement the students posed the question, "Where did they come from?" Today they'll begin finding the answer. What follows is Ms. Lowell's plan for an activity in which they'll decide where to look for information.

Objective The students will choose appropriate data sources.

Activity
1. Review discussion of ethnic origins; ask student to restate problem.
2. Assign groups task of discussing ways of finding answers to question. Groups should report on two or three ways on chart paper.
   • Review groupwork procedures.
3. Have group reports.
   • Discuss group problems.

Evaluation
1. Observe groups at work.
2. Completed charts—check appropriateness.

Materials
1. Chart paper.
2. Felt markers.

For purposes of illustration this plan has been simplified and deals with a very short learning activity. With one group of children this might be the total activity. With another, Ms. Lowell might also have them plan to gather data from the sources they've chosen. As her students work in groups with this activity, Ms. Lowell will be circulating through the class—observing, answering questions, and offering help.

Synthesis: Working Toward Your Own Planning Style _____

At the beginning of this chapter we indicated that, in reality, different teachers had personal planning styles, considering different elements of the process we have described at different times. Some, for example, begin by thinking about activities. The purpose of this section is to help you begin working toward your own personal style of planning. To do this I'd like to share an insight about planning I have had and what I see its implications to be for your work.

This insight comes from my own work as an elementary school teacher and is bolstered by some of the reading of the research on planning I have done. Put quite simply, it appears that a greater amount of in-depth thought occurs at the initial stages of planning. If a teacher first considers goals, for instance, there is a good probability that a proportionately greater amount of time will be spent thinking about these than about activities. Thought about the former lays the groundwork for the latter, which tend often to fall into place.

It would seem, then, that as we plan we should first consider those elements that need the most thought. If we work from the assumption that each of the elements of the planning process is important then it would seem that we should begin our planning with the element with which we feel least secure. The additional time we spend with the first stage of planning—

whatever it may be—should gradually help us feel more secure with that stage.

My suggestion here is that we avoid developing our own style of planning by focusing on the things with which we feel more comfortable. Instead, start with those that are most uncomfortable and understand how to deal with them. Once this has been accomplished we can begin with the more comfortable elements—the things we feel good about—with the assurance that the other elements will, indeed, fall into place. Our initial endeavors with them will provide us with the experience, and knowledge, to allow this to occur.

The choice of the unit planning model described in this chapter was a deliberate one. It has been my experience as an educator of novice elementary social studies teachers that they feel most uncomfortable with the goals and content of the social studies. This is understandable because this area encompasses affective considerations as well as ideas and processes from a minimum of six academic disciplines. The use of this model helps beginning teachers become more comfortable with goals and content and allows them to move to their own style with the assurance that they are planning thoroughly for their social studies instruction.

We can end this chapter by indicating that an awareness of how one plans a unit from scratch, if you will, should not be thought to preclude use of a textbook as a major resource. If anything, it can only strengthen your use of the textbook. This knowledge will allow you to be certain that the purposes for which the text was written will be met. It will also allow you to supplement the text, thus insuring that the needs and interests of your students are recognized.

Springboards to Discussion _____

1. Visit the resource center of a local school district to determine the various resources (for example, films, artifacts, and so forth) that they have available. Examine these to determine what units of study they might support. Based on what you found, generate several goals that your unit might have. Try to generate goals of more than one type, that is, conceptual, process, and affective.
2. Interview a teacher about the process he or she uses in planning a unit. Focus on the steps taken and the sequence with which they are taken. Ask the teacher to share what he or she considers to be the most important curricular decisions that need to be made in this planning.
3. Choose a unit topic for a grade with which you have some familiarity. Then, following the process we have discussed choose and develop one conceptual goal that would be appropriate for that unit. Analyze the goal and determine if you can incorporate process and affect. Then, from your analysis, develop objectives and plan learning experiences. Finally, for your first objective, develop a daily lesson plan.

References _____

FRAENKEL, JACK. "The Importance of Learning Activities," in William W. Joyce and Frank L. Ryan (eds.), *Social Studies and the Elementary Teacher: Promises and Practices,* Bulletin 53. Washington, D.C.: National Council for the Social Studies, 1977.

GRONLUND, NORMAN E. *Stating Objectives for Classroom Instruction.* New York: Macmillan Publishing Company, 1978.

LYDECKER, ANN FAVOR. "Teacher Planning of Social Studies Intructional Units." Paper presented at the annual meeting of the American Educational Research Association, Los Angeles, April 1981.

ROBERTS, ARTHUR D. "The Roberts Checklist—Selecting and Evaluating Social Studies Materials," *The Social Studies* (May/June, 1980), pp. 114–117.

TABA, HILDA, et al. *A Teacher's Handbook to Elementary Social Studies: An Inductive Approach.* Reading, MA: Addison-Wesley, 1971.

TABA, HILDA. *Curriculum Development: Theory and Practice.* New York: Harcourt, Brace and World, 1962.

TYLER, RALPH. *Basic Principles of Curriculum and Instruction.* Chicago: University of Illinois Press, 1949.

Implementing

CHAPTER

11

Activity-Oriented Learning Experiences

CHAPTER OBJECTIVES _____

After reading this chapter you should be able to:

1. Describe learning experiences designed to simulate real-life situations:
   - Simulations.
   - Dramatic play.
2. Elaborate upon the different types of learning experiences in which children make things related to the topic being studied:
   - Construction.
   - Processing, the replication of activities in which people engage to meet basic needs and wants.
3. Discuss those creative experiences that can be included in the curriculum:
   - Music and dance.
   - Dramatic experiences.
4. Describe experiences that allow children to gather information firsthand:
   - Study trips.
   - Interviews with resource persons.
5. Describe experiences that are appropriate for children with handicapping conditions.

In introducing this book I asked what your memories of social studies in the elementary school were. I ask that question quite frequently when I work with pre- and inservice teachers. When we analyze what made for a positive recollection of elementary social studies we tend to come up with similar results time after time. Aside from teacher characteristics ("She was interested in us." "You could tell he really liked social studies and wanted us to like them"), the most important contributing factor to the type of memory a person had was the learning activities done. They either made social studies exciting and meaningful or as one student said, "dull as dishwater."

When we look further to determine what made these experiences meaningful to the students we usually again come up with similar results. They forced the student to *actively* consider the subject matter in some way. Either the students were physically doing something or, if they were working with reading materials, they could clearly perceive the purpose for what they were doing. Social studies, for them, was not a constant, "Read the chapter and answer the questions at the end."

In this section of the book we'll consider ways of making social studies meaningful by involving students with subject matter. The present chapter will be devoted to a consideration of a number of doing-type experiences, such as construction and simulation, which for the most part, require some type of physical activity on the part of the children. In the next chapter, we'll consider how language-related activities, such as text usage, can also provide for active involvement on the children's part. In the concluding chapter of this section we'll examine ways of insuring that these experiences are successful, considering various learning experiences as well as strategies for organizing our classrooms for learning.

As we consider each of the experiences we'll also give some indication of what your role as teacher will be as children engage in them. In the synthesis sections we'll suggest some general guidelines for insuring that the learning experiences are successful in helping students meet their objectives.

Characteristics of Learning Experiences

We are using the term *learning experiences* in this chapter instead of learning activities. This is done purposefully. As you will shortly see, the nature of the experiences is such that they usually require that the students engage in more than one activity before any type of closure is reached. In a given dramatic play session, for example, they might engage in three different activities: make props, act out a situation, and then engage in research for the purpose of making their future play more realistic. A learning experience, then, is usually made up of a series of activities.

As you read about the different learning experiences we have chosen to include in this chapter you will notice that the activities they entail can be easily fit into Fraenkel's (1977) four categories of learning activities, which we discussed earlier. Some will allow for student *intake* of information. Some serve the purpose of facilitating the *organization* of this data. Others will permit *generalizing* and *creating*.

There are any number of ways of categorizing learning experiences and activities. For our purposes, the ones being discussed here can be thought of as belonging to one of four groups:

1. Those that provide the opportunity for the children to engage in problem solving in a simulated environment.
2. Those that emphasize construction and making of different tangible products.
3. Those that emphasize creative endeavors in one way or another.
4. Those that emphasize the use of social-science-type investigative skills.

Simulating Human Activities

The first group of learning experiences we will consider are ones that place children in simulated real-life situations and have them deal with these to the best of their ability. These experiences include simulations and dramatic play. Both are designed to give the students some understanding of how the world and its people function and/or give them the opportunity to use different thinking processes in dealing with real-life problems. They are suited for use in the elementary classroom because they make content come alive for the student; children can, for example, vicariously experience what life was like during early colonial days, work on an assembly line, or decide how to run a business. They are also appropriate because they provide for active involvement on the part of the students.

Simulations

1. It's after school and nobody is home. John has been making toast in the toaster when he notices smoke. It's coming from the toaster cord. John knows not to touch the wire. He goes to the telephone.

    As he makes his telephone call John's third-grade classmates observe. Later, with their teacher's help, they will discuss the appropriateness of whom John called and what he said.

2. The fifth grade "family" sits at a table deciding how they will spend their monthly income. So much for food. So much for clothing. And this month they're going to get a medical insurance policy after paying the doctor's bill for Junior's broken wrist. (They really didn't expect that expense, and it set them back!) After everything is paid, there won't be much money left for entertainment.

    Once their budget is completed they'll pick up an "Events" card to see if anything is going to affect their income next month. They're not worried about another broken wrist, but they sure hope that there won't be an increase in grocery prices.

3. Lee is really feeling pleased with himself. So far his apple business has been showing a good profit. Now he has to decide how much he wants to charge for them tomorrow. After he punches his decision into the computer it will give him a sales report for the next day, telling him how many he sold and how much income he has.

These situations are examples of three different types of simulation that can be used in elementary classrooms. The first is a commercially prepared one (Glazier, Moore, and Wiener, 1971). The second was teacher-designed. The third is a computer simulation (*Sell Apples,* Minnesota Educational Computing Consortium, 1983). Later we'll discuss each of these types. At this point, however, we can analyze these examples for the purpose of determining what makes a simulation a simulation.

Essentially, simulations have two basic characteristics. First, they are *abstractions* of real-life situations. They encapsulate the essential elements of the situation and present these elements to be dealt with by the students. In *Help!*, for example, the two major elements are an emergency and a telephone call that needs to be made in order to get help in this emergency. In some respects this encapsulation simplifies reality. A good simulation, however, will not distort reality as it simplifies it. Instead, it will include its most essential elements. So in *Sell Apples* the focus is on price and income.

The second characteristic of a simulation is its emphasis on *decision making*. Individuals are usually required to decide upon something—be it who to

call or how much to spend. The interesting thing about simulations in respect to decision making is their ability to provide individuals with data
about the outcome of their decisions. Usually there is some mechanism
provided for feedback on what will occur as a result of the decision—the
consequences of a given choice are provided to the students. *Sell Apples*, for
example, tells you what happened the next day.

In addition to these major characteristics, all simulations usually have
other things in common. They all, for example, put individuals into *roles*
that parallel those in the real-life situation—be it mother, father, or entre-
preneur. They also impose the *rules* or restrictions that would prevail in that
situation. Finally they have *rounds*. Individuals make decisions more than
once in a simulation; consequences of actions in previous rounds can be used
as data for making the present round's decisions.

Simulations are appropriate for helping students develop social science
understandings. (*Sell Apples*, for example, helps illustrate the relationship
between price and income.) Their very nature is one that helps students
develop and exercise various problem-solving skills. They can also help develop affective capabilities, such as perspective-taking skills, by putting
individuals into the roles of others and allowing them to experience what it
is like to be in those roles. Thus, they can be used to help develop the types of
social studies goals we have been discussing. Further, they can be used with
students of varying ability and achievement levels.

Categories of Simulation. For the purposes of our discussion, simulations fall into three different categories. First, as in the case of *Help!*, there
are those that have been developed and published by individuals and
groups. Related to these are the second group, computer simulations, which
are commercially prepared. Finally, there are teacher-constructed simulations, which may or may not utilize the computer. The following briefly
describes these.

Prepared Simulations. Although not as plentiful as those available to
older students, there are still any number of simulations that have been
developed for use in the elementary classroom. In her review of elementary
classroom simulations that could be used with large groups, Muir (1980)
found eighty-eight; these included content from all of the social sciences and
history. (Unfortunately, the bulk of these were designed to be used in grades
four and above.) These vary in cost from nothing to more than fifty dollars.
The former can be found, accompanied by complete descriptions of how to
prepare and run them, in such journals as *Social Education, The Social
Studies,* and *Instructor.* There are also books, such as *Paper, Pencils and
Pennies* (Hyman, 1977), that contain simulations for classroom use. With
these it is the teacher's responsibility to prepare necessary materials. More
expensive simulations usually come packaged with all necessary materials
and are available from commerical publishers or clearing houses such as
Social Studies School Services (P.O. Box 802, Culver City, Co. 90230). A
good source of information is Stadsklev's (1975) *Handbook of Simulation
Gaming in Social Education: Part II: Directory,* which describes and evalu-
ates various simulations and indicates where they might be obtained.

Computer simulations provide quick feedback on decisions students make.

Computer Simulations. A natural outcome of the increased usage of computers in the classroom has been the development of software for the social studies. Included in this software are simulations. Although there are ways in which computer simulations can be used with total class groups, the interactive nature of these simulations (the need to respond to computer-generated questions and directions) makes them more appropriate for use by individuals and small groups.

As with the previously discussed prepared simulations there is a wide variety of sources for programs. Such professional journals as *Classroom Computer Learning* and *Social Education* often will print programs for simulations that can be copied as well as information about programs that are available for purchase. (The latter journal, incidentally, frequently publishes a feature section on computer courseware.) Another source for computer-assisted simulations is the Minnesota Educational Computing Consortium (MECC, 3490 Lexington Avenue North, St. Paul, MN 55112). This consortium gathers and packages computer software for all areas of the curriculum and makes these available, through subscription, to school districts that are permitted to copy them. Included with the discs are manuals (including student materials) that can also be copied.

One concern that has been often voiced about instructional simulations is that they often simplify reality to the point of distorting it. This is necessary in many cases because the complexity of events would serve to confuse students, and the purpose for which the simulation was developed would not be served. Fortunately, computer-assisted simulations are often able to circumvent this problem. Data can be built into the program to be presented only when necessary in relation to student decision making. Otherwise, it remains stored in the computer's memory.

The number of available computer simulations is not as high as other types of simulations. It is anticipated that this will increase in correspondence to computer usage in the elementary school. Because many textbook publishers are moving into the production of computer software it is also anticipated that simulations (and other course-related materials) will soon be available as adjuncts to textbooks.

The choice of commercially prepared simulations, computer or otherwise, should be made judiciously. Schug and Kepner (1984) suggest that twelve criteria be employed. Although they were specifically addressing computer simulations, these criteria are just as appropriate for other types of simulations. They include the following:*

1. Helps to meet existing social studies course objectives.
2. Develops content and skills not easily addressed in traditional materials.
3. Presents educationally sound social studies content and skills.
4. Provides multiple opportunities for students to interact with the simulation.
5. Has clear directions and simple routines for students to follow.
6. Presents graphics and sound which contribute to learning.
7. Is playable without using inappropriate amounts of time.
8. Has adequate support materials for teachers.
9. Provides materials and activities to prepare students to play the simulation.
10. Has specific directions to guide the debriefing session.
11. Uses examples and language which are nonsexist and nonracist.
12. Is not excessively violent or competitive.

Computer simulations should be used judiciously. They are attractive to children because many have a gamelike quality (e.g., in MECC's "Oregon Trail," which simulates a wagon-train trip during the westward movement, there is an opportunity to hunt deer or shoot at bandits in a shooting-gallery-like context). This attractiveness may cause the simulations to be used for purposes other than intended; for example, as a rainy-day time-filler. This diminishes their potential for meaningful learning experiences. (We know, for example, of a school district that has forbidden the use of "Oregon Trail" in all grades but the fifth, for whom it was originally purchased. This occurred because it was being overused in earlier grades, and fifth graders saw it only as a game!) Simulations are meant to be learning experiences and their independent use outside of a unit of study is probably best reserved until after their use as learning experiences has been accomplished. At that point they may serve to reinforce learning.

Teacher-Constructed Simulations. It is possible for teachers to design their own simulations for classroom use. Sometimes they are quite simple;

*From Mark C. Schug and Henry S. Kepner, Jr. "Computer Simulation in the Social Studies," *The Social Studies*, Vol. 75:5 (September/October 1984), pp. 211–215. A publication of the Helen Dwight Reid Educational Foundation. Reprinted with permission.

many teachers have invented some type of "assembly line" simulation to illustrate concepts associated with production such as *division of labor* and *interdependence.* Sometimes they get quite elaborate; for example, the classroom is transformed into a mini-economic society with budding young capitalists inventing businesses, selling stock, and going bankrupt. And sometimes simple simulations develop into quite elaborative ones. We observed a teacher initiate a mini-economy simply to insure that classroom management and housekeeping tasks ran smoothly. Gradually this activity evolved into a simulation where businesses were being invented and stocks were being sold!

The development of a classroom simulation parallels planning for other types of learning experiences; essentially you need to decide what you want your students to accomplish and how they will accomplish it. The literature dealing with simulations has described this development in terms of a series of steps to be taken and factors to be considered. The following synthesizes the important steps found in this literature.

1. Select a *topic* for the simulation. Here you will decide upon which aspect of the larger unit topic the simulation will address. In selecting this topic you will, of course, have learning objectives in mind. For the most part these will be the same as those of the larger unit; however, it is possible for the simulation topic to suggest additional objectives.

2. Select a *model* or *context* for the simulation. Essentially, this step requires you to decide upon *how* the topic will be approached; for example, in "Oregon Trail" the westward movement is approached by having students move along the trail on a simulated map.

3. Decide what *form* the simulation will take. Here, your concern will be with *how* to best present the simulation to the students. What will be the overall goal of the simulation (survival? making money? and so on)? How will they approach this goal (as explorers, family members)? How will they know how to approach this goal (What information will they be given? When? How will they know what to do with it?)?

4. Consider the *roles* the characters will take, what *resources* they will have, and the *rules* that will guide their behavior.

5. Consider how *reality* will be emphasized. What aspects of life are going to be introduced in addition to those stipulated in the prior step? Here you might consider whether problems, such as unforseen loss of resources or medical emergencies, will be brought into the simulation and when they will be introduced.

6. Decide how *rounds* will be structured and when the game will *terminate.* Your job here is to determine how decision making will occur in the simulation. You will also need to consider when to end the simulation, the point at which it is most probable that its objectives will have been met.

7. Select *evaluation* strategies to determine if, indeed, the objectives have been met.

These steps, of course, are basic ones and you will need to make other decisions as you go through them. For example, you'll need to consider the materials the simulation will require and what information the students will need. One way to get a sense of what these are (as well as a sense of what is entailed in the basic design steps) is to examine and play commercially prepared simulations.

Dramatic Play

Kari was upset at "her" students. They had misbehaved all day while attending her Dame School in Colonial New England. She really didn't think that children would really act that way in those times.

"Well," her teacher asked, "why did you guys misbehave?" As different children chimed in with bits of information the basic problem became apparent; they had nothing to do! As their discussion progressed they realized that, if their play was going to be authentic, they would need to find out what the early colonial children did in school.

Their teacher had anticipated this problem and had prepared a short lesson on the hornbook. The total class group examined a replica of one that had been obtained from the school district's instructional materials center. Then the entire class read a prepared handout that gave basic information about hornbooks. Finally, the school group made plans to construct their own hornbooks.

This vignette, which we actually observed, captures some of the aspects of dramatic play. Children attempt to recreate some aspect of the human experience. They take the roles of individuals in a given situation and attempt to act as those individuals might. As the play progresses they are encouraged to make it as authentic as possible. (The resolution of Kari's problem made her school situation a bit more authentic.) This usually requires some research and data gathering on the children's part, and the results of the research should be immediately applied to the situation.

In many respects dramatic play may be considered to be a simulation—children take the roles of individuals, act as they would, and often encounter problems typical of the situation. It differs somewhat from the simulations we have been discussing in that what occurs in dramatic play is very spontaneous. It follows no set script; the direction it takes is dependent upon the children's needs and interests. The only restriction placed on the children is that they attempt to make their play as authentic as possible.

Dramatic play evolves through several stages. The first of these is the exploration of an arranged environment by the children. This environment, which might be located in a certain part of the classroom, will contain various resources that are related to the general topic the teacher has chosen for the play. These resources might include different types of realia, clothing, pictures, books, and so on. Three examples illustrate such arranged environments.

1. For a first grade class, a play house was located in one corner of the room. It contained a table, chairs, a variety of mock utensils and appliances, and a box of dress-up clothes.
2. On a table in one corner of a third grade class were a variety of restaurant menus, different food magazines, trays borrowed from the cafeteria, and small order-pads.

3. The Navajo corner of a fifth grade class was decorated with brightly colored Navajo rugs and blankets, as well as posters of the Navajo people at work. On the table there were a variety of books dealing with the Navajo. The most popular items, however, were the drop spindle (a top-shaded tool for spinning wool—wool is spun as the spindle is spun, then dropped), a carder (for cleaning and preparing wool for spinning), several clumps of raw wool, and a loom.

Prior to exploring the environment children may be told that they will be engaging in play about a certain topic, or they may not be. In any case they are encouraged to make use of this environment—to examine, touch, and manipulate. Once they have done this exploration they are encouraged by their teacher to act out situations suggested by the environment.

Following the initial acting out, which is usually relatively short, the pupils are brought together to plan the next play period. Problems the children encountered, such as not knowing what a drop spindle was and what it was used for, are elicited. Plans are made to deal with these problems, and suggestions are made about what the children will do in the next play.

Following this initial play and planning stage, the dramatic play follows a cyclical pattern. The children engage in the play and are observed by the teacher who notes any problems. Then they are brought together to discuss and evaluate the play. At this point they may indicate any problems they encountered. The teacher may also point out any difficulties he or she has observed. Next, plans are made to deal with these problems; the children or the teacher may indicate any research that needs to be done before the next play to make it more authentic. Finally, the children engage in whatever research, construction, etcetera, will be necessary for the next play period. Prior to that period they will meet briefly, in a group led by the teacher, to discuss their plans.

A dramatic play about a specific situation or topic can last for varying amounts of time. Usually the daily play is relatively short; however, it is possible for the total play to last anywhere from a few days to several weeks. When to stop the play, of course, will be based on the teacher's judgment as to whether the students have (or will be able to) achieve the maximum benefits from the play. That is, the ending of the play will be based on student motivation to continue as well as the teacher's judgment as to whether they are developing understandings and skills as a result of their experiences.

Dramatic play should not end abruptly, however. It is the teacher's responsibility to help the students achieve closure. That is, they should be helped to reflect on the experiences they have had in terms of what they have learned about the situation, the various skills and processes they have used, and the different interpersonal skills and understandings they have developed.

"Making" Experiences _____

The two types of learning experiences we will focus upon in this section are concerned with the children making things that are in some way related to the topic being studied. Although construction and processing are related they differ in that, in the latter, the purpose of making things is to replicate the steps of the production processes used by contemporary people *and* people from the past in meeting their needs and wants.

Construction

There are four different purposes for including construction activities in a social studies unit.

1. To develop models of things being studied. These models may be of any scale and, depending upon various capabilities of the students, may vary in the degree to which they actually model the real objects. Kindergartners may make a model neighborhood using blocks for houses, while upper graders, who have an understanding of the concept of scale, might actually construct a neighborhood to scale. Some models we have observed in classrooms include modes of transportation of the past, present, and future; homes in other lands; early American homes and furnishings; different inventions; models of appropriate and inappropriate soil conservation projects; an Aztec temple; and, with upper graders, various types of contour maps.

2. To illustrate something that the students have learned. Construction activities are appropriate means of synthesizing understanding of various concepts and processes in tangible ways. Included in this category would be bulletin boards; dioramas (scenes in which there are an illustrated back and sides) constructed using shoe or larger-sized boxes; and panoramas, in which a three-dimensional scene is constructed on, say, a tabletop. These differ from models in that the plan for illustrating what is learned is the student's; essentially there is no object to be copied.

3. For use as adjuncts to other activities that are occurring in the unit of study. Construction is especially appropriate with dramatic play, and other dramatic activities, when it is necessary for the children to have props of various kinds.

4. To facilitate problem solving. Sometimes children (and adults for that matter) function best with problem solving when they can deal with the problem manipulatively. Shaftel, Crabtree, and Sherman (1971) provide an illustration of younger children dealing with the question of how oil spills can be contained throught the use of various tools they constructed. I, myself, worked with a group of upper-grade students as they constructed a full-sized replica of an archaeological site (from the site map) and then developed inferences about the people who inhabited the site. (Incidentally, the quality of their inferences was much higher than that of a group who worked solely with the map.)

Construction in the Classroom. It should be obvious from our discussion of the various purposes that construction serves that it is appropriate for helping children achieve different types of goals, both conceptual and those that are more process-oriented in nature. In order to insure that these goals are met, teacher guidance is necessary throughout the construction.

Planning is crucial to a successful experience. Although the teacher may do some planning beforehand (determining objectives, procedures, materials), cooperative planning with the students is imperative. At the minimum this will entail a consideration of what the activity is to accomplish and the steps necessary for this to occur. The children should have a good grasp of what the outcome of the experience will be. The planning will also need to include a review of safety procedures, and, because construction can get noisy, a consideration of how the activity can proceed without unnecessary distraction to others.

As the activity proceeds, the teacher will need to monitor what is occurring, offering advice and assistance when needed.

The construction experience does not culminate with the completion of a product. Time needs to be taken to cooperatively evaluate what has been done. The product is considered in light of original plans. It is equally important that the process (both the group and construction) used to arrive at the product is jointly critiqued by the teacher and students.

Construction differs from many other types of activities that occur in the classroom in the amount of resources it requires, including a variety of different tools and building materials. At times schools may include funds for these resources in their budget. More often than not, however, they don't. This means that you will need to consider alternative and low-cost ways of getting materials. In the past, lumberyards and building supply houses could be counted upon for scrap materials; however, the standardization of many materials has caused this supply to dwindle. A source that has not changed is the parents of the students. A letter sent home indicating what your goals and needs are may provide you with necessary supplies. Similarly, the school PTA may also be a good source.

Construction can be messy. It's a good idea to try to contain the mess in some way. One way, of course, is to have clean-up procedures. Another way is to locate materials and tools in a specific area of the classroom. Some teachers do this with a construction center with bins for materials and a pegboard (with tool shapes outlined) for hanging the tools.

Processing

Processing experiences are essentially an offshoot of construction. Here, the focus is on having children replicate various activities that people utilize, or have utilized, in meeting their needs and wants. They entail having the children produce things while using the same step-by-step process that the people being studied would use. The following illustrate some of the different types of processes that are appropriate to elementary classrooms.

Food Production and Preparation. There are any number of processes entailed in moving food from its raw, natural state to the table; children can be given experiences with each. It is sometimes possible to grow food in class gardens, or to pick various fruits and vegetables at a farm. (These are especially interesting to children whose only experience with food has been on supermarket shelves.) Other food experiences are concerned with refining raw foods for further use. Grinding corn into cornmeal using a metate, or churning butter or ice cream, would be examples of this type of experience. Still other activities would focus on food preservation: for example, making apple butter, fruit leather, or drying various fruits and vegetables.

Cooking is a favorite activity of children and a good way to give them experiences that people of other cultures, and times, have had. One precaution, in addition to safety considerations, that needs to be taken with cooking experiences—especially those that are cross cultural in nature—is that they should not teach stereotypes. Canned pineapple does not a luau make! Nor should the food prepared be so exotic to the children that the culture is perceived as strange. Familiar ingredients, prepared in new ways, do much to encourage understandings about a culture's effect on meeting basic needs.

Industrial Processes. As with food, industrial processes encompass everything from gathering raw materials and refining them to the production of finished products. Gathering would include such activities as gathering various plants (and vegetables) to make natural dyes for cloth, which might then be tie-dyed or batiked. In a different vein it might also include (as we observed in California) the students panning for gold. Examples of refining activities would include the spinning of wool or the carving of fruits, vegetables, or soap to make ink or paint-printing implements. The making of finished products could be exemplified by weaving, quilting, soap making, and candlemaking. With older children this might move into the industrial arts area, with various types of construction projects.

Crafts. Related to industrial processes are various crafts experiences children might have. Crafts allow modifications to be made in the steps of a process or in the finished product. Thus, simple weaving is an industrial process; when a pattern is introduced it becomes a craft. Because of this, craft experiences can be creative experiences for children, and creativity should be encouraged.

Children can be given experiences with a variety of media. Cloth can be dyed, embroidered, and appliqued. Yarn can be woven, made into God's Eyes (a Mexican ornament), or glued to cardboard backing to make yarn pictures. Clay can be used to make various types of pottery and other objects. Baskets can be woven out of a variety of materials. Wood, stone, or soap can be used for carving. And there are any number of uses for papier-mâché—including masks, piñatas, and different types of small figures.

As with construction, cooperative planning and evaluation is a must for processing activities. The students must be aware of the steps of the process and any specific techniques they will employ. Materials need to be available. When the children have completed a process they need to be helped to reflect on what they have done. This reflection should focus not only on the process but also on the social studies understandings that might be generated by the experience.

Creative Experiences _____

Creative experiences can occur in two ways in the classroom. Students can be exposed to the creative expressions of other people; that is, they can be helped to appreciate varied forms of art, music, and literature. Or they can be encouraged to use their own creativity to illustrate something they have learned. Often these two types of experiences will occur together; for example, reading a number of haikus may lead to the students writing their own. We will consider both of these ways of providing creative experiences together in the following discussion.

Music

Tooze and Krone (1958), who have written extensively about the use of music in the social studies curriculum, strongly encourage its use because, as they so eloquently state, it represents a "distilled essence of [people's] values and experiences" (p. 3). They indicate that to know the music of a people is to know the people themselves.

There are a variety of ways that we can foster this musical knowledge. The first of these involves having students listen to different types of music. One of the major musical ways of learning about a people or, for that matter, the people of an era is through their folksongs. Thus, for example, a study of

These cloggers reflect one of the cultural groups at their school. They are sharing their culture through dance.

the antebellum South might be enhanced by listening to the spirituals sung by the slaves. Or, a unit on the westward movement might be accompanied by the exploration of the songs sung by the pioneers.

Of course, music is played as well as sung, and other listening experiences would focus on instrumental music. These experiences might include the instrumental music of a group of people; for example, sitar music of India, the piped music of Peru, or flamenco or fado music of Spain and Portugal. They might also include music composed to evoke images of people, places, or times. Examples of this type of music would include Dvorak's *New World Symphony*, Copeland's *Grand Canyon Suite*, or the steel-drum music of the Caribbean. Finally, the experience might focus on listening to a single instrument as it is characteristically played; for example the ram's horn (shofar) as it is blown to signal the end of Yom Kippur, the Jewish Day of Atonement, or the "talking drums" of Equatorial West Africa as they are used to communicate across distances.

Usually children are not satisfied to sit and listen for very long—they want to be part of the music making. Most children will gladly join in singing songs of other times and people, even if these songs are not in English. They will also join in providing the background rhythms and, when necessary, sound effects for the songs.

The third way of utilizing music in the social studies is through the use of musical instruments. At times it is possible to obtain musical instruments used by other cultures and have the children explore the different sounds and melodies these can produce. In some cases children can also make their own instruments. These may be quite authentic (such as rattles made out of dried gourds and filled with stones—an instrument used by, among others, some West African, Native American, and Caribbean peoples).

The singing of songs and the making of instruments can quite naturally lead to the children's developing their own music, both instrumental and sung. This might be *about* the topic being studied. It might also be music that is in the *style* of the era or people being studied.

A final way of incorporating music is through dance. Most cultural groups have characteristics dances that, in their simplest form, rely on a few basic steps. These steps can be taught to the students and, once mastered, can be elaborated upon. (Many also have the advantage of not requiring partners. From my experience this avoids many problems that occur when students are at an age where they are hesitant to dance with partners of the opposite sex.) Some examples of different dances I have successfully taught to my students include: Greek line dances, such as the *Hassapiko*; the Philippine *Tinikling*, which is done between two bamboo poles as they are clapped together; the Israeli *hora*, which is done in a circle; and the West African *High Life*, which is a cha-cha type dance. I have also observed children being taught dances, such as clogging and square dances, which are typical of their own region or subculture.

A teacher need not be an accomplished musician to use music as part of the social studies curriculum. There are any number of resources that can be consulted. There are books of songs and music, such as that by Tooze and Krone (1958) noted earlier. *Social Education* (October 1985) devoted an entire issue to music in the social studies, citing a variety of resources for teachers to consult. Usually a school library or a school district's media center will contain a number of such resources. There are also records that contain both music and instruction for dances. Again, these can be obtained from various media centers. A school or school district will also contain people who are willing to help in the selection and teaching of music activities. These might be teachers who are music specialists. They might also be members of the community, including parents, who are willing to volunteer their time and expertise. (In the school I taught in in California, for example, we often called upon a student's aunt, who had been a professional dancer in Mexico. She was thrilled to share her talent.) Your job is simply one of finding and using these resources.

Dramatic Experiences

Children enjoy stepping into other people's shoes and acting as they do. Two of the strategies we have discussed earlier in this book allow them to do this. Both role play and dramatic play are creative activities that are included in the category of dramatic experiences. Because we have discussed them in detail we won't do so here; instead we'll focus on two other related types of dramatic experiences.

The first of these has been referred to by others as *dramatic play* (McCaslin, 1980) or *reality practice* (Shaftel, 1982). Essentially, this entails having the children spontaneously act out real-life situations. It might take the form of the child imitating the actions of others: for example, first graders may act as parents and children in the play house; third graders might assume the role of community workers; or fifth graders might synthesize their learnings about the legislative branch of government by acting out the process by which a bill becomes a law. It might also take the form of children acting out different types of life situations they might encounter; for example asking or giving directions, seeking help if they were lost, talking on the telephone, and so forth. McCaslin (1980) indicates that this latter type of activity is very appropriate for younger students; it gives them practice in dealing with life situations in a nonthreatening atmosphere.

The second type of dramatic experience is often referred to by the term *creative dramatics*. Here, a story line is decided upon, roles are assigned, and the children spontaneously work through the story. Usually, one person acts as a leader; depending upon the experience of the students this may or may not be the teacher. Some props may be used in creative dramatics, although it is most often done without costumes.

The story line used for the enactments may be created by the children. It may, for example, be some such historical episode as a winter's day at Valley Forge during the Revolutionary War. Or it may depict some aspect of life in a cultural group other than the children's own. Choosing such a story line is not difficult—it has been my experience that, with encouragement, children are very quick to pick up on episodes for enactment from the content they are studying. The story line may also be derived from stories the children

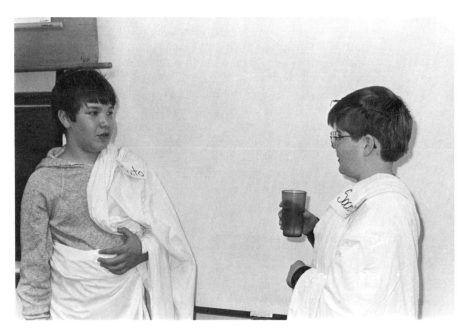

Dramatic presentations need not be elaborate; some research and two sheets yield a dialogue between Plato and Socrates.

have heard or read. In this situation, the children spontaneously act out the story, adding their own interpretations. Benninga and Crum (1982) indicate that this approach to creative dramatics is especially appropriate for fostering the development of perspective taking—discussed earlier—in younger children.

Both of these types of dramatic experiences can not only be done with the children being the actors but also lend themselves to the use of puppets, which can be made by the children from a variety of materials. Papier-mâché molded over small balloons can be used for puppet heads; so, too, can old tennis balls with holes cut in them. Other puppets can be made from lunch bags turned upside down so that the bottom crease is the puppet's mouth, or simply by pasting paper faces on sticks. Puppets have the benefit, in some cases, of permitting normally reticent children to express themselves through the puppets. (Similarly, I have also found them to be useful with students who speak English as a second language. They seem to be less hesitant to speak English when the puppet is doing the speaking.)

The dramatic activities we have been discussing are characterized by their spontaneity. Children decide on a situation and act it out as they think it should be acted out. This may or may not be done with a classroom audience.

Because of their spontaneity, the preparation for these dramatic experiences need not be very structured. A short discussion of what the episode will be about, what roles will be taken, and how characters might act is sufficient. Greater preparation may have the effect of decreasing creativity on the part of the students.

Investigative Experiences _____

Investigative learning experiences provide opportunities for the students to gather information about a topic being studied through first-hand experiences. They allow the students to see places they have studied about, observe different processes, and interact with people. They include study trips and the use of resource people in the classroom. In this section we'll discuss what these experiences are about and how we can ensure that they facilitate student attainment of learning goals. Chapter 13 outlines how you might find the resources for these investigative experiences.

Study Trips

The term *study trip* is used to describe an experience in which students travel to a specific place for the purpose of obtaining information relevant to the topic being studied. A study trip should help students attain specific unit objectives. Although students indeed may derive pleasure from these trips their primary purpose is learning. Thus they differ somewhat from field trips, such as one to an amusement park, whose primary purpose is fun. (Fun trips, of course, do have a place in the curriculum.)

Regardless of where you will be teaching, the area that surrounds the school within a short driving radius will contain places that can be visited for learning purposes. These might include the following.

- Businesses and industries, including factories and service-oriented businesses.
- Government buildings and offices, including those that are service-oriented such as the post office and the police, fire, and health departments.
- Voluntary and civic organizations, such as the Red Cross.
- Museums of various types.
- Communication agencies, including the telephone company, newspaper offices, and radio and television stations.
- Different types of parks—historical homes and sites as well as those containing unique physical characteristics.
- Farms.
- Transportation centers such as terminals of different types, docks, and railway stations.

Most of these will allow, with prior arrangements, visits from class groups.

Before taking a group on a study trip, it is advisable, if possible, for the teacher to take a preview trip to the site. This is done so that the teacher can not only note the features that should be observed by the students, but also for practical considerations. If a guide is to be used, the teacher will want to confer with this person to discuss what will be observed as well as share specific characteristics of the students (attention span, for example) of which the guide should be aware. The teacher should also inquire about any safety precautions that need to be taken by the students. It is also wise to inquire about the number of adults needed to supervise, the availability of adequate restroom facilities and drinking fountains. For field trips that require a large portion of the school day, it is wise to inquire about a place for the students to eat lunch.

Preparation for the study trip includes more than a site preview. Other practical considerations will entail arranging for transportation, obtaining additional adults to accompany the children, and securing parental permission for the trip. (Usually schools or districts have standard permission forms.) All of these arrangements need to be made well in advance of the study trip.

Students need to be prepared for the trip so that they can understand its relationship to what they are studying. They should be aware of the objectives of the trip and know what they will be expected to get out of it. The teacher may wish to elaborate upon those things to be observed and the reasons why they will be observed. Student questions to be answered during the trip should be elicited and strategies for insuring that they are answered should be discussed.

Practical aspects of the trip also need to be cooperatively planned just prior to the trip. Students need to be assigned to chaperones and it is probably wise to assign students "buddies" to insure that no one gets lost. Safety procedures, as well as potential problems (and what to do about them) should be discussed. Appropriate behavior standards need to be established. And, just prior to embarking on the trip, students should be given the opportunity to visit the restroom and water fountain. Following this, a "nose count," which will be repeated during the trip, should be made.

A study trip doesn't end with a visit to a site; follow-up is crucial to insure that its objectives have been met. Students need to be given the opportunity to reflect on their experience in order to reiterate what has been learned. Questions, established before the trip, should be reexamined and their answers discussed. (And, if they haven't been answered, alternative approaches to finding the answers should be considered.) Findings should be synthesized in some way. In addition, of course, some of this time should be spent in writing thank-you notes to individuals—such as guides and chaperones—who helped with the study trip.

Resource Persons

Just as there are a variety of places to visit in the area of the school, so too are there any number of people in the community who have different areas of expertise that they may be willing to share with our students. These individuals may engage in different occupations that are of interest to the students. They may belong to a different subcultural group or have lived in a different cultural environment. They may have lived in a time that is history to our students. Or, they may have different talents and skills they can share. These individuals can be invited into our classrooms, or our students might be taken to visit them.

The contribution that resource persons can make to our curriculum should be established before they actually meet with our students. Many teachers

Resource persons, such as this Cherokee basket maker, are especially interesting when they bring things that can be seen and touched.

contact these individuals well before a unit begins to discuss the possibility of a future visit. During this discussion the teacher determines the individual's specific area of expertise and the general times when the individual might be available to interact with the students. These are noted, for future reference, on a file card that also includes the resource person's name, address, and telephone number.

The resource person should be contacted twice prior to the actual visit. During the first contact the teacher will arrange the time for the visit and generally discuss the topic with which the resource person will deal. The second contact, which occurs just prior to the visit, goes into specifics. The teacher will want to outline exactly what the students have been studying and specific questions that they will have. The teacher will also want to share specific characteristics of the students that the guest should be aware.

These might include developmental characteristics; for example, that, if possible, younger students prefer doing to seeing and listening. They might also include such factors as attention span.

Students need to be prepared for the resource person's visit. With the teacher's help they can generate and list the specific questions and topics with which they wish the resource person to deal. They can also be helped to consider how they will interact with the resource person, practicing different questioning and interviewing techniques. At this time it will also be wise to review different behavior standards—how they will greet and make the guest feel comfortable, and so on.

The follow-up of a resource person's visit is very similar to that of the study trip. Time should be devoted to the students in order that they may synthesize what they have learned. Questions, and their answers, can be reviewed and, if necessary, the students may make plans for further follow-up on the subject. It may also be necessary for the students to evaluate their interaction with the person, suggesting, for example, ways that they might more effectively interview resource people in the future.

Good resource people are an asset to our curriculum, and we'll want to ensure that they look upon the experience as a positive one. We, and our students, will want to make them feel warmly welcomed in our classroom. One way to do this is to ensure that they have the student's attention; other tasks should be put aside during the visit. Another way is to express our appreciation for the time they have taken to be with us. A personal thank-you note from the teacher, and one that is cooperatively written by the individuals with whom the resource person worked, are a good way to do this.

Learning Experiences and the Mainstreamed Child _____

Mainstreaming refers to the integration of children with handicapping conditions into the regular classroom. This integration is both social and instructional. The handicapped children are part of the classroom group and receive instruction with their nonhandicapped peers.

Mainstreaming is not a matter of choice for schools; it is a mandate. Public Law 94–142, the Education for All Handicapped Children Act, requires that handicapped children be educated to the greatest extent possible with their nonhandicapped peers. This means that you may have a handicapped child working in your classroom for all or part of the day, depending upon the type of assistance they need from special teachers.

The integration of the special child is not done haphazardly. PL 94–142 requires that, once a handicapped child is identified, an Individualized Education Program (IEP) be developed. The IEP is developed cooperatively by representatives of the school system—including regular classroom teachers—the child's parent or parents and, if appropriate, the child. It will include long-range goals for the child, short-term objectives, evaluation procedures, and criteria (along with an evaluation schedule), an indication of the special services the child is to receive, and an indication of the amount of time the child is to be in the regular program.

Although you most likely will receive help from a resource teacher (and if you don't you shouldn't hesitate to ask for it) you will need to make decisions about the most appropriate learning experiences for your handicapped students. In order to do this you should be aware of the characteristics of specific disabilities and the implications these have for the learning situation.

Before we begin our examination of these characteristics, two points need to be made. First, special educators appear to be unanimous in their belief that exceptional children are more *like* unexceptional children than they are different. The two will have many characteristics in common. Second, the characteristics that they don't have in common are the ones that you'll need to consider. Both of these points suggest that, as you plan for the special child, you consider the special characteristics of the child, *not* the label (e.g., "learning disabled") attached to the characteristics. Thus, you'll find that many activities are appropriate in teaching both the handicapped and nonhandicapped child.

Characteristics of Handicapped Students

Mental Retardation. Public Law 94–142 defines mental retardation as significant subaverage intellectual functioning coupled with deficiencies in adaptive behavior. The former is usually determined in terms of scores on standardized intelligence tests. Where the mean IQ is 100, with a standard deviation of 15 points, subaverage intellectual functioning is defined as an IQ of 70 or below. Students in the upper range, 50–70 IQ, are referred to as *educable mentally retarded* and are the mentally retarded who are most often mainstreamed. Deficiencies in adaptive behavior refers to the lack of development of such things as social and self-help skills and the ability to apply reasoning.

Mentally retarded students have a slower learning rate than their non-handicapped peers, and they need more practice with new concepts and skills. Thus, the quantity of things that they will learn will be less than their peers. This implies that we need to be careful in choosing what we want them to learn. Our choices should be based on what is most relevant and functional to their present and future lives (Schulz and Turnbull, 1984).

In working with mildly retarded students we should be aware that they probably have difficulty with reading. They will also have difficulty dealing with abstract reasoning. These facts, coupled with the fact that they will have short attention spans, would suggest that the learning experiences we provide be as concrete as possible for these children. Many of the experiences we have discussed in this chapter—dramatics, construction, and processing—would be appropriate.

Learning Disabilities. According to Public Law 94–142 a learning disability occurs when there is an "imperfect ability to listen, think, read, spell, or do mathematical calculation" (*Federal Register*, 1977, 42478). This is due, it says, to a disorder in one of the basic psychological processes involved in using or understanding language.

Learning disabled students will experience difficulty with school subjects. Yet, according to Schulz and Turnbull (1984) we cannot generalize and say that they won't do well in a specific subject or subjects. They indicate that individual strengths and weakness are particularly striking with these children. Further, they indicate that they may have deficits in one or more learning modalities (e.g., reading or listening). This suggests, as we have said in various parts of this book, that we employ a multimodal approach to learning, that we _not_ use one type of learning experience solely.

Learning disabled students may be easily distracted, especially when there may be a variety of stimuli vying for their attention (for example, cars passing on the street outside the classroom). This suggests placing the students away from possible distractions and in a position to attend to what is relevant. It also suggests teaching the children strategies for monitoring their own behavior as well as for monitoring the behavior of their peers. Fowler (1986) found that a carefully developed routine for activities, paired with strategies for peer monitoring, then self-monitoring of individual actions, led to a substantial decrease in disruption and nonparticipation among children with behavior and/or learning problems.

Behavioral/Emotional Disturbance. As with all other handicapping conditions, PL 94–142 defines emotional disturbance as a condition that is exhibited over a marked period of time and adversely affects educational experience. Some of the characteristics that could indicate emotional disturbance include:

1. An inability to learn that cannot be attributed to intellectual, sensory, or health factors.
2. An inability to develop or maintain satisfactory interpersonal relationships.
3. Inappropriate behavior or feelings for a given situation.
4. A tendency to develop physical symptoms or fears associated with personal or school problems.

An individual who exhibits one or more of these characteristics could be considered to be emotionally disturbed.

Emotional disturbance can affect learning. So too can learning (or lack of it) affect one's emotional well-being. Schuncke (1978) indicates that in some classrooms the organization is such that boys perceived by their teacher to be of low ability were similarly perceived by their peers. This, in turn, was reflected in the affect (liking) and power structures of the classroom. Academically low boys were low in all areas. Other research (Glidewell and Kantor, 1966) indicates that individuals who are low in these areas tend to exhibit one of two types of behavior—they are passive and withdrawn or aggressive and hostile. These behaviors are characteristic of emotionally disturbed children.

PL 94–142 focuses on _serious_ emotional disturbances; children with less serious problems are technically not classified as being emotionally disturbed. Yet, there is a good probability that we will see children with characteristics—such as the passive or aggressive behavior noted, or with an inability to complete work, or with difficulty adjusting to change—of the emotionally disturbed. As we said earlier, regardless of label, we can work to change these characteristics.

How can we do this? With acting-out behavioral problems we need to set standards that the child understands and realizes that we will consistently uphold. We can also structure activities so that there are times for the child to be physically active and use energy that might otherwise be used disruptively. This does not necessarily mean having a recess. Many of the experiences cited in this chapter (e.g., construction, and music activities) would be appropriate physical breaks. We can also teach the child strategies for monitoring his or her own behavior. (I once had a sixth grader who gradually learned to take "time out" when he felt he was going to have a disagreement with his peers.) The passive child, according to Schulz and Turnbull (1984) is often overlooked by the teacher. So, one of our first jobs is to notice this child. From there, Schulz and Turnbull suggest that we use strategies for helping the child to build the trust necessary for interpersonal relationships.

As far as learning problems are concerned, experiences for these children should be appropriate to the child academically and appeal to his or her interests. Activities should be highly structured so that the child knows what to do each step of the way and knows what the intended outcome is. In addition, they should be relatively concrete in nature.

Hearing Disabilities. There are essentially two types of hearing disabilities: deafness and hearing impairment. The latter can range from mild to profound. The major educational effect of hearing loss is in the area of communication. Without intervention it is difficult or impossible for a child to process spoken information. This intervention takes different forms depending upon the severity of hearing loss.

Totally deaf children usually are not mainstreamed in the early years of school. Instead they are given intensive training in communication—in some cases lip reading and oral communication, in other cases manual communication (signing). Usually they are mainstreamed when they have developed proficiency. Children who have some hearing can usually be mainstreamed immediately. Hearing aids, as well as devices in which the teacher wears a microphone that transmits to a device worn in the student's ear allow oral communication to be heard to some extent.

Regardless of the extent of hearing loss special considerations need to be made for children with hearing disabilities. Most obviously, some experiences in which hearing is not necessary are appropriate. However, understanding oral communication is important and these children should not be deprived of opportunities to sharpen their skills in this area. To help them do this we should seat them where they are able to see both the teacher and other students since understanding is facilitated by their seeing lip movement. Schulz and Turnbull (1984) indicate that it is not necessary to exaggerate our pronunciation or speak loudly. It is important though, to be certain they can see our lips. Avoid positioning yourself so that things such as glare from windows impairs seeing. Also, when writing on the blackboard, avoid talking while facing the board.

Vision Disabilities. As with hearing disabilities there is a range of vision handicaps that moves from total blindness to vision that is impaired to some degree. PL 94–142 defines a visual disability as one that, *even with correction,* impairs a person's ability to learn.

Adjustments will need to be made when visually handicapped students are in the classroom. Written materials will need to be in Braille for blind students and it may be necessary for the teacher to learn to write in Braille. For partially sighted students these will need to be in large type. Learning experiences will need to be developed so that other sensory channels can be used, especially the senses of touch and hearing. When possible, students should be given the opportunity to handle concrete objects. Auditory substitutes can be made for printed materials. Written material can be read either into a tape recorder or by someone in the classroom. Such objects as pictures can be visually described.

In addition to considering learning experiences, the teacher of a blind student will need to help the child to be able to move about freely in the classroom and school. This will initially require that the student be oriented to the layout of the areas, and be given practice (preferably when no one is in the area) in moving about in them.

Physical Disabilities. Physical disabilities include orthopedic conditions, such as the absence of a limb or cerebral palsy, which impair an individual's mobility. They also include health impairments of a chronic or acute nature, such as epilepsy, asthma, or leukemia, which affect the child's strength or vitality. To be a physical disability, in terms of PL 94–142, these conditions must adversely affect a child's educational performance.

It is difficult to generalize about the educational effects of orthopedic disabilities and ways of intervening. In some cases, student mobility can be helped through use of braces and wheelchairs and through the removal of architectural barriers in the school. Other orthopedic handicaps may require that more time be allowed for a child to complete an assignment or may render a child incapable of engaging in some of the learning experiences, such as construction, which we have been discussing in this chapter. Consultation with the resource teacher will allow you to determine what is appropriate and inappropriate.

With physical disabilities it is necessary for you, as the teacher to know several things. First, you should be aware of the disability. The health section of each child's cumulative records should be checked at the beginning of the school year. Then you need to know whether any special action will be required on your part; for example, if a child is epileptic, you should know what to do in case of seizure. This can be learned through conference with the child's parents and other resource people. Finally, you'll need to know what implications the disability will have for classroom activities; for example, whether the child will tire quickly and, thus, need shorter assignments. Learning experiences should be chosen with these factors in mind.

Synthesis: Making Sense of Learning Experiences _____

In his classic book *Experience and Education*, John Dewey (1972) discusses some of the factors that make an experience, in his words, "educative." One of these factors is the need for reflection on the experience; children need to think about what they learned and did. This is true of the learning experiences we have been discussing. Children may have a grand time, say, constructing a model or engaging in a computer simulation without deriving any of its potential learnings. Unless they can be helped to see its relevance, it is possible for them to engage in an experience without ever attaining any of its objectives.

One of the ways that we can help children make sense out of their experiences is through a debriefing discussion, one in which the activity is examined and evaluated. In this discussion the teacher's role will be that of a facilitator, drawing out the students' perceptions and ideas. Let's briefly examine some of the techniques that can be used to this.

The major technique used in encouraging a discussion is *questioning*. In Chapter 6 we discussed questions that were based on Bloom's taxonomy. These can be used to guide the discussion. For example, in discussing strategies used to obtain data in dramatic play, students might initially be asked a memory question, "What sources did you use?" to begin the discussion. At some point later they might be asked to evaluate the effectiveness of these sources. After a simulation they might be asked to state a generalization based on their experiences (synthesis). Strategies for structuring such questions may be found in Chapter 6.

Hilda Taba and her associates (1971) have developed two strategies, employing questions that are especially appropriate for helping students develop concepts and generalizations based on their experiences. In one strategy students develop concepts by: (1) listing what they have observed or experienced; (2) grouping items from this list; and (3) indicating why they perceive the items to belong together. The strategy for developing generalization also begins with the students elaborating on what they have observed. They are then asked to look for similarities and differences among these things. Next, they are asked to explain why they believe these similarities and differences occurred. Finally, they are asked to develop a generalization based on their explanation for similarities and differences. Taba and her associates suggest a structured series of questions to be used with both of these strategies. Examples of these questions can be found in their book *A Teacher's Handbook to Elementary Social Studies* (1971).

In the debriefing discussion, teacher questions will be used for a variety of purposes, including bringing forth ideas to be discussed, keeping the students on track, probing for further ideas, and getting the students to elaborate upon statements. Of course, there are other techniques that can be used to keep the discussion moving. One of these helps students clarify what is being said. This requires teacher's rephrasing what the student has said in the form of a question ("Are you saying that . . .?"), or it can be done by having the teacher or another student tell what they heard a student say

("What I hear you saying is . . ."). Another technique asks the student for elaboration by restating exactly what has been said, but in a questioning tone ("You didn't like it when the children wouldn't listen to you?").

The amount of time spent on a debriefing discussion will vary with what the children have done in the learning experience. With some experiences it will be quite obvious when the children have met the learning objectives, and the debriefing will not be overly long. With others the outcome may not be so obvious, and the discussion will need to be more structured to insure attainment of objectives. Regardless, our experiences indicate that some type of debriefing is necessary. It serves the function of reinforcing what has been learned and bringing closure to the activity.

Springboards to Discussion _____

1. Examine the elementary social studies computer programs that are available from the Minnesota Educational Computing Consortium. (These can usually be found in your college's curriculum materials center or in a local school district's resource center.) Work through some of the programs. For each program determine the level for which it is appropriate, what the program is helping to teach, and the specific content with which it might be used.
2. Many teachers are afraid of teaching with dramatic play—until they've tried it once. Design a dramatic play experience that might be used with a group of students in a given grade. Plan the arranged environment you might use and consider some strategies that you could employ to lead the children into the play after they have explored the environment. If possible, try the dramatic play with children and evaluate what occurs.
3. Examine a textbook for a given grade with the idea of supplementing it. Examine the objectives for each chapter and the content that is used. Then, determine which of the learning experiences discussed in this chapter would extend and enrich the material presented in the text. Indicate how the learning experience would be developed and what you would need to do to insure its success. Also, suggest how you might evaluate what the students have learned as a result of the experience.

References _____

BENNINGA, JACQUES S., AND CRUM, RUTH ANN. " 'Acting Out' for Social Understanding," *Childhood Education,* Vol. 58 (January/February 1982), pp. 144–147.

DEWEY, JOHN. *Experience and Education.* New York: Collier Books, 1972.

FOWLER, SUSAN A. "Peer Monitoring and Self-Monitoring: Alternatives to Traditional Teacher Management," *Exceptional Children,* Vol. 52, No. 6 (April 1986), pp. 573–581.

FRAENKEL, JACK R. "The Importance of Learning Activities," in William W. Joyce and Frank L. Ryan (eds.), *Social Studies and the Elementary Teacher: Promises and Practices,* Bulletin 53. Washington, DC: National Council for the Social Studies, 1977.

GLAZIER, RAY, MOORE, M. KEITH AND WIENER, KAREN. *HELP!* Cambridge, MA: Abt Associates Inc., 1971.

GLIDEWELL, JOHN C., KANTOR, MILDRED B., et al. "Socialization and Social Structure in the Classroom," in Martin L. Hoffmann and Lois W. Hoffman (eds.), *Review of Child Development Research.* New York: Russell Sage Foundation, 1966, pp. 221–256.

HANNA, LAVONE A, POTTER, GLADYS L., AND REYNOLDS, ROBERT W. *Dynamic Elementary Social Studies.* New York: Holt, Rinehart and Winston, 1973.

HYMAN, RONALD T. *Paper, Pencils and Pennies.* Englewood Cliffs, NJ: Prentice-Hall, 1977.

JOHNSON, DAVID W., AND JOHNSON, ROGER T. *Learning Together and Alone.* Englewood Cliffs, NJ: Prentice-Hall, 1975.

McCASLIN, NELLIE. *Creative Drama in the Classroom.* New York: Longman, 1980.

MUIR, SHARON PRAY. "Simulation Games for Elementary Social Studies," *Social Education,* Vol. 44 (January 1980), pp. 35–39, 76.

SCHUG, MARK C., AND KEPNER, HENRY S., JR. "Computer Simulation in the Social Studies," *The Social Studies,* Vol. 75, No. 5 (September/October 1984), pp.211–215.

SCHULZ, JANE B., AND TURNBULL, ANN P. *Mainstreaming Handicapped Students: A Guide for Classroom Teachers.* Boston: Allyn and Bacon, 1984.

SCHUNCKE, GEORGE M. "Social Effects of Classroom Organization," *The Journal of Educational Research.* Vol. 71, No. 6. (July/August 1978), pp. 303–307.

SHAFTEL, FANNIE R., CRABTREE, CHARLOTTE, AND SHERMAN, VIVIAN. "Problems—Resolution in the Elementary School," in Richard C. Gross and Raymond H. Muesseig (eds.), *Problem-Centered Social Studies Instruction.* Washington, D.C.: National Council for the Social Studies, 1971.

SHAFTEL, FANNIE R., AND SHAFTEL, GEORGE. *Role Playing in The Curriculum.* Englewood Cliffs, NJ: Prentice-Hall, 1982.

Social Education (October 1985).

STADSKLEV, RON. *Handbook of Simulation Games in Social Education: Part II: Directory.* Institute of Higher Edcucation Research and Service, The University of Alabama, 1975.

TABA, HILDA, et al. *A Teacher's Handbook to Elementary Social Studies.* Reading, MA: Addison-Wesley, 1971.

TOOZE, RUTH, AND KRONE, BERTHA. *Literature and Music as Sources for the Social Studies.* Englewood Cliffs, NJ: Prentice-Hall, 1958.

12

Language and Teacher-Facilitated Activities*

After reading this chapter you should be able to:

1. Explore the relationship between social studies and language.

2. Identify reading and language-related study skills that are necessary for students of social studies.

3. Demonstrate how social studies teachers can reinforce these skills.

4. Identify and explain methods for matching students with social studies materials and resources.

5. Present strategies that teachers can use to integrate the language arts with social studies.

Although we have frequently referred to "Your social studies curriculum," in reality it would be extremely difficult to isolate social studies from the rest of the elementary school curriculum. Even if it were easy, it would be undesireable. The isolation and compartmentalization of one school subject from all others convey the subtle message that life is simple, problems are easily dealt with in isolation, and there is no interrelatedness between people, ideas, and experiences. This is simply not true. Learning from a new experience is based on past experience, and new experiences lead to further experiences. The very term *social studies* implies cooperation and interaction. If something is social it cannot exist in isolation from everything else.

Thus, social studies can not and should not exist in isolation from other school subjects. The child in the classroom, just like the adult in our society, should be given numerous opportunities to perceive the complexity and interrelations of life. Although every subject can be incorporated into social studies in one way or another, the language arts are particularly relevant. The purpose of language is communication, and communication requires at least two people: one to send the message (through speaking or writing), and one to receive the message (through listening or reading). Language is at the heart of all social situations and it is an essential tool of social studies.

In this chapter we will explore the relationship between social studies and language. Because of the special importance of reading, we will begin with a

---

*This chapter contributed by Jean Benedict Raffa.

discussion of the reading skills students will need in order to cope with social studies materials. Following this we will discuss how to match children with appropriate materials and resources. Included in this section will be methods for assessing the readability of materials and the abilities and interests of children. Finally, we will provide several strategies that teachers can use for the integration of language arts. These will include activities involving listening, speaking, the reading of related literature, and writing.

Social Studies and Reading Skills

Few teachers would try to teach social studies without any written materials. Most would use a text to help organize, guide, and enrich discovery of social studies concepts. Most will use several other materials, such as maps, card catalogs, and encyclopedias, each of which requires reading. If students are to get maximum benefits from these materials, they will need to develop different reading and reading-related study skills, including using book parts; vocabulary; comprehension; finding and using information sources; and note taking (West, 1978). We can briefly examine each of these.

Using Book Parts

Reading to obtain information requires skills different from those needed when reading for pleasure. We cannot assume that because children have been exposed to books throughout their school years they will understand how to use the study aids provided in a social studies text. Students will need to receive instruction in the use of these aids throughout the elementary grades.

A good time to begin this instruction is when the books are first issued to pupils. Although this can be done in a number of ways, methods that require student involvement and discovery are apt to be more beneficial than lectures. For example, in introducing the title page the teacher can ask, "Who are the authors of this book? How did you find out?" To introduce or reinforce use of the table of contents, the teacher can ask, "How many chapters are in this book? On what page does Chapter 5 begin?" Questions for the index might include, "Where can we find out about the Louisiana Purchase?" "Does the book tell anything about Cuba?"

Questions and activities will vary, of course, with the grade being taught. In the primary grades, much of this instruction will be oral. In the intermediate grades, pupils can be given written exercises that require them to locate information in their texts by using various parts of the book. Activities of this sort should not be limited to the first day but should continue throughout the school year.

Vocabulary

Problems with vocabulary are a major cause for the difficulty that many students have learning social studies concepts. Because concepts are tied to vocabulary, it is important that instruction in vocabulary development go hand in hand with instruction in concepts. By carefully planning vocabulary instruction around each unit of study you will be influencing the linguistic development as well as the conceptual development of each student. Both kinds of development are crucial to successful functioning in society.

The social studies teacher must be concerned with two kinds of vocabulary problems: problems related to the recognition of the printed word and problems in understanding the meaning of the word. Both of these can be aided by teacher planning and instruction in the use of context clues, dictionaries, and structural analysis of words. Students must also be given help in recognizing and understanding many commonly used words, as well as the special and technical vocabulary words that are unique to social studies.

Vocabulary instruction is most effective when it becomes a regular, integral part of each lesson rather than when it is separated into isolated drills. Such activities as having students look up long lists of words in the dictionary prior to a new unit of study are rarely productive. On the other hand, discussing the meanings of key words as they appear in a reading selection, and relating these meanings to the major concepts that are to be studied, should be far more meaningful. For example, before a lesson, you can write out two or three of the sentences from the text that contain key words. Ask students to tell what they think these words mean. What do the sentences mean? What do they have to do with the concept being studied?

After the lesson these words can again be referred to. Students can be asked, "What does this mean to you now? Do you have any questions about what it means or why we are learning it?" Summarize the meanings of the new words and provide helpful examples from the students' own experiences. In succeeding lessons, you should use these new terms whenever possible.

Not all vocabulary study has to be written, however. Some of the most meaningful learning will arise from class and group discussion, field trips, role playing, and other activities. Teachers should take vocabulary development seriously in social studies, using every opportunity to teach new words and reinforce the meanings of those that have already been introduced.

Three Types of Reading Vocabulary. Simmons (1965) identifies three kinds of reading vocabularies that teachers are responsible for developing. The first is a general vocabulary. This consists of all those words that each student encounters, understands, and uses in everyday activities.

While every teacher will help students with these words, there are other more technical terms that are specific to certain content areas. This technical vocabulary is usually exclusive to one subject. Because these words may not be otherwise taught, it is up to the social studies teacher to inventory such terms and provide instruction in them. Examples of technical terms in social studies would include *veto, longitude, legislature, democracy,* and *civilization.*

Finally, there is a specialized vocabulary. This is composed of words that have a generally understood meaning, but when applied to social studies mean something different. An example would be the word *radical,* which means one thing to a math teacher and quite another to the social studies teacher. Other such words would include *cabinet, revolution, range, mouth,* and *fork.*

It is the responsibility of the social studies teacher to provide help with all three kinds of vocabularies. Following are three techniques commonly used by social studies teachers to enhance vocabulary development.

Context Clues. McCullough (1958) has identified nine types of context clues that are often used by writers in content areas. Understanding these clues can aid in vocabulary and concept development.

1. *Picture clues* show a concrete example of the vocabulary word. For example, "The sloping *banks* of the river were covered with flowers and grass."
2. *Verbal clues* are such that sentences before or after the unknown word explain the meaning. For example, "The president's *cabinet* meets weekly. These official advisors help the president determine policy."
3. *Experience clues* are the concrete experiences of the reader that help him or her to assume the meaning of an unknown word. For example, "When we came to a *fork* in the road we decided to go left."
4. *Comparison and contrast clues* occur when two words are compared or contrasted to each other. One is common and one may be unknown. For example, "The president *vetoed* the first bill but decided to *allow* the second one to become law."
5. *Synonym clues* are such that a sentence repeats the same idea, using a synonym for the unknown word in the repetition. For example, "The democratic party presented its *platform;* this *plan* must be voted on by the delegates."
6. *Summary clues* are found when several ideas result in an unknown word that is a summary of these ideas. For example, "What people know and believe to be true, how they do such things as educate children, and how they act on special occasions are all part of their *culture.*"
7. *Definition clues* are ones in which the actual definition of the unknown word appears in the sentence. For example, "To *lobby* is to accost, address, or solicit a legislator in order to influence legislation to one's own advantage."
8. *Mood clues* are apparent when the tone of the sentence suggests the meaning of the unknown word. For example, "His *disrespect* for his captors was evident in the way he scowled at them and spat upon the ground."
9. *Familiar expression clues* are such that the word can be recognized by its use in a familiar phrase or experience. For example, "The Christmas card said, 'Happy Holidays.'"

Teachers can reinforce the learning of these clues by pointing out their occurrence in social studies texts, and by devising exercises that require students to recognize and use them.

Dictionary. Reading and language-arts teachers introduce children to dictionaries in the primary grades; however, use of the dictionary should be reinforced by all teachers in all subjects. One of the most powerful instructional devices is the teacher's own modeling of his or her use of the dictionary when new or difficult words are encountered.

Glossaries are similarly helpful, but will not always contain as much information as is required. For example, a glossary in a social studies text may contain only one meaning of the word *primary*. It might be described as a noun that refers to a political election, whereas a dictionary will show several meanings for *primary* the noun and several more for *primary* the adjective. These differences must be noted by the teacher and pointed out to pupils.

Structural Analysis. Context clues and dictionaries are valuable aids in social studies vocabulary development. A third technique for unlocking the meaning of new words is called structural analysis. Usually taught in reading classes, this technique involves the recognition and comprehension of word affixes: roots, prefixes, and suffixes.

Mastery of the meaning of prefixes and suffixes can allow readers to determine the meanings of hundreds of unknown words. Donoghue (1979) notes that of Thorndike's list of the twenty thousand most common words in the English language, five thousand words, or 25 percent, have prefixes. Of this group 82 percent use one of fourteen prefixes. Knowledge of the meaning of these fourteen prefixes can therefore unlock the meaning of some 4,100 words. These fourteen prefixes are: *ab* (away from), *ad* (toward or to); *be* (overly or on all sides); *com, con, co* (together or with); *de* (downward, reversal, or from); *dis* (apart from, not, opposite); *en* (in, into, or to cover); *ex* (former or out of); *in* (not or into); *pre* (before); *pro* (for, before, or in favor of); *re* (again or restore); *sub* (beneath or under); and *un* (not or the opposite of). Similarly, knowledge that compound words can be broken into their parts, and an awareness of root words can do much to help children decode.

Based on the preceding information, teachers can devise many kinds of activities to help students learn the skill of analyzing the structure of words. From time to time teachers should also model the structural analysis of a new social studies word for the class. Choosing unusual words with interesting derivations and analyzing them with a problem solving approach can be highly motivating and memorable for pupils.

Comprehension

Being able to read a new vocabulary word does not always result in understanding. The problem is magnified when students are asked to read several words, sentences, and paragraphs in a social studies text and derive meaning from them. For this reason you should be familiar with techniques that can facilitate student comprehension of the written word. In this section we will deal with four major components of comprehension: (1) getting a general understanding of the main ideas that are being presented; (2) locating, understanding, and remembering details related to the main ideas; (3) recognizing the organization and sequence of ideas presented; and (4) being able to analyze or interpret what is read by making inferences, reading critically, detecting bias, anticipating outcomes, and so on.

Main Ideas. Three techniques are most helpful in aiding students to understand the main idea of a selection: (1) previewing for the general idea; (2) establishing a purpose for reading; and (3) recognizing topic sentences in paragraphs.

When a lesson is to be based on reading from the text or other printed material, it is essential that the students first be primed as to the general nature of the topic for study. An instruction to "Read pages 63 to 75 and be ready to answer questions," will do little to motivate learning or enhance comprehension of the selection. A more effective method would be as follows:

TEACHER: Let's all turn to page 63 in your social studies text. Who can read the title on this page?

MARK: It says "Farmington."

TEACHER: Right, Mark. "Farmington." Does that word make you think of any special kind of place?

JAMIE: It makes me think of a farm.

TEACHER: That's what it makes me think of too. But what do you suppose the *ton* at the end of the word *farming* means? Think of other words that end in *ton* like, Washington, or Lexington, or Riverton.

ANNE: Could it mean town?

TEACHER: Yes, that *is* what *ton* means when it's the suffix at the end of the name of a place. What do you think about this place that has the name of "Farmington."

JAMIE: I think it's the name of a town that has a lot of farms in it. Or maybe close by.

TEACHER: Yes, that's what this chapter will be about. Is there anything else on the next few pages that gives you another hint about this chapter?

ALLISON: There's a picture on page 66 that shows a dairy cow being milked, and then an arrow points to another picture showing the milk being put on a truck and then it's driven to town. Maybe the chapter will tell about some of the food that comes from this town, or some of the jobs people have there.

The discerning reader will have noted that, in the preceding exchange, not only was the general idea of the chapter established but the teacher and students also engaged in the structural analysis of a new word. They also began to examine and discuss a linear chart, a form of graphics mentioned in Chapter 7.

An essential ingredient of this preliminary discussion will also be to establish a purpose for reading. The teacher should already have read the chapter and determined what major concepts are being discussed. These can then be turned into questions that are put on the board or handed out in the form of work sheets or study guides. Or the purpose can be established in the form of an oral direction. For example:

TEACHER: Last week we discussed Metropolis and found out what life is like in a big city. We also found out what kind of jobs people have, the kinds of buildings they work in and live in, the kinds of transportation they use, and so on. When you read this chapter on Farmington I want you to notice how life in a smaller farm town is different from life in a big city. Every time you notice a difference, I want you to jot down a note on a piece of paper. Later, when you've finished reading, we'll see how many ways you've found that the smaller town is different from the city.

Notice, incidentally, that the children will be engaging in the exploration model of problem solving discussed in Chapter 5.

A final skill in recognizing the main ideas is to help pupils locate topic sentences in paragraphs. In the above lesson, the teacher could guide the beginning of the independent reading in the following way:

TEACHER: Read the first sentence of the first paragraph on page 63. What does it tell you about this paragraph?

ANNE: It says that not all communities are as large as Metropolis is. I guess that means this paragraph is going to tell about some other kinds of communities. Maybe it'll tell about Farmington.

TEACHER: Yes. Now read the rest of the paragraph and see if Anne's idea about the first, or topic sentence, was right.

Again, the teacher has established a purpose for reading the paragraph, while at the same time pointing out another aid to help students comprehend what the paragraph will be about: the topic sentence. Of course, further examination of several other paragraphs in different lessons will reveal the fact that the topic sentence is not always at the beginning of a paragraph. Sometimes it's in the middle, or even at the end. Sometimes a paragraph will not have a topic sentence. This too must be pointed out.

One kind of exercise the teacher can devise for reading a short selection is shown in Table 12.1.

Details In the previous discussion about Farmington, the teacher directed the pupils to list the ways in which a small town is different from a large city. Aside from establishing a clear purpose for reading, this exercise also insured that students would attend to specific details of the selection.

Another way of calling attention to the details of a reading selection is to give students a study guide that asks questions that must be answered, or makes statements with blanks in the place of important details. Students must then read carefully in order to complete the guides.

TABLE 12.1 Sample Exercise: Topic Sentences

Read the first four paragraphs on page 63. After you have read each paragraph, think about the sentence that best describes what the paragraph is about. Write that sentence below.

Paragraph 1: Topic Sentence _____

Paragraph 2: Topic Sentence _____

Paragraph 3: Topic Sentence _____

Paragraph 4: Topic Sentence _____

A guided oral activity that does not require writing might also be used. Here the teacher might say something like this:

> Turn to page 67 and point to the third paragraph. The topic sentence tells us that after the cows are milked, the milk is treated before it is sent to town. In one process, the milk is heated so the fat can be spread evenly throughout the milk. Find the word for that process. Who can tell me what that word is?

As important as details are to a reading selection, they are only important insofar as they help to clarify meaning, explain relationships, and develop concepts. There is no value in memorizing and recalling details that have nothing to do with important concepts or whose relation to these concepts is not understood by the pupils.

Organization. Every textbook contains organization aids that help students obtain meaning from the written words. A table of contents is a valuable aid that tells readers which main topics are discussed in the book and where the information about these topics may be found. Chapters are titled and followed by section heads. Important words or terms are often italicized or written in larger, darker type. Summaries precisely recap and reiterate chapter organization. Finally, some chapters end with questions for study that further help students to organize information.

Paragraphs and sentences are also ways of organizing information. Students need to learn that a paragraph usually deals with one topic. Furthermore, it usually begins with a topic sentence that is followed by important details that explain or enlarge upon the topic sentence.

Another form of organization that students must become familiar with is sequential. Words such as *first, initially, furthermore, in addition, second, last of all, finally, next,* and *moreover* can be valuable aids in helping students make sense of sequentially related information.

It must not be assumed that students will automatically recognize and use these aids. In fact, teachers themselves are often unaware of them. For example, are you aware of the organization of this book? Does it have sections (usually referred to as "parts" or "units") as well as chapters? Have you been reading the section heads and subheads within each chapter to help you determine what follows? See what we mean?

Teachers should analyze social studies texts to determine what organizational aids are available. Exercises can then be developed on the pupils' level that can help them comprehend the organization of the book and its subject matter. Whenever possible, teachers should point out words, phrases, sentences, and headings that help organize the material.

Interpretation. As we are considering it here, there are two aspects to the word *interpretation* as it applies to comprehension. It involves simply being able to interpret the author's intended meaning through the understanding of words, phrases, metaphors, and other figurative language, sentences, and paragraphs. Words that mean one thing in a picture book may mean something quite different in a social studies text. When many of these words and phrases apppear together, the comprehension of a child who does not have the ability to understand different connotations in different contexts will be limited.

Providing a purpose for reading and guiding this reading with questions that require students to locate main ideas and important details, as well as to read between the lines to sense relationships, find implied ideas, recognize feelings or moods, and predict outcomes, will be valuable experiences for students. Special activities can be devised to draw attention to the use of metaphors, similes, and such devices as contrast, comparison, and irony.

Intepretation in reading also involves the critical evaluation of the written and spoken word. It entails thinking skills beyond simple recollection or factual comprehension of details. It requires that students learn to distinguish fact from fantasy, identify the main problem, distinguish between relevant and irrelevant statements, know the difference between fact and opinion, determine the qualifications of the speaker or writer, identify bias, recognize the effects of deliberate efforts to influence an audience and draw conclusions about the information presented.

Elementary students are capable of critical reading and listening, but these skills do not come easily or naturally. In today's world, where the influence of the written word, (via newspapers, magazines, books, pamphlets, bumper stickers, etc.) and the spoken word, (via radio, television, movies, films, and tapes) is extremely pervasive and powerful, it is especially important that we given children the necessary skills to recognize and counteract any potentially negative messages.

Luckily, television, newspapers, magazines, and advertisements of all kinds provide abundant opportunities for students to learn to interpret the written or spoken word. Any of these materials can provide the basis for a lesson. Magazine ads can be compared and evaluated in terms of the images they are conveying, the subtle messages that accompany these images, sexual or racial bias, role stereotyping, or underlying or implied values.

Television commercials are an especially rich source of material that can be evaluated for the presence of propaganda techniques. With the sophisticated equipment available in most elementary schools today, teachers are able to tape, play, stop, reverse, and replay an unlimited number and variety of commercials that may contain any of the following propaganda techniques:

1. *Snob appeal* speaks to elitism, exclusively of a product.
2. *Bad names (or name-calling)* appeal to hate, fear, dislike.
3. *Glad names* gives pleasant names about people or products without supporting facts.
4. *Glitering generalities* appeal to love, generosity, brotherhood, the American way, and so forth.
5. *Bandwagon* appeals to the desire to be part of the crowd: "Everybody's doing it."
6. *Testimonial* associates the product with a famous person.
7. *Plain folks* appeals to the "average person"; good, plain folks.

An ideal source of written material is the newspaper. Newspaper articles, especially editorials and letters to the editor, are rife with written material that can be analyzed for fact or opinion, bias, emotional slant, lack of objectivity, and qualifications (or lack thereof) of the writer. Together you and your students can devise questions to evaluate news items. These might be concerned with the writer (Is this person an authority?); the writer's evidence (Is this fact or opinion?); and the motivation behind an item (Why is this written?).

Reading Materials

In Chapter 13 we will discuss some of the major materials and resources that are used by the social studies teacher, including textbooks, maps and globes, books and periodicals, and audiovisual and high-tech resources. Here we wish to make mention of other, more highly specialized kinds of reading materials that pupils will need to use in the elementary school.

The first is the card catalog. In some schools the media resource person is responsible for teaching pupils how to use this important reference aid. In other schools it is up to the classroom teacher. Regardless of who is responsible for the primary instruction, you will need to provide help, reinforcement, and review of the necessary skills such as alphabetization, knowing the difference between title and author cards, understanding abbreviations, and understanding the information printed on the cards. This will be especially necessary in the intermediate grades.

An atlas is a resource that is particularly valuable to social studies instruction. Unfortunately many classrooms do not have their own copies, thus students must go to the media center where they may or may not receive help in learning how to use one. You may therefore want to bring one to class on several occasions to point out its various parts, familiarize students with its organization, and help them to interpret the particular kinds of graphics used.

Intermediate grade students should also become aware of the various sorts of catalogs, indices, guides, and other special references available to the researcher. Some of these are *The Consumer Guide, Who's Who in America, Junior Book of Authors, World Almanac, The National Geographic Index, Education Index*, and *The Readers' Guide*. Because some elementary school media centers may not have these (despite the fact that many students could profit from their use), teachers may wish to plan a field trip to the local library to familiarize pupils with these aids. The ideal time to do this would be just before students need to use them in conjunction with a unit of study or the preparation of a research paper or report. Knowing how to use these special references could save students much time and energy that might otherwise be spent needlessly searching elsewhere for data that are readily available in such books.

Encyclopedias are such a commonly used source of information that only two points need to be noted about them here. First, the ideas we discussed in relation to comprehension are especially cogent when its comes to encyclopedias. Without emphasis on comprehension children tend to simply copy verbatim from the encyclopedia, often with little understanding. Second, some are more appropriate for elementary school readers. Two of the best and most popular for younger students are *Book of Knowledge*, published by Grolier, and *The World Book Encyclopedia*, published by World Book Incorporated.

Bibliographies can be found in many printed materials for children. Often they are ignored or neglected by teachers in the elementary school and their usefulness is rarely brought to pupils' attention before the junior high or high school years. Two kinds of bibliographies, however, may be of particular interest to the intermediate grade pupil. The first is the one that often appears at the end of a social studies text or informational book. Students can be encouraged to consult these for further information about a topic in which they are interested and wish to conduct further research.

The second kind of bibliography that may be useful is a booklist. Booklists are bibliographies of recommended children's books that are compiled by authorities. They are usually published in pamphlets, either monthly or annually. They can provide teachers and students with titles and summaries of outstanding literature for children than can be used to enrich and enhance units of study.

Examples of helpful booklists are "Children's Books of the Year," published by the Child Study Association; "Good and Inexpensive Books for Children," published by the Association for Childhood Education International; "Children's Choices," published annually by the Children's Book Council and International Reading Association Joint Committe. The American Library Association publishes "Notable Children's Books" each year. Finally, "Notable Children's Trade Books in the Field of Social Studies" is distributed yearly by the Children's Book Council (CBC) and is a project of the National Council for the Social Studies–CBC Joint Committee. All of these can be found in city and university libraries. Later in this chapter we will deal in greater depth with the selection and use of related children's literature.

The vertical file is a file containing printed or graphic materials that have been clipped out of magazines, newspapers, and pamphlets, and filed in envelopes. Many media centers contain a vertical file. It will be organized according to the needs of the particular library. Students may find it useful to look through a vertical file for pictures, recent news items, and other data that may be helpful when conducting research or giving reports on various social studies topics.

In summary, you will have many opportunities to teach and reinforce reading skills. You will need to help students use parts of books, interpret graphics, build vocabularies, comprehend reading material, vary reading rates according to time and purpose, and use a variety of sources of information. In order to give students instruction that will be of maximum utility, you will also need to know how to match students and their language-arts abilities with appropriate materials and resources. The following section addresses this issue.

Matching Children, Materials, and Resources _____

Most teachers are fully aware of the difficulties that children have with social studies and other content area texts. Despite the efforts of publishers to provide texts on appropriate reading levels for each grade, there are always students who either can't or won't study books if left on their own. This may be due to difficulty of the reading material, or it may be due to such learning problems as lack of interest or motivation, poor study skills, reading problems, low self-esteem, and so on. In this section we will discuss ways of assessing reading materials to determine their difficulty. Following this we will look at the learner. Only by having a general idea of the characteristics of both will you as a teacher be in a position to match children with appropriate materials.

Assessing Readability

When making personal judgments about the suitability of written materials, teachers should ask such questions as the following:

1. Are the topics ones that will be of interest to these students?
2. Can the students grasp the concepts? Are pertinent and relevant examples provided?
3. Is the material presented in a motivating or challenging manner and is the writing understandable?
4. Will the written and graphic material appeal to a wide variety of ethnic and religious groups?
5. Are the topics ones that will be of interest to both boys and girls or does the material seem to be slanted to one sex?
6. Are enrichment activities that can appeal to students of varying intellectual and developmental abilities provided or suggested?

When you are still unsure about the difficulty of written material, you many wish to make a more formal assessment. This necessity might arise when a particular group of students is atypical in terms of average reading ability, or when the approximate reading level of certain written materials is unknown. Teachers can select from a large number of readability formulas or alternative techniques.

Readability formulas are quantitative techniques that focus on the reading achievement level that students will need in order to get the most from written material. There are over thirty such formulas available to classroom teachers. For more information see Fry (1977), Guthrie (1974), or Hittleman (1978). Most of these formulas involve measuring sentence length and word difficulty to arrive at a rough estimate of text difficulty. They do not measure word meanings, concept load, or cognitive difficulty; thus, matching the readability score of a textbook with the reading achievement scores of students will not automatically result in comprehension.

Although most readability formulas, especially the Fry Readability Graph, can be useful to the elementary teacher, they are somewhat limited in scope. We would like to recommend an alternative technique that assesses the difficulty of the concepts *and* the reading level, while also revealing the reading abilities of individual students. It is called the *Cloze Procedure*. It is extremely easy to construct, administer, interpret, and use.

The cloze technique takes advantage of the psychological principle of closure, which is the human tendency to complete a familiar but unfinished pattern. For example, most of us feel a little uncomfortable when a person stops talking in the middle of a sentence; we want him to finish, or else we want to finish for him. The same is true of a story, joke, symbol, or song. When applied to reading, it simply means that students are required to supply the missing words that have been systematically deleted from a passage of written material. Vacca (1981, pp. 270–73) provides a clear description of how it works.*

1. *Construction*
   a. Select a reading passage of approximately two hundred seventy-five words from material that students have not yet read, but that you plan to assign.
   b. Leave the first sentence intact. Starting with the second sentence, select at random one of the first five words. Delete every fifth word thereafter, until you have a total of fifty words for deletion. Retain the remaining sentence of the last deleted word. Type one more sentence intact. For children below grade four, deletion of every tenth word is often recommended.
   c. Leave an underlined blank fifteen spaces long for each deleted word as you type the passage on a ditto master.

2. *Administration*
   a. Inform students that they are not to use their textbooks or work together in completing the cloze passage.
   b. Explain the task that students are to perform. Show how the cloze procedure works by providing several examples on the board.
   c. Allow students as much time as they need to complete the cloze passage.

3. *Scoring*
   a. Count as correct every *exact* word students supply. *Do not* count synonyms even though they may appear to be satisfactory. Counting synonyms will not change the scores appreciably, but it will cause unnecessary hassles and haggling with students. Accepting synonyms also affects the reliability of the performance criteria since they were established on exact word replacement.
   b. Multiply the total number of exact word replacements by two in order to determine the student's cloze percentage score.
   c. Record the cloze percentage scores on a single sheet of paper for each class. For each class you now have from one to three instructional groups that can form the basis for differentiated assignments: i.e., below 40%, between 40% and 60%, and above 60%.

4. *Interpretation*
   a. A score of forty to sixty percent indicates that the passage can be read with some competence by students. The material will challenge students if they are given some form of reading guidance.
   b. A score of above sixty percent indicates that the passage can be read with a great deal of competence by students. They may be able to read the material on their own without reading guidance.
   c. A score below forty percent indicates the passage will probably be too difficult for students. They will need either a great deal of reading guidance to benefit from the material or more suitable material.

*From Richard T. Vacca, *Content Area Reading,* pp. 270–273. Copyright © 1981 by Richard T. Vacca. Reprinted by permission of Little, Brown and Company.

Assessing Children

Matching materials to children requires that assessments be made of the students too, and not just the materials they will read. Student assessments, like reading material assessments, can be qualitative or quantitative.

Qualitative assessments examine children's interests, preferred ways of working, and past experience and will include things such as check lists, interest inventories, personal reports, rating scales, questionnaires, and interviews. Some of these methods require personal reports from the students. Others make use of teacher observation. The interview combines personal report with teacher observation. All of these methods will be discussed in Chapter 14.

More specific information about reading ability, however, will be derived from more formal reading tests. These tests can be standardized, which give an estimate of reading grade level and are given to an entire group of students; diagnostic, which give a more detailed analysis of reading problems and are usually given by specialist to individual students; or placement tests, which are developed by the publishers of reading materials in order to aid placement of the students in those specific materials.

Elementary school teachers are usually required to administer standardized tests once or twice a year. These scores are usually available in the permanent record of the student. Teachers who require more information about a student's reading ability will need to request additional diagnostic testing by the school counselor or reading specialist. Information derived from these tests can aid teachers in determining which skills a student needs special help with. Placement tests should be used only for placement in the specific materials for which they were devised.

A final kind of test is the informal reading inventory. These tests are teacher-made and are based on the textbook and other reading materials used. Like the Cloze technique, the purpose of an informal reading inventory is to determine students' abilities to read these materials. However, it does not assess the difficulty of the material itself.

When making a group reading inventory, you should plan it so that it will not take more than one class period to administer. You should use from 26 to 30 questions. Each of these questions is written by you to measure pupils' abilities to use specific reading skills. Some questions will require students to refer to their textbook. Others will be based on a single reading selection from the text. Once the tests have been evaluated you can construct a chart that will summarize the abilities and problems of each student in each of the skills tested. Activities can then be provided to help pupils to learn those skills in which they are deficient.

West (1978, p. 38) suggests that the following eight skills be tested for reading in social studies texts. We have included sample questions for each. (The number of questions in parentheses are suggested by West.)

1. *Using part of the book (five questions)*
   Sample question: On what page would you find the map that shows (name of map)? (This tests ability to use map table found in front of book.)

2. *Using source materials (four questions)*
   Sample question: "What library aid will tell you the library number of the book_____so that you would be able to find the book on the shelves?" (Test knowledge of function of card catalogue.)
3. *Using maps, charts, etc. (four questions)*
   Sample question: "What do the black areas (or some other special feature) on the map on page_____represent?" (Tests ability to read information from a map.)
4. *Understanding vocabulary (three questions)*
   Sample question: "What does *opportunity cost* mean?" (Word or term to define from the comment must be pointed out to pupils by underlining or italics.) (Tests contextual meanings.)
5. *Noting main ideas (three questions) (Have students read a selection then answer questions asking for main points of information.)*
   Sample question: "Why were the colonists rebelling against England?"
6. *Noting details (three questions taken from a specific selection.)*
   Sample question: Give one example of how the colonists rebelled.
7. *Drawing conclusions (three questions calling for answers not completely found in reading selection.)*
   Sample question: "What does *this* tell you about what the Amish feel is important?"
8. *Noting organizations (three questions)*
   Sample question: "If you were to outline the material that you have read, what would be the main topics of your outline?

The benefit of such an informal reading inventory is that, like the diagnostic test, it is keyed specifically to the test or other materials being used. It can also give you a pretty good idea of how well each student can handle the reading skills required. However, it does not tell you how difficult the material is to comprehend or give you norms or standards by which to compare the performance of each student. You might therefore want to combine an informal reading inventory with some other technique, such as the Cloze.

Ultimately the methods you use for matching reading materials with a particular group of students will depend upon what you know about the materials and what you know about the students. When all the testing is complete, however, don't forget the importance of direct instruction from you, the most important resource your students will have. Regardless of the reading materials you choose, you will want to provide additional instruction in the form of help with new words or terms, giving a purpose for reading, guiding the reading, and reinforcing the printed material with previews, discussions, reviews, summaries, and related hands-on activities.

Reading Materials for the Mainstreamed Child

Having conducted the necessary assessments, you will undoubtedly find that a few students are unable to read on the level at which most of your materials are written. Special materials will need to be prepared for these students when the assignment is to read a portion of the text. Teachers can rewrite textbook passages for the appropriate level using the following guidelines.

First, identify such key vocabulary words from the selection as any technical terms that are exclusive to the content area and have no synonyms. Examples of such words are *World War I, Congress, suffragette,* and so on. These words will have to be included in your rewritten version.

Next, identify the major concepts that are crucial to the passage. At the same time, take note of information that is not essential to student understanding and may thus be eliminated.

Finally, rewrite the passage using general vocabulary words the students should know and the key words you have identified. Define any of the key terms that may be new to the students within the passage itself. As a general rule, lower reading levels require short sentences and short paragraphs. For example, at the second grade reading level, a child can usually manage about four to eight words per sentence with about four to eight sentences per paragraph. Students reading at the fourth grade level can handle seven to ten sentences per paragraph, with seven to ten words per sentence. In the primary grades, no more than one difficult word should appear in each paragraph; in the fourth through sixth grades, there can be two or three difficult words per paragraph at most.

The following table shows how this was done for fourth grade students reading on a second grade level.

TABLE 12.2 Textbook Adaptation

Title of Textbook: Using the Social Studies

Grade Level of Text: 4   Reading Level of Student: Level 2

Chapter or Passage Title: Equal Job Rights, page 227

Equal job rights. In 1917 the United States entered into the First World War. As men left their jobs to serve in the armed forces, women often replaced them. Women began to work in offices and factories that would not hire them before the war. Many women also worked as nurses and in volunteer programs.

The suffragettes felt that this was the time to get an amendment to the Constitution. Women were working in almost every type of business and factory. They were now working at almost every kind of job that men were. Suffragettes felt sure that enough members of Congress would now be willing to vote for suffrage for women.

Adaptation for Level 2			
Word List:	World War I	volunteers	laws
	treated	Congress	suffragettes
Concepts to be Developed:	Congress	World War I	laws
	volunteers		

Rewritten Passage:

Before World War I men and women were not treated the same. The men had to go to the war. So the women did the men's jobs. Some women even did the job without any pay. They were called volunteers.

After the war, some women worked to ask Congress to change the laws. They wanted men and women to be treated the same. Women wanted to vote too. These women were called suffragettes.

Strategies for Integrating Language Arts and Social Studies _____

In the social studies, language-arts activities are not taught for their own sake, but are tools to help students learn the necessary concepts, processes, and skills. The kinds of language-arts activities you will use can be divided into four categories: those that involve listening, speaking, reading of literature, and writing. The remainder of this chapter will discuss activities in these four categories that you might wish to use in your teaching.

Listening

The experts have identified many different kinds of listening. We particularly like Donoghue's (1979) classification into three basic types: appreciative, attentive, and critical.

Appreciative Listening. Appreciative listening is the ability to listen for enjoyment or pleasure. The response to appreciative listening is creative. In this kind of listening, pupils are relaxed. They are not expected to respond in a predetermined manner, but are encouraged to enjoy and appreciate the sounds they are listening to. Music, poetry, literature, and drama lend themselves especially well to appreciative listening.

Attentive Listening. Attentive listening is the second type of listening identified by Donoghue (1979). Attentive listening requires the ability to respond to directions and explanations and to comprehend and recall information presented orally. Students are expected to be able to apply the knowledge they have acquired through this kind of listening in a manner that indicates comprehension. The required response is cognitive, not affective. Following directions, answering questions about the content of a presentation, and summarizing what has been heard would be the result of attentive listening.

Critical Listening. The third type of listening is critical listening. Here the required response is evaluation. Earlier in this chapter we discussed the need for critical reading skills. The same skills apply to critical listening, with the obvious exception that they do not require reading ability. For example, students should be able to listen to a radio or television commercial and then determine bias, propaganda techniques, point of view, fact versus opinion, and so on. They should also learn to listen for background music and sound effects in regular shows for the purpose of determining the effect these audio stimuli are having on the listener. All other oral communications, such as speeches, lectures, interviews, debates, committee reports, stories, reports of factual experiences, conversations, and discussions should be listened to with the same criteria used for critical reading. After such listening experiences students should be able to form critical judgments and substantiate their opinions by citing examples.

Speaking

Speech is the major means of human communication. It is probably the single most powerful and influential tool that humans can use in their social interactions. But just as some tools are more roughly made and less useful than others, some speakers are less polished and effective than others. When students are unable to express themselves clearly and logically they are handicapped to an extent that they are sometimes unable to become productive members of society. The maintenance of a free society is dependent to a great extent on the clear, logical thought of its members; yet, in many classrooms students are rarely engaged in oral language activities. It is far more common for teachers to require students to engage in the passive and receptive language activities of listening and reading rather than the active ones of speaking and writing. This is unfortunate because expressing thoughts in speech or writing are extremely effective ways for students to gain proficiency in thinking and language skills.

You should give your students many opportunities to think and speak out loud. Teacher-guided conversations and discussions are two speech activities that can involve groups of students at all grade levels.

Primary grade pupils can learn to give directions to each other and can engage in informal classroom sharing or reporting. Learning how to make announcements and introductions are activities that will be enjoyed by students in the middle elementary grades. These and older students will also benefit from more formal activities like making committee reports and conducting interviews.

Fifth and sixth grade students are capable of speech activities that require more logical and critical thinking skills. Examples of such activities are debating and following parliamentary procedure. Not only are these last two activities excellent for practicing thinking and speaking skills but are also invaluable preparations for life in a democratic society.

Learning derived from such activities can be enhanced when students are taught to evaluate speech activities. Primary grade children can learn to observe that story dramatizations are more enjoyable when the actors speak loudly and clearly. Third and fourth graders can devise guidelines for giving reports, participating in discussions, or conducting interviews. When these activities are completed, they can be critiqued according to the class-established guidelines.

Fifth and sixth graders can learn the rules that guide debates and parliamentary procedure. They can establish their own rules for panel or round-table discussions. The effectiveness of these activities can be evaluated according to three general criteria: (1) Were the rules adhered to?; (2) Was the content presented logically and clearly?; and (3) Were the speakers effective in terms of such physical skills as use of voice, hand gestures, posture, eye contact, and body movement?

It is important for teachers to create an understanding, nonthreatening environment if students are to feel comfortable about expressing their thoughts and ideas through speech. When a teacher is critical of student questions, students learn very quickly not to speak up, even when they don't understand. If a teacher ridicules poor speech habits or allows students to ridicule each other very few students will have the confidence to participate in speech activities.

Reading Literature

Earlier in this chapter we discussed the reading and study skills that you will need to help your pupils with. The chief concern in that section, "Social Studies and Reading Skills," was the reading of textbooks and other printed social studies materials. Here we wish to stress the importance of supplementing that reading with good children's literature.

There is an abundance of excellent literature, both fiction and nonfiction, that is highly relevant to social studies. There are biographies and autobiographies about famous historical characters, informational books about every conceivable subject, and folk tales, fables, and myths that portray the values and customs of every society. Historical fiction provides valuable insights into important eras, and realistic books honestly and tactfully deal with problems of modern society which might confront the children. Even humorous books, adventure stories, animal books, and poetry that can enrich and extend almost any topic for study can be found.

Opportunities to read and listen to good literature should be provided to all children on a daily basis. A special shelf for books that are related to the current topic of study can be a permanent part of the classroom. The selection of books can be changed periodically and can be added to by teachers, students, and the media specialist. Posters, riddles, questions, bulletin boards, and interesting captions can be positioned near the shelf to encourage students to browse through the collection. Skits, TV programs, commercials, character dress-up days, and games such as twenty questions can be fun ways of reporting on these books and motivating others to read them.

Daily oral reading by the teacher should also be a regular part of the routine of every elementary classroom. This can be a time when teachers can enthusiastically expose children to books that are too difficult for them to read yet, or that they might never choose to read on their own. Often these books can be chosen because they relate to a social studies unit.

In choosing books for stocking the shelf or reading aloud, you should be aware of a few important considerations.

1. Whenever possible, select books that will provide a racial, religious, and sexual balance. If most of the books are about white Protestant boys, the needs and interests of a large portion of your students will not be met.
2. Provide books with a broad range of reading difficulty. Make sure there are some books that are appropriate for your poorest readers, and some that will challenge your best.
3. Try to provide books in several different genres and not just historical fiction, for example. This will broaden student tastes, interests, perspectives, and knowledge.
4. Select books that are of high literary quality. Too many students will never be exposed to good literature if they are not guided to it by concerned teachers.

Several sources are available to teachers to aid them in the selection of appropriate books. *Social Education*, the journal of the National Council for the Social Studies, has a special section every spring called "Notable Trade-books," which focuses on books related to different social studies areas. In the Sources of Information section of this chapter we noted that the American Library Association publishes a well-known booklist each year called "Notable Children's Books." Two other selections aids that can be found in most libraries are *The Best in Children's Books*, edited by Zena Sutherland, and *Children's Catalog*, published by the H. W. Wilson Company. Both of these provide annotations for each book listed. Finally, teachers can be assured that any children's book that has received a Caldecott medal (given to the best illustrated picture book each year), or a Newberry medal (given to the author of the most outstanding children's book each year), will be of the highest quality. Lists of these award-winning books are available in most libraries.

Writing

The importance or writing is receiving renewed emphasis in education today. Like speech, writing is an expressive activity that requires clear, logical, organized thinking. Unlike speech, it requires additional skill in spelling, penmanship, capitalization, and punctuation. For this reason, it is the last of the four major language-arts skills to develop. It is also the most difficult to perfect.

Despite recognition of this difficulty (or perhaps because of it), schools have provided scant opportunities for students to develop good writing skills. Writing activities are rarely assigned, and when they are, students are given so little help and yet are graded so stringently that both students and teachers very quickly lose any excitement they might have had about writing.

Daily writing should be a part of the curriculum from kindergarten through high school, yet this is rarely the case. This may be because teachers feel uncomfortable with writing; they lack the skill to teach and evaluate it. Another reason often cited is class size and the impossibility of grading so many papers from so many students.

New research, however, is pointing to new techniques for teaching and evaluating student writing. We offer the following suggestions for you to integrate writing into your instruction. For more information on how to organize the classroom and help students with daily writing activities, see Graves (1983) and Turbill (1982).

1. Focus on clear and logical ordering of information, not spelling and punctuation, etc. If correct spelling of new social studies vocabulary or concepts is your goal, let the students know this ahead of time and provide help for those who are having difficulty.
2. Give students many writing activities that will not be graded for language-arts ability. These can be summaries, answers to questions, outlines, evaluations of themes or major ideas, and so on. Students can then get into groups to discuss what they have written. Just as students

are not graded every time they open their mouths to speak, they should not be graded every time they put pencil to paper. Much practice is necessary before perfection can be achieved.

3. When a writing assignment is to be graded, let the students know in advance, and give them guidelines or requirements. For example, an eight-point paragraph on "Three reasons for the Western movement," could be graded like this:
   - 1 point for a good topic sentence.
   - 2 points for each of 3 sentences that give clear, correct reasons.
   - 1 point for a good closing sentence.

   We particularly like the above guidelines because they focus on what is important to the assignment: understanding the social studies ideas and being able to express the information in a clear, logical manner. In this way, writing is used as a tool for expression, not as an end in itself.

4. When a written assignment is to be graded according to previously determined guidelines, allow students time to write a first draft and share it with others for questions and opinions before rewriting.

5. Let students choose their own topics as much as possible. When they write about things that really interest them, their writing is apt to be far more creative and interesting.

6. Occasionally publish something they have written. (Publishing means being put into a final correct form and shared with others.) This could be in the form of a monthly class newspaper that is shared with other classes, a typed and duplicated collection of student essays and poems about relevant issues they have been studying, or just a bulletin board with a sentence or caption written by each child. The publishing stage is extremely important because it gives students an awareness of their audience and reinforces the need for correct mechanics and logical thinking.

7. Give pupils many opportunities to share their writing with each other: one to one, in small groups, and with the whole class.

Social studies content is ideally suited to writing activities of all kinds including captions, headlines, want ads, editorials, lists, paragraphs, summaries, essays, poems, reports, radio and TV advertisements, diaries, myths, legends, journals, proverbs, short stories, biographies, skits, plays, letters, flyers, minutes of meetings, travelogs, speeches, and many others. Many of these activities overlap with listening, speaking, and reading, thus providing enrichment in all the language arts as well as social studies. Table 12.3 suggests sample writing activities that can be used by social studies teachers in all elementary grades.

Table 12.3 suggests three kinds of poetry that you may be unfamiliar with: cinquain, biopoems, and haiku. Here are directions and samples for each. Many third graders can write cinquains and biopoems, and most students beyond the third grade can write all three.

Cinquain. A cinquain is a five-line poem that does not rhyme. Each line has a special purpose.

TABLE 12.3 Sample Writing Activities in Social Studies

Grade Level	Social Studies Topic	Writing Activity/Teaching Strategy
K–2	Family and Community Helpers	Shopping lists: have students dictate the names of items they would like to have their mothers buy at the grocery store. Teacher writes these names on the board. Each student chooses some items for his/her own shopping list, copies the names, and beside each name pastes or draws a picture of the item.
K–2	Holidays (any)	Children make and illustrate greeting cards for friends, family. Class decides on a message or messages, which teacher writes on board and students copy; or students dictate their own messages, which the teacher writes and they copy.
3–6	Advertising	Students imagine they have just invented a new toy and write an advertisement about it.
3–4	City or State	Students read several examples of cinquain poetry. They write their own cinquain poems about their city or state.
4–6	Settling the West	After reading some traditional ballads and/or tall tales from the United States children write their own about imaginary heroes.
5–6	American History	Students choose a favorite historical figure and write a biopoem about him or her. These are compiled into a class book.
5–6	Other Countries	Students listen to poetry from the country being studied; then, using the same formats, write their own. Example: Japanese haiku.

Line 1: A one-word title.
Line 2: Two words that describe the title.
Line 3: Three words expressing an action.
Line 4: Four words expressing a feeling.
Line 5: A one-word synonym for the title.

Examples:

Florida
• Tropical vacationland
• Beaches slowly eroding.
• Cars and boats polluting.
• Paradise.

Puppies
• Friendly buddies.
• Tails always wagging.
• Happiest when you're near.
• Pets.

Biopoems. A biopoem is a poem that is a biography of a person. The person can be real (yourself or a friend) or imaginary (a historical or made-up character). Following are two formats: one for a real person, and one for a historical character.

    Line 1: Your first name only.
    Line 2: Four traits that describe you.
    Line 3: Sibling of (brother or sister of).
    Line 4: Lover of (3 people or ideas).
    Line 5: Who feels (3 items).
    Line 6: Who needs (3 items).
    Line 7: Who gives (3 items).
    Line 8: Who fears (3 items).
    Line 9: Who would like to see (3 items).
    Line 10: Resident of (your street name or your city).
    Line 11: Your last name only.

Variation for a historical character:

    Line 1: First name.
    Line 2: Title.
    Line 3: Four words that describe the person.
    Line 4: Lover of (3 things or ideas).
    Line 5: Who believed (1 or more ideas).
    Line 6: Who wanted (3 things).
    Line 7: Who used (3 methods or things).
    Line 8: Who gave (3 things).
    Line 9: Who said (a quote).
    Line 10: Last name.

Example:

Matthew
- Tall, slim, smart, good.
- Brother of Julie.
- Lover of football, spaghetti, and my dog, Peri.
- Who feels happy when I'm playing a sport, excited about traveling and contented when my dog licks my face.
- Who needs the friendship of my dog, the love of my mom and dad, and a little time each day to watch television.
- Who gives care, friendship, and funny comments.
- Who fears getting an "F," the way I'm going to die, and burglars.
- Who would like to see people getting well, 100 pounds when I step on the scale, and myself driving a Porsche.
- Resident of Maitland.
- Rogers.

Haiku. A haiku is a Japanese poem of 17 syllables: five in the first line, seven in the second, and five in the third. Every haiku is written about nature and takes place at the present moment. It usually describes an outer event or scene and implies a relationship with another idea, event, or scene. It is usually written in one or two complete sentences.

Examples:

The angry waves toss
gigantic ocean liners,
then kiss my bare toes.

The storm clouds gather
in the north. I sit inside,
cozy by the fire.

Synthesis: Appropriate Language Activities _____

Two important points need to be made about language activities that are included as part of your social studies curriculum. As with previous topics we have considered in this book, one has to do with the appropriateness of language activities to children's developmental levels. The second point has to do with how these activities fit into the curriculum.

Young children, at Piaget's preoperational and concrete operational stages of cognitive development, have difficulty learning solely through language. This is not to say that language activities are not to be used with them. Rather, it should be interpreted to mean that these activities should be used in conjunction with other, more experiential, activities. For example, younger children might dictate (and illustrate) a story about a study trip they have taken. Or, older students might discuss the points a resource person has made. Similarly, reading activities should be structured so that the children can in some way relate what is being read to their own experiential backgrounds.

When language activities are used in conjunction with the children's own experiences, each type of experience complements the other. The verbal complements the active and vice versa. In the process two things may happen. First, we will be providing children with alternative ways of learning. Secondly, by using different types of activities together, rather than alone, we can provide a breadth of understanding to the topic under consideration.

As children move through the grades, of course, we can expect that they will be capable of learning more through verbal means. Still, we should not depend on these solely. Think about your own experience as an adult learner. Aren't there times when a concept or idea becomes clearer when it is learned through some avenue other than reading or the spoken word? Aren't other, more concrete, types of experiences just as appropriate?

The second point to consider about language activities in the social studies curriculum is their function. As we have noted throughout this chapter, language activities are a means for helping children attain the ends of our instruction: the goals we have established. Care must be taken to insure that, in the social studies, these do not become ends in themselves and overshadow what we are trying to accomplish. We can, and should, teach language in the social studies context, and vice versa. However, we don't want to place so much emphasis on, say, the grammatical correctness of a student's written project, that we stifle that student's production of ideas. There can be a balance.

It is important for teachers to view social studies contents and instructional practices as being closely related to the language arts. We should use instructional strategies and teach content that is related to reading, literature, drama, writing, speech, and listening. Ideally, students will leave the elementary school with a strong sense of the interrelatedness of things, ideas, and people. Ideally, they will have developed language tools that will prepare them to communicate in meaningful ways with each other and with society. Isn't that what the social studies are really all about?

Springboards to Discussion

1. There are four primary language-arts skills: listening, speaking, reading, and writing. Which one of these do you think is most essential to the social development of the human being in society? Why? Write a paragraph defending your choice. Now select the skill that you think is most crucial to the learning of social studies content in the schools. Write a paragraph defending this choice. Did you choose two different skills? If so, do you think there should be a difference between the primary way we teach socialization in everyday living versus the way we teach it in schools? Share your ideas with a classmate who selected different skills.

2. Choose a social studies text from the fourth, fifth, or sixth grade. Locate a passage that you think should be rewritten for a reader on a second grade reading level. Rewrite it following the guidelines in this chapter. Locate another passage that you would not rewrite if you were the teacher. Explain why you would not rewrite it.

3. Select a chapter or unit of study from a second grade social studies text. If you could select one language-arts enrichment activity that is appropriate for this topic and grade level, what would it be? Now do the same for a fifth grade text and topic. Share with a classmate and defend your choices.

References

CHENEY, ARNOLD B. *Teaching Reading Skills Through the Newspaper.* Newark, DE: International Reading Association, 1971.

DONOGHUE, MILDRED R. *The Child and the English Language Arts.* Dubuque: William C. Brown Company, Publishers, 1979.

FRY, EDWARD. "Fry's Readability Graph: Clarifications, Validity, and Extension to Level 17," *Journal of Reading,* Vol. 21 (1977), pp. 242–252.

GRAVES, DONALD H. *Writing: Teachers and Children at Work.* Exeter, NH: Heinemann Educational Books, 1983.

GUTHRIE, JOHN, et al. "The Maze Technique to Assess Monitor Reading Comprehension," *The Reading Teacher,* Vol. 28 (1974), pp. 161–168.

HARKER, J. (ed.). *Classroom Strategies for Secondary Reading.* Newark, DE: International Reading Association, 1977.

HITTLEMAN, DANIEL. "Readability, Readability Formulas, and Cloze: Selecting Instructional Materials," *Journal of Reading,* vol. 22 (1978), pp. 177–192.

McCULLOUGH, CONSTANCE. "Context Aids in Reading," *The Reading Teacher,* Vol. 11 (1958), pp. 225–29.

SIMMONS, JOHN S. "Word Study Skills," in Harold L. Herber (ed.), *Developing Study Skills in Secondary Schools: Perspectives in Reading No. 4.* Newark, DE: International Reading Association, 1965.

THORPE, LOUIS P., MEYERS, CHARLES E., AND SEA, MARCELLA R. *What I Like to Do: An Inventory of Children's Interests, Grades 4 to 7.* Chicago: Science Research Associates, 1954.

TURBILL, JAN (ed.) *No Better Way to Teach Writing!* Roseberry, New South Wales: Primary English Association, 1982. Distributed in the United States by Heinemann Educational Books, Exeter, New Hampshire.

VACCA, RICHARD T. *Content Area Reading.* Boston: Little, Brown and Company, 1981.

WEST, GAIL B. *Teaching Reading Skills in Content Areas.* Oviedo, FL: Sandpiper Press, 1978.

Organizing for Learning

After reading this chapter you should be able to:

1. Delineate guidelines for using the various types of printed materials available for the social studies curriculum.

2. Describe how various types of maps and globes can be utilized.

3. Describe strategies for using various audiovisual resources—films, filmstrips, slides, television, and videos.

4. Discuss the various uses of computers in the social studies curriculum.

5. Discuss the uses of artifacts and realia.

6. Describe strategies for locating resources.

7. Discuss the use and appropriateness of various forms of classroom organization:
   • Total class instruction.
   • Small groups.
   • Individualization.

8. Indicate criteria for choosing specific resources and forms of classroom organizations.

There are two curricular decisions that need to be made in relation to the learning experiences you will be providing for your students. The first is concerned with *what* things the students will require in order to have a successful experience—you will need to select those materials and resources that will most appropriately help the students meet their goals. Secondly, you'll need to determine *how* the students will engage in the experience. You'll need to judge whether it lends itself to total class, small group, or individual work. These organizational decisions are usually made in conjunction with the choice of the learning experience.

This chapter is concerned with providing you with some of the data necessary to making these decisions. Initially we'll examine the range of resources that can be employed in the learning situation. Included in this discussion will be a consideration of printed materials, audiovisuals, high-tech resources, and realia. We'll consider how you find these resources, how you determine their appropriateness to your situation, and how they're employed in the classroom. We'll also suggest ways of organizing these so that you'll know what you have available as you engage in your curricular decision-making. Following this, we'll turn our attention to organizing our students for learning. We'll look at different classroom organizational patterns—individualized instruction, small groups, and total class instruction—and suggest the appropriate conditions for using each of these.

Materials and Resources _____

In its 1979 statement of curriculum guidelines, the National Council for the Social Studies indicated that instruction in the social studies should rely upon a broad range of learning resources. It was noted that no one textbook is sufficient. Instead, this should be but one resource that is complemented by other printed materials, a variety of media, resource persons, and other resources in the community.

We agree wholeheartedly with the National Council for the Social Studies. We are aware, however, that the textbook is the primary resource in most social studies classrooms. We're also aware that it is the most frequently used resource. Therefore, before considering the other resources noted by NCSS we'll briefly examine textbooks in terms of what you should be looking for in the text you will have in your classroom.

Textbooks

You will want to evaluate a textbook prior to using it with your students from at least three different perspectives. First, there is the curriculum perspective; is it directed toward all of the goals of social studies education? Second, as we saw in the previous chapter you need to examine the book from the students' standpoint; is it appropriate to them? Finally, there are your own concerns; will it help you do the best possible job?

There are several things that need to be considered in evaluating a textbook in relation to the social studies curriculum. The first of these are the goals of social studies education, and several questions need to be addressed:

1. *Is the book directed at the development of social science and historical concepts and generalizations?* Most teachers' manuals will contain some type of scope and sequence chart that will indicate the ideas to be developed in the text. An examination of this chart will give you some indication of whether the book will facilitate student attainment of established knowledge goals.
2. *How are the ideas developed?* As we indicated in an early chapter of this book we can understand a concept *denotatively*, by knowing how to define it. This understanding is less thorough than a *conotative* one in which we have some awareness of the attributes of the concept as well as the ability to describe some examples of it. We'll want the book to provide opportunities for children to develop these conotative understandings; examples of concepts should be provided in addition to their definitions.
3. *Does the book provide opportunities for students to develop problem-solving and thinking skills?* Again, an examination of the scope-and-

sequence chart should give some indication as to what process skills will be given attention in the book. In many cases this chart will focus only on skills, however. We have found that it is usually necessary to thoroughly examine the teachers' manual to get some idea of how different total processes—such as exploration or inquiry—might be employed in conjunction with the book. In addition, it is helpful to examine the children's text. In some cases the textual material will be written so that it models different problem-solving activities; for example, it might be written so that the decision-making process is illustrated in a step-by-step fashion. You'll also want to evaluate the quality of questions asked in the text. Are they all of the memory and comprehension type or do they allow for higher levels of thinking? If the former is the case, you'll also want to try to determine if the questions can be modified to allow them to engender higher-level questions.

4. *How does the book address affective concerns?* You'll want to examine both the teacher's manual and the student's text to see how affective concerns are handled. You'll want to note what values are conveyed and how they're conveyed. (Sometimes this is done very tacitly; for example, illustrations might convey a middle-class bias.) You'll also want to evaluate the text for the opportunities it presents for the development of various affective capabilities and skills, such as perspective taking, valuing, and values analysis.

5. *Is the textual material accurate and does it portray the world as it is?* You'll want to evaluate the data presented in the children's text to ensure that it has intellectual validity; it should give the students a good picture of social reality. Information should be accurate and data should be multicultural in nature. In addition, texts and pictures should be scrutinized for stereotypes as well as a balance of groups of different age, sex, ethnicity, and socioeconomic status. (Fortunately, publishers are very aware of this and their awareness is reflected in the books.)

As we said in the previous chapter, an examination of a text from the students' standpoint basically focuses on a determination of how attractive they will find it. Does the book have colorful illustrations to complement textual content and is there a relationship between content and illustrations? Is the text written at a level of readability that is at, or slightly lower than, the children's reading level? Are a manageable number of concepts presented in a given section or will the students be overloaded with ideas? Is the material presented in an interesting manner using a variety of literary styles, such as description and narration, or does it simply impart information?

More often than not children will find a text interesting when it is written with a cognizance of their developmental characteristics. In the elementary school, ideas should be presented as concretely as possible; children should be able to relate in some way to the materials. The textbook should illustrate an awareness of the children's developing concepts of time and space. In addition, the skills taught within the text should be those the children are capable of mastering. (See Chapter 7 for a discussion of when it is most appropriate to teach various skills.)

Finally, you'll want to evaluate the text in terms of how it will help you do the best possible job. This entails a thorough examination of the teachers' manual. Often, an examination of the students' text gives no indication of the richness of learning that can occur when it is used in conjunction with the manual. Look for the various directions that are given for using the text. (A number of teachers have indicated to me, for example, that they could ascertain no problem-solving opportunities in the text until they read the teachers' manual.) Determine how the manual can be helpful to you in developing the background knowledge necessary for teaching the various topics dealt with in the book. Does the manual contain this information or give any indication (bibliographies, for example) where it might be found? Also, determine whether the manual provides information as to how the data in the book can be supplemented. Does the manual suggest additional reading and activities for the students? A good teachers' manual will not only help you utilize the text effectively with your students but also offer suggestions for going beyond the text.

Many beginning teachers wonder whether it is necessary to follow a text from part one to the end. Or, they ask, is it okay to select parts of the texts to be used with their students and ignore other parts?

The answer to their question is a *conditional* yes—yes, it's okay to skip around under the right conditions. A text series is usually written, as we indicated in an earlier chapter, so that concepts are reintroduced at a higher level of complexity each year. This is referred to as a *vertical spiral* of concepts. In many cases a textbook will also contain a *horizontal spiral*; ideas are reintroduced (usually at a somewhat greater level of complexity) several times in a given text. To use one section of a textbook without the assurance that the students have the necessary background experiences and understandings is a risk. It's necessary to insure that the students are ready to deal with the idea as it is being presented in the text. Therefore, the condition under which it is okay to use sections of a text is that students have the understandings requisite for working with that section.

Periodicals

The classroom should contain a range of different types of books and periodicals in addition to the basic textbooks. Included among these should be reference books of various types, trade books, current events periodicals, and magazines of different types. These should be housed in a classroom library (in addition to the school library facilities) that is easily accessible to all of the children.

Because we considered different types of reference and trade books in the previous chapter we will now focus on periodicals. There are any number of these that have been published expressly for children and can be utilized in the social studies curriculum. They deal with topics that include current affairs, world cultures, consumerism, ecology, and conservation. Some come with directions for use in the classroom. The following is a brief list of some of these and their appropriate grade level.

Current Affairs

My Weekly Reader (K–6)
P.O. Box 16673
Columbus, Ohio 43216

Let's Find Out (K)
News Pilot (1)
News Ranger (2)
News Trails (3)
News Explorer (4)
Newstime (5–6)
Scholastic Magazines
730 Broadway
New York, NY 10003

World Cultures

Faces (3 and above)
(Written in cooperation with the American Museum of Natural History.)
20 Grove Street
Peterborough, NH 03458

Consumerism

Penny Power (all grades)
(By the editors of *Consumer Reports*.)
256 Washington Street
Mt. Vernon, NY 10053

Ecology and Conservation

Ranger Rick (1–6)
National Wildlife Federation
1412 16th St., NW
Washington, D. C. 20036
National Geographic World (3–6)
17th and M Streets, NW
Washington, D. C. 20036

Of course, periodicals in the classroom need not be restricted to those published for children. Some adult publications, especially those with abundant illustrations such as *National Geographic* can also be included as data sources. Older children may be able to read the articles. For younger children illustrations and pictures can be cut out and used to illustrate various concepts. (For example, we observed first graders going on a scavenger hunt for pictures of different families. They cut these out to make a collage.)

Newspapers should become a part of the classroom library in the intermediate and upper grades. In many cases, publishers offer their papers to schools at reduced rates (or occasionally at no cost). One of their main functions, of course, is to provide students with current affairs information. They, of course, can be used for a variety of other purposes; for example, children can sharpen their map-reading skills with weather maps, can learn to analyze political cartoons, and can analyze charts and graphs which often accompany articles. In many areas, newspapers sponsor *Newspapers in Education* inservice courses for teachers. These deal with the variety of ways the newspaper can be utilized in the classroom.

Free or Inexpensive Printed Materials. Guidebooks, pamphlets, booklets and brochures can often be employed as data sources in a unit of study. These can be obtained at little or no cost from a variety of sources such as departments of the federal government, tourism departments of various states and countries, information agencies of countries, museums, and historical societies. Many businesses and industries also distribute printed materials about their product or ideas related to it, and are usually happy to distribute these to schools.

Although these materials may help students achieve learning objectives, many have been written for other purposes. It is necessary for you to evaluate these materials to insure that their purposes do not greatly deviate from your goals. They should be examined, among other things, for stated and unstated objectives; sources of data; assumptions; and the promotion of a particular product or type of product. The results of this evaluation should indicate whether and how the materials can be used.

Maps and Globes

Every school should have a supply of different types of maps which can be taken to different classrooms for use. Included in this collection might be as follows:

1. Political maps that show cities, states, and nations and their boundaries.
2. Physical maps that illustrate, among other things, land masses, water areas, and elevations.
3. Economic maps showing how land is used and what is produced.
4. Specialized maps, such as those showing climate.
5. Regional maps showing specific areas being studied during a given year in some detail.

Of course, it is not necessary to have separate maps of each of these types. Different types are often combined on a single map.

If possible, maps should be available in a variety of forms. These would not only include the flat wall maps with which we are all familiar but also washable versions of these, which can be written on with felt markers. Relief maps that can either be hung or laid on flat surfaces are also quite appropriate for classroom use. Topographical maps, which are quite detailed, are available for any area of the United States from the U.S. Geological Survey and may be appropriate. So, too, may be picture maps taken from satellites, which are also available in slide form at a nominal fee from the U.S. Geological Survey (EROS Data Center, Sioux Falls, SD 57198).

As we noted in our discussion of map and globe skills (Chapter 7) there tends to be some consensus that the learning of map skills should progress from the students actually making their own maps to the use of commercially prepared maps. This implies that, in addition to (and prior to working with) the types of maps mentioned above, the classroom should also contain maps made by the students. In the early grades these might be three-dimensional models or simple drawings. In the later grades these would be extended to include larger outline maps drawn with the help of an opaque projector (an audiovisual device that projects an image directly from a printed page), maps drawn by the students through the use of grids, and three dimensional topographical maps constructed from a salt-and-flour paste, papier mâché, or clay.

Every classroom should also include at least one globe. Although systematic instruction concerning the globe is probably not appropriate to any extent until the intermediate grades, as we noted earlier, the globe can serve as a reference in all grades. Thus, even though younger students have little concept of the distances between places on the globe, it can be used to help them realize the relationship among places on earth.

Audiovisual and High-Tech Resources

Audiovisual resources include films, sound filmstrips, and television. Even though they don't technically fit into this category we are also including slides and nonsound filmstrips. High-tech resources include everything related to computer usage—from the computer itself to its software (the various programs that have been developed for it). Because of their intrinsic attractiveness to children, both types of resources can be invaluable to our social studies program. They permit learning through seeing, hearing, and doing.

The attractiveness of these resources can also act as a deterrent to learning in some ways. Both types are perceived by children as sources of entertainment. Many children watch television, including movies on pay television, for a greater amount of time than they go to school. Similarly, many homes are now equipped with personal computers that are usually accompanied by a variety of video games. Children use these to be entertained, not to learn. Unless they can see the purpose for utilizing these resources in the classroom, they may perceive them in exactly the same way. Therefore, careful planning is necessary in order to derive their educational benefits.

Films and Filmstrips. Films and filmstrips can make a topic come alive for students. They allow students to see and hear things that they might not otherwise be able to experience. This value is recognized by schools; most are equipped with projectors. In some cases they also have a library of films. In just about all situations, the learning resource (or media) center of a school district will have a library of film holdings. They usually publish a catalog describing these holdings by subject and/or title. Teachers are free to order these for classroom use.

The procedures that teachers need to follow for using these two types of media effectively are similar. Initially, it is necessary to preview the film, filmstrip, or slides prior to showing them to the students. During this preview the teacher will want to determine the appropriateness of the medium to what he or she hopes it will accomplish. One criterion for appropriateness, of course, is content based. Does the medium introduce or reinforce concepts for the children and help extend their understanding of the topic? Will they understand the film? Another criterion will be the up-to-dateness of the film. In one case this has to do with the accuracy of the content in portraying current social reality. Also, this up-to-dateness has to do with the vintage of the film. Some older films are appropriate as far as content is concerned but may have anomalies (dress, for example) or technical qualities that distract the student. (I once showed a film to sixth graders that perfectly illustrated what I wanted them to see. Unfortunately it was made at a time when films were projected at a different speed. People walked fast, antique cars whizzed by, and the students roared!)

As you are previewing the film you'll also want to note important points, ideas about which you want the children to be aware. Prior to the presentation you'll want to share these with the students in question form or simply as things you want them to look for. This preparation is important; it has been my experience that a student who is prepared to observe will get more from the medium than the student who has not been so instructed. Of course, students should also be encouraged to ask questions that they'd like answered.

Children should be prepared by the teacher to view audiovisual materials.

With filmstrips it is often possible to stop the presentation in order to refer to important points. In some cases it may be preferable to do so with films. Frequently, however, we have found that children tend to find this annoying and prefer to see the film through to the end. We have also found, in the case of short films, that children do not mind a rescreening when they have missed important points.

In order to derive the educative benefits of the medium, a follow-up is necessary. Students should be asked to respond to the points that you and they brought up prior to the showing. This might be done in a large-group discussion or in small groups and will serve to give an indication of whether or not the objectives for using the film have been met. During this time additional questions and concerns can also be raised.

Watching a film or filmstrip in the classroom, then, differs from watching one on television or in a movie theater in two important ways. First, there is a purpose in addition to being entertained and children are made aware of that purpose. Secondly, there is follow-up; children are held accountable for what they observed.

Slides. There are commercially prepared sets of slides dealing with a variety of subjects, and often these will be included in the audiovisual catalog of a school district. In many cases they are accompanied by background information for the teacher. The procedure for using these is the same as that of films and filmstrips: teacher preview, student preparation, and follow-up. With slides it is very natural to discuss important points as they come up; the pacing of the slide show is done by the person showing the slides.

Frequently, however, slides that are shown in the classroom are not commercially prepared. Instead they have been taken by the teacher or a resource person such as a parent. In many cases these can be much more effective than commercially prepared slides because the person showing them usually has a great deal of firsthand information and will probably be able to respond to spontaneous questions asked by the students. Of course, unless some preparation is made for the slide presentation it can just as well be ineffective.

We have found that one appropriate way to prepare a slide presentation is to decide beforehand exactly what ideas are to be developed through the presentation and then select only those slides that *directly* contribute to the development of those ideas. Thus, in helping my students develop ideas about cultural, technological, and environmental effects with respect to the ways in which people meet basic needs, I show a slide presentation of different types of housing that I photographed in West Africa. Only slides that systematically portray each of the effects are shown. I show, for example, a picture of the rain forest and then a home that would be found in this area. If I were having a resource person work with my students I would ascertain the specific ideas their slides would illustrate and suggest the most appropriate type of slide to be shown. I would also apprise this person of the characteristics of my students to insure that the presentation were not, among other things, too technical or too long.

Television. Many school districts are in areas served by educational television, either directly or by cable. Often these stations carry programming that is appropriate to the social studies curriculum. In fact, we are aware of several instances in which programs have been developed to complement a year's course of study. In North Carolina, for example, a program called "Carolina Carousel" has been developed to directly parallel the fourth-grade textbook about the state. In many cases, program producers will also publish supplementary materials, such as teachers' manuals, to go along with the programs.

In the past, schools that were not in an area served by educational television could not reap its benefits. Those schools who were served had to tune into a program when it was being shown, regardless of how it fit into whatever else was being studied. Thus, educational television was good, but limited. With the advent of videotape recorders, videocassette recorders, and videodisc recorders these limitations could be minimized. Now, programs are often available on cassettes; schools can borrow or rent them from the television stations. In addition, these recorders allow programs to be taped at one time in the school and then shown at the most appropriate time. In both cases teachers can choose programs for viewing when their content best fits what is being studied. Recorders have allowed television programs to be integrated into the curriculum at the most appropriate point.

Video recorders also allow children to experiment, and work with, the medium of television. Children can tape presentations and dramatizations to be viewed by their classmates and others. For example, we recently visited a school where fourth, fifth, and sixth graders were responsible for a weekly news program that was shown to all of the grades. They were responsible for all aspects of the show—from preparation of scripts to rehearsal to taping.

As with any of the other media we have been discussing, a television program should not be something that children watch and forget. There needs to be preparation and follow-up. (Recordings, incidentally, have another benefit in that they permit the teacher to preview the program as part of his or her preparation.)

Computers. In the age of "computer literacy" it isn't necessary to describe what a computer's various components are. Instead, we'll focus on what the computer can do for the social studies curriculum and the social studies teacher. We'll do this by examining the types of programs that have been developed for teaching and the different types of experiences it is possible for students to have while interacting with the computer.

At the present time there are four broad general categories of software that have been developed for use in the social studies curriculum. The first of these are programs that have been designed to directly teach a concept or skill. We observed a program, for example, that utilized computer graphics to explain the reason for the different seasons on earth by showing the relationship of the earth's tilt to the sun. Often these programs include an evaluation component. Students are questioned about ideas; a wrong response triggers the information being re-presented. The second category of program is designed for drill and practice. These allow students to work with previously learned facts, concepts, and skills. A program such as *Nomad* (Minnesota Educational Computing Consortium [MECC], 1981) allows students to practice using basic directional terms (forward, right) as they drive a car on a map to Gramma's house. "States," another MECC program, requires students to name a state that is highlighted on a map. Usually, these drill and practice programs provide students with feedback on the correctness of their responses. The third category of software, which we discussed in Chapter 11, is the simulation in which the student is put in a real-life decision situation. These, too, provide feedback about the decisions. A fourth category of software is archival in nature. That is, a large amount of data can be stored on a program and "called up" by the student. These data discs differ from other such archival sources as encyclopedias in that the data can be presented in ways that the computer user desires. If the program is capable, the data may be presented in numeric order, alphabetically, or in chart form. An example of such an archival program is one that is currently being field tested in North Carolina by the State Department of Public Instruction. This disc contains a variety of data about all of the counties in North Carolina. Students can request information about a specific county or they can request information, such as per capita income or elevation, for all the counties.

Other benefits of classroom computers,—particularly word processing and programming—are derived from what children can do with them. Word processing is essentially the composition of written communications on the computer. An elementary word processing program, such as *Bank Street Writer*, will allow even the youngest student to type and edit stories, reports, presentations, and so on. (In Chapter 4 we noted the use of a word processing program for a current events program.) Some of these programs are even equipped to catch errors and point them out to students. Word processing is a nonthreatening way to encourage student writing.

In the process of writing their own programs, students sequentially lay out a series of commands that they wish the computer to execute. On one line, for example, they might tell the computer to ask a question. On the following line the computer will be told what to do if the answer is correct. The following line might tell the computer what to do in case of an incorrect answer. Students can program tutorials, simulations (see Michael Rossler, "Moving Canadian Studies into the Computer Age," in *Canada in the Classroom*, William W. Joyce, Ed. [NCSS Bulletin No.76] for a complete description of how this is done), and generate their own data bases. One benefit of programming is that it allows the student to work with and apply ideas they already possess. A fifth grader who develops a program requiring the computer user to identify different types of government is working with these concepts in his or her own head. Another benefit of programming is that it requires the student to think logically. One of the fundamental commands in programming is the "if, then" statement: *if* this happens, *then* the computer should do that. If the commands are not given to the computer in a logical sequence the computer will either be unable to execute the program or will execute it in a way unintended by the programmer. As a result, it actually forces the student to think in a step-by-step sequence.

Computers and Videos. Advances in technology have allowed the integration of computers with videotapes and -discs. Called interactive videos, these expand the computer's ability to present data in audiovisual form; actual (as opposed to computer-generated) pictures and sound are used. Because interactive videos are relatively new there are not a wide range of them. Most have been developed for tutorial and archival purposes, although some do have simulation elements. *The Voyage of the Mimi*, developed by the Bank Street College of Education and published by Holt, Rinehart and Winston, details a voyage whose purpose is to study whales. The program is designed to help children learn about scientists and requires critical thinking and problem solving. It includes a simulation element as children identify whales. An example of an archival disc is the *Videodisc Encyclopedia of the Twentieth Century* (New York: CEI Educational Resources) which contains film and video footage of recent events. Students can command that any of the events be put on the monitor. There are also videodiscs of encyclopedias (Grolier), the entire holdings of the National Gallery of Art, and, in the near future, the entire visual reference materials of the Library of Congress.

Realia

Realia are tangible objects—things that can be seen, touched, held, and smelled—that give students a real-life experience with the topic they have been studying. Realia include artifacts or things that the people they are considering use or have used. These artifacts can encompass everything from works of art to cooking implements. Realia also include reproductions and models.

Realia can be used for a variety of purposes. As we noted earlier they can be an integral part of dramatic play. We observed that one group of children in California used authentic gold pans in their play concerned with the forty-niners. Another group, mentioned in our discussion of dramatic play, used model hornbooks. Realia can also be a data source. The writing contained on the hornbook told the children something about what the early colonists believed to be important and, thus, needed to be conveyed to their children. Similarly, things such as diaries, clothing, and toys can help children determine what life was like in the "olden days." Finally, realia can be used as springboard. We've seen children ask "What's this?" with any number of items—from the drop spindle, mentioned in our discussion of dramatic play, to a dowsing rod that was lent to a teacher for a unit on Appalachian culture. (What is a dowsing rod, anyway? And how is it used?)

In any community there is a variety of sources of realia. One of the most prevalent is the media or learning-resource center attached to a school district. They will usually contain any number of artifacts and models. If they don't, the director of the center is usually willing to attempt to find what the teacher needs. Many museums and libraries have collections of artifacts and models they are willing to let schools borrow. Sometimes they will also send individuals to work with the children. Individuals in the community, including you, your students, and their parents, are also sources of realia. In a later section of this chapter we will discuss how we can find these sources.

When most children want to "see" something they really want to hold and manipulate it. Therefore, caution should be exercised in deciding what realia should be brought into the classroom. Fragile, easily breakable items should be avoided. So too should irreplaceable ones, which if lost or damaged would cause discomfort for the owner. Things that might lose value if smudged or dirtied are also probably not appropriate for classroom use. The best realia are those things strong enough to be handled (and dropped) and either impervious to dirt or easily cleaned. There are quite a number of things that will fit this description.

Finding Resources

The resources we have discussed in this chapter certainly don't encompass all that can be employed in your curriculum. We have, in other chapters, referred to such additional resources as music and people, which could also be an integral part of the learning experiences provided for your students. Essentially, the resources you use are limited only by your ideas and your willingness to seek them out.

There are systematic ways of finding and organizing resources and we can conclude our consideration of media and materials by briefly considering two of them, the *resource unit* and the *community search*. In actuality, the two are not discrete; something you find in a search of your community may fit quite well in a resource package. They differ in *how* you look for your resources. For a resource unit you would be gathering media and materials that are appropriate to a specific topic. With a community search you're looking for all available resources. These might fit a variety of topics.

Resource Units

As we noted previously, a resource unit is a collection of materials and references that deal with a specific topic. Usually, the development of a resource unit begins with an idea about something (people, place) you'd like your students to study. This idea is a general one because you're probably not certain at that point exactly what you'll find. In fact, you'll probably let the specific things your students will study in a unit be dictated to some extent by the resources you find.

Once you have your general topic you can begin your search. Although different teachers do their searches differently it has been my experience that the best starting points are you yourself and other teachers; both will have a good idea of a variety of different resources. Next the media center of your school and the learning resource center of your school district should be consulted. You'll want to depend upon them as much as possible; if they have few resources available you may want to question how practical the resource unit is.

You'll want to examine what is available to determine what learnings they can foster and how appropriate they are to your students. A good way to keep records of your search is to note on a file card the category of resource (e.g., film), its name, where it can be found, and any restrictions on using it. You may also want to include any personal evaluative comments about the resource. (This isn't to say that you won't actually gather materials; you will. The file cards, though, are a ready reference.)

At some point you'll want to branch out into the community and beyond, looking for people who can act as resource persons, places to visit, organizations who can supply various sources of information, and sources of realia. Again, you'll want to note what you find on file cards.

Gradually you will see the resource file begin to take shape and you'll be able to identify specific topics with which your resources deal. For example, as I was developing a set of file cards on West Africa I found a film on a day in the life of Nigerian children, showing them playing games; several books dealing with West African folktales; a book about games around the world; a Kallah ("African checkers") gameboard; a finger piano and drums; several records of West African dance music (with directions for the dances); and various other items concerned with play and entertainment. These suggested a unit topic to me: "How West African Children Entertain Themselves." As your resources begin to suggest specific unit topics you'll begin to focus your search around these topics.

One source you will want to tap in your search are the families of your students. A note sent home indicating what you will be studying and asking for help in terms of speakers, demonstrations, slides, realia, and leads to other resources can have surprising results. Incidentally, these notes should be sent out well before the unit begins. They should also not be sent home on Friday; the weekend causes people to forget to respond!

The nice thing about resource files is their permanence. Once you have started one it can be added to year after year. In fact, some of the items in the file will become part of your classroom resource collection.

Community Search

Once I lived in a small town in Florida that many people described as having a stop light, two convenience stores, and a gas station. What people didn't think about was the fact that it had an iron foundry and an oil railway station. They didn't know about the archaeological dig where various fossilized bones, including those of a giant sloth, were uncovered. They probably weren't aware that an event that affected the outcome of the Civil War, the capture by Union forces of a Confederate gold train bound for Cuba, occurred within the town limits. And, they probably didn't think it important that the town also contained several close acquaintances of Marjorie Kinnan Rawlings, author of *The Yearling*, who had lived in nearby Cross Creek.

Communities, even one-stoplight ones, have a variety of resources that can enrich our social studies curriculum. As teachers what we need to do is find out what these resources are: this is the purpose of a community search. It is very similar to the development of a resource file. However, it is more broad ranging. No topic is used to guide this search; instead, we essentially look to see who and what is available.

In a community search we look for people to interact with our students, to demonstrate and to teach. We look for places, such as factories, museums, and historical sites, that our students might visit. And we look for realia that can be brought into the classroom or experienced in its natural setting. (The town I lived in also has a working mule-driven sugar mill, for example.) Like the resource file, we note these people, places, and things on file cards—indicating what the resource is, where it is located, and how it can be used.

We also need to indicate to what topic our resource would lend itself. We would indicate this on the upper corner of the index card for reference. Thus, the woman I found two blocks from my school who made tortillas by hand was indexed under "Mexican food." Sometimes, resources that are found fit more than one topic and it is helpful to cross-reference these. Mrs. Serrano, who made tortillas, was also willing to tell stories about Coyote, the central character in some Mexican folk tales. Therefore, I made two additional cards for her: "ethnic folk tales" and "Mexican folk tales." On each of these cards I simply wrote "Serrano-Mexican food," telling me where to look for a description. Thus, because Mrs. Serrano was willing to visit our classroom, I could use her services for several different topics.

It has been my experience, and the experience of other teachers, that people in the community are usually very pleased to act as resources. They perceive being asked to demonstrate, guide, teach, or interact with students as a compliment. They also tend to see this role as a civic duty. Therefore, we shouldn't hesitate to ask them.

Classroom Organization

There are three different ways of organizing students for learning in the social studies. In some cases, which we refer to as *total-class instruction,* every student will be working on the same learning activity. In other cases, some (or all) of the children will be interacting with small groups of their peers to accomplish some task. Finally, there will be times when a student will be working alone on an activity that may or may not be done by the other children.

The decision of which type of organization to use with a given learning experience will be affected by a number of factors. One of these is the type of experience; some naturally lend themselves more to specific types of organizations. It's difficult, for example, for the total class to work with one computer. Similarly, in most cases it would be impolite to have small groups at work at the same time you have a resource speaker. Another factor will be the needs and abilities of the students. In a lower grade class you may be judicious in your use of small groups because of the students' lack of interpersonal communication skills. In an upper grade you may decide to use groups frequently because of a perceived need for students to practice those skills. A third factor will be the objective of the activity, as we shall see in the following discussion of the three types of organizations and how we use them. Different organizations are appropriate to different types of goals.

Total-Class Instruction

The following are some examples of total-class activities that might occur in an elementary social studies classroom. An examination of them should give you some idea of what their purpose is.

1. A fourth grade teacher is teaching her class the concept *role* by citing several examples of it. She then follows these by alternating examples of roles with examples of things that are not roles. She ends the lesson by having her students identify things that are and are not roles.
2. A group of first graders role play various solutions to a problem concerning whether a boy should tell on his best friend who has broken another child's toy. As they do this, their classmates observe. Then all discuss what they perceive the most appropriate solution to be.
3. Third graders discuss how they will greet their visitor from China, and then have their teacher list the questions they will ask the visitor.
4. At the end of a unit, a class develops an experience chart as a way of synthesizing what they have learned.

Why do we have a total-class instruction? Although the examples may appear to be such that the students are working toward different specific objectives (and they are), the general goal of the activities is the same throughout. It is the presentation of ideas and experiences that the teacher believes the total class needs and from which they can benefit. These ideas might be concepts that are required for broader understandings, as seen in the first example. They might be the broader understandings themselves that are the result of the children having a number of unit-learning experiences, as seen in the fourth example. They might be ideas about ways of dealing with a situation or plans that the group generates as the children did for the visitor from China. Or, as seen in the second example, total class instruction might be a means by which ideas that represent different levels of thought can be presented to students as a means of facilitating the development of various capabilities.

The four examples we have provided, of course, do not encompass the total range of total-class instructional activities. There are also observation activities, such as study trips or watching a film, that could be included. Listening to a resource person would be an appropriate total-class activity, as would singing the songs of various cultural groups. So too would competitive games be used to reinforce certain concepts and skills. The list could go on and on; however, instead of elaborating on specifics it is more appropriate to share two general guidelines you can use to help you decide if an activity is appropriate for the total class:

1. Is the experience one which has potential benefits for the total class? Are the concepts, skills, or whatever else will result from the activity ones that all the children need? Or, do some children already possess these? If so, is the activity appropriate (say, to reinforce) or is there a possibility that it will have negative consequences (boredom, misbehavior)?

2. Can the total-class activity occur in such a way that it addresses the range of abilities and interests present in the group? Will everyone understand (and be able to sit still for) what's going on?

Often, total-class instruction is narrowly defined as the teacher *telling* the students. In some cases—such as the first example, in which the teacher was helping students attain a specific concept—it is. This, however, represents one end of a continuum; the other end is one wherein the teacher acts as a facilitator, and most of the instructional activity is done by the students. One example of an activity at this other end would be a classroom discussion in which the students talk with one another, being guided by the teacher through the judicious use of questions, such as those based on Bloom's Taxonomy, which we discussed in Chapter 6.

Small-Group Activities

Small-group activities can serve a variety of purposes in the social studies. According to Johnson and Johnson (1975), they are especially appropriate for learning experiences that require some type of problem solving, such as inquiry and decision making, and/or that require creative thinking. Working with a small number of peers allows children to engage in synergistic thinking, the building upon of ideas so that the outcome of the experience represents something that is more than could be expected of any one group member.

Many new teachers experience difficultly in employing small groups in their classroom. Often they find things getting out of hand and the children never accomplishing the learning goals that have been set. Much of this is avoidable if, in planning the group activity, consideration is given to two related factors: how the activity is to be structured and presented to the students; and the previous experiences the students have had working in groups. How the former is done is very dependent on the latter.

The structure of group activities is based on the two characteristics of cooperative ventures that make them different from activities—such as total class instruction or individual work—that are not cooperative in nature. The first characteristic is that a group activity has a *group goal* as opposed to a set of individual goals. This goal, which might be among other things the development of a plan of action, the formulation of an idea or generalization, or the development of some product—should be thought of by group members as "ours." It is understood that the contribution of one group member is facilitating the movement of all members toward the goal. What this group goal is should be considered in planning. The second characteristic of a cooperative activity is that there is provision for *interdependence* among group members. Quite simply, this means that if the group goal is going to be attained, the members will need to communicate with one another. Group work just doesn't occur in silence! Therefore some thought needs to be given to how this interaction will occur.

One necessary ingredient of productive group work is *conflict*. Individuals need to question each other's ideas and to suggest what they perceive to be better ideas. Unfortunately, at times it is possible for this conflict to be misunderstood; rather than a conflict of ideas it is seen as a conflict of personalities. It is necessary in planning for groupwork to consider how the situation can be structured so that the conflict has positive rather than negative outcomes.

Research indicates (Deutsch, 1962, Bloom and Schuncke, 1979) that perceptions of conflict tend to be related to the experiences individuals have had with groups. Individuals with little group experience see it as interpersonal in nature; those with experience see it as relating to the group task. Therefore in planning you'll want to consider the group experience the students have had and structure the activity accordingly. For students who have had little or no experience you'll want to minimize the opportunity for unneeded conflict by: (1) being very explicit about the outcome that is expected from the group endeavor, and (2) specifying the exact steps the students will need to go through to achieve the outcome. They should know exactly what they're expected to do and how they're supposed to do it. As students become more experienced, less specificity is desired; they can be given the opportunity to decide upon their goals and how to reach them. So, if you wanted an inexperienced group to illustrate the changes that have occurred in St. Augustine, our nation's oldest city, you might (after having taught the students how to make a time line) give the groups the assignment of showing which countries were in possession of St. Augustine by drawing a time line from the date St. Augustine was founded to the present. Then you might have the group put the names of the different countries over the dates that the city comes into their respective possession. For experienced groups your instructions might simply be, "Show, in some way, changes that St. Augustine has undergone" (Schuncke, 1979).

How do you ascertain how experienced your students are? If you're a lower grade teacher you'll probably want to assume they have little or no experience and plan for simple, straightforward group tasks. With upper graders you may wish to speak with the teachers your students have had in the past, determining the extent to which they used groups. Or, you may initially wish to give the group rather open-ended tasks, such as the latter assignment ("Show, in some way. . .") and evaluate how well they perform. Future tasks can be planned using the data you gathered from this initial experience.

As you plan for group activities you'll want to think about two questions of a more practical nature. The first of these is "How do I decide which children to put in which group?" There are a number of different criteria you might use:

1. *Interest.* Groups would be formed by allowing children to choose the topic they would like to pursue. At times, the children's choices may reflect factors other than interest—such as a desire to be with one's friends—and you will need to determine if, indeed, being in a group based on this latter criterion is in the best interests of a given child.
2. *Sociometric.* You may wish to examine the social structure of your classroom by administering a sociometric test. This test will contain items such as "Name three people you'd like to have in your social studies group." The children's responses to this question (in the form of names) can be tabulated and illustrated graphically on a sociogram.

(See Norman Gronlund, *Sociometry in the Classroom* [1959] for a thorough discussion of both sociometric questions and the construction of sociograms.) Responses will indicate who, indeed, would like to work with whom. They will also indicate sociometric *stars,* individuals chosen quite frequently, and *isolates,* children, who for one reason or another, are chosen infrequently, if at all. Groups can be constituted in a variety of ways using these data: you may wish to put children with whom they have chosen; or at times, you might wish to enlist the aid of a *star* in bringing an *isolate* more into the group.

3. *Capabilities.* Knowing the various capabilities of your students you may wish to constitute the groups so that there is a balance of these. For example, you may want to insure that a group is not composed only of nonreaders. Or, perhaps, you'd like an artist or an individual who has certain map skills in each group. By constituting groups in this way you can insure that the group's tasks can be approached efficiently.

There are, of course, many other criteria that you might employ. These may be particular to the group with whom you're working. One year, for example, I had a class in which Mexican-American students wanted to work with Mexican-Americans and Anglos with Anglos. I decided that this "in-class" segregation was unhealthy and, therefore, composed mixed groups.

The second practical question in planning for group work is "How many students in each group?" Earlier we mentioned that one benefit of group work is the synergy that occurs. For this synergy to occur there needs to be communication among group members; everyone must have the chance to contribute. The larger the group, the less the probability that everyone will have this chance. Because of this it is therefore best to limit the size of the group to between four and six individuals.

As with many other things we have discussed in this book, the capabilities (such as interpersonal skills) necessary to function effectively in a group are learned through experience. Children need to have experiences working in groups and then be given the opportunity to examine and evaluate what has occurred. We have found that a good way to do this is to spend a short time, at the end of the group session, discussing "What was good" and "What wasn't good." The next time the group meets, the students are reminded of these suggestions. At the end of this group meeting they are asked to evaluate the effectiveness of the suggestions.

Individual Activities

On different occasions the most appropriate learning situation will entail that the child work individually on a learning task. One of these occasions will be when the child indicates an interest in something that he or she would like to study, an interest not shared by the other students. If possible, the pursuit of these interests should be encouraged. One way to work with the individual students in these situations is through the individual conference. Initially this might focus on planning—determining exactly what the student wants to know and how he or she might go about finding this. As the child moves into the study intermittent teacher-student meetings would be scheduled for progress reports and the planning of future activities. When the study is completed the focus would be upon achieving closure. The activities would be synthesized in some way and what has been done would be evaluated.

Individual activities are also appropriate for helping students develop specific concepts and skills, according to Johnson and Johnson (1975). One way to do this, of course, is for the teacher to work with the child on a one-to-one basis. Although this is necessary at times, it isn't always; sometimes children can work on their own with minimal direction from the teacher. A vehicle to facilitate this independent work while insuring that the student is indeed attending to the concept or skill, is the *learning activity packet* (LAP). As its name implies, a LAP is a package (an envelope or manila folder, for example) that contains one or more activities dealing with a specific idea. (Some teachers prefer a package to contain only one activity; others will include all activities dealing with the concept or skills.)

Because the student will be working without direct assistance from the teacher the LAP needs to be constructed very carefully to insure that its purpose is achieved. At the minimum it should include:

1. A statement of the objectives of the activity in terms the students will understand.
2. Directions for completing the activity. This includes a step-by-step delineation of what the student will do.
3. Materials necessary for completing the activity, or clear directions for obtaining these materials.
4. Directions to the students as to what to do with the activity when it is completed. (Turn it in to the teacher, use an answer key to determine if responses are correct, share with a classmate, and so on.)

The following is an example of a learning activity packet that a fifth grade teacher used to teach simple measurement of distance using scale on a community map.

Objective: At the end of this activity you will be able to measure the distance from place to place on a map using a ruler.
Directions: Included in this packet are three items: a map, a ruler, and a cassette tape. Check to see if you have all three. You will also need a tape recorder and headphones and a pencil and paper.
After you have gotten these, put the cassette into the recorder and follow all directions.

At this point the activity is directed through the tape. The teacher indicates the legend and has the students line up their rulers with the scale. Following this they are told how to find distances. They are frequently told to turn off the recorder while they work, and when they turn it back on the correct answer is given to them. After several examples are given they are told to find distances between pairs of places on the map and write these on their paper. The activity ends with their being told to put all materials, with the exception of the paper that will be given to the teacher, back into the packet.

Learning centers can be used to integrate social studies and other curricular areas.

Different types of learning activities may be included in a LAP: those that teach concepts or skills, such as the example we just examined; those that extend or reinforce learning; those that allow ideas to be applied to a new situation; and those that evaluate. As we said, a learning activity packet may contain more than one activity. These don't necessarily need to be of the same type. As we have seen, it is possible to have both instructional and evaluative activities together.

In the upper grades children may be sufficiently mature to be able to use a LAP without teacher direction. We have found, however, that it is usually wise for the teacher to introduce the LAP prior to its use. Briefly telling students about a LAP and explaining procedures for its use will do much to insure that students will work with it effectively.

Many teachers employ learning centers for use with individualized work. These can be generic in nature; a section of the classroom will be designated as the social studies center. It will contain a variety of different materials—LAPS, books, filmstrips, construction materials, maps, pictures, and so on—that can be used for different learning experiences.

Learning center may also be unit-specific. That is, they may be constructed in such a way that they contain materials and activities that deal with specific concepts and skills to be developed in a unit.

Some teachers rely much more heavily on individualized activities than others. Those who do have found that some type of record keeping—who has done what and who is supposed to do what—is very important. They have found that, rather than note what every student is doing in their plan book, individual contracts with students can accomplish this. These contracts indicate what a student is supposed to do in a given period of time. A third grade teacher of our acquaintance, for example, had contracts that indicated what a student was supposed to accomplish in a given week. In some cases she dictated the terms of the contract. In other cases, the contract was cooperatively developed between the teacher and the child, with each suggesting objectives. She found these contracts to be quite effective. She was able to prescribe not only for individual needs but also to help students develop their decision-making capabilities. In many cases they could decide *when* they would complete the activity.

Synthesis: Facilitating Learning

In our discussion of unit planning (Chapter 10) we indicated that there were certain criteria that needed to be applied as we chose learning activities for our students. These included developmental considerations; namely, the activities must be ones that our students are capable of handling. They also included practical considerations. We would want, for example, to choose those activities that are most economical in terms of time needed, materials required, and so on. The same type of criteria need to be considered as we make decisions about resources and classroom organization.

Developmental considerations basically focus on the determination of whether our students will be able to work effectively with a resource or in a specific type of classroom organization. With respect to resources we might ask such a variety of questions as:

1. Do they have the necessary reading abilities for use of specific reading materials or are the books and periodicals written at a reading level beyond that of the students?
2. Do they have the conceptual and skills background necessary for effective use of the resource?
3. Is the material contained in the resource presented in such a way that they can understand it?

These of course do not exhaust the questions we will ask. Many questions, in fact, will be resource-specific. For example, if we were considering having a resource person come to our second grade class we might try to determine if the person were capable of interacting with second graders (some people aren't). Or, if we were considering some type of media, we would evaluate it for the amount of information it presents (too much or too little) and the amount of time it will require. All of the questions we do ask should be directed at determining whether there is, in our professional opinion, an acceptable match between what our students can realistically be expected to do and what is required of the resource.

We'll also want to be certain that our students will be able to work effectively within a given type of classroom organization. This is especially true when small groups and individual work are being utilized because they do not allow every student to have simultaneous sustained contact with the teacher. (Of course, total-class instruction doesn't necessarily guarantee this either.) We'll want to make certain that we structure these activities in such a way that the students don't spend an inordinate amount of time trying to determine what to do and how to work. Thus, if we know that students have had little experience in small groups our group assignment will be very specific. Similarly, initial attempts at individual work will require a great deal of direction and guidance.

From a practical standpoint our choice of resources and organization should be guided by a principle of economy. The resource we select to supplement a learning experience should be the one that allows the students to attain a learning objective in the most efficient manner. We wouldn't, for example, have the students read a description of some process, say, carding wool, when a demonstration (where they might actually do it) would not only be quicker, but possibly more illuminating. Similarly, we'll want to choose the form of classroom organization that is best suited to our purposes. If it is necessary, for example, for every child in the classroom to know a given concept, then whole-class instruction is probably more economical. On the other hand, if every child but one understands the concept we wouldn't want to waste the total class' time by reteaching it to everyone. Here we'd work with the individual child while small groups apply the concept to some new situation.

Springboards to Discussion _____

1. In this chapter, we discussed the various resources that could be found in the small town in which I lived in Florida. Many people are surprised at what is available in communities they think have no resources whatsoever. If you think your community has nothing to offer you may wish to do a community resource search. Use the guidelines discussed in this chapter to do it.
2. Read "Mainstreaming and Cooperative Learning Strategies," by Johnson and Johnson (1986), which discusses the use of groups in the mainstreamed classroom. Using their suggestions, develop a plan to introduce a cooperative activity to a group of children with whom you are familiar. Specify the steps you will take before, during, and after the activity to insure its success. Then tell how you'll evaluate whether it was a success from both a learning and groupwork standpoint.
3. Choose a specific concept or skill that you would like to teach a student. Then develop a Learning Activity Packet to teach it. Be certain to include all of the components we have discussed in this chapter.

References _____

Bloom, Joan R., and Schuncke, George M. "A Cooperative Curriculum Experience and Choice of Task Organization," _The Journal of Experimental Education_, Vol. 48 (Fall 1979), pp. 84–89.

DEUTSCH, MARTIN. "Cooperation and Trust: Some Theoretical Notes," in M. R. Jones (ed.), *Nebraska Symposium of Motivation.* Lincoln, NE: University of Nebraska Press, 1962.

GRONLUND, NORMAN. *Sociometry in the Classroom.* New York: Harper & Row, 1959.

JOHNSON, DAVID W., AND JOHNSON, ROGER T. *Learning Together and Alone.* Englewood Cliffs, NJ: Prentice-Hall, Inc., 1975.

JOHNSON, DAVID W., AND JOHNSON, ROGER T. "Mainstreaming and Cooperative Learning Strategies," *Exceptional Children,* Vol. 52 (April 1986), pp. 553–561.

National Council for the Social Studies. "Revision of the NCSS Social Studies Curriculum Guidelines," *Social Education,* Vol. 43 (April 1979), pp. 261–273.

ROSSLER, MICHAEL. "Moving Canadian Studies into the Computer Age," in William Joyce (ed.), *Canada in the Classroom.* (NCSS Bulletin No. 76). Washington, D.C.: National Council for the Social Studies, 1985.

SCHUNCKE, GEORGE M. "Using Groups in Social Studies Classes," *The Social Studies,* Vol. 70: 1 (January/February 1979), pp. 38–41.

14

Evaluating Learning

CHAPTER OBJECTIVES

After reading this chapter you should be able to:

1. Describe the various functions for which evaluation is used.

2. Discuss the relationship between evaluation and grading.

3. Describe formal evaluation instruments.

4. Identify informal evaluation strategies:
   - Observation.
   - Work samples.
   - Teacher-made tests.

5. Delineate criteria for choosing appropriate evaluation instruments.

6. Examine the relationships that exist among goals, learning experiences, and evaluation.

Having considered goals and ways of helping children move toward them we can now focus on ways of determining if the goals have been met. To do this we will discuss evaluation from two different standpoints.

The first section of this chapter deals with what evaluation is, when we do it, and the purposes for which it is done. We'll consider the various uses that can be made of evaluative data. Although this section is somewhat theoretical in nature and discusses evaluation in general, it does, however, provide the necessary background for understanding what follows.

The major portion of the chapter is devoted to an examination of specific evaluation strategies and tools. It begins with a discussion of formal evaluation strategies: standardized tests. It then moves to consider the more widely used informal evaluation strategies, the ones you would develop for your class. A wide range of these are considered, from observation to teacher-made tests.

In the synthesis section of this chapter we'll briefly consider how what we have discussed in relation to evaluation fits with other ideas we have encountered in this text.

Evaluation: What, When, and Why?

Evaluation, as we will be considering it in this chapter, is concerned with the appraisal of what our students have learned in relation to the goals and objectives we have set for them. Because it is concerned with this child-goals relationship it is not directed solely at determining how our students are doing. It is also concerned with how our teaching is doing; that is, whether the learning experiences we have planned are meeting their purposes. Thus, if a child is not progressing as anticipated we look to both the child *and* to the learning activities he or she is engaging in for clues to this lack of progress.

Evaluation begins very early in the planning process. As we begin to consider what we will be teaching in a unit we look to the children to ascertain, among other things, their capabilities, interests, and previous experiences. We use this information to help define our learning goals. Then, as we saw in an earlier chapter, we analyze these goals. We determine what our students will need to know, or be able to do, in order to attain them successfully. We essentially construct a blueprint of the potential steps the students will need to take to achieve the objectives. The steps are the basis of the learning experiences our students will have. They are also potential indicators of the points at which we should be consciously evaluating learning. Having considered these points briefly in our chapter on planning we can examine them here.

Diagnosis

In the planning process we initially decide upon the end of the instructional process, the goals we wish our students to attain. We then speculate upon the steps that are necessary to achieve those ends—we basically say to ourselves, "First the students will need to know how to do this. Then this, and so on." For purposes of our discussion let's think of these steps as falling in an A, B, C order until the goal has been met. Sometimes our students will have to start at A. We may, for example, want our first graders to develop some understanding about families, and realize that in order to do this they initially need to understand the concept *family*. Here, we begin the instructional process by helping them develop that concept. At other times our students may understand A and B. In this case it may not be practical or judicious to start the instructional sequence at A. A group of fourth graders, for example, may have an adequately developed concept of family and need not be taught it. In order to decide whether to begin at A or B or whatever, we need information. This information is supplied through *diagnosis*. We ascertain whether the students have acquired the knowledge, or skills, required for each step of the learning sequence beginning with A and moving onward. The instructional sequence would begin at that point where we find the students do not possess the requisites. (It may well be that different students will be at different points and, we'll need to plan learning experiences that take these differences into account.) Diagnostic data may be obtained in a variety of different ways. Students may have demonstrated knowledge of a given concept or skill in previous units, and we can use our knowledge of this as data. For example, if our students have previously worked in groups we can probably safely assume that they have some groupwork skills. At other times we may need to use some type of evaluation strategy. If an integral part of the learning sequence entails working with maps you'd want to determine the maps skills your students possessed.

Possibly you'd have them do this by working several map exercises that emphasize the skills they'd need. Or, in a different case, you might give the students some form of written pretests.

Diagnosis is important. If it doesn't occur, one of two things may result. Either you and the students will be covering ground that doesn't need to be covered (my experience has been that when you do this the students will quickly let you know in one way or another) or you won't be covering grounds that needs to be covered (this tends to result in student frustration due to lack of requisite knowledge and skills). On some occasions you may find that, even after diagnosis, students may have difficulty. This could be the fault of the learning activity in some way or another and you may wish to replan it. Or, you may not have considered all of the steps in the learning sequence.

Formative Evaluation

Having determined the sequence for learning experiences and determined where the students would enter this sequence, you'll now want to make certain that they successfully progress through it. You'll want to ensure that they've mastered B and C and so on. Thus, you'll evaluate their work at each step, determining if they understand the ideas and skills that will allow them to ultimately attain their learning goal. This is called formative evaluation.

In addition to gauging student progress, formative evaluation can give you some idea of the effectiveness of the learning experiences you are providing for them. Suppose, for example, you developed a learning activity package designed to teach simple map scale. This package contained activities that introduced the skill by having the students listen to a tape while simultaneously completing a worksheet. If, upon examining these worksheets, you were to find several students making similar errors you might want to reevaluate the tape to determine how (and where) it might be causing them to make errors. Thus, formative evaluation allows for in-course corrections.

We have found that one of the most common errors teachers make with this type of evaluation is that they neglect to do it (Schuncke, 1981), assuming that it isn't necessary to evaluate until the end of an instructional sequence. Usually, this sin of omission becomes obvious—either when children have difficulty with subsequent activities or at the end of the sequence. Then it's necessary to reteach some of the skills and ideas that should have been but weren't evaluated.

Summative Evaluation

Summative evaluation culminates an instructional sequence or unit. It's basic purpose is the determination of whether the students have attained the preestablished goals. We use summative evaluation as a means of determining whether our students have developed the understandings, processes and skills that the various learning experiences were directed toward developing.

Summative evaluation is often thought of in terms of one large end-of-unit test covering all of the important ideas and skills that have been dealt with in the unit. This needn't be the case all of the time. In many cases learning experiences are built on one another in such a way that the different formative evaluation data can be combined to form a clear and unified summation of what has been learned. So, for example, an understanding may be developed by the students learning one concept, then another, and then combining these. The formative evaluations would provide information about the learning of each concept; the summative evaluation would focus on the understanding.

Evaluation and Grading

Evaluation is done for purposes other than determining whether an individual has achieved an objective or whether a learning experience has been effective. Data from formative and summative evaluations are often used by teachers for the purposes of assigning grades to students. How grades are assigned depends on how the data are interpreted. There are two ways in which this interpretation might be done. In discussing evaluation to this point we have been considering evaluation as *criterion referenced*. That is, the learning objective indicates a criterion the student needs to meet in order for us to be satisfied that specific ideas, skills, and so on have been learned. Our evaluation indicates the extent to which this criterion has been met. The assignment of grades using criterion-referenced data can be done in a number of ways:

1. The criterion for each objective can be set at a realistic minimum point (e.g., the child will identify five of ten examples of concepts). This would represent a minimum passing grade around which other grades could be assigned for the given objective. Thus, a child who achieves more than the minimum criterion would achieve a higher than minimum passing grade. Grades to be reported would represent an average of the grade attained for each objective.
2. The achievement of all of the objectives is considered to represent optimum performance and would merit the highest grade on whatever grading scale the teacher is using (A, B, C, D, etc.). Lower grades would be given based on the number of objectives attained (Gronlund, 1976).
3. Grading is done on a satisfactory-unsatisfactory or pass-fail basis. Here, the teacher sets a minimum standard of acceptable work. Work at or beyond this standard is considered satisfactory; below, unsatisfactory. Because it works from the attainment of objectives, criterion-referenced grading allows a teacher to decide whether the same standards will be used for all students in a given classroom or whether different standards will be used for different students.

A second way of interpreting evaluation data for the purpose of grading is to look at a child's performance in relation to the performance of other students. A child performing better than the others would receive a higher grade; those not performing well, a lower grade. This is referred to as *norm-referenced* grading. In theory, it is based on the assumption that, in a given classroom, student performance will be *normally distributed* on a bell-shaped curve, with given percentages of students scoring at different points above and below the average score. In practice, it is rare to find a class that is normally distributed. Therefore, norm-referenced grading tends to be based on a predetermined decision made by the teacher or school as to what percentage of students will receive a given grade. Usually, this decision is one in which a relatively small percentage receive the highest grade, a small percentage receive the lowest grade, and the bulk of the students receive the grade(s) in between.

The difference between *criterion-referenced* and *norm-referenced* grading is that the latter requires that students be ranked—some people will receive higher grades than others. With the former it is possible for all children to attain the same grade.

Evaluation: How? _____

Individuals who work in the field of tests and measurement place evaluation instruments in two categories, *formal* and *informal*. The former receive their designation because they are developed using formalized test construction techniques. Their validity (the fact that they are testing what they are supposed to test) and reliability (an individual responds to similar items in a similar manner) are discovered. In addition, norms are obtained using appropriate sampling techniques from an appropriate population. These are most familiar to people when referred to as *standardized* tests. The latter encompass various strategies that teachers themselves develop and use. The designation *informal* is given because there is less stringency in the development of these instruments.

Formal Evaluation Strategies

The formal evaluation instrument with which most people are familiar is the achievement test. Referred to as standardized tests, these are normed on large populations (frequently nationwide) and will indicate how a student performs in comparison to other students of a given grade. These are administered under standardized conditions (time, etc). usually contain multiple choice items, and are usually machine scored. The following are some examples of standardized tests which have a social studies component.

> *Metropolitan Achievement Tests* (New York: Harcourt, Brace, Jovanovich), Test 9: Social Studies (Intermediate Battery) focuses on knowledge and skills for students in grades 5–7.
> *Stanford Achievement Test* (Social Science) (New York: The Psychological Corporation) gauges understanding of concepts from the social sciences and history for grades 2–9.
> *Sequential Tests of Educational Process* (Social Studies) (Reading, MA: Addison-Wesley) gauge social studies knowledge and skills for students beginning in grade three.

Other standardized tests do include social studies in the area which they examine; however, they do not focus on them solely. The *Stanford Early School Achievement Test* (New York: The Psychological Corporation) includes social studies items, along with those for other curricular areas, and is appropriate for kindergarteners and first graders. The *Comprehensive Tests of Basic Skills* (Monterey: CTB/McGraw-Hill) include tests of social studies knowledge and skills along with tests from other curricular areas. For a description of the range of tests that can be used, Mitchell's *Tests in Print III* (1983) is recommended.

Interpretation of standardized test scores is difficult as far as social studies is concerned. This is because, unlike other curricular areas, there is not complete consensus as to what should be included in the curriculum. This will vary from school district to school district. Thus standardized instruments that deal with conceptual knowledge may not be completely testing what has been taught. They may give some indication of what the children don't know but ignore what has been learned. In addition, because of the diversity of social studies content, some instruments heavily test skills, such as those associated with map reading, and place less emphasis on concepts and content. These too would not provide a complete picture of student learning.

Informal Evaluation Strategies

The term *informal evaluation* should not be interpreted to mean that these teacher-developed instruments do not have integrity. When conceived and developed appropriately these strategies should be *valid* measures of student learning. That is, they should gauge attainment of the objectives that have been established and for which learning activities have been developed. All should clearly and unambiguously address the question of whether the objectives have been met.

The informal evaluation strategies we will discuss in this section may be considered to fall on a continuum that falls from those that are *unobtrusive* to those that are *obtrusive*. An unobtrusive measure is one in which students are evaluated in the course of their everyday activities and may not actually know that they are being evaluated. Teacher observation could be an unobtrusive evaluation strategy. Obtrusive measures, on the other hand, are ones in which the students are aware that they are being evaluated. A written test would be an example of more obtrusive strategy. We will start with a consideration of the more unobtrusive and move to the obtrusive.

Observation. As we indicated in the preceding section, observation can be one of the most unobtrusive evaluation strategies. Because of this it can be especially good with students who suffer test anxiety, who may understand something but "freeze up" when confronted with it in a formal testing situation.

Observation is especially appropriate with activities in which there is *observable behavior* on the student's part and with activities that lend themselves to the *production of observable end products* (Ten Brink, 1974). Thus, this strategy will be appropriate to our process goals—for example, it can be

Small-group work often lends itself to evaluation through observation.

used to evaluate how students work through problems, use different skills, and so on. It is also appropriate for affective components of the curriculum; we can gauge, for example, how students engage in social interaction or how they perceive and respond to the feelings of others. It is less appropriate to conceptual objectives.

As we shall shortly see, an observation, to be effective, usually needs to be structured by the teacher. One situation where the observation is not structured is when it is used as a basis for *anecdotal records*. These can be used for a variety of purposes; the chief of these are to examine social interaction among students and to determine patterns in an individual student's behavior. An anecdotal record consists of a factual (as opposed to inferential) description of a student's behavior. The teacher notes, without interpretation, what occurred in a given situation. Usually, these records are jotted on file cards and include, in addition to the description of the behavior, when and where it occurred, as well as any special circumstances that might be relevant to the situation.

Typically, anecdotal records have been used with children who are behavior problems and tend to focus only on incidents of negative behavior. This has probably occurred because the keeping of such records is time consuming. They are just as appropriate for positive behavior, however. An examination of children's "good" times, along with their "bad" times may provide needed information for structuring the curriculum and the classroom environment.

Observation is done for a purpose. In order to help keep this purpose in mind, and to help keep their observations objective, many teachers structure their observation using aids, such as *checklists* and *rating scales*. These indicate the behavior or product that the teacher wishes to see and provide a format for noting what has been observed. They differ in the degree to which the teacher can note performance.

Checklists would be used to provide information on whether or not a student has demonstrated a given behavior. As its name implies a checklist simply contains a listing of what the teacher wishes to observe along with a space that can be checked when it is observed. A teacher who is concerned with developing groupwork skills might use a checklist with items such as "Listens to others," and "Contributes to discussion." Another teacher might evaluate a student-constructed bulletin board on American ethnic groups with items such as "Identifies ethnic groups," "Gives examples of significant contributions of group members," and so on.

Rating scales perform the same function as checklists in that they help the teacher discover whether or not students have exhibited a given behavior. They go one step further, however, in that they also allow the teacher to indicate the extent to which it is being exhibited. The teacher observing students as they work in groups might use a rating scale with the statement "Contributes to group discussion" followed by indicators of frequency (always, usually, seldom, never) that could be circled or checked. Other indicators might deal with the quality of student work (excellent, good, fair, poor).

Observation is usually not a one-time occurrence. Rather, to insure that you are getting as complete a picture of student behavior it should be done a number of times. The checklist or rating scale used for previous observations can be used to focus subsequent observations; it will indicate what needs to be noticed. As you do the observation it is probably best not to make notations on the checksheet or rating scale because this will cause the observation to become obtrusive and (as anyone who has ever been observed by a supervisor can attest) may negatively affect student performance.

Before moving on to consider other types of informal evaluation we should briefly note that, although checklists and rating scales are useful tools to help guide observation, their use does not need to be restricted to observation alone. As we shall see later they can be used to synthesize data obtained through a number of different evaluation strategies. They can also be used for self-evaluation by the student. A third grade teacher we observed prepared a checklist for her students on "Being an Investigator." On this checklist she listed the various steps of exploration. ("Pick a topic you'd like to find out about." "Decide where you can find information—books, talking to people. . ." and so on.) As the children completed each step they checked it off.

Work Samples. Related to observation is a second evaluative strategy, the collection of student work samples. Although a bit more obtrusive than the former this evaluation technique tends to be accepted by students simply because of the frequency with which it is employed in the classroom. In most classrooms students are very accustomed to turning their work in to the teacher as a matter of course. Work samples, of course, need not just be papers completed by the students; they can be anything produced by the students.

As with observation there needs to be some structure attached to the evaluation of work samples. To obtain evaluative data the students' work cannot be looked at simply in terms of something being right or wrong. Instead, the work should be utilized to get some indication of how and what individual students are thinking. Work samples of the same activity gathered from a number of students can be scrutinized to find patterns of errors among students. These patterns might suggest difficulties attributable to the learning experience or our teaching.

Two examples illustrate why work samples should be analyzed rather than simply graded.

My son, Mark, who was a first grader at the time, brought home a worksheet he had been doing as part of an animal unit. On the worksheet were the directions "X the animal that does not belong." Below were pictures of a snake, a lizard, a turtle, and a frog. Mark had X'd out the snake but his teacher had marked his selection wrong and circled the frog. Why? After a few minutes his quizzical father realized that the frog was not a reptile. (In one sense, Mark was correct because all of the animals but the snake had legs!)

This one wrong item could suggest several different things to the teacher: (1) Mark didn't know the difference between reptiles and amphibians; (2) he couldn't apply the knowledge if he did know; (3) he couldn't see the connection between what he was studying and the worksheet; (4) he took the directions too literally and analyzed the pictures from a very simple perspective; and (5) the directions on the worksheet were too vague. If knowledge of the difference between reptiles and amphibians were a crucial objective the teacher would probably want to check these ideas out.

A fifth grade teacher was surprised that all of the students who completed a learning activity packet on using map scale got the simplest problems wrong. These problems asked them to measure from place to place "as the crow flies." Investigating this, he found out that, indeed, the students could use scale. The problem was they just didn't know what "as the crow flies" meant.

These examples show work samples being employed for formative evaluation ("Can the children differentiate between reptiles and amphibians?" "Can they work with scale on maps?" "If not, why not?"). Work samples can also be used diagnostically and summatively. The key to using them effectively is to be well aware of what objectives are to be met and how the work sample will show attainment of these objectives.

It is very difficult to see growth over a period of time; just as we don't see children increasing in height we often don't easily perceive growth in conceptual understanding or skills development. We really don't notice how effective the sum total of learning experiences we provide are. The periodic collection of work examples can help us see this. Some teachers will collect a work sample from a given area on a monthly or biweekly basis throughout the year. These are then kept in an individual child's folder. When they are examined for a period of time it is possible to see growth (or lack of it). Thus both individual work samples and collections of these can provide us with evaluative data. It has been my experience, incidentally, that collected work samples are invaluable aids during parent-teacher conferences.

Verbal Techniques. Student verbal interaction is constantly going on during the school day. Students talk with one another and to the teacher in both structured (e.g., class discussions) and informal situations. The following considers some of these situations and how they can be exploited for evaluative data.

Independent Small Group Discussion. In this type of discussion the teacher is not an active participant; the students have a group task to accomplish and do it on their own. To obtain evaluative data the teacher listens to what is occurring in the group. Thus, in this situation the techniques we discussed in relation to observation are appropriate. The teacher has some evaluative criteria in mind as he or she observes the students and uses the observation to note whether or not these criteria are being met. Data obtained from these discussions may be noted on a check sheet, rating scale, or in the form of written notes.

Group discussions are very appropriate contexts for ideas to be considered; thus, it is possible to obtain evaluative data concerned with conceptual objectives. One strategy that can be employed to help increase the probability of getting this data is to structure the group task in such a way that the students are aware of what they are to discuss. (You may also wish to have each group record its ideas.) This structure should be based on your instructional objectives and will serve as an evaluation guideline for you. Thus, with an upper-grade group that has been studying the various factors (cultural, physical, etc.) that affect how people meet their needs you might have children work in groups examining houses around the world. For their group assignment you might tell them that they are to come up with reasons why houses are built the way they are throughout the world. These reasons, you tell them, must hold for houses in more than one part of the world.

Teacher-Led Discussion. Teacher-led discussion can be done with groups of varying sizes, from four or five children to the total class. It differs from the independent discussion, just considered, in that the teacher provides the structure. This is done as the discussion progresses by using the evaluative criteria, decided beforehand, as a basis.

For a group discussion to provide evaluative data it is necessary that the teacher keep several things in mind, in addition to the preestablished evaluative criteria. First, although it is very difficult to evaluate all of the students in a large-group discussion, you will want to get information from as many students as possible. You will therefore want to provide opportunities for as many students as possible to contribute and not allow one or two students to monopolize. Because, ideally, a group discussion is one in which students speak to one another (as opposed to the teacher) this monopolization problem is a real one. If you see this occurring you may wish to step in by directing the discussion to another student ("Suzanne, what can you add to what Richard is saying?") or by redirecting the discussion with a new question ("OK. We agree that the type of houses people live in is affected by climate. Dorene, can you suggest some other thing that might have an effect?")

The second thing to keep in mind is that *you* should not monopolize either. You should be wary of having the discussion turn into a recitation (teacher

Evaluation data can be obtained through group discussion.

asks question, student responds, teacher asks question) if, indeed, you want a discussion. You should also be wary of other things such as answering your own questions or elaborating upon student responses (they can be asked to do this).

Finally, you will want to have questions in mind that can be employed to get the evaluative information you need. In most cases you will want to include questions at all levels of the cognitive domain. You may want to plan these questions ahead of time and consider the sequence in which they will be asked.

The major problem with discussion as a strategy for gathering evaluative information is that, in a large group, it is difficult to get data from all students. Some students hesitate, for one reason or another, to actively participate. Pushing them to do so may cause discomfort on their part and be counterproductive. Further, time constraints (e.g., how long the discussion can be productively carried out) may prohibit getting adequate data from all students. Therefore, it is probably best to utilize discussion in conjunction with other evaluative strategies.

Conferences. There are occasions when it is appropriate for the teacher to have a one-to-one conference with a student for evaluative purposes. These might include situations when a new child enters the classroom and diagnostic data is needed, when other evaluative strategies have not provided needed information, or when other information indicates that the child has not met an objective but you have reason to believe that this is not the case.

As with the other strategies we have been discussing the conference uses the instructional objectives as its basis. After a short period of time in which the student is made to feel comfortable in the one-to-one situation, the teacher can begin discussing each of these with the student using appropriate questions. Student responses to these can then be followed up with other questions; however, the interview should not be a rapid-fire grilling. During the conference the student can also share and explain other (e.g., written) work that has been done.

One attractive feature of the conference is that it allows for the teacher to probe for data; student responses can be followed up until the teacher obtains the necessary information. This, however, produces a negative aspect—conferences are very time-consuming. It would be very difficult to interview every child in a class in relation to every objective. Therefore, it has been our experience that teachers use conferences only when other, more easily obtainable, data are not available.

Teacher-Made Tests. The evaluation strategy with which we are probably most familiar is the written test, and all of us are aware of the format that the various item on these tests take. In this section we'll examine some of these different types of items and discuss appropriate ways of constructing each of them.

Fill-in the Blank. "Fill-in the blank" is a statement in which one or two important words or phrases are replaced with a blank that is to be filled in by the student. The following are examples of such items:

The lines running from North to South Pole on a globe are called meridians, or lines of _____.

Money collected from people and businesses by governments to provide services for people is called _____.

You may notice from these examples that this type of item is most appropriate when your objective is one of having students recall factual information. Thus, with some exceptions, it is probably more appropriate for diagnostic and formative evaluations where we want to ascertain basic understandings of material with which students will work further.

The construction of fill-in-the-blank items is relatively straightforward and entails removing only a key word or phrase from the statement. The primary concern that teachers should have is that there is no ambiguity attached to this missing term. The statement should be such that, if the student understands the material he or she should be able to fill in the blank. Thus, the teacher constructing the first item wanted to make certain that the students knew what a line of longitude was. Had the item been written "North-south lines on a globe are _____," a variety of answers (meridians, longitude, black, 15° apart) would have been possible. The statement also should not unnecessarily lead the students to the correct response. Care should be taken that cues (such as the use of the articles *a* or *an* before the response) are not given.

Fill-in-the-blank items can be used for purposes other than recall of specific information. They can be used as part of *interest inventories,* whose purpose is to obtain information about the children's interest, past experiences, likes, and dislikes. Fill-in-the-blank items on an interest inventory might include questions such as the following.

My favorite hobby is _____.
I would like to travel to _____.
I would like to learn about _____.

Administered at the beginning of the year, these inventories can provide the teacher with ideas for units and activities. They can also provide insights about the characteristics and special needs of the students.

A variation of the fill-in-the-blank item is the *unfinished sentence*. As its name implies this item consists of the stem of a sentence (e.g., "When I think of Mexico, I think of. . .) which is completed by the student. Because of its open-endedness the unifinished sentence is not as appropriate as other strategies for determining achievement of specific objectives. It is useful as a diagnostic tool, however; it can not only help give some indication of what students know but also some idea of the stereotypes students hold and the attitudes they have.

Alternative-Response Items. With respect to alternative-response items, a student is asked to choose one of two responses as typifying a given statement. The student is told what the alternative choices are. Although many people tend to think of alternative response items primarily in terms of true-false questions, there are other different types of alternatives we can use. In fact, Ten Brink (1974) suggests that, because it is difficult to produce items that are clearly true or clearly false, these items tend to be limited to gauging knowledge at the lower levels of cognition. Some other forms of alternative-response items that can be employed would include items that ask students to differentiate between *examples and nonexamples of a concept; statements of fact and opinion; statements that require students to differentiate between related concepts* (natural or people made, producers of goods or services, consumer or producer, and so on).

In developing alternative-response items we, of course, start with our objectives and use them as a basis for selecting our alternatives. Thus, if our objective focused on being able to identify examples of, say, the concept *role,* we would first identify examples of *role.* Then we would identify nonexamples. Finally, we would decide the order in which these would be presented to students and write clear directions for responding. As we said earlier, the two types of correct responses would be indicated in these directions.

The major difficulty with alternative-response questions is that, more than any other type item, they are susceptible to the student guessing an answer; thus they have a fifty-fifty chance of choosing the correct response. To get more valid evaluative data, which indicates that the students indeed know what it is we are trying to measure, it is necessary to include a relatively large number of this type item.

Alternative-response items can be used to deal with affective concerns. When employed in this manner they are usually of a format that asks the students whether they like or dislike something or agree or disagree with a statement. The following are examples of alternative-response questions used for affective purposes.

1. Answer yes or no. Would you like to
   a. visit another country?_____
   b. have someone from another country visit you?_____
2. Tell whether you agree or disagree.
   a. People on welfare should work for the money they are given. _____
   b. People can feel differently about the same thing. _____

Matching. With respect to exercises requiring matching, the student is given two lists of items and asked to indicate which items on each list belong together. When joined, the items on both lists would form statements that would be included in the following categories:

1. *Problems and solutions.* In the social studies we might have students match different items found on a map with their functions (what symbols identify, information contained in different parts of the maps). We might have them actually use different map skills (locate places, determine distance, determine direction, and so on.) We might also use these items to have them identify where different data sources would be appropriate. (When to use the encyclopedia, atlas, or almanac, for example.)
2. *Concepts and their examples.* In matching concepts and their examples, a listing of different ideas studied would be accompanied by appropriate examples. This could be used with both concepts and generalizations.
3. *Cause and effect.* Some of the understandings we will be working with are causal in nature—if one thing happens, then another thing will result. For example, when supply is high and demand low (cause) this usually results in low cost (effect). Or, if a person violates norms (cause), sanctions will be imposed (effect). Causes and effects can be separated to make the two lists that will be matched.

Other types of matching items that might be included would ask students to match words and definitions or events and the dates on which they occurred. Unlike the former types, which have the potential for eliciting higher levels of cognition on the students' part, these latter items tend to focus on memory. Thus, they would be more appropriately used for evaluation early in the instructional sequence.

It is unwise to include several different categories of matching items on a single test unless these categories are related in some way. When this is done it is possible for the student to narrow down the number of correct responses because they belong to the same category as the item to be matched. Thus, if three different categories were used on, say, a ten-response test the student, knowing the category, only needs to choose among three or four responses.

Constructing a matching test requires that we initially identify the items and their responses. Ten Brink (1974) suggest that these be made into simple declarative statements, which will then be broken apart. Following this, a list of plausible distracters is generated. These are responses that could be matched to the first column if the student does not understand the idea or skill being tested. Thus a list of responses for the causal statement, "When supply is high and demand is low, cost tends to be. . ." would include "high," "low," and "not affected." Unless the student understood the total proposition, any of these would be plausible. In a matching test the response column will contain roughly two times as many items as the statement column.

Multiple-Choice Items. Multiple-choice items are related both to the alternative-choice and matching items. They are related to the former in that they present the children with options for responding. These, however, number more than two alternatives. They are related to the latter in that the items included with the correct response are plausible distracters. They usually take the form of a stem (the question) followed by two, three, or four responses, one of which is correct. The following would be an example of a multiple choice item based on the supply-demand-cost generalization discussed above: "When supply is high and demand is low, cost tends to be (a) high, (b) low, or (c) unaffected."

The process used in the construction of multiple-choice items is very similar to that of matching. Initially, the teacher translates the idea or skill that represents the learning objective into a statement or statements. This statement will contain the stem, which is essentially the question being asked, and the correct alternative. A simple example of such a statement would be: The best resource for finding out when a famous person was born is (stem) the encyclopedia (correct alternative). After this, the teacher generates plausible alternatives. For our example these might be the dictionary, the almanac, and the thesauras. Then the stem and the alternatives are written out. The responses can be listed alphabetically or however the teacher chooses.

Multiple-choice items can be written so that they ask the student to identify correct responses. They can also request the incorrect response. ("Which of the following is *not* . . .") In the latter case care should be taken to emphasize the negative aspect of the question by underlining or completely capitalizing the word *not*.

The choice of a stem and plausible distracters is sometimes difficult, and care must be taken that they do not inadvertently give the students cues as to the correct response. This would mean that the alternatives grammatically follow the stem and that such grammatical hints as the using of "a" and "an" as the last word of the stem be avoided. Further, the distracters should be equally plausible. The following is an example of a question where all are not equally plausible:

1. The affect that climate may have on industry is best illustrated by
   a. artichoke production in California.
   b. steel production in Pennsylvania.
   c. automobile production in Michigan.
   d. furniture production in North Carolina.

Even if the students did not know that the coastal climate in mid-California makes it the artichoke production center of the country they could easily figure out the answer because all of the other alternatives are activities that occur indoors. All they need to do is equate *climate* with *outside* and they have their answer.

We have been discussing multiple-choice items in terms of our conceptual and process objectives. Like alternative-response items they can also be used with affective goals. One device for measuring attitudes presents the students with a position and asks for a response in terms of strongly agree, agree, undecided, disagree, strongly disagree (Donlon, 1974). Similar devices can measure social distance, the degree to which a student would feel comfortable with a given group of people. Herein, the stem of the question is the name of a group of people (e.g., Cubans) and the alternatives would be such items as "Would have as a friend"; "They could live in my neighborhood"; or "I would not want them in my neighborhood."

Short-Answer Questions. Short-answer questions are items to which short responses (a word, a phrase, or one or two sentences) are written by students. According to Ten Brink (1974) these are most appropriate for gauging understanding of a *single idea*. At times they can be like fill-in-the-blank items in that they can ask for a very specific answer; for example, "Name the two city-states of ancient Greece." In this case, the desired responses would be ones of lower (e.g., memory, comprehension) levels of cognition.

If they were only like fill-in-the-blank items there would be no reason, other than variety, for using short-answer questions. There are times, however, when understanding of concepts and skills can be demonstrated in a variety of ways. For example, the question, "what are three examples of interdependence among people?" can have any number of correct answers. It would allow some students, who might not provide the expected answer on a fill-in-the-blank item, to demonstrate that indeed they understand the idea. Thus, this type of item is appropriate when there can be a number of correct responses.

The key to writing a good short-answer item is to make it as straightforward and unambiguous as possible. As we said earlier, it should measure one idea, and there should be no confusion on the students' part as to what this idea is. In writing these questions it is a good practice to ask ourselves if there is any possible way for the question to be misinterpreted. For example, the question, "On your map, what is the distance from Ogden to St. George?" can be misinterpreted because it does not specify whether the distance by road or the shortest distance, "as the crow flies," is desired.

Essay Questions. Essay questions are items that pick up where short-answer questions leave off. In some cases they can actually be considered to be extended short-answer questions; that is, they ask that students discuss a single idea but that this be done in more than two sentences. The item, "Discuss three causes of the Civil War," would be an example of such a question.

Essay questions, of course, can go well beyond simply being extended short-answer items. In fact, essay questions are often appropriate for eliciting synthesis and evaluation-level thought. We observed an example of a synthesis-level essay question being given to a fourth-grade class who had studied industry in their state. They were given a map of a fictitious island. Printed on the map were resources of the island. The question accompanying the map asked them to make a proposal for an industry to be located on the island and telling why it would be appropriate. An evaluation-level question given to sixth graders asked them to discuss three causes of the Civil War and tell which one they thought was most important and why.

The writing of an essay question, as with other evaluation items, begins with the objective you want to test; this will supply you with what the question should be asking. This should then be translated into a question that can be understood by the student. This translation will result in asking the students for one of two types of responses: closed or open. In formulating a closed question you would tell the students more or less exactly what was expected (list three causes, tell which you thought was more important). A closed response may also be restricted as to length. An open response, on the other hand, gives students the freedom to answer in any way they choose. As with the map exercise, they can use any appropriate ideas they choose, including ideas that may not have been studied in the unit prior to the evaluation. At the most open level, students would be able to choose the format their answer would take (e.g., "Illustrate changes that have occurred in your city since it was founded").

The process for evaluating essay tests is similar in some respects to both closed and open responses. Upon constructing the essay question the teacher would then set the parameters for an acceptable response. That is, an outline of what would be expected would be made. This outline (which is sometimes called a model response) is then consulted when the essay is read. The evaluation of open responses usually requires a more general outline than that of closed responses because the teacher will probably go beyond this outline and look at the response more subjectively. In this manner, such concerns as internal consistency (Do the ideas hang together logically?), organization, and relevance to the topic would also be considered.

Which Informal Strategy?

In this section we will examine a number of strategies that teachers can use with their own classes. Included among these are the following.

Observation.
Work samples.
Verbal techniques.
Teacher-made tests.

Because these will be the strategies you will use most often in your classroom, at this point we can consider their appropriateness to a given situation. We'd like to offer four guidelines for deciding on which evalution strategy you will use.

The first factor to consider is the *child*; it's necessary to consider the type of evaluation activity he or she is capable of doing. You should know intuitively that younger children will have difficulty with written evaluation strategies. Although you can devise simple written tests (which may be in picture rather than word form) you'll probably want to rely more on observation, work samples, and different verbal strategies. Even with older students you'll need to consider whether or not a written test is appropriate.

Will it be evaluating their reading and writing skills rather than what they've learned in social studies? In all cases it's probably better to use an eclectic approach to evaluating—relying on a number of different strategies rather than a single one.

Your second consideration should be on the type of *goal* being evaluated. We have seen in this chapter that some strategies are more or less appropriate to the different types of goals. Knowledge is best evaluated with work samples, written tests, and verbal strategies (when there is structuring of the discussion). Process can be evaluated with all of the strategies we have discussed, as can effect. However, with the latter some types of items in teacher-made tests (e.g., matching) may not be as appropriate as others. You'll want to judge which strategy is most appropriate for your goal.

Our third guideline focuses on the type of instructional *objective* being measured and at what point (diagnosis, formative, summative) the evaluation is occuring. Different types of strategies are appropriate for different types of *objectives*. This is especially pertinent with written tests. We have seen, for example, that certain types of items, such as fill-in-the-blank and true-false, are appropriate for gauging lower levels of learning (e.g., memory). These would be appropriate for diagnosis and for objectives formulated for learning activities early in the learning experiences. They would be less appropriate for summative evaluion. In the same light, if your objective focused, say, on demonstrating something, you would want to use observation.

Finally, you would want to consider the type of *activity* the children have engaged in as you choose your evaluation strategy. Different activities lend themselves to different types of evaluation. For example, if the activity is one that entails reading, you might use a written test or verbal strategies. With a research project you might choose to take a work sample. Group activities might lend themselves to observation. The evalution strategy you choose should be a natural outgrowth of the activities the children do.

Synthesis: Putting It All Together _____

In this book we have discussed what we consider to be the three major elements of the social studies curriculum. We examined the three types of goals—knowledge, process, and affect—that contribute to the attainment of the primary goal of social education: world citizenship. Then we moved on to look at ways in which we could plan for, and actually facilitate, goals attainment. Finally, we moved to a consideration of how we could get some indication that the goals, indeed, had been met.

Of necessity, we had to consider these elements separately. Although we occasionally mentioned one element as we considered another, most of our discussion of an area focused on that area alone. In reality, there is such an intimate relationship among these elements that they cannot be considered separately; they need to be considered holistically. Let's examine some of these relationships to see why this is so.

The first relationship that we can consider is the one that exists among the goals. It is almost impossible to work toward one type of goal without working toward one, or both, of the other types. We might think that we are simply helping children, say, to learn a concept. Yet there is a good probability that we are also dealing with some aspects of process (i.e., gathering data) and affect (perceptions of people in the world, for example, or how the children feel about the social studies.) Because we're actually teaching more than one thing, we have suggested in this book that conscious attention on your part be given to all three goals as you plan, teach, and evaluate.

It's quite natural as you are considering goals to be simultaneously considering how your students are going to work toward meeting them. You'll be thinking about what they'll actually need to learn (your objectives) and how they'll go about doing this (the learning experiences). Although we considered the process of planning as being relatively sequential, what you'll find happening, as you become a more experienced teacher, is that the sequence, instead of being somewhat linear, becomes more or less circular. As you consider objectives you start thinking about activities. These in turn cause you to think of other objectives, which in turn are the progenitors of more activities. This is not to say that the relatively linear planning process we discussed is only theoretical and that in reality you do something else. No, as we said in our planning chapter we (and the new teachers we have worked with) have found it to be a good starting point. It suggests what you need to consider and where you ultimately need to be going. You still consider the same things and wind up in the same place as your planning becomes more circular.

It's probably not difficult for you to see the third relationship, that which exists among evaluation and the other areas. Just as they suggest learning experiences, your objectives essentially tell you what it is that you need to be evaluating. They specifically indicate what the child is to know and be able to do; evaluation tells you if, indeed, this has occurred. Similarly, as we have mentioned in a previous section of this chapter, the type of learning experience you plan will suggest the type of evaluation strategy you will use. Thus, your goals suggest *what* is to be evaluated and your activities, *how*.

A consideration of these three elements of the social studies curriculum would be incomplete if we did not also keep a fourth, and most important, element in mind. That element is the child. The children you teach will be unique. Each child will have a distinct personality and will have had a variety of life experiences that no one in the class has had. To insure learning, your planning must take the uniqueness of each child into account. It's vitally necessary to consider their personal backgrounds—their needs, interests, and experiences—in order to provide for meaningful learning.

It's also necessary to consider their commonalities. Throughout this book we have stressed one particularly area of commonality—how they develop. We have looked at cognitive development and the implications that it has for teaching and learning. We have also looked at how various affective capabilities develop. Keeping all of these in mind as we consider the other curricular elements will do much to facilitate the growth of our students as knowledgeable, active world citizens.

Springboards to Discussion _____

1. If they are available through your college's library, examine several of the standardized tests mentioned in this chapter. Consider what specifically they are testing (concepts, skills, etc.). Then determine what you perceive to be their strengths and weaknesses. If possible attempt to develop a generalization about standardized tests (e.g., "Unless a child can read at grade level, he or she will have difficulty with standardized tests"). Share this as an hypothesis to be accepted or rejected by your peers. They must have the data to accept or reject.

2. In Chapter 12 we presented an exercise in which you were to plan a small group activity. Develop a checklist that would allow you to evaluate the group activity while it was occurring.

3. In discussing criteria for choosing evaluation instruments we indicated that one factor which needs to be considered is the *child*. Although circumstances (e.g., the nature of the activity) will also affect the specific technique used some strategies will be less effective than others because of the child's capabilities. Rank order the informal evaluation instruments we have discussed in terms of the developing capabilities of children. That is, choose the instrument that is most appropriate for younger children and move up through the grades. Tell why you assigned a given rank to a given strategy.

References _____

BUROS, OSCAR K. *The Seventh Mental Measurements Yearbook.* Highland Park, NJ: Gryphon Press, 1972.

DONLON, THOMAS F. "Testing in the Affective Domain," ERIC/TM Report No. 4. Princeton: ERIC Clearinghouse on Tests, Measurement, and Evaluation, 1974.

GRONLUND, NORMAN E. *Measurement and Evaluation in Teaching.* New York: Macmillan Publishing Co., 1976.

MITCHELL, J. V. *Tests in Print III: An Index to Tests, Test Reviews and the Literature on Specific Tests.* Lincoln, NE: University of Nebraska Press, 1983.

ROID, GALE H., AND HALADYNA, THOMAS M. *A Technology for Test-Item Writing.* New York: Academic Press, 1982.

SCHUNCKE, GEORGE M. "The Uses and Misuses of Evaluation," *The Clearing House,* Vol. 54 (January 1981), pp. 219–222.

SUPERKA, DOUGLAS P., VIGILIANA, ALICE AND HEDSTROM, JUDITH E. *Social Studies Evaluation Sourcebook.* Boulder: Social Science Education Consortium, 1978.

TEN BRINK, TERRY D. *Evaluation: A Practical Guide for Teachers.* New York: McGraw-Hill, 1974.

Index